THE JACOBIN LEGACY IN MODERN FRANCE

Vincent Wright 1937–1999

The Jacobin Legacy in Modern France

Essays in Honour of Vincent Wright

Edited by Sudhir Hazareesingh

OXFORD
UNIVERSITY PRESS

*This book has been printed digitally and produced in a standard specification
in order to ensure its continuing availability*

OXFORD
UNIVERSITY PRESS

Great Clarendon Street, Oxford OX2 6DP

Oxford University Press is a department of the University of Oxford.
It furthers the University's objective of excellence in research, scholarship,
and education by publishing worldwide in

Oxford New York

Auckland Cape Town Dar es Salaam Hong Kong Karachi
Kuala Lumpur Madrid Melbourne Mexico City Nairobi
New Delhi Shanghai Taipei Toronto
With offices in
Argentina Austria Brazil Chile Czech Republic France Greece
Guatemala Hungary Italy Japan South Korea Poland Portugal
Singapore Switzerland Thailand Turkey Ukraine Vietnam

Oxford is a registered trade mark of Oxford University Press
in the UK and in certain other countries

Published in the United States
by Oxford University Press Inc., New York

© Sudhir Hazareesingh 2002

ISBN 978-0-19-925646-4

PREFACE

ONE of the many wonderful things about the late Vincent Wright was the community of scholars surrounding him—a multinational collectivity, straddling several disciplines, and committed through their various endeavours to the common ideals of the Republic of Letters. These men and women were also his friends, with whom he kept in touch, invariably visited when he was abroad, and invited to Nuffield and to his homes in Oxford, France, and Italy.

I begin by offering my warmest thanks to the contributors to this volume, all of whom knew Vincent very well and agreed—generously, and without the slightest hesitation—to participate in this homage to his historical works on France. I am grateful to them for their diligence, punctiliousness, and dedication, all of which greatly facilitated my task of editing this book. Through them, and their marvellous contributions, this work stands as a tribute to the values cherished by Vincent in his professional life: scholarship and the dissemination of research, intellectual cooperation across boundaries, hospitality, and above all friendship.

This book would not have seen the day without the support of Dominic Byatt, my editor at Oxford University Press. I want to take this opportunity to thank him for his constant encouragement and assistance; I also owe a great debt to the two anonymous OUP readers who warmly endorsed this project and made very helpful specific recommendations about its overall structure and content. Amanda Watkins, Gwen Booth, and Michael James displayed their customary efficiency in steering the book through its various phases of production, and Frank Pert's craftsmanship has again supplied a wonderful index.

Equally decisive has been the warm and generous support given to this project by Sir Tony Atkinson, the Warden of Nuffield College, Oxford. I am also greatly in the debt of Marion Rogers and Stephanie Wright, from Nuffield as well, for various forms of assistance provided with courteous efficiency; Valerie Grundy, who braved wintry conditions in the Ardèche superbly to translate Chapters 4, 8, and 10 from French into English; and Ian Fraser, who rendered the English version of Chapter 9. Basil Smith graciously supplied the photograph of Vincent Wright which adorns the inside page. My warmest thanks, finally, go to Glynis Baleham, Senior Tutor's Secretary at Balliol College, Oxford, for her prompt and decisive help with the final preparation of the index.

This book was conceived at a time when I was applying to the British Academy for support to work on the political and intellectual history of the French Left since the mid-nineteenth century. It was in this context that I encountered the concept of 'Jacobinism' and thought of deploying it as the overarching framework for this book—although, as we shall see, modern 'Jacobinism' is of course no longer exclusively on the left. Having been fortunate enough to be successful in my application, I began my research leave in October 2001. I would like to express my deep gratitude to the British Academy, thanks to whom I have been able to finish this book *dans les plus brefs délais*, and especially to use some of my research in the writing of Chapter 1.

My thanks, finally, to my mother, Thara Hazareesingh, for all her assistance; and to my accomplice Karma Nabulsi, for her invaluable critical eye and for helping me to define and think through this project which honours our great friend Vincent.

Sudhir Hazareesingh
Paris, February 2002

CONTENTS

NOTES ON CONTRIBUTORS

SUDHIR HAZAREESINGH is Official Fellow and Tutor in Politics at Balliol College, Oxford. He specializes in modern French politics and the history of French political thought. His books include *Political Traditions in Modern France* (1994), *From Subject to Citizen* (1998), *Intellectual Founders of the Republic* (2001), and *Francs-Maçons sous le Second Empire: le Grand Orient de France à la veille de la Troisième République* (with Vincent Wright) (2001).

OLIVIER IHL is Professor of Political Science at the Institut des Etudes Politiques, Grenoble, and associate member of the Centre de Recherches Politiques de la Sorbonne at the University of Paris (Panthéon-Sorbonne). He is a specialist of modern French political and socio-cultural history. He has published *La Fête Républicaine* (1996) and *Le Vote* (2000), and edited *Le Protocole ou la Mise en Forme du Politique* (with C. Haroche and Y. Déloye) (1996) and *Un Cérémonial Politique: les Voyages Officiels des Chefs de l'Etat* (with J.-W. Dereymez and G. Sabatier) (1998). His forthcoming book *La Formation des Sciences de Gouvernement XIXe–XXe siècles* will appear in 2003.

DOUGLAS JOHNSON is Emeritus Professor of History at the University of London, and has written extensively on modern French political, social, and cultural history. He is the author of *Guizot* (1963), *France and the Dreyfus Affair* (1966), *A Concise History of France* (1971), *The Age of Illusion: Art and Politics in France* (with Madeleine Johnson) (1987), *Michelet and the French Revolution* (1990), and *How European are the French?* (1996).

MAURICE LARKIN is Emeritus Professor of History and Honorary Fellow of the University of Edinburgh, where he held the Richard Pares Professorship of History between 1976 and 1999. He has written extensively on modern French social and political history, and is the author of *Church and State after the Dreyfus Affair* (1974), *Man and Society in Nineteenth Century Realism* (1977), *France since the Popular Front* (second edition, 1997), and *Religion, Politics, and Preferment since 1890: La Belle Epoque and its Legacy* (1995).

JEAN-PIERRE MACHELON is Professor of Public Law at the Université René Descartes—Paris 5, where he directs the Maurice Hauriou Centre, and Directeur d'Etudes at the Ecole pratique des Hautes Etudes in Paris (Professorship of the History of European Institutions). His works include *Les idées politiques de J.L. de Lolme* (1969) and *La République contre les libertés?* (1976). His recent publications have focused principally on history, constitutional law, and administrative history. He has co-edited *La Constitution de l'an*

III. *Boissy d'Anglas et la naissance du libéralisme constitutionnel* (1999) and *Les communes et le pouvoir. Histoire politique des communes françaises de 1789 à nos jours* (2002).

YVES MÉNY is Professor at the Institut des Etudes Politiques, Paris, former Director of the Robert Schuman Centre, and President of the European University Institute, Florence. He is the author of numerous books on French and European politics, including *Centre-Periphery Relations in Western Europe* (1983) and *The Politics of Steel* (1985) (both co-edited with Vincent Wright), *Centralisation et Décentralisation dans le débat politique français* (1974), and *La Corruption de la République* (1991). He is the co-author of *Par le Peuple, Pour le Peuple: le Populisme et les Démocraties* (2000) and the co-editor of *Democracies and the Populist Challenge* (2002) (both with Yves Surel).

KARMA NABULSI is a Prize Research Fellow at Nuffield College, Oxford. She is the author of *Traditions of War: Occupation, Resistance, and the Law* (1999). She is the Project Leader of a British Academy-sponsored networks programme on republican movements in Europe. She is currently working on two books: *Patriotic Politics: The Republican Tradition of War in Europe*, an examination of the political culture of republican war between the mid-eighteenth century and the Spanish Civil War, and *Inventing Europe*, a book about the founding of the semi-secret republican society Young Europe.

PHILIP NORD is a Professor of History at Princeton University and a specialist of modern French political history. He is the author of *Paris Shopkeepers and the Politics of Resentment* (1986), *The Republican Moment: Struggles for Democracy in 19th Century France* (1995), and *Impressionists and Politics: Art and Democracy in the 19th Century* (2000). He is presently working on a book on conservative reformers in France, 1930–50.

DOMINIQUE SCHNAPPER is Directrice d'Etudes at the Ecole des Hautes Etudes en Sciences Sociales in Paris. She is the author of numerous books and articles on French politics and society, including *Jewish Identities in France* (1983), *La France de l'Intégration* (1991), *La Relation à l'Autre* (1998), *The Community of Citizens* (1998), and *La Démocratie Providentielle* (2002).

1

Vincent Wright and the Jacobin Legacy in Historical and Theoretical Perspectives

SUDHIR HAZAREESINGH

I T is still difficult, more than two years after his death, to come to terms with the fact that Vincent Wright is no longer with us. His departure has removed from our midst a dear friend, a wonderful colleague, a conscientious teacher and dedicated supervisor, and above all a scholar who was at the height of his intellectual powers and who still had huge contributions to make to the various academic fields with which he was engaged during his distinguished career. Indeed it is a tribute to the range, depth, and creativity of his scholarship that his passing will be marked by Oxford University Press by two commemorative volumes: *Governing Europe*, edited by Jack Hayward and Anand Menon, devoted to comparative and European politics,[1] and the present collection of essays, centred on modern French political history.

France was a privileged focus for Vincent Wright's work throughout his academic life, from his doctoral thesis on the Basses-Pyrénées through his studies of French administrative history and his two seminal works, *Le Conseil d'Etat sous le Second Empire* (1972) and *Les Préfets du Second Empire* (with Bernard Le Clère, 1973).[2] Even when he embraced comparative and European politics after moving to an Official Fellowship at Oxford in 1977, he continued, as he put it, to 'close the door at Nuffield and write history'.[3] From his flat on Boulevard Bonne-Nouvelle and his country house near Cahors he worked painstakingly in Parisian and departmental archives, gathering material for a biographical dictionary of the prefects of the republican Government of National Defence (1870–1)—a work on which he had made considerable progress by the summer of 1999. In collaboration with his Nuffield colleague Karma Nabulsi, he was also exploring conceptual and historical dimensions of the conflicts within the French republican camp during the Franco-Prussian

---

[1] Oxford, forthcoming 2003.
[2] See the Appendix for a complete bibliography and bibliographical details of Vincent Wright's works.
[3] 'The Path to Hesitant Comparison' (1997).

war. His last major piece of French historical research, jointly written with this author, was a study of the provincial Freemasonry on the eve of the Third Republic.[4]

Vincent Wright thus remained actively engaged in the field of French history for a period of more than 30 years. Although he wrote about earlier and later periods with equal ease and insightfulness, Wright was most at home in the remarkable half-century which began with the 1848 Revolution and ended with the consolidation of the Third Republic in the late nineteenth century. These were the years which in many respects shaped the contours of modern France, most significantly with respect to the definitive triumph—if we discount the Vichy aberration—of republicanism over its Bonapartist, Orleanist, and Bourbon royalist competitors.[5] Wright used this period to make sense of the fundamental questions raised by the science of politics, notably about political leadership and administrative power; the transition from authoritarian to democratic rule; the preconditions of democratic governance; and the sources of political legitimacy. There were three overarching themes to his analysis of political and administrative power: the history of the administrative institutions of the State, the territorial dimensions of power, and the study of elites and networks, both social and political.[6] Shattering conventional wisdoms and ideologically-constructed self-images of the French State, he showed how power could become fragmented and dispersed through spatial and sociological constraints. At the same time, he drew out the permanent elements of State power which survived across time and ideological ruptures. Through this dialectic portrayal of change and continuity, Wright revolutionized our understanding of the nineteenth-century French State and especially its administrative elites, whom he greatly admired; and his scholarship largely helped to rehabilitate two of France's least known and most caricatured nineteenth-century regimes, the Bonapartist Second Empire and the republican Government of National Defence of 1870–1.

From the very outset, Wright came to be regarded, both inside and outside France, as one of the leading administrative historians of the *hexagone*. This recognition could be seen at all levels: he was awarded the *Légion d'Honneur* by the French State; he established close and fruitful intellectual partnerships with leading French scholars, institutions, and networks—most notably, in Paris, the Institut des Etudes Politiques, the University of Paris, the Ecole Pratique des Hautes Etudes, and the Conseil d'Etat; and by the late 1970s his works had become classics, read by successive generations of French teachers and students, held in university and public libraries, and cited in all serious

[4] Sudhir Hazareesingh and Vincent Wright, *Francs-maçons sous le Second Empire* (2001).

[5] For an excellent recent study, see Jérôme Grévy, *La République des opportunistes 1870–1885* (Paris, 1998).

[6] For further discussion see Sudhir Hazareesingh and Karma Nabulsi, 'The Ambivalent Jacobin: Vincent Wright as a Political Historian of Modern France', *Modern and Contemporary France*, 8 (2000), 371–80. A French version of the same piece, 'Un Jacobin ambivalent: Vincent Wright, historien politique de la France moderne', appeared in the *Revue Française d'Administration Publique*, 93 (January–March 2000), 7–17.

studies of French political history in the second half of the nineteenth century. For example, one of the standard overviews of the 1852–70 period, Alain Plessis's volume in Seuil's highly successful series 'Nouvelle Histoire de la France Contemporaine'. There are references to Wright's works throughout the book, and the early section on the evolution of the administration under the Second Empire is drawn almost entirely from his scholarship.[7] His works enjoy an equally authoritative status when it comes to the republican Government of National Defence of 1870–1. In Stéphane Audoin-Rouzeau's *1870: La France dans la guerre*, one of the best recent works on the Franco-Prussian war, the author acknowledges that his portrayal of the administrative elites—and especially the prefects—is entirely reliant upon Wright's published research.[8] Similar tributes appear in the works of social historians of nineteenth-century France.[9]

Wright's contribution to nineteenth-century French history may be simply summed up. He is one of the handful of non-French academics who succeeded, during their own lifetimes, not only in challenging but also in changing the way the French perceived their own history. The scale of this achievement is all the more monumental when we consider the extent of his professional engagement with comparative and European politics after 1977, the sheer tenacity of certain ideological and institutional myths in France— notably about republicanism and the role of the State—and above all the extraordinary difficulty for any foreign scholar to have his work published in France, let alone receive the sort of anointment bestowed upon Wright's *oeuvre*.

Vincent Wright's Scholarship

What were the specific qualities and characteristics of Wright's work and approach to French history which made possible such a *sacre*? He was intellectually radiant, as all those who knew him—or even met him for a brief moment—will remember. But he was also an indefatigable worker, who knew that the complete mastery of a subject required hard, persistent work as well as thoroughness and scrupulous attention to detail.

His command of sources, both primary and secondary, was awesome. He seemed to know everyone who had lived in the second half of the French nineteenth century, and to have read everything ever published on the subject of its political, administrative, and social history. He was also an old *habitué* of the Archives Nationales, and he remembered the halcyon days

[7] Alain Plessis, *De la fête impériale au mur des Fédérés* (Paris, 1979), esp. 60–70.

[8] 'Les lignes qui suivent doivent beaucoup à Vincent Wright, qui a complètement renouvelé l'histoire administrative de cette période, permettant de jeter sur plusieurs aspects de celle-ci un regard neuf.' Stéphane Audoin-Rouzeau, *1870: La France dans la guerre* (Paris, 1989), 358.

[9] See for example Christophe Charle, *Histoire sociale de la France au XIXème siècle* (Paris, 1991), esp. 77–80.

when there were few limits on the daily number of documents which could be ordered. Furthermore, he had combed through the relevant *fonds* of every departmental archive in metropolitan France—especially the M series, which held no secrets to him—as well as a large collection of privately held archives. His memory was remarkable, and remained so until the very end. In the late spring of 1999, at a time when his physical powers were beginning to decline, I recall telling him that I was having difficulty locating a portrait of the republican philosopher and member of Parliament Jules Barni. He looked up and instantly replied: 'Look in the February 1876 issues of *Le Temps*', he said. 'They ran a series of pieces on outgoing republican deputies before the elections, and the article on Barni was accompanied by a drawing.' Needless to say, he was right.

Another striking Wrightian quality was his open-mindedness. He loved to engage with colleagues who were working in areas similar or adjacent to his own, and he always retained a fondness for collaborative work. His personal archives are full of letters to French historians—and replies from them—discussing the availability of sources and the interpretation of evidence, and asking for specific information about individuals or groups; marriages, family connections, and personal fortunes were systematically tracked down for his biographical dictionary of the prefects of 1870–1. Often these letters led to further exchanges and meetings which sometimes developed into lasting friendships. He regarded these 'networks' not only as essential means of gathering information but also as a way of opening himself to new evidence and fresh perspectives. Ultimately, this open-mindedness was a means of remaining humble and shielding himself from the perils of complacency. Wright never rested on his laurels: even after his historical works on France became classics he continued to challenge himself, to acknowledge his own occasional misconceptions, and to learn from the work of others—the mark of a true scholar.

This open-mindedness naturally fuelled Wright's ingrained sense of scepticism, which was both one of his most renowned characteristics and one of the principal sources of his creative thinking. Vividly described in his intellectual autobiography,[10] his years at the LSE under the formative influence of Michael Oakeshott instilled in him an intense dislike of 'theoretical' intrusions into history—or for that matter political science—whether in the form of models, inductive generalizations, or psychological assumptions about agents; and he always displayed a healthy contempt for game theory and rational choice approaches to social explanation. Armed with this scepticism about theoretical abstractions and grounded in a robust empiricism, Wright was perfectly placed to take on conventional wisdoms and orthodox viewpoints. This Saint George helped to slay many mythological dragons in nineteenth century French history: the omnipotence of the Bonapartist *préfets à poigne*; the brutality and odiousness of the Second Empire; the incompetence of the

---

[10] Wright, 'The Path to Hesitant Comparison' (1997).

republican Government of National Defence; the political subordination of the Conseil d'Etat to the executive; the ideal of the French administrative system 'open to all talents'; the political subversiveness of the provincial Freemasonry and its domination by republicans; the penetration of the republican State by Protestantism after 1871; and the inherent Jacobinism of the republican elites in the 1870s.

Hard work, open-mindedness, and scepticism all came together in what was perhaps the most important source of Wright's intellectual fertility: his commitment to interdisciplinarity. He believed that only by combining the tools of political science, historical enquiry, and sociological observation could one arrive at an understanding of the complexities of the exercise of power in nineteenth century France. His overall *démarche* was in this respect strikingly Weberian, as were his conclusions about power. He constantly sought to distinguish political and juridical power from authority, and stressed that the formal instruments of governance were often not the real sites where power was exercised. Informal networks, such as those based on family traditions or cultural affinities, could prove extremely powerful, both at national level— through the penetration of administrative institutions—and at local level—through the exercise of *pouvoir notabilier*. This methodological pluralism was extremely advantageous to Wright's historical scholarship, in both a negative and a positive sense. It prevented him from being 'boxed in' by the disciplinary constraints of history. His writings were thus entirely unaffected by many of the more recent turns taken by the profession, notably the emphasis on 'gender' and 'culture'. As an open-minded and inclusive scholar, he welcomed the achievements brought about by these new trends. However, he also believed that these advances had been achieved at an inordinately high cost: the de-contextualization, de-territorialization, and depoliticization of the historical subject.

More importantly, this methodological pluralism allowed Wright to illuminate the objects of his historical investigations with insights and instruments drawn from political science and sociology—even though, as Karma Nabulsi points out in her contribution, he did not elaborate the precise intellectual relationship among these disciplines.

Conceptualizing the Jacobin Legacy

The overarching theme of this commemorative volume is the 'Jacobin legacy' in modern France. What we understand by Jacobinism here is not the Revolutionary political movement which rose to prominence in the aftermath of the 1789 Revolution and reached its apogee in the period 1793–4 under the leadership of Robespierre and the Committee of Public Safety: the Jacobinism of Robespierre, Marat, and Saint-Just, which proliferated in organized clubs across the country, confiscated State power, exalted republican virtue, patriotism, and centralized government, suspended the *état de droit*, and unleashed

the Terror which eventually consumed it.[11] Rather, this book is concerned
with later forms of Jacobinism—clusters of ideas, principles, and values, as well
as myths, which came to occupy an increasingly central position in French
political culture as from the end of the Restoration and were aptly characterized by the Revolutionary historian François Furet as a belief in one or more of
the following dispositions: 'the indivisibility of national sovereignty, the vocation of the State to transform society, governmental and administrative centralisation, the equality of citizens guaranteed by the uniformity of legislation,
the regeneration of men by republican education, or merely a fastidious
attachment to national independence'.[12] To this list we might also add other
threads which have also frequently figured in this Jacobin fabric: the conception of the State as the guardian of the 'general interest', a commitment to
rationalism and progress, a belief in the possibility of national unity through
the transcendence of sectional divisions, and a suspicion of all intermediate
groupings between State and society—most notably religious groups.

How did the meaning of the term 'Jacobin' shift and acquire such elasticity?
For much of the nineteenth century 'Jacobin' and 'Jacobinism' referred in
France to two overlapping but relatively limited contexts in time and ideological space: the ideas, experiences, and memories of the 1790s; and the doctrines of those who subscribed to 'ardent democratic ideas' in France and
Europe.[13] With the advent and institutionalization of the Third Republic,
however, Jacobinism took on a broader significance, at the core of which was
the vigorous defence of the State and a strong hostility to anything which
might lead to its dismemberment.[14] In the early stages of assuming this wider
meaning, Jacobinism remained an essentially pejorative term, used by conservatives such as the Goncourt brothers to describe the perceived threat of radical republicanism in the 1870s;[15] and a generation later by liberal
philosophers such as Alain to stigmatize the doctrinal inflexibility of the
Republican State and its Ministers.[16] By the late Third Republic, monarchist
opponents of the Republic routinely associated Jacobinism with all the 'perverse' manifestations of French democracy. Léon Daudet, for example, wrote
of 'the excessive centralization, originating from Jacobinism, consolidated by
Bonaparte and "electoralized" by the Third Republic'.[17]

These semantic shifts prepared the ground for the wider connotations of
'Jacobinism' which have become common since 1945: its association with

[11] On Jacobin clubs see Michael Kennedy's trilogy, *The Jacobin Clubs in the French Revolution* (Vols
I and II, Princeton, 1982 and 1988; Vol. III London, 2000). For a recent regional study, see Danièle
Pingué, *Les Mouvements jacobins en Normandie orientale 1790–1795* (Paris, 2001). Two contrasting
evaluations of the Jacobin experience are offered by Lucien Jaume, *Le discours jacobin et la démocratie*
(Paris, 1989); and Patrice Higonnet, *Goodness Beyond Virtue* (Cambridge, MA, 1998).
[12] François Furet, 'Jacobinisme', in François Furet and Mona Ozouf (eds), *Dictionnaire critique de la
Révolution Française. Idées* (Paris, 1992), 243.
[13] Emile Littré, *Dictionnaire de la langue française*, iii. (Paris, 1877 edn), 165.
[14] See *Trésor de la Langue Française. Dictionnaire de la Langue au XIXe et XXe siècle (1789-1960)*, x.
(Paris, 1983), and Alain Rey (ed), *Dictionnaire historique de la langue française* (Paris, 2000 edn).
[15] Edmond and Jules de Goncourt, *Journal* (Paris, 1879), 8.
[16] Emile Charter (Alain), *Eléments d'une doctrine radicale* (Paris, 1925), 60.
[17] Léon Daudet, *Maurras* (Paris, 1928), 158.

'authoritarian' republican parties of the Right and Left, such as the Gaullists and the Communists, and with all those in today's France who champion centralization and the role of the State, the principle of sovereignty, and the cultural unity of the nation. The polemical dimensions of the concept have remained powerful; indeed, in contemporary France assorted politicians—generally when in opposition—publicists, and journalists regularly rail against the excessive 'Jacobin' characteristics of the State whenever they draw up a list of the country's political and cultural dysfunctions.[18] The relative ideological re-emergence of liberalism in France has also spawned some interesting studies of anti-Jacobin thought, both within and outside the republican fold. The most recent exemplar is Renzo Ragghianti's *De Cousin à Benda: portraits d'intellectuels antijacobins*,[19] a philosophical investigation of the writings of Victor Cousin, Ernest Renan, Etienne Vacherot, Georges Sorel, Emile Durkheim, and Julien Benda—a gathering which shows how the line between supporters and advocates of Jacobinism historically cut across traditional ideological cleavages.

The Revolutionary historian Michel Vovelle has coined the term 'transhistorical jacobinism' to refer to the post-Revolutionary manifestations of the phenomenon.[20] Vovelle stresses the roots of these post-Revolutionary forms of Jacobinism in the history and memories of the 1790s. For him, however, this neo-Jacobinism was distinctive in two respects: first in that it was a way of being rather than a clear and comprehensive ideology—an echo of Furet's 'dispositional' view; and second in that it characterized itself 'in terms of organizational structures, of a theory—and especially a practice—of power and a vision of the State'.[21] Both of these points are essential to understand the complex nature and multiple trajectories of this French 'Jacobinism'. Complexity, in the sense that we are dealing with values and principles which can 'inhabit' a diverse range of actors and sites: the State itself, taken as an abstract entity—notably its constitutional principles and juridical norms; particular political and administrative institutions within the State; political parties, both in power and in opposition; associational movements, especially those with links to the State; and specific social groups, as for example the republican 'Jews of State' described by Pierre Birnbaum.[22] Multiple trajectories, also, because these 'Jacobin' elements have proved compatible with a very broad range of regimes, ideologies and systems of thought, and mass political sentiments—which partly explains the remarkable longevity and potency of this 'Jacobin' culture in modern France.

---

[18] For a recent sample of this genre, see Alain Garrigou, *Les Elites contre la République. Sciences Po et L'ENA* (Paris, 2001); Laurent Joffrin, *Le Gouvernement invisible. Naissance d'une démocratie sans le peuple* (Paris, 2001); Jean-Christophe Comor and Olivier Beyeler, *Zéro politique* (Paris, 2002); and Jean-Marie Colombani, *Les infortunes de la République* (Paris, 2002).

[19] Paris, 2000.

[20] Michel Vovelle, *Les Jacobins, de Robespierre à Chevènement* (Paris, 1999), 5.

[21] Vovelle, *Les Jacobins*, 6.

[22] Pierre Birnbaum, *Les Fous de la République: histoire politique des Juifs d'Etat de Gambetta à Vichy* (Paris, 1994 edn).

Three basic distinctions may help to map out more clearly the different manifestations of this 'Jacobinism' in France since the early nineteenth century. First, it is essential to distinguish between 'republican' and 'revolutionary' forms of Jacobinism. Ever since the late 1790s, the heritage of the French Revolution has been claimed by relatively moderate constitutionalist political groups as well as more radical movements on the Left and extreme Left. While they were united in their appreciation of centralization and the role of the State, their celebration of the 'people' and its sovereignty, their ardent patriotism, and their hostility to intermediate organizations, these movements also disagreed about both ends and means—about how much equality was consistent with the republican good life and about the extent of violence which could legitimately be deployed to achieve republican ends.[23]

Two related but parallel Jacobin 'traditions' can thus be traced, both steeped in the historical memories and mythologies of the Revolution of 1789. On the one side stood a 'republican' version, which came to life in the early July Monarchy, briefly held sway in the early days of the 1848 Revolution with the likes of Ledru-Rollin and Louis Blanc and during the 'dictatorship' of Gambetta in 1870–1, and then through the Radical Party became the dominant voice of constitutional republicanism under the Third Republic. In opposition to this republican Jacobinism, sometimes literally across the barricades,[24] there emerged a 'revolutionary' strand which came to the fore with the conspiratorial republicanisms of Babeuf and Buonarroti, gathered momentum in the Blanquist, socialist, and 'Montagnard' groups of the Second Republic and the underground resistance to the Bonapartist *coup d'état* in the early 1850s, and reached its nineteenth century apogee under the 1871 Paris Commune.[25] Thereafter the standard-bearers of this 'revolutionary' Jacobinism were the Guesdists and Blanquists, and nearer our times the French Communist Party (PCF).[26]

A second axis which provides useful indicators of the unity but also diversity of this 'Jacobinism' is the classic distinction between the Left and the Right. Born in Revolutionary France, this division, which defined French and European political alignments for much of the modern era,[27] illustrates both the cross-cutting character of Jacobin dispositions and their defining nature. The Right, as we all know since René Rémond's pioneering work, can be broadly subdivided into three groupings since the early nineteenth century: a traditionalist pole, committed to religion, social hierarchy, and social conservation; a liberal strand, devoted to elite governance and economic freedom under bourgeois rule; and a populist tradition, stressing the values of order,

[23] See our chapter on 'The Republican Tradition' in Sudhir Hazareesingh, *Political Traditions in Modern France* (Oxford, 1994), 65–97.

[24] On this theme see the stimulating contributions in the work edited by Alain Corbin and Jean-Marie Mayeur, *La Barricade* (Paris, 1997).

[25] For a useful recent overview see John Merriman, 'The French Revolutions 1830–1871', in Isser Woloch (ed.), *Revolutions and the Meaning of Freedom in the 19th Century* (Stanford, 1996).

[26] Jean Touchard, *La Gauche en France depuis 1900* (Paris, 1981 edn).

[27] See Marcel Gauchet, 'La Droite et la Gauche', in Pierre Nora (ed.), *Les Lieux de mémoire*, iii. (Paris, 1992), 395–467; and Norberto Bobbio, *Droite et gauche: essai sur une distinction politique* (Paris, 1996).

nationalism, and charismatic leadership.[28] 'Jacobin' tendencies have been strongly marked in the second—the 'statist' liberalism of the Doctrinaires, and most notably Guizot, who consistently refused to distinguish State from society[29]—and especially the third strand, whether in its Bonapartist variant in the nineteenth century or in its modern manifestation, Gaullism.

Were we to identify, in a similar vein, the subcultures of the Left across time, we might also come up with three broad strands: a 'Montagnard' component, which eventually developed into French Communism, committed to national unity, social regeneration, and revolutionary change through centralized State power; a progressive pole, around which gravitated different groups committed to an incremental and 'reformist' socialism; and a libertarian tendency, whose theoretician was Proudhon and which was long symbolized by anarchism and anarcho-syndicalism; this libertarian Left rejected the State—and often the very notion of politics—and sought to promote decentralized and associational forms of social change. Here, too, we find powerful 'Jacobin' resonances, especially the Montagnard/Marxist Left but also—and this is one of the strong cultural differences with the socialist movement in Britain—among the progressives; Jaurès used to say that if he had been a member of the Jacobins he would have sat next to Robespierre.

Indeed, the point may be pressed further. What is striking, when both the French Left and Right are viewed in historical perspective, is the preponderance of 'Jacobin' elements over their respective rivals within their own camps—in this respect a continuation of the drama of the 1790s, which saw the crushing of the Gironde by the Jacobins. Despite the efforts of legitimists and individualist liberals for much of the nineteenth century, the Bonapartists and the Orleanists—both impeccably 'statist'—remained the dominant voices on the French Right; the Fifth Republic was likewise marked by the political and intellectual hegemony of Gaullism over its right-wing competitors. On the other side of the ideological divide, similarly, the federalist voice of Proudhon was always drowned out by Jacobin and 'municipalist' conceptions of citizenship in the republican camp;[30] and most of the history of the modern Left—until the late 1980s—was a narrative of Marxist and Communist domination over socialist and republican groups, not only in terms of political and organizational power but also from the ideological and programmatic points of view.[31]

Finally, we may borrow an important distinction made by Lucien Jaume, albeit in a different historical context, between 'State' Jacobinism and 'Jacobinism of action'. For Jaume, this distinction captured an important duality in the Revolutionary era, when Jacobinism was both a movement which was critical of the post-1789 State—and especially its practice of representation—

[28] René Rémond, *Les Droites en France* (Paris, 1982).
[29] See Lucien Jaume, *L'Individu effacé* (Paris, 1998).
[30] On this theme see our work *From Subject to Citizen: the Second Empire and the Emergence of Modern French Democracy* (Princeton, 1998).
[31] See Tony Judt, *Marxism and the French Left* (Oxford, 1986).

and, at the same time, became committed to the capture and institutional transformation of the State and ultimately its reinforcement.[32] If we think of French
political and administrative practice since the early nineteenth century, this distinction tells us something very important about French political culture,
namely, that 'Jacobin' principles and values were capable all at once of defining
the *Weltanschauung* of the French State—and any French State committed to the
broad principles of 1789, not just a republican State—while at the same time
providing the conceptual and mythological foundations of its radical critique.
As in its Revolutionary incarnation, modern Jacobinism thus remained both a
creative and a destructive force.

This Jacobinism has been the inspiration of French collective legal reasoning since the foundation of the modern Republic, 'one and indivisible'.
Indeed, despite the 'pluralistic' advances of the 1980s and 1990s, some of
which are highlighted in this book, this unitary and centralist philosophy
arguably remains the guiding principle of French public law—as we may
observe almost every week in the rulings of the Conseil d'Etat and the Conseil
Constitutionnel. For example, ruling No. 99-412 of the Conseil Constitutionnel (15 June 1999) rejected the ratification of the European charter of
regional languages on the grounds that French law and the unity of its people
'deny any recognition of collective rights to any group, whether defined by
community of origin, culture, language, or belief'.[33] But the same bedrock of
values can also underlie the passionate clamours of all those oppositional
movements—historically Blanquists and Boulangists, Communists and
Gaullists; and Jean-Pierre Chevènement in today's France—which sought and
continue to aspire to a radical overhaul of the French political system by
invoking the confiscation of State power by sectional groups, the emascula-
tion of the sovereignty of the people, the corruption of the republican fabric
by venal interests, and, most importantly of all, the threat of national dissolution. In an article written in 1999 entitled 'Dépasser le faux débat "jacobins-
girondins"', Chevènement thus categorically reaffirmed his commitment to
republican centralization and his hostility to any devolution of substantive
powers to the regions: 'the addition of twenty-six local policies would not
make a national policy. Let us not forget that the Republic is a collective project, or it is nothing.'[34]

These distinctions between republican and revolutionary, Left and Right,
State and action Jacobinism highlight the elasticity of the phenomenon in
modern French political culture. The synthetic power of Jacobinism, its capacity both to feed upon diverse political movements and at the same time to
mould them into its own shape, can also help to explain its pervasiveness and
durability over time. In fact, its greatest force—and this is the dimension

---

[32] Lucien Jaume, *Echec au libéralisme. Les Jacobins et l'Etat* (Paris, 1990), 74.

[33] Cited in Annie Fitte-Duval, 'Droit et pluralisme dans l'Etat unitaire', *Revue Politique et
Parlementaire*, 1008 (September–October 2000), 69.

[34] Jean-Pierre Chevènement, *La République contre les bien-pensants* (Paris, 1999), 166. For a recent
biography of France's most prominent self-styled Jacobin, see Laurent Chabrun and Franck Hériot,
Jean-Pierre Chevènement, une certaine idée de la République (Paris, 2002).

which was privileged in Vincent Wright's own research—was its capacity to 'occupy' the inner recesses of the French State and to give voice to the very particular conception of territorial, administrative, and constitutional power which has been the defining feature of all modern French governments. This 'State' Jacobinism is not a pure emanation of the republican tradition; in some respects it perpetuates the 'statism' of monarchical absolutism. Even more importantly—and we shall return to this point—this 'State' Jacobinism is heavily indebted to Bonapartism, in both its First and its Second Empire man-ifestations.

Exploring the Jacobin Legacy

Having set out the richness of post-Revolutionary Jacobinism, we can now offer a few thoughts about how and why this overarching concept can provide an ideal framework for this collection of tributes to Vincent Wright's histor-ical scholarship.

Several elements stand out here. Wright was entirely happy to label himself a 'Jacobin', not only in conversation and discussion but also in his writings.[35] In terms of his personal political philosophy, and in light of the distinctions we have offered above, he was most definitely a 'republican' Jacobin—with more than a few Bonapartist trimmings—and not a 'revolutionary' one, although he was always fascinated by French Communists and had a particu-lar soft spot for the 'Jacobin' Communards of 1871, including the really depraved ones such as the Blanquist Prefect of Police Raoul Rigault.[36] And he was even more emphatically a 'State' Jacobin; two of his favourite political leaders were Gambetta and Clemenceau, both complex figures who straddled the divisions between republican and revolutionary, Left and Right, and State and 'action' Jacobinism during their political careers.[37] He would certainly have signed up enthusiastically to the principles listed by Furet: a belief in cen-tralization and a defence of the State as the upholder of the general interest, civil equality, and republican education; the virulence of his anti-clericalism was also reminiscent of the tirades of Paul Bert and the *père* Combes. The pos-sible exception here is the notion of 'national independence', which offended his cosmopolitan culture, his genuine embrace of human universality, and, in the last two decades of his life, his commitment to the project of European political and economic integration.

---

[35] See for example Vincent Wright, 'Questions d'un jacobin anglais aux régionalistes français' (1981).

[36] See Charles Prolès, *Raoul Rigault: la Préfecture de Police sous la Commune* (Paris, 1898); and the entry on Rigault in Jean Maitron (ed.), *Dictionnaire Biographique du mouvement ouvrier, II (1864–1871)*, viii. (Paris, 1970).

[37] Both men began their careers on the republican extreme left and moved considerably to the right later; both exercised the highest functions in the State, and also brought down governments (Clemenceau) and regimes (Gambetta). For two good recent biographies, see Jean-Baptiste Duroselle, *Clemenceau* (Paris, 1989); and Pierre Antonmattei, *Léon Gambetta, héraut de la République* (Paris, 1999).

Second, as mentioned above, this 'Jacobin' theme also resonated very strongly in Wright's own scholarship. Indeed, without his ever explicitly putting it in such terms, it is clear that his concern to explore the territorial, administrative, and elite manifestations of State power in modern France was driven by a quest to make sense of this 'State' Jacobinism. Or, to put the same point differently, this 'Jacobin' culture was often at the heart of the institutional and elite values he spent so much of his time studying, most notably in the Prefectorate and the Conseil d'Etat and in the upper reaches of the French administration. Furthermore, in conceptual terms, the 'Jacobinism' which we have defined here was a quintessentially Wrightian notion: not a 'model' or ideological doctrine but an amorphous ideational assemblage, powerful but often entirely unarticulated—perhaps we should say powerful *because* entirely unarticulated; not an abstraction created by historians or political scientists but a concept which was rooted in French historical experience and shaped by it; and not a smooth and linear phenomenon but rather an entity which was clearly definable at its core but was at the same time highly ambiguous, complex, and paradoxical in its manifestations.

The final reason why this 'Jacobinism' provides an excellent vehicle for this collection of essays in honour of Vincent Wright is that its existence and impact over time have been somewhat neglected by French historians and political scientists. In the words of Gérard Maintenant 'many domains remain to be explored in order to make sense of the scale of Jacobin influence on French and foreign culture'.[38] To avoid any misunderstanding, let us repeat that this claim of neglect is not directed at the 'historical' phenomenon of Jacobinism in the 1790s. If anything, the 1790s proved so controversial that they occulted later manifestations of the phenomenon. For those who abhorred the principles of 1789, such as Joseph de Maistre, Jacobinism was seen as the essence of the Revolution and the manifestation of its perversity; and later French counter-revolutionary thinkers—for example Blanc de Saint-Bonnet, Hippolyte Taine, and Augustin Cochin—concentrated their attacks on the Jacobins' destructiveness, sectarianism, and 'rationalism', as well as their inordinate love of centralization.[39]

But for republicans, too, the Jacobinism of the 1790s was a highly contested object, and therefore much spoken—and written—about. For much of the nineteenth century, and with exceptional intensity at certain periods, notably between the 1840s and the late 1860s, the 'Jacobin' degeneration of the Revolution into the Terror was a source of bitter ideological controversy, with the likes of Jules Michelet, Edgar Quinet, Emile Ollivier, and Jules Ferry leading the charge against a political movement and system of thought which had

---

[38] Gérard Maintenant, *Les Jacobins* (Paris, 1984), 126.

[39] Antoine Blanc de Saint Bonnet, *De l'affaiblissement de la raison par suite de l'enseignement en Europe depuis le XVIIIe siècle* (Paris, 1853) and *Politique réelle* (Paris, 1858); Hippolyte Taine, *Les Origines de la France contemporaine* (3 vols) (Paris, 1878–1885); and Augustin Cochin, *L'Esprit du jacobinisme* (Paris, 1921/1979). On Cochin and the wider historiography of the Revolution, see also Fred Schrader, *Augustin Cochin et la République Française* (Paris, 1992).

in their view systematically negated the principles of 1789.[40] Later generations of republicans, most notably Radicals, rejected this attempt to drive a wedge between 1789 and 1793, and asserted in the celebrated expression of Clemenceau that the Revolution was a 'bloc'.[41] As an historical object, Jacobinism was also given a new lease of life by the Russian Revolution of 1917 and its political and intellectual consequences in France. For much of the twentieth century, the historiography of the French Revolution resembled a pitched battle between a Jacobin-Marxist tradition, broadly sympathetic to the aspirations of the Mountain—even if it was critical of its mistakes and short-comings—and a liberal strand, which essentially drew upon and amplified the attacks launched by anti-Jacobin intellectuals, both liberal and republican, of the nineteenth century. These liberals belatedly triumphed over their adversaries in time for the bicentennial commemorations of 1989, which witnessed the canonization of François Furet as the leading Revolutionary historian of his generation.

Beyond doubt, then, the furore caused by the events of the 1790s, both within the republican camp and outside it, concentrated the attention of French historians to the detriment of the post-Revolutionary manifestations of Jacobinism. Furthermore, as mentioned earlier, 'Jacobinism', in this wider, post-Third Republican sense, was for a long time a derogatory term used by its opponents rather than assumed fully by its advocates and practitioners. Constitutional republicans, for example, generally preferred to eschew the term 'Jacobin' to describe themselves, if necessary going so far as to coin new words, as for example Gambetta's self-definition as an advocate of 'French centrality'.[42] There is also the fear of anachronism, which indeed looms large, particularly when one writes about the nineteenth century, where 'Jacobinism' still essentially retained its ideological associations with the ideas and practices of the 1790s.[43] But some scholars have resolutely confronted and surmounted this obstacle, as we may observe in the lead given by the Revolutionary historian Michel Vovelle. His account of the reluctance of the historical confraternity to analyse this 'Jacobin' legacy dwells essentially on conjunctural factors, the most significant of which is the present 'crisis' of the Jacobin model itself, challenged outside France by European integration and globalization and within the country by the economic retreats of the State, the rise of regional and multicultural aspirations, the growing emphasis on 'civil society', and the decline of traditional integrative institutions such as trades unions and political parties.[44]

[40] On the controversies of the 1860s, see François Furet, *La Gauche et la révolution au milieu du XIXème siècle. Edgar Quinet et la question du Jacobinisme 1865-1870* (Paris, 1986).
[41] Clemenceau speech, 29 January 1891, cited in Barral, *Les fondateurs de la Troisième République* (Paris, 1968), 114.
[42] 'La centralité française'. Speech of 18 September 1878, cited in Barral, *Les fondateurs*, 318. This conceptual innovation did not make it into everyday usage.
[43] On the resonances of the Revolutionary era in nineteenth-century France, see the excellent study by Dominique Aubry, *Quatre-vingt-treize et les Jacobins* (Lyon, 1988); also François Furet and Mona Ozouf (eds), *The French Revolution and the Creation of Modern French Political Culture*, iii. (Oxford, 1989).
[44] Vovelle, *Les Jacobins*, 157-61.

There are, however, deeper reasons why this wider 'Jacobin' legacy has been overlooked, and they can be appreciated at the intersection of the historiographies of the French State, the 1789 Revolution, and the republican tradition. As Pierre Rosanvallon has noted, the history of the modern French State is still in its infancy, with the broad theoretical frameworks of Constant, Tocqueville, Marx, or Louis Blanc still being preferred to detailed empirical investigations and modern conceptualizations.[45] He perceptively identifies the 'specificity' of the French State created by the Revolution, a State which is 'erected as an instrument of production in the social realm and becomes the principal unifying agent in an atomized society'[46]—precisely what many would call a 'Jacobin' State. But Rosanvallon himself carefully eschews the term, and his colleagues have largely followed his lead in this respect.

What of the historians of the French Revolution? Here the problem is of a different order. In addition to their reluctance to venture too far beyond the 1790s—1848 tends to be the point at which most Revolutionary historians 'draw the line[47]—the historiography of the 1790s and its aftermath has to some extent suffered from an over-investment in the Marxist problematic and in the historical correlation between Jacobinism and Bolshevism. For too long, both of these factors have resulted in attention being focused on the 'revolutionary' aspects of Jacobinism at the expense of its 'republican' variant. Furet himself is an excellent example; although he devoted his life to opposing the rigid imposition of the Leninist interpretative grid on the 1790s,[48] and while he also recognized the essential elements of continuity between the 'Jacobin tradition' and the constitutionalist republicanism of the Third Republic, he nonetheless believed that it was its 'revolutionary' manifestations which typified the Jacobin traditions in the nineteenth and twentieth centuries.[49] Behind this specific case lurks a deeper question, which continues to impede our understanding of the modern French political experience: the excessive polarization of historical and theoretical research on the distinct entities of 'republicanism' and 'liberalism', and the reluctance of intellectual and political historians on both sides of this divide to recognize the profound interpenetration of these two realms since the mid-nineteenth century.

Indeed, if historians of the Revolution have shied away from the wider aspects of the Jacobin legacy, historians of French republicanism have not done much better. Here, too, the relative paucity of conceptual and intellectual histories of French republicanism in the nineteenth and twentieth centuries is striking. While it has rightly been received with critical acclaim,

---

[45] Pierre Rosanvallon, *L'Etat en France de 1789 à nos jours* (Paris, 1990), 10.

[46] Rosanvallon, *L'Etat en France*, 96.

[47] With the notable exception of Furet, whose two-volume work *La Révolution* (Paris, 1988) explores the historical and ideological impact of the 1790s up to the establishment of the Third Republic.

[48] On this theme see François Furet, '1789–1917: aller et retour', in *La Révolution en débat* (Paris, 1999), 155–88.

[49] Furet, 'Jacobinisme', 247.

Claude Nicolet's wonderful *L'Idée républicaine en France*[50] has triggered relatively little by way of further research on the history of French republican thought; and it is even more striking that there is still no comparable work on the twentieth century peregrinations of the republican idea. Ever the land of paradox, France thus consistently celebrates the achievements of its dominant political tradition but its historians have done little to explore how this 'republicanism', and especially its 'Jacobin' component, has adapted and evolved since its modern foundation in the Third Republic. An important aspect of the problem is that republicanism has been seen largely through the prism of the *guerres franco-françaises*: in other words, as a source of political division and ideological confrontation rather than as a basis for drawing political families and political groups together around core principles and values.

This modern republican function as a common denominator—'the regime which divides us the least', in the celebrated expression of the early Third Republic—still awaits its full and comprehensive conceptual and philosophical narration.[51] This is especially the case when we think of the history of the French Left, where the significance of republicanism has been consistently undervalued. The contribution of this book will in this respect be to underscore the cementing role of 'Jacobin' principles in this integrative republican tradition.

The Contributions and Themes of this Book

Now, finally, to the specifics of this collection of essays and what they reveal about the modern French political experience. The nine contributors to this book were all friends and colleagues of Vincent Wright, and they collectively represent almost the full range of disciplines and fields which he engaged with during his academic career: constitutional law, administrative history, political science, political thought, and sociology.[52]

Their contributions follow an essentially chronological format while at the same time highlighting the different facets of the French 'Jacobin' legacy since the early nineteenth century. The book substantively opens with two chapters on one of the defining themes of Jacobin practice and imagery: war. Karma Nabulsi's piece focuses on the political culture of republican war in the early 1830s, the 'combat phase'—in the words of Louis Blanc—in the construction of the modern French republican movement. She highlights the material and intellectual sophistication of this insurrectionary republican culture and the passionate nature of intra-republican debates during this period. We also

---

[50] Paris, 1982.

[51] For an ambitious recent effort in this field, seeking among other things to explore the connection between classical republicanism and its modern French variants, see Blandine Kriegel, *Philosophie de la République* (Paris, 1998).

[52] Wright was also an economist, and he regarded political economy—in the old-fashioned sense of the term—as an important sub-discipline. Much of his work on European politics in the 1980s and 1990s sprang from his interest in questions of political economy.

rediscover the pivotal nature of the July Monarchy generation of republicans: on the one hand the continuators of the political and intellectual legacy of the 1790s, and thus of Jacobinism, and on the other hand the direct, if unacknowledged, inspiration for republican theory and practices during the Second Empire and early Third Republic, as evidenced by the powerful resonances of the debates of the early 1830s in the dilemmas confronted by the republicans during the Franco-Prussian war.

My own chapter offers a very different variation on this war theme, examining the fate of war veterans of the 1792–1815 period—thus also including many 'real' Jacobins—in the joyful setting of the ceremonies of 15 August, France's national festivity under the Second Empire. Through an analysis of this civic interface between State authorities and local communities, and the public honouring of Jacobin and Napoleonic war veterans, we hear the continuing echoes of the myths and memories of the Revolutionary and imperial eras and witness the vitality of popular Bonapartism in mid-nineteenth century France. But this chapter also provides a specific example of a phenomenon which became an integral component of the modus operandi of the modern Jacobin State: its assumption of the task of defining the historical and political identity of the nation, and its exhortation of the citizenry to celebrate this 'invented tradition': essentially the same exercise which has been carried out by the Republic with the *fête du quatorze juillet* ever since 1880.

The next four contributions take us through some of the important mutations and adaptations of French Jacobinism between the early Third Republic and the Liberation. In Chapter 4, Jean-Pierre Machelon provides a complex and nuanced description of republican prefects appointed between 1870 and 1914, the 'heroic' foundational years of the republican regime. Despite introducing some modest changes to their status and functions, the triumphant Republic essentially continued to deploy prefects as political agents, making them responsible for the political surveillance of their department and the organization of 'good' elections. Through his account Machelon affords us with key insights into a fundamental aspect of the early Third Republic: its explicit reinforcement of State institutions, at both national and local levels. Yet this 'strong' State could be curiously porous, as we discover in Maurice Larkin's chapter on the quest for State favours between 1900 and 1926 in the principal Masonic organization, the Grand Orient de France. Drawing on archives of local lodges, Larkin paints a rich and evocative portrait of the provincial Freemasonry during this period and demonstrates the close connections between Masonic and republican elites, and the more than occasional penetration of the latter by the interests and values of the former.

Chapters 6 and 7, by Philip Nord and Douglas Johnson respectively, take us forward to the period between the Popular Front and the Liberation. We have here splendid contrasts on the theme of continuities and ruptures in the French State. Nord tells of the transformation of the Institut des Études Politiques in Paris (Sciences-Po), both from the 'internal' perspective of its curriculum and teaching staff and from the 'external' aspect of its status as a public institution. This is a compelling story of modernization and renewal but also a tale, repeated on countless occasions in similar encounters between the Jacobin State and 'private' groups, of elite adaptation, accommodation, and co-optation. By the Liberation, Sciences-Po had managed to head off the challenges of the Popular Front and Vichy, and successfully to manoeuvre the post-war republican State into adopting a 'reform' which left it with considerable autonomy, ultimately allowing it to retain its position as one of the leading tertiary institutions in France.

In neat counterpoint, Douglas Johnson's chapter looks at the reconstruction of the French State from the single and imposing perspective of General de Gaulle. Here, too, we find the same duality: strong elements of rupture, most particularly in de Gaulle's aspiration to break with Vichy and rebuild a powerful State which provided the leadership which the Republic had failed to offer the French people; at the same time, Johnson shows how the Resistance leader drew on existing notions of the republican good life, particularly in his conception of sovereignty, the necessary revival of party political competition, and the unity and indivisibility of the Army and State. Focusing as it does on the role of individual leadership, Johnson's piece wonderfully draws out the place of the contingent in the making of history, as well as the role of mistakes and false perceptions. More broadly, we also witness one of the defining moments of twentieth century French history: the embrace of the republican tradition by what was to become the dominant political movement of the French Right.

The last three chapters of *The Jacobin Legacy* bring us into the contemporary realm, with the overarching theme of the capacity, and willingness, of the Jacobin State to mould collective identities in France. In a powerful and thought-provoking chapter, Olivier Ihl explores the proliferation of meritorious awards by the French State in the modern era and especially under the Republic. His argument is that this policy of systematically honouring citizens has to be seen from a dual perspective: on the one hand the reinforcement of the 'majestic' attributes of the republican State, and on the other the social control of the citizenry through the public definition of criteria of virtuous conduct. Underlying this inexorable process is the unfolding of bureaucratic power: a stimulating Foucaldian twist to Tocqueville's classic argument about the transcendence of politics by the power of French State institutions.

In Chapter 9, Yves Mény casts his expert eye on the territorial order of the Republic. At the aspirational level, here too we find a strong proclivity rigidly to impose a common order on the whole of society, based on the Jacobin principle of 'unity as uniformity'. However, the reality proves much more complex, and Mény draws attention to widespread instances of exceptions, derogations, and 'loose' applications of the Jacobin territorial model, both in the operation of local administration and, perhaps even more so, in the workings of local democracy. Indeed, so different is the reality from the discourse that it raises the question of why the political rhetoric does not change. The answer, implies Mény, is that mythologies play an essential role in all

political systems, and the Jacobin myth remains—for want of a better alternative—the defining articulation of modern French political and civic life.

   This disjunction between rhetoric and reality is also strongly underscored in
Dominique Schnapper's chapter, which closes this collection of essays. The
Republic sought to create a unified citizenry and effectively used its educational and military institutions to integrate the native and immigrant populations into its new civic order. But, far from destroying specificities, this project
incorporated particularistic identities, both territorial or religious, which were
recognized by the State as the indispensable mediators in the formation of the
new republican order. In contemporary France, Schnapper concludes, the
retreat of the Jacobin State is uneven: it has been forced to retrench—especially in the economic realm—in the face of European integration and globalization; and it has effectively recognized the existence of particular 'groups',
notably in its social policies and even in the hallowed realm of education. But
in other areas, notably the 'special' status of public sector workers, Jacobin
principles and practices remain entrenched, even if their future no longer
appears as secure as in the golden age of 'heroic' public policies and ideological certitudes.

Looking Forward

Republican and revolutionary, Left and Right, State and action Jacobinisms
have thus all contributed to give France her current political, administrative,
and cultural physiognomy. The breadth of this Jacobinism can also be emphasized in terms of the historical influences which have shaped it over time: a
point which was repeatedly emphasized in Vincent Wright's own scholarship.
Modern Jacobinism is an integral component of republican political culture,
but this book makes clear that it is not an *exclusively* republican construct: it
has evolved by incorporating absolutist elements, liberal principles and values, and also significant aspects of the Bonapartist legacies of the First and
Second Empires, most ironically so given how much Napoleon and the
Jacobins detested each other. Jacobinism is thus both less and more than
republicanism: less in the sense that it is not a comprehensive ideology and
more in that it contains elements, most notably the cult of the State, which
are not necessary features of the French republican tradition.

   Chateaubriand deplored the fact that, having suffered the physical despotism of the Jacobins and Bonaparte, France seemed condemned to endure the
despotism of their memories; they had 'disturbed even the future'.[53] With his
characteristic sensitivity and prescience the author of *Génie du Christianisme*
had appreciated the depth of the imprint which would be left by these two
forces, the joint founding fathers of modern 'Jacobinism'. Fortunately, how-

---

[53] Quoted in Françoise Mélonio, *Naissance et affirmation d'une culture nationale. La France de 1815
à 1880* (Paris, 2001), 275.

ever, its legacy proved rather more mellow than Chateaubriand had feared. Modern Jacobinism not only adapted itself to the requirements of a democratic polity but also flourished into something approximating the defining character of 'Frenchness'. And while it would be unseemly to enter into the polemics which have often marred French discussions of the nature and impact of post-Revolutionary Jacobinism, we should make clear our sympathy with Vincent Wright's positive appreciation of its overall achievements. But this, as Dominique Schnapper points out so well in her contribution, is surely a conclusion with which all reasonable men and women should concur, for to dissent from it is in some significant sense to reject out of hand not only the core features of the French polity as we know it today but also the battles which generations of militants in France, and elsewhere, have fought to uphold the Jacobin principles of *liberté-égalité-fraternité*.

But such sympathy—and this too takes us back to Vincent—should exclude neither a sense of sobriety nor a willingness to identify the paradoxes of the French Jacobin legacy and to criticize its shortcomings. Its synthetic attributes, which have done so much to ensure its success and adaptation over time, also go some way towards explaining the multiple contradictions of modern France, many of which are highlighted in this book: a land where Jacobinism can be both a doctrine of State power and an instrument of its radical critique; where the State reigns supreme but where groups are routinely permitted to use violence to challenge, resist, and even overturn public policies—the legitimacy of 'the street' in France is undoubtedly one of the most vivid political legacies of the Jacobin era; where the civic order celebrates the principle of 'equality' as an irreversible conquest of '1789' but where women are still severely under-represented in the political system and where social differences based on culture, honorific distinctions, and much else are explicitly recognized and actively promoted; where all groups repeatedly invoke the myth of 'unity' but where social fragmentation and institutional corporatism continue to fissure the body politic; and, most paradoxically of all, where State dignitaries repeatedly celebrate their 'patriotic' credentials and their particularistic commitment to the defence of French culture but where these same elites abolish the national currency at one fell swoop and resolutely push their citizens into wider and deeper integration into the European Union.

Can this Jacobin culture survive the acceleration of the process of European integration in the twenty-first century, which many in Britain—and some in France too—see as threatening the very notion of the modern sovereign State? Vincent Wright constantly warned against showing undue haste in burying the French State.[54] Following his lead in this respect, the contributions offered in this book show both the resilience of the Jacobin culture which is rooted in the French State and its considerable capacity for adaptation. Furthermore, especially in France, political discourse and especially political mythologies

---

[54] See for example his piece 'L'Etat n'est pas mort', in Dominique Jacques-Jouvenot (ed.), *L'oeil du sociologue* (Besançon, 1998).

are much harder entities to break down than constitutions, political institutions, or even regimes. French politicians may today celebrate liberal individualism and social pluralism, welcome the advent of a Europeanized and globalized world community, award the Légion d'Honneur to Sylvester Stallone, and even on occasion speak English. But their essential utterances—notably in moments of national crisis and during the polarizing elections to the Presidency—continue, *pour le meilleur et pour le pire*, to be made using the vintage terminology and imagery bequeathed to them by their Jacobin political ancestors. Jacques Chirac achieved his re-election as President in 2002 on an immaculately Jacobin platform, rallying the nation around the themes of republican unity, social fraternity, and the defence of democratic principles against the threat of political factionalism and national dissolution.

So are we witnessing the end of Jacobinism? We should simply echo Zhou-en-Lai's response when asked to assess the impact of the French Revolution: 'It is too early to tell.'

2

'La Guerre Sainte': Debates about Just War among Republicans in the Nineteenth Century

KARMA NABULSI

> Today the Prussians surround Besançon, and are threatening the valley of the Rhône. No more delays! The republican populations of the Midi must rise collectively in a *levée en masse* so as to prevent the invaders from defiling any further the soil of the *patrie*.
>
> *Manifeste de la Ligue du Midi*, Marseille, 25 October 1870[1]

THIS exhortation comes not from the Revolutionary era but from an official call to arms to the people by the French republican organization, the Ligue du Midi, in October 1870. The original poster was given to me by Vincent Wright in the spring of 1999, while we were working on a piece together, drawing from Vincent's extensive archives of the 1870–1 war period. Our article focused on the range of disagreements between Gambetta's new republican prefects and France's army generals, all of whom had been appointed by the old regime of the Second Empire. Both of these actors were charged with organizing the defence of the country as it was being invaded by Prussia. And Vincent and I had given ourselves the ambitious task of setting out precisely the nature of the quarrel between them and its manifestations on the local and national levels. We set out to classify and explore, within the literature on the Franco-Prussian war and wider debates in the academic literature, a typology of conflicts between these two parties. Yet every day our discussions on the nature of our joint piece inexorably took us into the realm of another, more fascinating quarrel concerning the conflicts that flourished within the republican camp in 1870–1.

Indeed, the Ligue poster sums up some of the paradoxes of the new republican Government of National Defence between September 1870 and February 1871. It was published as an official declaration on behalf of the French government and issued in Marseille by the regional prefect, Alphonse Esquiros.

---

[1] Archives Départementales du Rhône, Lyon, 1 M 118.

This call to arms, however, did not happen to have the sanction of the leadership in Paris; the army was even less sympathetic to the notion of arming citizens. Why did Esquiros, the author of the Ligue's proclamation, nonetheless publish it and believe he was acting on legitimate authority in so doing? Esquiros was somewhat typical of the generation of republicans that came into administrative power under Gambetta. Vincent had been engaged upon a detailed study of Gambetta's prefects for over 20 years and had amassed a wealth of archival and other primary sources on them as well as on the 1870–1 war during which they had been appointed. Wright's file on Esquiros undoubtedly contained more personal details about him than would have been found even in his police files under the Second Empire. His maternal grandfather's occupation, that of his uncles, the dates of his siblings' births and deaths: all were neatly entered in the Esquiros family file under the general heading 'FAMILY: a family of good bourgeois stock from Paris'.[2] Also included—after an extended entry on his 'position of fortune'—were his 'religious opinions'. This contained a description of his civic funeral taken from an administrative report in the departmental archives of the Bouches-du-Rhône: 'the population gave him a magnificent funeral . . . more than ten thousand people followed the procession: his burial was a scandalous manifestation of atheism, and his tomb would become a site for the manifestation of free-thinkers.'[3] Under the heading 'POLITICAL OPINIONS' Vincent had entered a single phrase: 'radical: Montagnard under the Second Republic; and in the National Assembly he sat on the extreme left.' It is also worth noting that Esquiros was a defender of the Jacobins; indeed his *Histoire des Montagnards* (1847) praised the Robespierrists as the saviours of the French nation.[4]

The person who appointed Esquiros to his post and was at the forefront of the French war effort after September 1870 was Léon Gambetta, the Minister of Interior and War in the republican Government of National Defence. Gambetta and Esquiros had much in common. They both had a remarkable way with words—Gambetta as a public orator, Esquiros as a writer and poet; they were both perceived as 'radical' republicans under the Second Empire; in 1869 both stood as republican candidates in Marseille; and both even shared membership of the same Masonic lodge in the city, La Réforme. But there were also differences between the two men. Gambetta's provincialism, his more humble social origins, and the relatively recent assimilation of his family into France all contrasted with Esquiros's Parisian bourgeois background. Esquiros was also a typical republican of 1848 who had spent much of the Second Empire years in exile, creating a vacuum into which younger and more ambitious young republicans such as Gambetta entered the political fray during the 1860s. Gambetta made his name in Paris during the Baudin trial, during which

---

[2] Vincent Wright Private Papers.
[3] Archives Départementales des Bouches-du-Rhône, Marseille. 1 M 1422.
[4] Alphonse Esquiros, *Histoire des Montagnards* (Paris, 1847).

he astonished the imperial court by challenging the legitimacy of the Bonapartist State.[5]

Such differences within the republican camp can be identified in several spheres, and can be usefully broken down and then set into a very Wrightian model of three variables: political, functional, and ideological. Functional differences emerged over where the locus of power should reside in the Republican State: in Paris or the provinces; among political or administrative elites; between civilian politicians or army generals. The ideological differences were between those that felt that the republican assumption of power should actually herald the onset of the Revolution and those who emphatically thought it should not. The republicans were also divided along generational lines—between the older generations of republicans from 1848 and the younger, more radical strands—that often overlapped with political and ideological differences, although this division was also about experience, philosophical affinities, and personal ambition.

The quarrels of 1870–1, however, still belonged within a particular world: the contingent sphere of the Franco-Prussian war and, by implication, a world in which the extraordinary claims of war, invasion, and occupation supervened over 'normal' politics. But another way of understanding the conflict within the republican camp is to appreciate that war was integral to the political culture of French republicanism in the nineteenth century. Republican views and practices on war in 1870–1 drew upon earlier generations of practitioners in the nineteenth century: these republicans were the definers of republican ideology and principles and the possessors of a rich and complex philosophy. By illustrating the world of French republican war of the 1830s we shall see how the ideational was always informed by the concrete world of political action and also the reverse: the realm of abstract principles informed and shaped the practical realm of war. As we explore this diachronic relationship within the French republican tradition, the impact of the 1830s generation on the remainder of the nineteenth century emerges.[6] Indeed, we shall see how the functional, political, and ideological differences of 1870–1 were all subsumed within the same just war debate. The arguments and divisions between republicans in the 1830s were all a part of a republican tradition of war, as will be demonstrated below.

The Republic of War at the Start of the July Monarchy

The early years of the decade—1832, 1833, 1834—were described by Gabriel Perreux as the essential years for the development of both republican thought

[5] Philip Nord, *The Republican Moment* (Princeton, 1995), 132.

[6] Jean Claude Caron's body of work on the 1830s shows, among other things, the manner of the influence of the French Revolution on the 1830s generation, but also the particular impact that the 1830s had on later generations. See for example his 'Inscrire la Révolution dans l'Histoire. Les Trois Glorieuses: coda, appendice ou palimpseste de la Grande Révolution?', in Michel Biard (ed.), *Terminée La Révolution...Actes du IVe Colloque Européen de Calais (26 et 27 janvier 2001)* (Calais: Bulletin des Amis du Vieux Calais, special issue, 2002), 56–67.

and action, the great 'period of effervescence and enthusiasm' for republicans.[7] And their enthusiasm was for a distinct course of action, that of creating republican states through war. The world of republican war, both its passions and some of its more theoretical principles, as well as its successes and its many harsh failures, clearly connects the ideology of republicanism to the types of actions republicans actually took. War was called the 'only sure path to freedom', and it was the main road taken by many republicans of the period.

At the fall of the day, the working men respectfully removed the tricolour flag, accompanying it into the courtyard and put themselves in a circle around it. All the republicans in the prison descended, reunited by the religion of Equality, and came with joy to render homage, all placed themselves haphazardly, stirred by the memories of other times and repeating, in chorus, the inspirations of our revolutionary poets. One of the assistants intoned the *Chant du Départ*; soon all the voices would lift, in concert, to repeat the refrain. We would go on to other hymns of liberty; how they were noble, elevated, sublime! Patriotism would be rekindled, the heart would revive and become passionate, and the soul would rise. Nothing could disturb this enthusiasm! All these strong and resonant voices, this silence, this place, this revered liberty, exalted, this presence of the three colours, all these men with their overflowing faith, whose conviction emphasized their words and rendered them so vibrant, all these formed a touching solemnity, a type of festival where hope was worshipped.[8]

These instances not only created a moment in which to live the dream of the future republic that was to be created but were practical tools of war as well, used as a means of strengthening the moral forces necessary to do battle in order to achieve it. Sometimes the songs themselves would become hard weapons in the battle of republican war. These republicans of the 1830s generation had come together initially committed to this collective goal, the realization of a republican state. This was understood as the real matter that bound them to each other in a common cause and to their collaborative work. Yet the practice of war attached them just as closely to each other as it was the very process by which they endeavoured to become part of this future republic. War was therefore the correct means to both build and to be in the republic. The way they saw themselves, the way they saw their predicament, how they interpreted what they were in the midst of: in all these areas we find the unifying concept of war. Republicans defined themselves as the 'Gladiators of the People'.[9] They perceived themselves in terms of the dangers of their goal, of the risks: 'Republicans are those who, dominated by an ardent love of justice, renounce their particular interests in order to establish, at the cost of their lives, the laws of justice and of reason.'[10] This battle was often described by

---

    [7] Gabriel Perreux, *Au Temps des sociétés secrètes. La propagande républicaine au début de la Monarchie de Juillet* (Paris, 1931), 384.
    [8] Emile Couret, *Le Pavillon des princes. Histoire complète de la prison politique de Sainte-Pelagie* (Paris, 1891), 110–11.
    [9] *Documents saisis de Berrier-Fontaine (1834)*, Archives Nationales, Paris, CC 664.
    [10] *Manifeste du Comité des Droits de L'Homme et du Citoyen*, in Girod de l'Ain, *Affaire du Mois D'Avril: Rapport fait à la Cours des Pairs*, i. (Paris, 1835), 33.

republicans as a continual political condition and as a constant search for liberty; it was also seen in distinctly religious, national, idealistic, as well as in pragmatic terms.

French republicans were participating in a broader debate and coordination with republicans from other parts of Europe. The engagement in a war to establish republics united this 1830s generation of European republicans across all types of divides: cultural, national, social, and linguistic. Although enjoying the benefits of peace under the July Monarchy, members of the republican Société des Droits de l'Homme et du Citoyen in Paris not only saw themselves as warriors entering a battle but felt that entering war was as sacred as taking the vows of marriage. 'Understand well your mission. It is sublime, and you are the only ones capable of accomplishing it! So work without respite, sure of that day which, fixed for the Battle, will be the definitive day of our betrothal to Liberty.'[11] The idea of being at war united republicans, yet had numerous meanings for them: they were in the midst of a war to create a republic, and in the midst of a war quite simply to remain a republican, as persons and as members of a republican group, of a republican party. The republican historian and politician of the period, Louis Blanc, wrote that the 'republican idea' was, during this period of the 1830s, in its 'phase of combat'.[12] These concepts were essential and the idea of war contained many deep-seated notions of the republican good life. War could even serve non-republicans as the vehicle for their conversion to republicanism. In a petition to Louis-Philippe, entitled 'Protestation des sous-officiers de l'armée', French soldiers claimed to find themselves suddenly sensing that they were no longer soldiers of the king. Rather, they now realized they were soldiers of the nation. Therefore it followed that they belonged 'on the frontiers defending the nation, and not invading others', and that the better form of government for them was now a republican one.[13]

The political centrality of war, thus defined, was set out by Jean-Jacques Rousseau in his *Social Contract*, a book relevant to this 1830s generation as a useful and eminently practical manual for their everyday business of working to construct republics and which they relied upon, not merely as theory or as an abstract philosophical text, together with their plans and charts and maps. It was reflected in the way they lived and thought, and the references they made to it. What Rousseau pointed out, and which was evident to these republicans, was that this state of war also had to do with confrontation and resistance, with not surrendering, even if one was the weaker party or not in authority. It was a book they could apply to their own predicament: 'I say that a slave made during wartime or a conquered people owe no allegiance to their master, except to obey him as much as compelled.' The state of war continued,

[11] 'Ordre du Jour' of the Legions Révolutionnaires, addressed to members of the Société des Droits de l'Homme. Archives Nationales, Paris, CC 664, document no. 40.

[12] From his *Discours Politiques*, cited in Iouda Tchernoff, *Le parti républicain sous la Monarchie de Juillet* (Paris, 1901), 321.

[13] 'Insurrection d'Avril à Chalon-sur-Saone et Besançon', document no. 484, Archives Nationales, Paris, CC 582.

even if one was the weaker party, because 'to renounce one's freedom is to renounce one's qualities as a man, to the rights and even the duties of humanity'. The republican, by virtue of his values and principles, had a duty to fight.

Thus, from whichever angle we examine things, the right of slavery is meaningless, not only because it is illegitimate, but because it is absurd and signifies nothing. These words, slavery, and right, are contradictory ; they are mutually exclusive. Whether from one man to another, or from one people to another, this kind of discourse will always remain equally absurd.[14]

Increasingly, republicans in France identified with this doctrine of resistance as Louis Philippe introduced more and more repressive and restrictive measures in 1832 and 1833. They saw themselves suffering under a regime that was entirely illegitimate, based as it was upon the power of the king and not of the people nor their elected representatives in parliament. In this sense they believed they were in a common battle with republicans across Europe who were fighting the Russian, Prussian, and Austrian empires.

As Rousseau had articulated, the rights to resist which were claimed by republicans were seen as having concomitant duties: the commitment to fighting the much more powerful enemy. This was an inexorable dynamic for republican action. One may not have institutional force or command official armies of the state. But one still had moral force, and even a moral obligation to resist tyranny. Obedience was owed only to just governments, not tyrannies. 'Let us therefore agree that force does not make law, and that one is compelled to obey only those authorities which are legitimate.'[15]

Republican war occurred at different levels and in distinct spheres: in the arguments laid out in pamphlets, in conspiracies and counter-conspiracies, in parliamentary debates, on battlefields, in prison cells, on city streets, and in besieged towns. It took place through different channels and modes: in private conversations, through public readings of republican brochures on factory floors, through chanting songs of insurrection, through planning them, through the military maps, signs, and secret meetings, through guns and swords, and long night marches. Republican war also took place using very diverse methods: from the merely political and theoretical in thought and action to the violent and the lethal in practice. Within this spectrum, one could find an enormous variety of types and methods of republican war. It could be engaged upon secretly or publicly, by small groups or by crowds of people, by leaders or by those who were, in other circumstances, normally led. Yet consistent throughout all of these terms, levels, spheres, methods, individuals, and groups, the notions of struggle and fight, of battle and resistance, unceasing, persistent, remained.

Two things united these republicans: the desire to create a republic, and the notion that they were in a state of war until it was built. The types of French

---

[14] Jean-Jacques Rousseau, Le Contrat Social, in Œuvres Complètes, iii., Book I Ch. IV, 'Sur L'Esclavage' (Paris, 1964 edn), 356, 358.

[15] Rousseau, Contrat Social, Book I, Chapter 3, 'Du Droit du Plus Fort', 355.

republicans that worked together were diverse in their ideological strands and traditions. And, once we advance through and beyond the perception that they were united in a common cause of struggle, we discover that there was a bewildering range of approaches to this common cause. We will see that, although much was commonly understood amongst republicans, it is more rare to find the smaller questions commonly agreed between them, especially on what it meant to be at war. The differences, as we will see, were ideological, contextual, tactical, and strategic; and they mattered enormously. They mattered because war was then, and remains, an issue of life and death; the way to live and think as a republican at war therefore had to be exactly right. Yet what will unfold here is an image of a common political culture that united these republican fighters and activists within France and right across Europe. For it is only within this same culture that their debates and dissensions occurred. Cultures are neither homogeneous nor united, and that of republican war was no exception.

The Enemy in Republican War

How did these republicans come to believe that such a destructive and violent mechanism as war was the solution to their political situation in France, and the best way to create a peaceful republic of liberty and equality, especially one where all men were brothers, living together in harmony? It was through an understanding of what it was they were confronting: their understanding of the enemy. They saw the enemy in two ways: as a concept and also as a material obstacle to their goal. Republicans generally acknowledged that in order to wage a successful war it was essential to have a good understanding of exactly who their enemy was. But, although the relationship between these two levels was also seen as crucial, they were not always disentangled. This was because the idealized principles, the future goal, and the more unpleasant reality were all hopelessly intertwined in practice. Yet it was clear to republicans that it would be impossible to change this implacable present if both the principles and the goal of defeating the enemy were not correctly set out. And there was a wide range of views on how they saw the common enemy, their current condition, and the nature of their predicament. So many of the battles were not merely about how to fight the enemy, or even the pleasure of fighting it; first, it had to be understood who the enemy was. This was the first battle that had to be won.

   The enemy was most commonly seen as a tyrant, a despot, or an emperor: in all these respects a ruler who enslaved his people. In Lyon, on the last days of the momentous insurrection of 1834 and as it was being crushed by the national troops, a poster went up in several places in the Croix Rousse area: 'No doubt it is terrible that blood must spill in order to fight tyranny, but this blood cannot fall back upon us, since our enemies have already assassinated us before we could dream of taking up arms. We are republicans and we know all the virtues.'[16] Here too was a reference to the justness of a war of self-defence against tyranny that was evoked by all republicans irrespective of their particular ideological strand. War was the only possible response to enslavement by the tyrant.

The republican society Aide-toi le ciel t'aidera had no concern that it might lose support by broadening its definition of the nature of the enemy. The loathed despot became more than simply an oppressive political ruler, it also included the reactionary practices of the Catholic Church. In its 'Last Advice to Electors' the society published a small brochure with the reminder that if one voted for the enemy the result would be: 'Humiliating wars of conquest like those of Algeria, or one which had, as its object, the maintenance and support of despotism and of the priests, like the war in Spain.'[17]

Divergences over the definition of the enemy and its social and political interpretations were to provoke the most heated debates within republican discourse during the battle to create the republic or even once it had been established. But the urgency of war overrode many of these problems. And the reliance on republican virtues meant that republicans could always draw upon another source for unity. Most republicans of the period was anxious to discover, and maintain, a definition of the enemy as all inclusive as possible. A combination of republican principles with virtues was essential for this weaving together of disparate views. Pierre Lortet's use of Fichte's famous essay *De l'idée d'une guerre légitime*, on the rights and duties of resistance against Napoleon, is one such example. His core values of republicanism were so universalist that he found sources of inspiration within the very arguments used against his own nation's army. 'It was always thus that Lortet was a partisan of the war of propaganda, and he found the arguments of the German philosophers and publicists who had resisted [French] oppression extremely useful.'[18] A medical doctor at Lyon, his republican activities were phenomenal. A founder of the Carbonari in that town in the 1820s; head of that town's Philhellenic committee during those years; a close associate of Buonarroti; head of the Committee for the Polish refugees; head of the reformed Charbonnerie democratique universelle of 1833, Lortet was also a scholar and the translator into French of the writings of Fichte and Kant.[19] He republished Fichte's essay with an introduction in which he encouraged the people of Lyon to revolt against their own government.

Several passages of the work that I have translated here seem to be written just for the era that we are now living in, and apply perfectly to the events that we are currently witnessing. The reader will seize all too easily the allusions for it to be necessary that I indi-

---

[16] E. Carrier, the commander of the Croix Rousse area of Lyon, 11 April 1834. Requisitoire, Cours des Pairs, *L'Affaire d'avril 1834* (Paris, 1835), 177.

[17] 'Papiers Saisis au domicile de Marchais'. No 25, 1833. Archives Nationales CC 614.

[18] Fernand Rude, 'Entre le Libéralisme et le Socialisme: Quelques médecins Lyonnais aux temps Romantiques', *Lyon et la Médecine*, special issue of *Revue Lyonnaise de la Médecine* (1958), 177.

[19] On his friendship and association with Buonarroti and the Carbonari see Lehning's classic 'Buonarroti and his International Secret Societies', *International Review of Social History*, 1 (1956), 133.

cate them in the preface. But read in this manner, [this book] could be seen as a document of the times.[20]

An argument made against the evils of foreign invasion which was then turned against domestic tyranny and which also set out clearly the guiding principles and virtues of republican war was *The Idea of a Just War*, republished by Lortet in 1831. It found a ready echo amongst republicans of his town, who were deep in preparations for the uprising that was to take place in the coming months. As Lortet asserted in his introduction to Fichte's call to arms: 'We cannot mistake the tyrant.'[21]

The Battle Ahead, the Battle Behind, the Battle Within

Republicans setting out to wage this war well understood that the physical and material forces the enemy possessed had to be confronted with all the united energies that they could bring to bear. An accurate evaluation of the nature of these forces was therefore vital. Tyranny and empire could not be seen in isolation from an appraisal of current conditions which obtained in both the enemy's camp and their own. How they conceived of their adversary's position and its capacities emerged from their principles as republicans.

But it also rose directly, and in some cases primarily, from the forges of their many heated encounters with the enemy in various arenas. What the practical experiences fighting empire had taught them about the nature of its forces also shaped their more abstract notions of their enemy, in a manner that pure republican theory, on its own, never could have done. Moreover, it was from this basis that they constructed their political and military plans for the battles ahead. The battle ahead depended, above all, upon republicans agreeing on a common narrative of what had transpired in the battle behind, which had been fought recently or even in the distant past. These were some of the most burning issues over which disagreements raged.

Some had the imaginative capacity to rely upon the battles waged by others and to draw upon others' experiences. As one of the young republican leaders who had led the street fighting in Paris which had overthrown the monarchy in July 1830, it was said of Godefroy Cavaignac that he was 'one of the first to fight, one of the most courageous, and generous, and was amongst those that planted the *tricolore* in the Tuileries'.[22] Yet Cavaignac decided against fighting for the installation of a republic as there appeared to be some popular opposition to it in the summer of 1830. He was the son of a member of the

---

[20] Pierre Lortet, 'Préface', in Johann Fichete, *De l'idée d'une guerre légitime: trois leçons faites à Berlin, en Mai 1813* (Lyon, 1831).
[21] Ibid.
[22] C. Ambert, *Portraits Républicains: Armand Carrel, Godefroy Cavaignac, Armand Marrast, Le Colonel Charras* (Paris, 1870), 88.

revolutionary Convention, and he often said this personal understanding of revolutionary history informed his assessment of how to measure the enemy's forces but, more importantly, how to confront the battle ahead. When congratulated by some liberals for his restraint in allowing the installation of Louis Philippe in 1830, rather than a republican government, he repudiated their gratitude, replying: 'You are wrong to thank us: we ceded only because we were not in force . . . Later it will be different.'[23]

The fact that, during the early years of the 1830s, republican insurrections all over Europe were meeting with failure after failure became the common starting point for published calls to arms, the point being that these attempts were not fruitless or doomed before they began. One placard put up at Lyon towards the end of the 1834 uprising urged the people to rise and overcome the despair of failure: 'Citizens! You must throw away the discouragement amongst us, the military authority has sent a message to the mayor in which it mentions that the town has submitted.' It went on, but 'there is nothing to this! The republicans, full of courage and ardour, are resisting with advantage: imitate them, continue our defence . . . be always unanimous in our efforts . . . and soon we shall hear the songs of victory—Long live Liberty and Anathema to Tyrants!'[24] At nearly the same time, in Paris, orders were going out that began in the same manner:

Citizens! Once again we have seen our hopes deceived, once again we have seen the paving stones of the street red with our blood of our brothers. But, as always, we have lifted ourselves up again even stronger, helped by our experiences in this defeat, without ceasing for an instant to be profoundly convinced of the infallibility of our principles. Put therefore to profit this past of sorrowful memories.[25]

And it was not only encounters with the tyrant and tyrannical rule that could prove fierce. Disputes over the battles recently fought and lost were what led to most of the skirmishes within the republican camp. Disagreements raged over the causes of these defeats. Tactics and strategy, both political and military, became tangled inside the political and ideological principles for which republicans were fighting. Flawed planning, flawed politics, faulty overall strategy, obsessive rows over minor tactics, or combinations of all of the above were published in brochures and argued over in barracks, in public halls and private rooms, in the prisons, and in the cafés. The tenor of these debates was so passionate simply because the stakes were very high: the final judgement of the causes for their previous defeats was also their benchmark for a future course of action. The wrong analysis was perilous to both life and limb, and the right one needed to persuade a sufficient number to embark upon it in order for it actually to become the right one.

Between 1832 and 1834, arguments within the republican camp always began with a critique of what had gone before. Arguments thus were partly

[23] George Weill, *Histoire du parti républicain en France (1814–1870)* (Paris, 1900), 25.

[24] Requisitoire, Cours des Pairs, *l'Affaire d'avril 1834*, 178.

[25] 'Ordre du jour' of the *Legions Révolutionnaires*, Archives Nationales, Paris, CC 664, document no. 40.

intrinsic and partly instrumental. But, for republicans poring over the causes of the last wars, one could never separate means from ends. The reasons they had lost, they argued, were that it had not been a republican war or that the battle had not been republican enough. Thus, in political battles as well as in the military ones, both the general and the particular, the ideological and the strategic, the principles and the numbers of dead counted were intermeshed with each other.

What Can Be Done and What Cannot Be Done

'The spirit of combat that drove the republicans pushed their authors to an exaggeration of theory more apparent than real', a historian of the French republican party said in their defence when faced with their bellicose prose.[26] But the theory of just war was not as distinct from its practice as some would have liked: the principles which inspired republicans drew them, on the whole, towards war rather than away from it. For the Poles and the Italians this issue was already settled; they were suffering tyranny and despotism. It was their right and their duty to resist it. However, for the French the question was much more complicated. Were they under a tyranny? If so, could they use violence to overthrow it? These issues were set out with great clarity by the founder of the society Aide-toi le ciel t'aidera, Garnier-Pagès, who wrote a lucid overview of the debate in the introduction to the *Dictionnaire politique* with his own piece, 'On Political Science':

The first duty, when one lives under a despotic government, is to look for ways to deliver liberty to one's country. The most certain means, and one can say the only means to render a country free that is not, is insurrection. Conspiracies that prepare insurrections and insurrections themselves are therefore a duty in countries that suffer under despotism. In countries where one enjoys liberty without, however, possessing equality of rights, one should only have recourse to insurrection at the last extremity, and one should not conspire. One should not rely on insurrection except in the last extremity, because insurrection carries with it very grave ills, it is not permitted to have recourse to such a terrible method as long as others are available. In countries where sovereignty of the people is established in both law and deed, conspiracies and insurrections are the greatest of all crimes.[27]

Garnier Pagès here captures beautifully the mainstream republican view of the period on just war principles. Yet the actual battles, as he well knew, were not always defined with such rigour as in the *Dictionnaire*. Questions ranging from which means could be used to fight or which methods were banned according to republican principle could not be dissociated from the matter of what tools of war could be used, where, and when. Equally important was the issue of who could fight, where they were permitted to fight: that is, in which

---

[26] Tchernoff, *Le Parti républicain sous la Monarchie de Juillet*, 321.
[27] Garnier-Pagès, Introduction, *Dictionnaire Politique*, xxiii. (Paris, 1860).

physical arenas, as opposed to political ones, these wars could take place. However, once these questions were agreed it could become less a matter of principle than a matter of tactics for republicans. 'Questions of insurrections are, for a people, merely questions of opportunity; and as for a party as for a man, questions of honour are always opportune', noted one newspaper columnist.[28]

Yet both the geographical and the political differences between republicans in Europe were vast, and their principles were fashioned to a large extent by their particular predicaments. So what went for the French was not at all what went for others. Under the July Monarchy violence was seen as a last resort. Louis Blanc noted that 'all republicans under the monarchy of July preferred legal action', reserving the 'resort to violent action if exceptional laws removed the means to resist by the press, by association'.[29] And Ledru-Rollin said 'it is beautiful to fight only with the weapons of law, the effort of the intelligence alone', although he was also clear that under despotism, under tyranny, and under an unjust system 'these means were useless'.[30] Armand Marrast, the editor of the republican *Tribune* took the same view: insurrection was justified when the freedom of the press and the rights of association had been repressed. When the State is 'thrown into chaos by its very leaders, each citizen returns into his individual right, and civil war has been declared by the power itself. What impedes a people, to rise in mass, and invade the public place ?' When the law is 'violated in its own legality, it is by deeds that one must return to its right sources'.[31] But he also believed in the general principle that both peaceful and violent means were equally justified for republicans.

To arrive at the perfection that is possible of society, from the point of departure that we are at, there are two routes: one violent, that of revolutions ; the other, peaceful education of public opinion. Both of these are popular, the *Tribune* accepts them both.[32]

Although there were real differences in the types of battles to be fought and choices to be made between a political or a military battle, between the small skirmish and a general insurrection, it was not so easy in practice to prevent one from turning into another. A search of the house of an arrested republican activist revealed this letter from a law student in Paris: 'everything is preparing for the great day—since 8 days now cartridges have been distributed: I've received mine; the moment for courage has arrived; it is clear it is no longer a small uprising, but rather a war unto death between the *juste milieu* and the Republic!'[33] For Polish and Italian republicans, however, these types of questions on conditions for a just war had ceased being discussed decades ago: generations of them had been fighting foreign oppression by 1830. The right to wage war in their situation represented clear sets of republican rights

[28] *La Tribune*, 17 March 1831.   [29] Louis Blanc, *Histoire de dix ans*, ii. (Paris,1848), 45.
[30] Tchernoff, *Le Parti républicain sous la Monarchie de Juillet*, 327.
[31] Armand Marrast in de l'Ain, *Affaire du Mois D'Avril*, ii., 8.
[32] Armand Marrast, *La Tribune*, 31 January 1833.
[33] 'Correspondence Communiquée par le Garde des Sceaux et le Ministre de l'Intérieur', Dossier 9. AN CC619.

as well as republican duties. As we shall see, it was not until 1870 that the republicans in France found themselves in exactly this position, and this had a strong effect on their articulation of the conditions for just war.

Republicans of all ideological strands and national predicaments debated another key question: *who* could be permitted to join in this battle? During a war of invasion and occupation, everyone was called to arms in the *levée en masse*.[34] 'Everyone' in this instance meant men, for the occasions when women participated were turned into illustrations of the unusualness of the situation, or the absolute justness of the particular cause, or to represent the emblematic and iconographic heroism of a people. Even when it was not a foreign invasion, the presence of women was often taken as an expression of the popular basis of struggle. 'We saw', said Baune, 'the wives of the workers, new Spartans, binding the wounds of their own at the very place of the fighting, restoring their courage and sending them back to the fire.'[35] There were often children with paving stones at the barricades of Lyon and Paris, carrying flags on the barricades of St Merri and Carrouge: 'these little unfortunates showed the greatest disrespect of danger, and some had a total disregard for life itself', as one historian of Lyon remarked reprovingly.[36] Yet republicans saw these battles as a peoples' war and, no matter how much republicans tried, 'the people' would not always remain restricted to men.

As a general principle of just war, republicans believed that all citizens had a duty and a right to fight for their liberty and for the establishment and preservation of the republic. The resonances of the An II, and of the Revolutionary era more generally, were extremely powerful here. In the early 1830s republicans formed the Société des Droits de l'Homme et du Citoyen; its founding principles were based on the 1793 Declaration presented by Robespierre to the Convention. In a brochure entitled 'Soldiers of Liberty', the Société stressed that the 'soldier' was anyone that received an education. 'Education begins in public schools, and should be pursued into the army, which must itself become a school of civic education, where the soldier obeys only a leader whom he has elected, where war is to be defensive only.'[37] A further question arose over participants and centred on the direction and leadership of the battle. Who had the right to lead the call to arms? This question was aimed at two distinct types of leadership. The first was of groups of people, of militias, or guerrillas, or insurrections. The second concerned the leadership of peoples as a whole.

The types of commanders and the virtues they had to possess was either a point of agreement or a source of bitter division. It also concerned who could lead the general insurrection in Europe, since insurrection was envisaged on

---

[34] For a legal and political history and definition of the term and practice of the *levée* in the nineteenth century, see my *Traditions of War: Resistance, Occupation, and the Law* (Oxford, 1999), 17–18, 52–5.

[35] Fernand Rude, *L'Insurrection lyonnaise de Novembre 1831* (Paris, 1969), 424.

[36] J. B. Monfalcon, *Histoire des insurrections de Lyon de 1831 et de 1834 d'après des documents authentiques* (Paris, 1834), 33.

[37] Girod de l'Ain, *Affaire du Mois d'Avril*, iv, 548.

an international basis rather than on a merely national or regional one, and plans needed to be harmonized accordingly. Etienne Cabet, one of the rare republican deputies of the period, was even more rare among French republicans in believing that leadership should not come from the French: 'No revolts, no conspiracies! We must learn how to wait! The time for our defence will arrive!' Until then, he added, 'we must take a count of ourselves, build up our ranks, keep our eyes open, and keep guard! It is those in foreign lands who will give us the sign to begin battle!'[38] Still common at that time was the notion of republican expansion and conquest. One of Napoleon's former generals Gustave Damas published an appeal for the creation of a Lafayette Legion so that they could 'awaken liberty from the Pyrenees, or carry help with our arms to those brave Poles; since it is altogether better to live and die free on foreign soil than to live as a slave on one's own'.[39] He wanted the men to carry a *tricolore* on the second expedition to liberate the Savoy, in 1834, and it had to be pointed out to him by the Savoyards that this would not be seen as liberation but as invasion and occupation.[40] His view of war was more Napoleonic than republican.

Republicans more often believed they were permitted to help others when they were struggling for the establishment of a republic by just means against a tyrant. Did one need to be asked first? There were differences of opinion here too. Many believed that helping others would jeopardize one's own battle. According to some, such actions on the part of a few could destroy their own plans for national insurrection. Further, some seemed to feel they had the right to impose their republicanism upon others. The Carbonari's 'cosmopolitanism' argued from such a premise, but most of the younger republican movements of the period believed in a type of fraternal action which relied upon the recognition of the rights of those national groups to decide their own needs. Republicans tended to send arms and people to help other peoples only once this aid had been requested. The French Société des amis du peuple sent republican volunteers to Belgium in 1830, as well as guns to the Italians. Michel-Ange Périer, the editor of Lyon's *La Glaneuse*, who had fought in the Trois Glorieuses in Paris in July, went to Belgium with his brother Joany, who was the standard bearer of the society's flag.[41] When offered two battalions of the Lyonnais national guard by the French republican and *carbonaro* Baune to assist their invasion into the Savoy, the Italian refugees in France refused his aid. They did not dare accept this generous offer which they believed could only jeopardize the success of their venture. The Volontaires du Rhône who made up the expedition left Lyon 'neither equipped, nor armed, nor dressed, but for the most part wearing miserable rags'. Still, 'rifles, powder, and munitions of all sorts had been directed in advance towards the mountains of Bugey

---

[38] Etienne Cabet, *Révolution de 1830 et Situation Présente (Novembre 1833) Expliquées et Eclairées Par les Révolutions de 1789, 1792, 1799 et 1804* (Paris, 1834), 191.

[39] *La Tribune*, 16 February 1831.

[40] Harro Harring gives a detailed account of the search for the correct expedition flag in his *Mémoires sur la Jeune Italie* (Dijon, 1835).

[41] Rude, *L'Insurrection lyonnaise*, 287.

in order to be distributed to them there'. This help they accepted without hesitation.[42]

Armand Carrel's gradual evolution into a moderate republican was largely a product of his increasing sense of shame at the manner in which the July Monarchy conducted her foreign affairs. He constantly attacked Louis-Philippe's ministers for their non-interventionist policy towards Europe in his newspaper *Le National*.[43] The external policy of the French republicans, as for all republicans of Europe, was closer to that of Carrel, even before he became a republican: 'deliver Germany, deliver Italy, call the peoples against oppressive aristocracies—such was the foreign programme of republicans'.[44]

So there were fine distinctions in the ways that republican war could be waged. However, for men such as Kersausie, and his infamous and mysterious secret Société d'Action—a splinter of the Société des Droits de l'Homme—action was to occur at all times, in all places, with whatever means were to hand, and with whatever friends he could round up to join him. All rules were permissible against the empire and the tyrant. In Sainte Pelagie prison, where the republicans were awaiting trial in 1835, one beleaguered warden wrote this report to his superior at 4 a.m.:

5 p.m. Kersausie and Gervais started a meeting, six or seven of them, singing republican songs, more and more outrageous, against the king, against the royal family, and the government in chorus and in full cry. They allowed themselves to be locked in as usual, but suddenly, at exactly 10 p.m., each began to break all the furniture in their room; chairs, tables, bottles, before throwing them into the courtyard. After that they began to break the boardings, the windows, ripping up the planks of the floor, etc. etc. A little before 11 p.m. a general cry could be heard: 'Come on, Citizens, to work!' This exclamation was swiftly followed by blows made with paving stones, blows with hammers, on the doors. This racket was mingled with loud cries of 'A bas Louis Philippe! Death to Gisquet! Persil and Thiers too!' This tumult was prolonged until 2 a.m. in the morning.[45]

The Tools and Techniques of Republican War

As we have seen, the world of republican war encompassed broad conceptual as well as physical battlefields. The tools and techniques used in this war were also very extensive and extremely inventive, and were used in both military arenas and in political conflict. The techniques which republicans acquired and then practised ranged across a spectrum of activities which began as often in editorial rooms as in military academies, sometimes in conspiratorial cafés as well as the barricaded street. As has been shown, many of those who sought to construct a republic in face of empire did not always find it possible to distinguish between political and military struggles in order to bring it about.

---

[42] Rude, *L'Insurrection lyonnaise*, 217; *Journal de Commerce*, 4 March 1831.
[43] Armand Carrel in the *National*, 21 September 1831.
[44] Weill, *Histoire du parti républicain en France*, 29.
[45] Archives Nationales, Paris, CC 664.

A central political tool of war was the printed word, and much of the planning of insurrection began in the printing presses which republicans bor-
rowed, rented, or ran. They were the essential arenas of republican battle in a
number of ways. Printing houses were where republicans of all ideological
flavours and all nationalities met, and often where they wrote their tracts of
republican action. Encouragements and appeals to insurgency were published
there, and those who wished to direct things had to make sure it was their own
call to arms which were published rather than some other group's.

The editorial rooms of the main French republican papers—for example, the
Tribune in Paris and the *Precurseur* in Lyon—were also the homes of the planning committees of the secret republican societies. They also published assistance and advice on the different means of conducting war: brochures,
newspapers, maps for insurrectionary expeditions, pictures and illustrative
cartoons, encouraging words, as well as subscription appeals to raise essential
funds for arms. The printed word was thus one of the most crucial weapons of
republican war. Brochures, flyleaves, and posters were used to call people to
arms, to enlighten them, to encourage them, and to bring them into the arena
of republican battle. Appeals and circulars were often used as means to entreat
the soldiers of empire to abandon their kings and join the people. As a technique of war, this propaganda was seen as so successful that it often met with
immediate and punitive reprisals. Brochures that were a fantastic blend of
ideas and values, rules of republican justice, of an organization's structure,
combined with extracts of poetry and appeals to be ready to rise, were considered to be as deadly as the bullets and explosives which were also being collected by their authors. All these weapons were hidden inside bottles and
under planks, in boxes of goods on ships, and inside books.[46] They were constantly being discovered by the agents, police, and soldiers of the Holy Empire.
Brochures with directions for action and principles of virtue were found in the
pockets of refugees and republicans killed or arrested in expeditions and insurrections all over Europe. One brochure, published by Kersausie's Société
d'Action, was boldly entitled *Le Catéchisme d'insurrection*.[47] Brochures of
republican societies were read on the factory floor of the Lyonnais silk workers until the government banned the criers that sold them.[48] Declamations
were the most powerful weapons of republican war, as the right ones could
raise a people to arms when they possessed none and were nearly defeated.

Two vital implements of republican war were poetry and songs. Both were
used extensively during this period by republicans of all political affiliations.
Charles Baudelaire, writing on the 1830s songwriter Pierre Dupont, remarked:
'when a poet, sometimes clumsy, but almost always brilliant, comes to proclaim the sanctity of the insurrection of 1830 in the language of fire . . . art
becomes inseparable from both morals and usefulness.'[49] They were useful in

[46] Archives Municipales, Lyon.   [47] Requisitoire, *l'Affaire d'avril 1834*, 120.
[48] They were called 'moving monitors of insurrection' by police chief de la Hodde in his *Histoire
des sociétés secrètes et du parti républicain de 1830 à 1848* (Paris 1851), 131–2.
[49] Quoted in Henri Lemaître, *Curiosités esthétiques. L'art romantique et autres oeuvres critiques* (Paris,
1990).

that the songs and poetry of the period brought together republicans that were divided over so many other issues, as we have just seen. These art forms bound them together, brought them strength to fight by raising morale, and the commitment to work together despite their differences, as they chanted together the words that meant something to each of them, as well as to them as a group. Further, their compositors played a special role in society, and they became leaders and heroes in their own right. The *Patriote Franc-Comtois* celebrated this role for music as their local garrison went to greet the Polish officers arriving into exile in France:

We hope that the music of the civil guard's band will do as good a duty as those of Colmar and Strasbourg, and all the other towns through which passed these heroes of liberty, and by hearing our patriotic airs which, in its energetic execution, we hope will make the whole of Europe tremble![50]

Other means of marking struggle and signalling the commencement of a particular battle were the toasts and celebration days of former famous republican battles, where commemorations became the spark, as well as the signal, for the next wave. The memorial of the June 1832 Paris riots became a site where revolution and republican principles were honoured, and it also acted as a signal for the launch of the 1834 revolt in Lyon. Certain techniques of republican war developed from the vital need to move freely and safely without being detected by the soldiers, agents, and police of the enemy, through the towns and villages of empire and back and forth across borders, so that republicans could organize their struggle with those of other nations. These towns and villages constituted abodes of varying mixtures of support and solidarity. But these villages, towns, and cities also contained a constant threat of danger for the foreigner, the exile, or even the local republican. This was a description by a republican of one of the border towns:

Nothing more gloomy than the town of Chambéry; one sees only military or police officers in the street; the well-to-do are in the countryside, and the other inhabitants don't show themselves. Have you an enemy, driven by the thirst for vengeance? Well, here he will introduce a brochure or incriminating papers, whatever, in your lodging, denounce you, and then: off you go! Into the dungeons![51]

The modes of transport for republicans to organize their insurrections against their regime or help others were whatever came to hand. At other times they walked, or marched, or were carried in boats or carts. In order for the timing of the insurrection in Paris to coincide with that of Lyon and Savoy uprisings in April 1834, the diminutive Kersausie got around Paris the fastest way possible, a tricycle.[52]

In order to recognize each other while moving through hostile territory, republicans used the passwords and watchwords and signals of their secret societies, so that they could then safely transfer their rifles and pistols and

[50] *Le Patriote Franc-Comtois*, 1 February 1832.
[51] Archives Nationales, Paris, CC 535, no. 144.
[52] Requisitoire, Cour des Pairs, *Affaire d'avril 1834*, 118.

brochures to allies and republicans in different towns and countries. Different branches of the secret societies were named after the famous historical landmarks of insurrection. In Paris, in 1834, some of the sections of the 1st and 2nd arrondissement's branches of the Société des Droits de l'Homme were named: Prise de la Bastille, Toussaint l'Ouverture, Contrat Social, 5 et 6 Juin, La Barricade 1er, 5 et 6 octobre, 14 juillet, Thermopyles, Ostralenka.[53] Gestures were often made in more graphic displays, through the ribbons and insignia of the societies, which were not just for decorative purposes but could display particular messages of affiliation and of political and military action.

Republican War and the Franco-Prussian War

The mountains of archival notes copied from the reports of prefects, mayors, generals, newspapers, and personal letters in Vincent's huge collection on Gambetta's prefects of 1870 showed very clearly that a republican culture of war was still operating at the outbreak of the Franco-Prussian war. His intent in gathering this material was to portray a much different world, one concerned with the technical aspects and functioning of local administration and central government in wartime. Yet the political framework and deeper ideological roots of the republican tradition of war constantly broke through. In the private and official letters and reports from functionaries which addressed such issues as political appointments, administrative operations, and decision making—or, rather, the breakdowns in decision making—between various governmental departments, the fact that these officials were dealing with, and sometimes driven by, a rich and coherent set of principles is apparent. Indeed, what emerges is that the thinking and the practices of French republicans, even those entrusted with local administration, were drawn from those of previous generations who were fighting to establish a republic in France. The context was clearly different from the early years of the July Monarchy—the assumption of power by the republicans without elections and also in the midst of a devastating foreign invasion—but the ideological framework drawn upon was firmly located within the republican tradition as outlined above. The outbreak of the war between France and Prussia; the manner in which French republicans viewed that war; the role of society and of the army; the nature of the enemy; the just causes and means to fight that war; the role of the citizenry: in all these respects can clearly be seen elements of the same political culture that had been flourishing in France since the early 1830s.

These republicans were fighting not only for the creation of a republic but also for its defence. Thus the fall of the Empire and the assumption of power by Gambetta was seen by republicans as sufficient evidence of the existence of an authoritative republican government, even without elections to legitimize it. No time was to be wasted. On the evening of 4 September, the Comité de

---

[53] Requisitoire, Cour des Pairs, *Affaire d'avril 1834*, 16, 17.

salut public of Lyon telegraphed to the neighbouring municipalities and departments: 'The Republic has been proclaimed in Lyon; immediately organize a republican government.'[54] The way this organization was to be achieved was similar to that earlier period: through local and regional republican societies and associations. The manner in which leaders were chosen was to be based on republican values and the virtues of patriotism. So the Ligue de l'Est demanded that all local committees be composed of men 'known for their patriotism and their republican convictions'.[55]

The role that citizens should play in the defence of *la patrie* was the most urgent issue before them. Many of the republican prefects who had been appointed by Gambetta relied upon republican doctrine to encourage the participation of citizens in the defence of their town, village, region. Sub-prefect De Marçay urged the people to organize into militias and reminded them of a crucial republican virtue: 'An hour of courage in a people, citizens, is more noticed than 20 years of despotism; an hour of courage will rehabilitate you in the eyes of the whole of Europe.'[56] Some prefects took this advice themselves, taking off from the *préfecture* with a rifle and a horse.

By 1870 the view of the military as tool of the Empire and an essentially hostile institution to the Republic—and the people—had become an integral part of the republican tradition, in contrast with the more ambivalent relationship that existed between earlier republican generations and the Army. This perception shifted as a result of the Bonapartist *coup* and the violent repression of republican activists of 1851–3, in which the Army played a significant role. However, republican intellectuals of the Second Empire generation, such as Gambetta, Simon, and Ferry, were not anti-war or anti-Army as a matter of principle; rather, they advocated universal military service which would give a 'popular' character to the army and eliminate its aristocratic culture and expansionary tendencies.[57] So they held the belief that the army could be transformed under a republican form of government and by means of republican ideals. Examples of these views during the 1870–1 war abounded from all over the country, but Vincent's sources from just the archives of the Haute-Garonne and Isère are evocative. After 4 September, a pro-republican Masonic lodge in Grenoble, the Loge des Arts Réunis, wrote to the Grand Maître that they had previously been hostile to war only because they had opposed all imperial wars; now that the Republic was proclaimed, they were 'clearly patriotic'.[58] But some of the soldiers that had been serving the Second Empire had apparently been republican all along. As the British diplomat Colonel Claremont reported worriedly to London on 26 September 1870:

[54] Rapport Préfecture d'Isère, 15 July 1871, Vincent Wright Private Papers.
[55] *Ligue de l'Est pour la Défense de la République* (Besançon, 1870). BN Lb 57 290.
[56] Neilz, *Journal d'un Vendômois. Cinq mois et dix jours d'invasion 1870–1871* (Vendôme, 1887); entry for 11 December 1870.
[57] Raoul Girardet, *La société militaire dans la France contemporaine* (Paris, 1953), 31.
[58] Fonds Maçonnique, Bibliothèque Nationale, Paris. FM/1-219, letter dated 14 December 1870.

The feelings of the people here are getting so excited that it is almost unsafe to walk about the streets and certainly to go on the line of the fortification . . . On the 18th Sept. General Ambert who commands a section of the fortifications made a stirring speech to the officers under his command, they cried 'Vive la République' to which he did not respond, they insisted and as he still would only cry 'Vive la Nation', they arrested him, tore his clothes nearly off his back and took him to the Ministère de la Guerre where he is now kept in concealment.[59]

The *garde nationale* was always a locus of a more popular expression of republicanism, and since the 1830s these locally-based militias were often full of republican activists. In 1870–1 this radicalism was graphically displayed, notably in the wake of the 'treason' committed by Marshal Bazaine in the surrender of Metz in October 1870. Here is a report from Toulouse, which demonstrates the comprehensive nature of the republican platform proposed:

A review of the national guard, inspired by a desire to protest against the treason [the capitulation of Bazaine], took place today, in the midst of popular support and with the strongest patriotic enthusiasm. The Republic and the Government of National Defence were acclaimed. The population in arms demands the *levée en masse*, the expulsion of the Jesuits, the dismissal of all the generals and the absolute subordination of the military command to civilian authority.[60]

The manner in which republicans participated in public life was through organizations and societies, much as in the 1830s. One can see through the platforms of the Committees of Defence that had sprung up across France in the late summer of 1870 that these were, almost to the last, republican in nature.[61] These committees were living expressions of the republican principle that it was both the duty and the right of citizens to defend their *patrie*. It was a core principle of republican doctrine even amongst the more moderate strands of republicanism, such as the Société républicaine pour la Défense Nationale in Grenoble, made up of the bourgeois notables of the town, in contrast with the more radical and working-class Association républicaine. The Société's statutes declared that, after France had become a republic on 4 September, it was no longer simply fighting a war of defence:

The war has changed character; we are no longer merely defending our invaded soil, our homeland soiled by the foreigner; we are fighting and we shall die for the Revolution of 89 . . . In order to achieve justice, let us abolish the magistracy. So that we may recover freedom of conscience, let the State achieve its freedom outside the Church. In order that we may recapture honour, morality, freedom, we must become a gigantic workshop where are forged, all at the same time, institutions and armies, ideas and actions.[62]

---

[59] FO 27/1829, VW Private Papers, dossier entitled 'Anti Military'.
[60] *Dépêche Télégraphique No. 24*, Toulouse, 30 Octobre 1870, from Prefect of Haute-Garonne, Armand Duportal, to the Prefects of Lyon, Marseille, Bordeaux, Poitiers, Limoges, Périgueux, Montpellier, and Nîmes.
[61] Archives Départementales Haute-Garonne, AD 4 M 91. Toulouse's Committee of Defence's simple charter was typical: '1. Refuse humiliating peace. 2. Fight till the death even if Paris falls. 3. Levy an extraordinary tax in each department. 4. Military organization of affiliated departments.'
[62] Report of the Préfet of Isère, 15 July 1871; *Reveil du Dauphiné*, 18 October 1870.

The belief that all citizens had to rely upon themselves and form local associations in order to unite the republic rather than break away from it did not emerge merely from grass-roots republican activists. It also came from above. On 4 November 1870, Gambetta went to this same town of Grenoble and spoke to a crowd of 'several thousand' citizens from the balcony of the Hôtel de Ville. He did not tell them to wait for orders from him or the government to act:

Citizens, I am grateful to you for coming, in the midst of our suffering, to demonstrate the sentiments of solidarity which unite us. We shall not give up, however great the betrayals which we see around us. But first understand that it is enough to want to escape from our fate in order to do so; it suffices to *will*, we must will. And you must not, furthermore, believe that the government can and must do everything: you must act by yourselves. In all of France, in each town, in each village, you must assemble, band together, and each one of you must come nearer to your neighbour, in order to unite and form a compact whole . . . We must also cease to distinguish between open and closed towns, between what can and cannot be defended; in a word, everywhere we must triumph or die. The Republic will live if you want it to live; it will live if we take the initiative, if we are prepared to give generously our blood for it and for liberty. Thus you should make your own personal contribution to the defence of the *patrie*. Rely only upon yourselves; for it is the curse of this country that it does nothing for itself, and raises its eyes to those who govern, expecting everything from them. Take things into your own hands.[63]

Republicans of the 1870–1 generation still believed that their principles transcended national boundaries and that all republicans were united in the fight against despotism. Many declarations and proclamations attested to this continuity. On 16 July 1870, before the start of the war, the Toulouse newspaper *l'Emancipation* published an appeal to German workers: 'German brothers, in the name of peace, do not listen to the paid or servile voices which seek to hoodwink you . . . For any war would be a fratricidal war, and our divisions would only bring on both sides of the Rhine the complete triumph of despotism.'[64] Louis Blanc, so active under the July Monarchy, wrote from his exile in London in July 1870 to his friend Antonin Dubost, who was soon to become the prefect of the Orne, about the nature of the Prussian invasion. He articulated the simple catechism of republican battle, which was as true in 1830 are it was 40 years later: 'Peoples are brothers for us, and tyrants are our enemies.'[65] The socialist republican Jules Guesde described the nature of the enemy in republican war in the same way: 'For us, the enemy is not at the frontier. He does not come from Berlin and is not wearing a pointed helmet. He does not speak the language of Goethe and Kant. The enemy is arbitrariness in all its forms. It is, in the material sphere, poverty; and in the moral sphere, ignorance.'[66]

[63] Cited in Pierre Maquest, *La France et L'Europe pendant le Siège de Paris (18 Septembre–28 Janvier), Enyclopédie Politique, Militaire, et Anecdotique*, 2nd edn (Paris, 1877), 193–4.
[64] Nicole Rouje, 'L'Opinion Toulousaine en face de la Première Internationale', DES thesis, 1965, 33.
[65] Archives Départementales d'Isère, 1 J 38.
[66] *Textes Choisis de Jules Guesde, Républicain Démocrate* (Paris, 1946), 45.

The republicans of 1870 used the same tools of war as those who had fought to establish republics before them. Gambetta used his speeches to mobilize the crowd to republican war, but republicans also spontaneously drew upon their tradition to help them face the enemy. Poetry and popular songs were much used to mobilize and unite the people. At Auch, at a public meeting held in the theatre hall, the mayor read to the populace of the town 'diverse pieces of verse from *Les Châtiments* of Victor Hugo'.[67] But also the actions of the people inspired the poets: 'Poetry and war offered new resources . . . the patriotic sentiments of the population immediately inspired many poets.'[68] The printed proclamations of the *franc-tireurs* were full of published songs and poems, and the *Chant du Départ* played the same role of unification and encouragement in facing the enemy. Flown outside the *mairies*, the red flag was used not only as a symbol to contest the principles of moderate republicans who raised the tricolour but also to demonstrate a willingness to fight the invading Empire.

Conclusion

Vincent Wright was highly sceptical of the role of ideology and principle as motivating forces for human action. Writing about the widespread collective resistance to the 1851 coup in France, he asked: 'What were all these people protesting about? One wonders how important political ideology was to the mass of artisans and peasants. No doubt egalitarian principles had considerable appeal but one suspects that this was essentially due to their association with pressing economic and social grievances.'[69] It is true that egalitarian principles are—in some basic sense—'abstract', as is French republicanism's ideological framework, which sees order and justice emerging through the application of the principles of equality, liberty, and fraternity. But, as we have seen throughout this chapter, republicans were spurred into action by these principles, which defined their very identity as political actors.

This kind of separation, common in 'political science', between ideology and interests cannot be helpful in illuminating the nature of the contextual and the contingent and its relationship to the conceptual. Exploring these issues within a broader conceptual framework provides a far richer and more persuasive account of political agency. Further, such distinctions, by introducing a methodology which breaks down republican thought and practice into a variety of discrete components, have tended to exaggerate the lines of demarcation between its constituent elements. Differences between the likes of Gambetta and those provincial republicans calling for *levée en masse* are

---

[67] *L'Avenir*, 3 December 1870.

[68] J. Schlutter, *La Poésie de la guerre de revanche* (Paris, 1878), 55. See also Claude Digeon's seminal *La Crise allemande de la pensée française 1870–1914* (Paris, 1959), which also explores the role of popular novels.

[69] Vincent Wright, 'The *coup d'état* of December 1851: Repression and the Limits to Repression' (1975), 59.

liable to be overstated if we deem the former to be driven by interests and the latter by ideology. In reality, all these republicans were driven by a tradition that wedded these notions together. While a conceptual framework of republicanism can illustrate both moderate and radical strands within this tradition, it also offers a way of understanding the filaments that tie them together, one that they too understood as binding them in a common project.

This chapter began with an attempt to set out an understanding of the conflict between republicans and ended up showing the commonalities that still obtained between them. These commonalities—in purpose, principle, and practice—pertained to a single generation, as well as across time, to the generations that followed. In this respect we have seen the pivotal position occupied by the republican generation of the 1830s and their debates about republican war for the subsequent elaboration of the republican project. A tradition shows us that certain concepts and practices may be contested. But it can show us which ones are concepts and practices that are within an ideology, and it is their weight, their relevance, their precise definition that are being contested. It is also in this way that we can see how certain other concepts and practices can fall completely outside of that tradition and become concepts and practices that are understood not to be held by republicans, the prime example here being Bonapartism, which in the eyes of the republicans had by 1870–1 lost all its historical and ideological affinities with their own tradition.

This notion of tradition also demonstrates that it is unhelpful to emphasize the distinction—important though it is—between 'republican' and 'revolutionary' elements within the Jacobin tradition.[70] The Jacobinism of the Convention may well have been the model for the Société des Droits de l'Homme, but Cavaignac and his colleagues' interpretation of the 1793 principles did not actually adhere to a centralized political model of the Revolutionary era. Likewise Esquiros, the historian of the Montagnards, created a grass-roots republican organization which sought to enlighten and enfranchise the citizenry in the battle against foreign invasion. Revolutionary republicanism was not just about the destruction of existing empires; more important, it was also about the reconstruction and defence of the Republic. It argued for the need to have distinct bodies of representation with associational foundations at every institutional level: local, regional, and national. It was about civic action and democratic participation rather than the desire to impose a conception of the good life 'for the happiness of all'. Further, republican leaders such as Gambetta strongly endorsed many of the principles of these 'revolutionary' republicans, most notably, as we have just seen, the belief in the necessity of mass political participation and collective action to construct the Republic. Along with Esquiros, Gambetta shared a vision of the architecture of the body of the Republic that was to come into being in 1870, of the role of the citizenry in building it, and of the precise shape in which the

---

[70] See Chapter 1.

living parts of the republic connected to the whole; that is, its institutional parts, both central and local. This too united them in a tradition as much as in an ideology.

The Franco-Prussian war was in many respects the moment which consummated the rupture, which had begun in 1851, between republicanism and Bonapartism. Also, this war has been viewed as a turning point in the transformation of French nationalism and the starting point for the elaboration of a new, more negative, form of French patriotism.[71] But in respect of the creation of the republican State, the war of 1870–1 tends to be seen as an obstacle or even a counter-model: a period of republican political failure, of 'dictatorial' government and internecine conflict, and, with the communalist movement in Paris and the provinces, of the final fling of the republican insurrectionary tradition of the Revolutionary era. But this chapter has demonstrated the strength and openness of republican patriotism in 1870–1, its anti-chauvinistic universalism, as well as the common understanding—which united all strands of the republican movement—of the role of the citizen. This vision, which had profound roots in earlier republican doctrines, was carried forward into the civic order which underlay the Third Republic. In this respect, the Franco-Prussian war represented an important and creative moment in the affirmation of French republicanism, providing an important enhancement to the notion of republican citizenship.

This can be recognized even more clearly when seen from an organizational point of view. What united all these republicans, from the 1790s through the 1830s and 1840s into the Second Empire and the Government of National Defence, was a commitment to organize and help mobilize action in the public sphere. Seen in this light, republican associations, radical *and* moderate, made major contributions to the development of mass democracy in France, with respect to both the principle of popular sovereignty and the practice of popular suffrage. What has been highlighted here is the contribution of the political culture of republican war on 'mainstream' republicanism. This connection appeared in full force in times of war and military occupation, when republicans agreed that the locus of sovereignty lay with the people—even, and especially, if the State itself had collapsed. This common notion centred around the struggle to build a republic, whether under foreign rule or domestic tyranny. Carrel and Cavaignac, Cabet and Marrast, Esquiros and Gambetta, all shared this vision of the republic of war.

[71] Stéphane Audoin-Rouzeau, *1870, La France dans la guerre* (Paris, 1989).

3

'Honorable and Honoured Citizens': War Veterans of the Revolutionary and Napoleonic Eras under the Second Empire

SUDHIR HAZAREESINGH

O N 15 August 1866, the 1,100 inhabitants of the small village of Foix (Nord) awoke to the sound of Church bells ringing vigorously. As in every town and village in the country, the peals were marking the official celebration of the Saint-Napoléon, France's national festivity, as well as the Catholic fête of the Assumption.

For Dumont, the mayor of Foix, the day began normally enough with a distribution of bread and meat to the poorer members of his commune. The prefect of the Nord had sent a memorandum to remind him—not that he needed reminding—that the Emperor Napoleon III attached 'special importance' to the relief of the needy on 15 August. At mid-morning he welcomed the *fonctionnaires* and eminent citizens of the commune into the *mairie*. The municipal councillors, members of the Office of Charity, and the Médaillés de Sainte-Hélène, the former military servicemen of the First Republic and Empire, talked animatedly for a while, and then lined up in preparation for the traditional procession to Church.

In recent years this official civic procession had been accompanied to Church by a company of firemen (*sapeurs-pompiers*) in full uniform. This escort bore witness to the mayor's pride in the village's firemen, whose brave interventions had saved lives and protected valuable properties in recent years. But the most important function of the escort was to honour the military veterans of the Revolutionary and Napoleonic eras. Each and every one of these 'glorious relics' was known and respected in Foix. The older folk, some of whom were their exact contemporaries, still vividly remembered the day when these men had returned to the village towards the end of the First Empire, with their scorched clothes, blackened faces, and haggard expressions. France was then a defeated and occupied nation, and in 1815 its Emperor departed to his exile in

Sainte-Hélène, where he ended his life—and began the Napoleonic legend. Some of these soldiers had subsequently fallen into poverty, but others had successfully reintegrated civilian life; a few had even become pillars of the community. And all of them loved to regale the younger people with their memories of the Revolutionary era and accounts of their own military exploits in battles with such strange and resonant names as Wagram, Eylau, Austerlitz, and Marengo.

The Médaillés de Sainte-Hélène, in short, were the heroes of the village of Foix, as well as its living link to a glorious past.

In his report to the prefect of the Nord on the festivities of the 15th of August 1866, Mayor Dumont dwelled on the village's pride in these former foot-soldiers of the Republic and Empire, noting the joyful expressions on their faces during the Church ceremony and the singing of the *Te Deum*. He then went on to outline the events during the rest of the day. As had been the case each year, the Mass was followed by public games, which were held in different parts of the commune. These amusements were extremely popular among the villagers, especially with the younger folk. By late afternoon, helped no doubt by the heat and the generous flow of wine, the atmosphere was relaxed and festive. Foix seemed like any other village celebrating the 15th of August.

But there was a particular twist to this year's celebrations in the commune. Let us pick up the story as narrated by Mayor Dumont: 'Despite the animation with which the inhabitants were enjoying themselves, at around six in the evening the games stopped as if by enchantment. The bells of the Church were tolling again, informing the population that a funeral ceremony was about to take place; indeed the time had come to pay the last respects to a virtuous military serviceman of the First Empire, a man by the name of Saumin, holder of the Médaille de Sainte-Hélène, who had died on the 14th of August at the age of 84.'[1]

Saumin had clearly been one of the village elders of Foix. His funeral brought an end to the festivities of 15 August in the village and at the same time set the day in its true perspective. Upon hearing the Church bells, all the officials of the commune and indeed the overwhelming majority of the inhabitants gathered at the house of the deceased. The entire village accompanied Saumin's coffin to the Church and then to the cemetery, where he was to be buried. Before the coffin was lowered one of the First Empire veterans gave a speech celebrating the life of his distinguished comrade. Saumin had witnessed the revolution of 1789 as a little boy, then joined the Grande Armée where he had served with distinction in many campaigns. The orator especially reminded those present of the 'qualities of the soldier and the citizen which made Saumin a brave soldier, and an honourable and honoured man'.[2] Many of the villagers were moved to tears. The first magistrate of the com-

---

[1] Report of mayor of Foix to prefect of Nord, 17 August 1866; AD Nord (Lille), M 141 (95), Fête du 15 août 1864–1870.
[2] Ibid.

mune summed up what had just occurred: 'The fête ended amidst an imposing calm which gave rise to the most serious reflections concerning the duties
of the citizen towards his *patrie*.'[3]

Life and death, rejoicing and grief, glory and humiliation, wealth and
poverty, memory of the past and anticipation of the future, private affections
and public virtues, the secular and the sacred, local patrimony and national
mythology, Jacobinism and Bonapartism: the individual narrative of
Napoleonic war veteran Saumin brings out the rich tapestry of meanings
associated with the celebration of the 15th of August under the Second
Empire. It also demonstrates the complex ways in which memories of the
Revolutionary and Napoleonic eras were transmitted across generations in
nineteenth-century France.

War Veterans of the Second Empire: The Wider Contexts

Despite the presence of significant holdings in the Archives Nationales and
departmental archives, the fate of the hundreds of thousands of men like
Saumin after Waterloo has attracted surprisingly little attention among social
and military historians. We propose here to focus on their lives between 1858
and 1869, and to do so through the prism of the festivities of the 15th of
August under the Second Empire, in which they played an important and
often defining role. Placing the veterans in this festive setting will also enable
us to engage with a broader range of questions about French politics and society in the nineteenth century.

Central among these is the perpetuation of the Napoleonic legend.
Ménager's classic study has brought out the richness and diversity of 'popular'
Bonapartism in French political culture, especially between 1815 and 1848,
when there was often no hard and fast distinction between Jacobinism and
Bonapartism.[4] At the same time we still have much to learn, notably concerning the social and institutional underpinnings of Napoleonic ideology and
particularly the manner in which the memories and legends of the imperial
era were orally transmitted across generations. Through their speeches and
songs, their re-enactment of the epic battles in which they fought, and their
celebration of the heritage of their commander-in-chief the imperial veterans
of the Second Empire open up these important facets of the dynamics of popular Bonapartism.

The Médaillés de Sainte-Hélène also provide privileged access to the festivity of the 15th of August. This Napoleonic celebration under the Second
Empire has been little studied by French social and cultural historians, who
have tended instead to direct their gaze at the 'fête républicaine' of the 14th
of July, officially established as France's national festivity by the republicans

³ Ibid.   ⁴ Bernard Ménager, *Les Napoléon du peuple* (Paris, 1988).

in 1880.[5] Indeed the festivities of the 15th of August are typically presented as
the mirror image of their republican successors. In contrast with the exuber-
ant, spontaneous, folkloric, and popular character of the celebrations of the
quatorze juillet, the festivities of the Second Empire are viewed as rather stilted
affairs, dominated by religious institutions and religiosity, perverted by militarism and chauvinism, and fundamentally 'imposed' by the State on a passive
and recalcitrant society.[6] The roles of, and public responses to, the imperial
veterans in the festivities of the 15th of August will enable us to move away
from these stereotypical representations and to witness the distinct rhythms
of social, political, and cultural life in nineteenth century France away from
Paris and the larger French towns.

Also present here is the age-old theme of the place of the soldier in French
society and the social integration of the armed forces into the national community. With the publication of the studies of Bois and Woloch on the
eighteenth century and the Napoleonic era, it has been argued that the rein-
tegration of the soldier into the nation was substantively initiated by the
ancien régime; the Revolution and Empire merely completed the process.[7] But,
as Raoul Girardet has shown, the first half of the nineteenth century marked
a dramatic rejection of the Army in French political and intellectual circles.
Reviled by the bourgeoisie and aristocracy as a debauched propagator of
Jacobinism, the soldier was also despised by liberals and Saint-Simonians as a
relic of a barbarian age; until the late 1860s anti-militarism was also a dominant component of republican political culture.[8] It was only with the advent
of the Second Empire and the growing conservative fear of social revolution
that the Army came to be seen among conservative and liberal elites as a
defender of social order.[9] Even so, there is still controversy about how long it
took for popular mentalities to make this conceptual shift. Indeed, a recent
article, drawing largely on literary sources, argues that for most of the nineteenth century the war veteran essentially retained his 'disreputable qualities
as a vagabond, a spendthrift, a thief, a braggart and a libertine'. In this view it
was only under the Third Republic that mass attitudes towards French soldiers
changed fundamentally.[10] Public responses to the veterans of the imperial era
during the Second Empire will allow us to test this proposition.

It was the French State which instituted the decoration of the Médaille de
Sainte-Hélène and by this process helped to forge a new social legitimacy for
the veterans at the twilight of their lives. The political and ideological dynam-

---

[5] The defining work here is Olivier Ihl's *La fête républicaine* (Paris, 1996).

[6] The notion of an 'imposed festivity' is developed by Rosemonde Sanson, 'Le 15 août: Fête
nationale du Second Empire', in A. Corbin, N. Gérôme, and D. Tartakowsky (eds), *Les usages politiques
des fêtes aux XIXe–XXe siècles* (Paris, 1994), 134.

[7] J.-F. Bois, *Les anciens soldats dans la société française au xviiie siècle* (Paris, 1990); Isser Woloch, *The
French Veteran from the Revolution to the Restoration* (Chapel Hill, NC, 1979).

[8] This theme is developed in Sudhir Hazareesingh, *Intellectual Founders of the Republic: Five Studies
In Nineteenth Century French Political Thought* (Oxford, 2001), esp. 238–61.

[9] Raoul Girardet, *La société militaire de 1815 à nos jours* (Paris, 1998), 26–7.

[10] David M. Hopkin, '*La Ramée*, the Archetypal Soldier, as an Indicator of Popular Attitudes to the
Army in Nineteenth Century France'. *French History*, 14/2 (June 2000), 115–49.

ics which underlay the creation of this new civic decoration have many interesting things to tell us here, notably about the democratization of honours under the Second Empire and also the power of public authority to fashion a new 'public reputation' for a class of citizens—this is one episode in a long and ongoing narrative in France.[11] The question here, however, is how far the State actually 'created' the sense of respect and honour with which the imperial veterans were regarded, and to what extent its award of the medal merely granted legal recognition to an existing social fact.

Finally, the intertwined stories of the Médaillés de Sainte-Hélène and the festivities of the 15th of August open up a magnificent vista for exploring the development of nationalist and patriotic feelings in nineteenth-century France.[12] While these questions have been fruitfully addressed through the lens of the history of ideas and studies of nationalist ideologies, our exploration of the discourses and practices of the war veterans under the Second Empire offers a different type of source for investigating the complex question of the genesis of French 'national' sentiment.[13]

The Institution of the Award

The distinction of the Médaille de Sainte-Hélène was established by Napoleon III by a decree of 22 August 1857.[14] It was to be awarded to all those, both of French and of foreign nationality, who had fought under the national flag during the Revolutionary and imperial wars. The commemorative medal was made of bronze, and was to be worn at the buttonhole, suspended by a green and red ribbon. One side depicted the effigy of the Emperor, and the other carried the inscription 'Campaigns from 1792 to 1815—To His Companions of Glory, His Final Thought, 9 May 1821'.[15]

The ostensible purpose of this decoration was to honour the many surviving veterans of the French Armies of the Napoleonic era and to help identify those among them who were in need of material assistance and support. But there were also deeper symbolic and political dimensions at work here. Nineteenth-century French political regimes were obsessed with the legitimization of their lineage. With the Médaille de Sainte-Hélène the Second Empire sought to celebrate its links to the founder of the imperial dynasty, Napoleon Bonaparte. The dramatic reference to the moment of his death at Sainte-Hélène drew upon the romantic legend of the Napoleonic cult, which

[11] On the French honours system since the Revolution, see Olivier Ihl's chapter in this book.
[12] On this theme see Philippe Darriulat, *Les patriotes. La gauche républicaine et la nation 1830–1870* (Paris, 2001).
[13] For a similar approach see Rebecca McCoy, 'Alsatians into Frenchmen: The Construction of National Identities at Sainte-Marie-aux-Mines, 1815–1851', *French History*, 12 (1998), 429–51.
[14] The idea was floating around in Bonapartist circles as from the early 1850s. See for example *Relation historique de l'institution de la Médaille de Sainte-Hélène par un vieux soldat du Premier Empire* (Marseille, 1861); its author, Jean-Baptiste Schweitzer, claimed that in 1852 he had sent the Minister of War a drawing of what would later become the Médaille de Sainte-Hélène.
[15] L. Tripier, *Code des membres de la Légion d'Honneur* (Paris, 1859), LII–LIII.

exercised a powerful appeal to successive generations in nineteenth century France.[16] In the context of the workings of the Second Empire, Napoleon III also hoped to use these awards as a means of creating a 'popular nobility', thus demonstrating that his regime remained true to the Bonapartist ideal of a society in which talent and merit could be recognized irrespective of wealth or social origin. The Second Empire had already initiated the practice of awarding the Legion of Honour to mayors of small rural communes; the Médaille de Sainte-Hélène was from this point of view an extension of the process of 'democratizing' the honours system.[17]

All these features were to come together on the 15th of August of each year. The Médaillés de Sainte-Hélène were to be given pride of place in the ceremonial of France's national festivity, providing living proof of the regime's Napoleonic and popular credentials as well as demonstrating its benevolence and compassion towards the poor and needy.

The processing of individual claims, verification of entitlements, and issuing the medals began in earnest in the autumn of 1857. It was a massive operation, involving the French state bureaucracy at the national, departmental, and communal levels. In over 36,000 communes of metropolitan France, mayors invited former soldiers of the First Republic and Empire to come forward, and drew up nominative lists of candidates for the awards; applicants were asked to provide evidence of their incorporation or discharge from the Army. These nominative lists were passed on to the prefect of the department, who after an initial verification despatched them to the Grande Chancellerie de la Légion d'Honneur in Paris—part of the Ministry of State, headed by Achille Fould. The Grande Chancellerie, after consulting where necessary with the Ministry of War, then issued the requisite number of medals and certificates. These awards travelled back to their point of origin by exactly the same route: first to the prefects, who then handed them on to the mayors. The prefects were given responsibility for ensuring prompt delivery of the medals.

On the whole, the operation proceeded very satisfactorily. A summary table produced by the sub-prefect of the arrondissement of Epernay (Marne) for the whole of the year 1858 demonstrated that, of the 1,063 medals and certificates received by the department of the Marne by October 1858, 1,030 had been issued to their recipients.[18] What had happened to the 33 unclaimed medals? Around a third had not yet been distributed by the mayors. Some of the honorands may also have left the commune, although this, given their age and social conditions, could have applied to only a very small number of Médaillés. It was most likely that some of the veterans had died during the previous twelve months, and that others had become too ill, or simply too frail, to come in person to the *mairie*.

But we should not imagine that all the former servicemen were in a state of physical decrepitude. The records held in departmental archives across France

---

[16] Ménager, *Les Napoléon du peuple*.
[17] See Sudhir Hazareesingh and Vincent Wright, 'Le Second Empire' (2002).
[18] AD Marne, 16 M 1 (Médaille de Sainte-Hélène).

attest to the remarkable experiences and continuing vitality of many of the Médaillés. Take the example of Pierre Nollet, who originated from the village of Saudrupt (Meuse). In April 1813 he joined the Army and was immediately assigned to serve as courier for Napoleon. He performed this task for over a year, during which he was on the front line of several key battles in the French campaign.[19] Although in his early seventies by 1858, Nollet was still in good health and received his medal with alacrity. And what of former corporal Augustin Aubertin, born in 1778, who gave gallant service to the Armies of both Republic and Empire between 1798 and 1812? Aubertin did battle in the Italian and Spanish campaigns, and sustained two injuries, one at a skirmish in Tyrol in April 1798 and the other at the battle of Albuéra in May 1811. Already in his 80th year in 1858, he was still in excellent health and greatly looked forward to receiving his medal.[20] These individual stories reflected the remarkable odds which these former military servicemen had defeated in order to receive these awards, four or five decades after the conclusion of the Revolutionary and Napoleonic wars.

Hopes and Frustrations

But the bureaucratic procedure did not go smoothly everywhere. The process of vetting and delivering the medals also give rise to problems, especially among those imperial veterans who possessed no documents attesting to their years of service. Let us consider the case of André Poupon, a textile worker from Lyon. Poupon's was a tale of fortitude and misery in equal measure. Having enlisted as a volunteer in June 1807, he had fought in the campaigns of Wagram (1809), Holland (1810), Russia (1812), and Belfort (1815). During the Russian campaign he was made prisoner and sent to Siberia, where he was interned for 18 months; he developed rheumatic pains which plagued him for the rest of his life. Sent back to France through an exchange of prisoners in 1814, Poupon was discharged, but, being a passionate Bonapartist, he enlisted again during the Hundred Days. His body took a severe battering during his eight years of active service: his right arm was pierced by a Cossack lance at Smolensk; his feet froze during the retreat from Moscow; and a Prussian sabre cracked open his head at Belfort.

   And yet this was not the end of his troubles. Destitute and miserable, he spent the entire Restoration period in abject poverty. The Bourbons had nothing to offer the veterans of an Army whose commander-in-chief they had so bitterly opposed. After the change of regime in 1830, Poupon sent a petition to the Duc D'Orléans asking him for a state pension, attaching all his military service documents. His demand found no favour, and his papers were never returned. Two further decades of deprivation followed. Louis Philippe's regime

---

[19] Certificate issued by municipality of Saudrupt, 17 April 1856, in AD Marne, 16 M 1 (Médaille de Sainte-Hélène).
[20] AD Marne, 16 M 1 (Médaille de Sainte-Hélène).

was eager to exploit the Bonapartist legend to its own advantage, notably through the return of Napoleon's remains in 1840; but it showed little interest in the fate of the Emperor's loyal foot-soldiers. In 1850, under the Second Republic, Poupon again petitioned the prefect of the Rhône for help, stressing his old age, material destitution, and poor health. Still he received no reply. Three years later—by now we were under the Second Empire, and his hopes were high—he tried the Ministry of War. This time he received a letter back informing him that he was not eligible for any state support, as he had been officially classified as a deserter. This bureaucratic mistake—for it was one: his was an extremely common name—caused Poupon to fall seriously ill. Finally in 1857, still lacking any documents to prove his membership of the Grande Armée, he appealed directly to Napoleon III. Moved by his plight, the Emperor seems to have ruled in his favour.[21]

Similar dramas unfolded all across France, not always with the positive conclusion which marked Poupon's repeated and impassioned pleas. Thomas Aubert, a prison warden at Villefranche (Rhône), found his application turned down because his discharge papers were issued collectively to a group of around 30 soldiers in the chaotic end of the 1815 campaign. Despite the award of the medal to many of his companions in the same regiment, and several of them vouching for him, his pleas remained unanswered.[22] Others, such as Marie-Antoine Lardet, a textile worker, could not produce their discharge papers because they were destroyed in the 'wretched invasion of 1815'[23]—a reminder that many servicemen returned to their villages at the end of the Napoleonic wars only to face more hardship and misery.

Local officials sometimes weighed in on behalf of disappointed applicants. The mayor of St Lager (Rhône) was 'painfully affected' to learn that none of the ten applicants from his commune had been granted their medals. He appealed to the Sub-prefect to have their cases re-examined, stressing that it was of 'public notoriety' in his commune that all these men had served in the Grande Armée.[24] These reviews, which at times applied somewhat less stringent criteria for assessing the credentials of former servicemen, created opportunities for recognition and advancement which were eagerly seized by some local officials. In April 1858 Berthier, the mayor of Ville-sur-Jarnioux (Rhône), informed his sub-prefect that only two of the eleven applicants from his commune had received their medals and certificates. He respectfully asked for their cases to be reviewed, and for good measure added his own name to the list on the grounds that he had been a zealous Bonapartist during the Hundred Days.[25]

---

[21] His letter to the Emperor made its way to Lyon, where the prefect assigned him a medal. AD Rhône, 1 M 263 (Médaille de Sainte-Hélène).
[22] A copy of his letter to the prefect of the Rhône, dated 19 August 1858, is in AD Rhône, 1 M 263 (Médaille de Sainte-Hélène).
[23] A copy of his letter dated 30 March 1858 is in AD Rhône, 1 M 263 (Médaille de Sainte-Hélène).
[24] Mayor of St Lager, letter dated 10 April 1858, in AD Rhône, 1 M 263 (Médaille de Sainte-Hélène).
[25] Mayor of Ville-sur-Jarnioux, letter dated 8 April 1858, in AD Rhône, 1 M 263 (Médaille de Sainte-Hélène).

Delays in the issuing of medals also created difficulties among veterans. In the run-up to the celebration of the festivity of the 15th of August 1858, many potential Médaillés had still not received their decorations. This situation made for great embarrassment, noted one frustrated *propriétaire* from Givors. Speaking for all those who shared his predicament, he remarked that without their medals 'it would be difficult for them properly to attend the Fête and even less the banquet which will follow it'.[26] Those whose applications were categorically denied were in an even worse position. It is easy enough to imagine the devastating social consequences of such denials of official recognition, especially in a small rural village: these hapless veterans would be excluded not only from the festivities but also from the wider collective life of their communities. The logic of the situation was implacable: if those who were officially honoured became 'honourable' citizens, then those whose applications were refused could only become dishonourable. Many veterans who were already socially marginalized through destitution, ill health, poor mobility, and old age thus paradoxically found themselves even more excluded as a result of the process.

Those whose claims were rejected were also excluded from membership of veterans' associations. Many departments also established their own mutual aid associations to defend and promote the interests of their Médaillés. In the department of the Somme, for example, there were over 5,300 recipients of the medal by the late 1850s.[27] The Association des Médaillés de Sainte-Hélène was thus set up in December 1859 by the Prefect Sencier. Its membership consisted of all the medal-holders, who paid a modest annual subscription, as well as honorary members who paid a minimum of six francs a year. The Association's aim was to supplement through local subscriptions the aid given to imperial veterans by the State.[28] The organization was extremely active and raised significant funds: for the year 1861–2 the total amount generated was 7,328 francs, of which 4,010 were spent in grants to destitute Médaillés.[29] The records of the Association offer some insights into the social circumstances of the veterans. In the 1860 membership list for the arrondissement of Abbeville, for example, at least half of the subscribers could not sign their name. But almost all the veterans paid something. One of them, Antoine Hector Carré, was 87 years old, and paid his annual membership fee of ten centimes even though he was described as 'blind and poor'. The only exception was the 72-year-old Jean-Baptiste Lebrun, from the commune of Maison-Ponthieu, who was exempted altogether from paying his subscription. The entry in the 'observations' column noted that he was 'completely destitute and almost an

---

[26] Letter of Jean Fleury Cognat, Givors, 21 July 1858, AD Rhône, 1 M 263 (Médaille de Sainte-Hélène).

[27] AD Somme, 99 M 27 (Médaillés de Sainte Hélène).

[28] Statuts de l'Association des Médaillés de Ste.Hélène de la Somme, 15 December 1859. AD Somme, 99 M 27.

[29] Association des Médaillés de Ste.Hélène de la Somme, report for 1861–2 activities, Amiens 25 June 1862; AD Somme, 99 M 27.

invalid'.[30] In overall terms, however, the Médaillés of the Somme did not give the impression of being overwhelmingly devoid of resources. Out of a total membership of over 5,000, only 208 requests for financial help were received by the Association in 1861–2, from less than 5 per cent of all members.[31] In subsequent years the number of applications for assistance fell even further.

Indeed, by the mid-1860s the Association was thriving financially, with a budgetary surplus of 5,743 francs.[32] Public support through individual donations and departmental and communal subscriptions had gathered considerable momentum. Every year, though, the number of Médaillés was being considerably reduced through death. The 1865 report gives no figures but notes that 'a large number' of Médaillés had died over the previous five years.[33] For those 'glorious relics' who had cheated death on so many occasions on the battlefield, and had survived through the treacherous waters of the nineteenth century, the 1860s represented the final race against Death. This sense of the ebbing of time was poignantly conveyed in a short letter written by a group of Médaillés from the Hospice de la Charité in Lyon in early August 1867. They appealed to the prefect of the Rhône to allow them out to attend the Mass in the St Jean Cathedral on the 15th of August because many of them 'would perhaps not be there next year'.[34]

The Ceremonies of 1858

Let us now return to celebration of the festivity of the 15th of August. In large parts of provincial and rural France, this was the moment which defined the public existence of the Médaillés between 1858 and 1869. In a very small number of cases, such as in Mormoiron (Vaucluse) in 1861, imperial veterans refused to take part in the festivities because of their 'opposition to the government'[35]—a reminder that many Jacobins had fought for Napoleon but did not necessarily remain committed to the Bonapartist cause in subsequent decades.

But there is little evidence that such opposition to the Second Empire was widespread. Indeed, the presence of the imperial veterans gave an added civic and commemorative dimension to the festivities; and the central position they occupied in the ceremonial of the 15th of August reflected the strong public identification of the Fête with the Médaillés. Even before 1858 we find numerous instances of the presence of imperial veterans during the festivities,

[30] Liste des souscriptions (1860), arrondissement d'Abbeville, Association des Médaillés de Ste. Hélène de la Somme. AD Somme, 99 M 27 (Médaillés de Sainte Hélène).
[31] Association des Médaillés de Ste. Hélène de la Somme, report for 1861–2 activities, Amiens 25 June 1862; AD Somme, 99 M 27.
[32] General Assembly of Association, 1865, report by prefect of the Somme. AD Somme, 99 M 27 (Médaillés de Sainte Hélène).
[33] Ibid.
[34] Letter from Auclair to prefect of Rhône, Hospice de la Charité, Lyon, 6 August 1867. AD Rhône 1 M 165.
[35] Report of Mayor, 17 August 1861. AD Vaucluse, 1 M 880.

notably at Sainte-Claude (Jura) in 1852,[36] La Châtre (Indre) in 1853,[37] and Carcassonne (Aude) in 1854.[38]

The veterans' greatest moment, however, came during the ceremonies of 1858, during which they were issued with their medals and certificates. In the village of Gourdon (Var), the mayor noted in his report that because this year's festivity had coincided with the distribution of medals to the commune's veterans 'the whole of the population was keen to turn out'. This was no rhetorical statement. The award ceremony had been fixed for the early afternoon of 15 August and was to be held in the *mairie* in the presence of the municipal council. However, when the veterans made their way to the public room at the appointed hour they found 'hundreds' of inhabitants already waiting for them. These citizens had come spontaneously; the mayor had issued no summons. And each minute that passed brought more people, so much so that 'soon the room became too small to hold the crowd, and we had to move the meeting to the big square in the village'. The mayor then gave a brief speech in which he summarized the origins of the Médaille and underlined the 'respect' owed to all its recipients. Before calling the names of the honorands, he invoked the memory of Emperor Napoleon at Sainte-Hélène by reading out the inscription on the medal. The veterans received their decorations 'with hearts bursting with joy and eyes full of tears of gratitude'. The crowd chanted 'Long Live Napoleon! Long live the Emperor!'. A group of soldiers, on home leave from a nearby garrison, fired several rounds in the air 'to render full military honours to the happy old folk who had received this honorary distinction'.

In Lagardefreinet (also in the Var), the mayor noted a larger public presence than usual at the festivities of the 15th of August. There was no doubt in his mind that the reason for this greater attendance was the ceremony in honour of the imperial veterans. Clearly facing an audience which was yet to be fully won over to the Second Empire, the mayor used the distribution of awards to 19 Médaillés to remind the inhabitants of 'the services which these old veterans have rendered to the First Empire'. He then invited the honorands to 'perpetuate a similar sense of duty to their descendants in favour of the Emperor's worthy successor, Napoleon III, whose great benefits to France are not yet fully appreciated'. The atmosphere was festive and somewhat martial; the ceremony ended with the execution by the local musical band of the air 'Partons pour la Syrie'.[39] The protection of Christian populations of the Levant by French troops was a popular cause in the late 1850s and early 1860s. In some localities the celebrations of 1858 were extended by several days in order to provide a fitting tribute to the Médaillés. In the town of Pertuis (Vaucluse) the Sub-prefect noted that the festivities had taken place 'under conditions which had not been witnessed up till that point'. There were three days of rejoicing:

[36] Report of Procureur-Général, Besançon, 14 September 1852. AN BB30-373.
[37] Report of Prefect, 20 August 1853. AN F1C^{III}/Indre (6).
[38] Report of Prefect of Aude, 20 August 1854. AN F1C^1 110.
[39] Report of Mayor of Lagardefreinet, 15 August 1858. AD Var 6 M 18 (5).

the Emperor was feted on the 15th, with all the traditional religious and civic manifestations; a large agricultural fair was held on the 16th, with public amusements and distributions of prizes to farmers; and the festivities culminated on the 17th with a ceremony in honour of the commune's Médaillés de Sainte-Hélène. This event took place in the afternoon in the presence of most of the inhabitants of Pertuis. A large banquet then followed, and in the evening there was a spectacular display of fireworks. There was little doubt that, for the local population, the third day had represented the climax of the festivities.[40]

The Civic Procession

The important position occupied by the Médaillés de Sainte-Hélène in the ceremonial of the 15th of August after 1858 could be measured at all the successive stages of the proceedings, as we shall see. But their defining moment in the public sphere was the morning procession in which all the notables of the commune marched from the *mairie* to the Church. This was a moment which the Médaillés themselves awaited eagerly. At Bouzigues (Hérault) in 1859, the mayor was slightly put out to find the village veterans already assembled in front of his house at six in the morning. But their enthusiasm was infectious: he could not help marvelling at how 'these noble veterans were looking for each other, calling out at each other in order to come together, exchange views and together evoke the memory of their illustrious companion'.[41]

All over France between 1858 and 1869 civic processions of the 15th of August accorded a special place to the Médaillés de Sainte-Hélène. At Bouzigues the veterans were lined up immediately behind the mayor and the municipal council; they were thus placed ahead of all the other public functionaries of the commune.[42] Elsewhere they stood out by virtue of their small numbers, proud symbols of military valour and physical resilience. Reporting on the celebrations of the 15th of August at La Ciotat (Bouches-du-Rhône) in 1862, the police commissioner enumerated a long list of official figures who escorted the municipal council to the Church; in the midst of the procession, and surrounded by an atmosphere of respect and admiration, were 'two Médaillés de Sainte-Hélène'.[43] At Sérignan (Vaucluse) the language of the mayor's report was similarly revealing: he described the veterans as having accompanied all the other 'corps' of the commune to the Church. In other words, the Médaillés were here fully integrated into the public sphere.[44] The sub-prefect of Dieppe went one stage further, noting that the procession of the 15th of August in this maritime town had included 'the administrative, mili-

---

[40] Report of Sub-prefect of Apt, 20 August 1858. AD Vaucluse 1 M 880.
[41] Report of Mayor of Bouzigues, 20 August 1859. AD Hérault 1 M 506.   [42] Ibid.
[43] La Ciotat Police Station, report of 18 August 1862. AD Bouches-du-Rhône 1 M 643.
[44] Report of Mayor of Sérignan, 16 August 1869. AD Vaucluse 1 M 880.

tary, and judicial authorities together with the Médaillés de Sainte-Hélène'.[45] In their different formulae all these reports indicate that the veterans enjoyed equal status with the public officials of the commune, but were in many senses more equal than all the others—by virtue of their age, their bravery, the challenges they had overcome, and above all through their personal memories of the Emperor Napoleon.

In most towns and villages the solemnity of the civic procession was enhanced by the presence of an escort of firemen. This escort performed several critical functions in the carefully orchestrated ensemble of symbolic practices which characterized the festivity of the 15th of August. For one thing, it was a good way of accentuating the prestige of the elected representatives and public officials of the village. Mayors and municipal councils were acutely aware that their fate under the Second Empire was eventually determined by the ballot box. A well-organized and resplendent civic procession thus represented a valuable opportunity to put their authority on display, and they knew that village folk respected authority all the more when that authority seemed to respect itself. The firemen's presence was also a gesture of salutation towards the Catholic Church, where the procession was headed. It was a sign of reverence for the house of God, of course, but also a subliminal act of differentiation on the part of the democratic representatives of the community, an affirmation that the village's secular institutions were just as worthy of public status and respect as the Church.

The underlying purpose of firemen's escort, in other words, was to draw out the distinctiveness of the commune's civic order. And what better symbol of this individuality than the Médaillés de Sainte-Hélène? Little wonder, then, that the veterans were not only given a prominent place in the procession but were also entrusted with the emblem which most vividly symbolized the commune's civic autonomy: the banner. At Sollièr-Ville (Var) in 1866, the civic procession was led off from the *mairie* by a group of imperial veterans, one of whom proudly bore the tricolour.[46] At Fains (Meuse), the national banner was carried in turn by the firemen and the veterans; both groups surrounded the flag 'almost protectively' during the religious ceremony in Church.[47] In many parts of France, the veterans also marked the 15th of August by creating their own emblems. The 1866 civic procession in the town of L'Isle (Vaucluse) saw the imperial veterans carry 'their own magnificent banner, which bore the following inscription: 'Long Live the Emperor—The Médaillés de Sainte-Hélène'.[48]

Perhaps the most remarkable evidence of the centrality of the Médaillés in the processions of the 15th of August lay in the surrogate functions they were called upon to perform. In many communes of France, particularly in the 1860s, the revival of democratic politics was accompanied by the development

[45] Report of Sub-prefect of Dieppe, 21 August 1865. AD Seine Maritime, 1 M 352.
[46] Report of Mayor of Sollièr-Ville, 16 August 1866. AD Var, 6 M 18 (5).
[47] Report of Mayor of Fains, 16 August 1862. AD Meuse, 73 M 6.
[48] Report of Police Commissioner of L'Isle, 16 August 1866. AD Vaucluse, 1 M 880.

of overt political opposition to the Second Empire. Municipal elections saw the victories of republican and legitimist councillors, and often the mayor, appointed by the State, found himself completely isolated within his local assembly. These opposition councillors often abstained from attending the civic ceremonies of the 15th of August, leaving mayors in an acutely embarrassing position. Such absences reflected poorly on them, undermining their claims to preside over a harmonious and efficient administration. Just as importantly, gaps in the processions and empty seats in Church highlighted their incompetence in the eyes of their tutelary authorities, the prefects.

First magistrates responded by increasingly relying on the Médaillés to fill these glaring deficiencies in the civic order of the commune. The year 1859 marked one of the high points of the 15th of August festivities all across France as it coincided with the triumphant return of the French Army from the Italian campaign. Not so, however, in the village of Willems (Nord). On the previous day the mayor had summoned his municipal council in order to vote a special credit for the local celebrations. Only four councillors showed up, making the meeting inquorate. The mayor was thus prevented from organizing any public festivities. Mortified, he wrote to the prefect: 'Our fête simply consisted in attending the *Te Deum*, accompanied by the Médaillés de Sainte-Hélène.'[49] In many of the rural communes of the Hérault, in 1860, the police commissioner reported that the celebrations had taken place 'without any great enthusiasm'; the only exceptions were those localities with significant cohorts of imperial veterans.[50]

The following year, things had not improved; the same police officer reported to the prefect of the Hérault that the whole municipal council of the commune of Lansargue, made up 'almost entirely of republicans', had refused to join the civic procession and had not attended the religious ceremonies in Church. The only officials present were the mayor, his deputy, and the Médaillés of Sainte-Hélène.[51] The same tune was heard in L'Isle and Thor (Vaucluse) in 1867 and 1869: at the latter 'a major part of the municipal councillors were absent' and at the former 'none of the councillors attended the procession and the ceremony'.[52] If one reads between the lines of the reports, it is clear that in both cases it was the presence of the Médaillés which had saved the day.

Public Honour and Popular Esteem

So far we have followed the narratives of the imperial veterans largely from above—and outside—focusing on their bureaucratic incorporation by the State, and then catching glimpses of how public institutions in provincial and

---

[49] Report of Mayor of Willems, 18 August 1859. AD Nord, M 141 (93).
[50] Report of 16 August 1860, AD Hérault 1 M 506.
[51] Report of 16 August 1861, AD Hérault 1 M 507.
[52] L'Isle, report of 16 August 1867; Thor, report of 19 August 1869. AD Vaucluse 1 M 880.

rural France celebrated the Médaillés and accorded them a central position in the ceremonial of the 15th of August. But how did the veterans view themselves? What were the reactions of other groups and institutions in civil society, and indeed—beyond the encomiums offered in Bonapartist pamphlets[53]—what evidence is there of the wider public response to the presence of the Médaillés in their midst?

This theme of 'honour' was clearly one of the dominant questions in the minds of Napoleonic veterans. It played very strongly in the internal debates and practices of associations of imperial veterans which mushroomed all over France after 1858. One such organization at la Chapelle Saint-Denis (Seine) regrouped a hundred veterans living in this Parisian neighbourhood. At its founding meeting in May 1858 the association approved a constitution of 30 articles, and elected an executive bureau of six members presided over by Hébert, the mayor of La Chapelle.[54] The association's definition of the decoration was striking: 'The medal of Sainte-Hélène is an eminently honourable distinction for all those who have the right to wear it, as for those who do not have the honour of being decorated by it, but who know how to understand and appreciate its meaning.'[55] The aim of the Corporation was to foster solidarity among its members and to engender 'respect and honour' of the medal,[56] to ensure that it was always worn 'decently' and never 'dishonoured' by any action or insult.[57] Individual members who were in material need and wished to plead to the Emperor for assistance were required to have their appeals vetted by the Corporation first; again the point was clearly to preserve the reputation of the membership as a whole.[58]

Transgressions from this code of honour were severely punished. Any member who brought the Corporation's good name into disrepute by his 'scandalous conduct and depraved morals' was liable to be permanently expelled.[59] All members were also under obligation, when one of theirs died, to attend his funeral; failure to pay their respects to the last remains of their colleague was also grounds for dismissal from the Corporation.[60] The behaviour of the Médaillés towards each other had at all times to be marked by the 'decency which always has to be shown by men who respect one another'.[61] Elsewhere in France some associations, such as the Médaillés de Sainte-Hélène of Maine et Loire, adopted even more stringent criteria, reserving the right to deny membership to any imperial veterans who did not enjoy a 'social position, which alone can guarantee them the respect which they enjoy as individuals'.[62]

[53] There is a modest collection of this genre in the Bibliothèque Nationale. See for example Henry Courant, *Sur la Médaille de Sainte-Hélène* (Paris, 1858). LL24-2.
[54] Corporation des Membres Décorés de la Médaille de Sainte-Hélène en résidence à la Chapelle Saint-Denis. Règlement (Paris, 1858). Bib.Nat.LL24-11.
[55] Corporation des Membres, 7.   [56] Corporation des Membres, 1.
[57] Corporation des Membres, 8.   [58] Corporation des Membres, 2–3.
[59] Corporation des Membres, 4.   [60] Corporation des Membres, 5–6.
[61] Corporation des Membres, 7.
[62] *Préambule et Statuts des Membres Décorés de la Médaille de Sainte-Hélène*, Maine et Loire (1859). Bib.Nat.LL24-10.

As a collectivity, the imperial veterans were thus extremely sensitive to their status and reacted with appropriate feeling to any impropriety of conduct by public institutions towards them. The main culprits here tended to be the municipalities. At Balaruc-les-Bains (Hérault) in 1867 a Médaillé complained that he had received no invitation to take part in the municipal procession, despite having been included in the official list in previous years; he blamed the mayor for the 'lack of solemnity which had been given to this national festivity'.[63] The same problem occurred at Barbentane (Bouches-du-Rhône) in 1862; the sub-prefect of Arles noted that 'the mayor had not invited the Médaillés de Sainte-Hélène'.[64] At Aix in August 1859 the municipality had also tried to get away with the strict minimum in terms of the organization of public festivities. There was thus no civic procession from the *mairie* to the Church, and only the mayor and his deputy attended the religious service. Even worse, the municipal posters which traditionally announced the national festivity to the population were not printed that year. Apart from providing details of the day's events, these posters also served as the official summons to attend the *Te Deum* in the cathedral, notably to all army veterans. The sub-prefect noted that the Médaillés were 'deeply offended by this oversight'.[65] This was, after all, the only time when their existence was publicly recognized as a group.

In the same year, even more offensive proved the behaviour of the curé of the parish of Vritz (Loire-Inférieure), who refused to allow the delegation of Médaillés de Sainte-Hélène to enter his Church bearing the tricolour they had flown during the procession. The reports do not mention whether the veterans came in without their banner or stayed outside in protest. In a letter of complaint to the Archbishop of Nantes, the prefect accepted that the priest had acted within his rights; he was after all statutorily responsible for maintaining order in his Church. However, the wider political context—Napoleon III's support for Italian unity and the concomitant threat to the temporal powers of the Pope—undoubtedly provided the motivation for the priest's symbolic act. In any event, noted the prefect, this priest had something of a track record of opposing the Second Empire; his gesture had thus provided 'new evidence of his hostile dispositions towards the administration'.[66] In other words, this was less an attempt to insult the Médaillés than a symbolic expression of opposition to Napoleon III's foreign policy.

These were relatively isolated incidents. The overwhelming majority of administrative reports on the festivities of the 15th of August spoke not only of the warmth and respect shown by local populations towards the Médaillés but also of the extraordinary effects their presence at times provoked. In the village of Sacy (Marne) in 1859 the official procession was made up of a strong contingent of imperial veterans; the mayor noted that 'everywhere on its pas-

[63] Letter of Antoine Cournet, 17 August 1867. AD Hérault 1 M 509.
[64] Report of Sub-prefect, 20 August 1862. AD Bouches-du-Rhône 1 M 643.
[65] Report of Sub-prefect, 16 August 1859. AD Bouches-du-Rhône 1 M 642.
[66] Letter dated 27 August 1859. AD Loire Atlantique, 1 M 675.

sage the procession was greeted with great fervour'. Indeed that year's celebrations in the commune—the first in which the Médaillés had taken a full
part—had proved the most memorable and festive to date.[67] At Cousancelles
(Meuse) the firemen elected to honour the imperial veterans in a special way.
The enthusiastic scenes which followed were depicted by the mayor:

The firemen in an impeccable outfit wished not only to escort the local authorities [to
Church], but insisted on the honour of fetching the Médaillés de Sainte-Hélène from
their homes and accompanying them together with the municipal council to the ceremonies of the day, after which they again escorted the veterans back to their homes,
where they presented their arms and gave a roll of honour. These old and brave relics of
our glorious armies responded to these military honours with energetic cries of 'Long
Live the Emperor', repeated a thousand times by the inhabitants who had spontaneously accompanied the escort.[68]

In the 1864 celebrations in the town of Armentières (Nord), the civic procession was made up of local officials, recently elevated Chevaliers of the
Légion d'Honneur, and Médaillés de Sainte-Hélène. The escort was provided
by firemen 'in grand uniform' with music provided by the local philharmonic
society. The mayor noted that 'a mass of people was pressing against the procession'.[69] At Nantes in 1869 events took an even more remarkable turn. The
mayor had invited, as was customary, the imperial veterans, together with the
veterans of the Crimean War, to gather in the forecourt of the municipality in
order to proceed to the Cathedral. Shortly before eleven in the morning, as the
gathering prepared to make its way, 'representatives of 36 workers' corpora-
tions, banners flying proudly, came spontaneously to join the procession,
which they accompanied all the way to the Cathedral'.[70] At Bergues (Nord) in
1864, the mayor's report stressed that the working class 'which had been most
favoured during the festivities, warmly expressed its deep sense of satisfaction'.[71] Indeed, in many localities it was apparent that the principal reason for
the large turn-out of workers during the festivities of the 15th of August was
the presence of the Médaillés de Sainte-Hélène.

But the veterans' appeal was not limited to one section of society. At Pignan
(Hérault) the civic procession was joined by 'the Catholic youth of the locality, who had brought with them a full complement of music'.[72] At Pérols, in
the same department, in 1864 large sections of the population were present
outside the *mairie* in the morning to witness the departure of the civic procession, which included a significant complement of Médaillés. However, as they
began to move it became apparent that the deputy mayor and a significant
proportion of the municipal councillors were absent. The mayor picks up the
story: 'At this moment all the young people who were in the crowd, with their

---

[67] Report of Mayor of Sacy, 23 August 1859. AD Marne 32 M 10.
[68] Report of 16 August 1858. AD Meuse, 73 M 6.
[69] Report of Mayor of Armentières, 16 August 1864. AD Nord, M 141 (95).
[70] Police Report 1869, Nantes. AD Loire Atlantique, 1 M 675.
[71] Report of Mayor of Bergues, 17 August 1864. AD Nord M 141 (95).
[72] Report of Mayor of Pignan, 17 August 1859. AD Hérault, 1 M 506.

banners and music, spontaneously came to join the procession in order to protest by their presence against the deliberate absence of the municipal officials.'[73] This popular guard of honour was not merely a gesture of support for the mayor but also a reflection of the public esteem for the Médaillés; the youth in this particular locality clearly regarded the absence of the municipal councillors as an unacceptable betrayal of the respect owed to the Revolutionary and Napoleonic veterans.

It is not surprising, then, that official reports typically dwell on the contentment of the ex-servicemen. Thus the Police Commissioner of Avignon in 1861: 'Everyone yesterday saw with pleasure the old Médaillés de Sainte-Hélène in the civic procession. The faces of these brave old folk were radiant with happiness.'[74] This was not merely because they were recognized and feted by all—although of course this was a huge source of satisfaction to them. There was something deeper. The Médaillés were happy because they saw that they possessed a special power: the capacity to enthuse local populations, to draw out all sections of society into the public sphere, and thus to generate mass fervour. On the large stage of the 15th of August, theirs was the act which the public applauded most passionately. This special place of the veterans in the hearts and minds of the French public was noted by state officials across France. The procureur-général of Colmar wrote in 1858 that 'the institution of the Médaille is very popular, especially in the countryside where there are still a substantially large number of relics of our old troops'.[75] This was echoed by the sub-prefect of Béziers: 'The presence and the enthusiasm of the Médaillés of Sainte-Hélène have produced a happy effect on public consciousness. By honouring them, the Empire has conquered the sympathies of even the most indifferent and rallied many hearts.'[76]

Feasts and Banquets

The pivotal position of the imperial veterans in the celebrations of the 15th of August came to a joyful climax during the various forms of entertainment laid out in their honour by local officials. The strength of communal sociability, the vigorous dissemination of Bonapartist ideology, and the physical resilience of the Médaillés themselves shine through the surviving accounts of these festivities.

In some communes the receptions for the veterans were held during the day. There were often two processions taking place on the 15th of August: a civic manifestation in the morning and a religious procession in honour of the Virgin Mary in the early evening. At Valseirs (Vaucluse) in 1868, the municipality offered the Médaillés a 'collation' at lunchtime, no doubt to help sus-

---

[73] Report of Mayor of Pérols, 17 August 1864. AD Hérault, 1 M 508.
    [74] Report of Police Commissioner, Avignon, 16 August 1861. AD Vaucluse 1 M 880.
    [75] Report of Procureur-Général, Colmar, 4 October 1858. AN BB30-376.
    [76] Report to Prefect, Béziers, 17 August 1858. AD Hérault, 1 M 505.

tain the veterans during this very long day.[77] But in general most of these gatherings were held in the evening. At Seillans (Var) in 1861, the processions having ended, the mayor invited the Médaillés into the town hall for a small reception. The atmosphere was festive, and the veterans were in excellent form despite their exertions of the day: 'On numerous occasions, their hearts brimming with joy and enthusiasm, they drank the health of the Emperor, the Empress, and the Imperial Prince.'[78] In the village of Heutrégiville (Marne) the mayor and the entire municipal council invited the Médaillés, together with the company of firemen to the Café du Commerce, the main establishment of the commune. The lengthy toasts and enthusiastic tone of the report suggest that its owner Monsieur Garnotel did very good business that evening.[79]

But in the majority of communes the festivities in honour of the Médaillés took the classic form assumed by nineteenth century French sociability: the banquet. At Avallon (Yonne) in 1861 the mayor gave an 'improvised banquet' for the imperial veterans.[80] In Fleury, in the same department, in 1863 the 32 firemen of the commune gave a banquet in honour of the eight Médaillés de Sainte-Hélène; the funds for this gathering were provided by the municipality.[81] At Althen-des-Paluds (Vaucluse) in 1864 the commune's eight imperial veterans were treated to a banquet during which they feasted 'with constantly renewed enthusiasm'.[82] In the larger towns these occasions were patronized by the entire administrative elite: at Toulouse in 1858 60 imperial veterans were the guests of honour at a banquet at the prefecture;[83] and at Rouen in 1859 the banquet in honour of the Médaillés was organized by the mayor, with the prefect of the Seine-Inférieure and the top military brass in attendance.[84]

No banquet would be complete without a proliferation of toasts. Their objects in this case were typically the Emperor Napoleon, his nephew Napoleon III—and the imperial family—and the Médaillés de Sainte-Hélène. At Marsillargues in 1858 a banquet for 36 guests was laid on by the communal authorities in honour of the imperial veterans. After the dinner the mayor invited all those present to drink to the health of Napoleon III and his family. The Police Commissioner then stood up:

Gentlemen, allow me in turn to offer a toast to the memory of the great man whose glorious memories still resonate powerfully in our hearts; to the glory and prosperity of his illustrious descendant, the founder of the noble legion of Sainte-Hélène; and to these veterans who by adorning their scarred breasts revive in the hearts of our little children feelings of enthusiasm and patriotism, and make heroes of all those humble conscripts who fought memorable battles in order to make France the queen of civilized nations.[85]

---

77 Report of Police Commissioner, 16 August 1868. AD Vaucluse, 1 M 880.
78 Report of the Mayor of Seillans, 20 August 1861. AD Var, 6 M 18 (5).
79 Mayor's report (undated). AD Marne, 32 M 10.
80 Report of Mayor, 16 August 1861. AD Yonne, 3 M³ 33.
81 Report of Police Commissioner, 17 August 1863. AD Yonne, 3 M³ 33.
82 Report of Mayor, 18 August 1864. AD Vaucluse, 1 M 880.
83 Report of Procureur-Général, Toulouse, 16 August 1858. AN BB30-421.
84 Draft report of Prefect to Minister of Interior, 1859. AD Seine-Maritime, 1 M 351.
85 Report of Police Commissioner, 16 August 1858. AD Hérault, 1 M 505.

   The distinctive appeal of the Bonapartist legend shines through here. This
was not merely an invocation of patriotism and nationalism through the great
figures of the Napoleonic dynasty. It was also a reminder of the powerful role
of the 'people' in sustaining the Bonapartist myth—a 'people' symbolized by
the Médaillés de Sainte-Hélène, and invested with the qualities of simplicity
and martyrdom and at the same time fortitude and pride. The notion of 'nobility' was also essential, conveying both an elevation based on honour and
virtue and a sublimation of social differences through effort and achievement.
In the Bonapartist scheme of things, nobility was not merely a matter of birth:
it could be acquired, and indeed acquired by the most humble *grognard* fighting for his country—an illustration of the close ideological proximity between
Napoleonic thought and the 'principles of 1789'.
   Not all toasts went exactly according to plan. The generous flow of wine was
often responsible for some embarrassing slips. At the same gathering in
Marsillargues the deputy mayor, clearly the worse for wear after the prolonged
libations, provoked general hilarity when he proposed a toast 'to the memory
of Monsieur le Maire'. The police commissioner reminded him that, far from
being dead, the mayor was sitting across the table.[86] The festive atmosphere
also gave new lease of life to the veterans. At the banquet in the town of Sarcey
(Rhône) in 1866, following the traditional toasts, the assembled Médaillés
stood up on a table and vigorously sang a succession of Napoleonic songs; they
paused at each couplet to chant 'Long Live the Emperor! Long Live France!'.[87]
At Monteux (Vaucluse), in the same year, the imperial veterans chanted patriotic songs in honour of the Bonapartist dynasty; after the end of the banquet
'the Médaillés processed through town, with flags and drums beating wildly,
breaking the silence of the night with their repeated cries of Long Live the
Emperor!'.[88]
   Most remarkable was the vitality shown by the 40 Médaillés of the commune of Chateaudouble (Var) in 1861. The day before the festivities they
felled a pine tree and carried it to the main square of the town, where they
chopped it into small logs to be used for the bonfire. On the 15th of August
they took a full part in two processions, one in the morning and the other in
the early evening, after which they gathered again at a banquet given in their
honour by the municipality. After the dinner the imperial veterans led the
guests out again into the town in a torchlight procession, which rapidly
attracted a large following. At midnight this merry band could still be heard
singing the refrain of Béranger's Napoleonic ditty, 'Parlez-nous de lui grand-
mère, grand-mère parlez-nous de lui'.[89] The festivities carried on until the
early hours of the following morning, when the Médaillés 'somewhat inebri-
ated, if truth be told, concluded this great national festivity with a breakfast
paid for from their own funds'.[90]

   [86] Ibid.   [87] Report of Mayor of Sarcey, 23 August 1866. AD Rhône 1 M 165.
   [88] Report of Mayor of Monteux, 19 August 1866. AD Vaucluse, 1 M 880.
   [89] On Béranger see Jean Touchard's seminal study, *La gloire de Béranger* (Paris, 1959).
   [90] Report of Mayor of Chateaudouble, 18 August 1861. AD Var, 6 M 18 (5).

Conclusion: Bonapartism, Nationalism, Peace

The Médaillés de Sainte-Hélène had a significant impact on French public consciousness between 1858 and 1869. Their prominence during the festivities of the 15th of August, which we have illustrated in a variety of ways here, reflected their deep entrenchment in their local communities as well as the respect and admiration they enjoyed in large sections of society.

One of the most striking features to emerge from our analysis is the sheer resilience of the Médaillés. It is true that the institution of the decoration by the Second Empire came too late for many of them; already in 1857—the year the Médaille was established—many communes had only one or two army veterans among the survivors of the Revolutionary and Napoleonic eras.[91] But, even though the process of natural attrition led to a gradual decline in their numbers during the 1860s, there were still enough of them for the veterans' presence to be strongly felt at public events. Indeed, funerals of Médaillés continued to be held well into the 1870s.[92] Resilience, therefore, and also robustness. These men, generally aged somewhere between the late sixties and the mid-eighties, took a full and active part in the ceremonies of the 15th of August. In many provincial and rural communes the veterans typically participated in two processions, one in the morning and the other in the afternoon. In many instances they also, as we have just seen, continued the celebrations well into night. Their stamina not only put to shame guests with significantly lower age profiles but also inspired a local poet from Rouen in 1865:

> Malgré tant de souffrance
> Malgré tant de revers
> Lauriers de notre France
> Vous êtes toujours verts![93]

Equally important is the sense of self-respect which the Médaillés possessed, and which was at the very least reinforced by the institution of the decoration. Administrative reports from all over France stressed the 'pride' with which the imperial veterans wore their medals.[94] Above all, our evidence underscores the depths of the public feelings of esteem, respect, and admiration for the war veterans throughout the period between 1858 and 1869. The institution of the Médaille de Sainte-Hélène was welcomed and poems written in its honour; inhabitants of towns and villages turned out in large numbers to witness the award of the decorations to the meritorious citizens of their commune; the

---

[91] See for example the report of the Mayor of Villeneuve-les-Béziers on the celebration of the 15th of August 1857; the official procession contained 'one former soldier of the Empire'. AD Hérault, 1 M 505.

[92] See *Discours prononcé par M. Pellecat sur la tombe de M. Jacques-Louis Philippe, Médaillé de Sainte-Hélène* (Rouen, 1874). Bib.Nat.LN27-27729.

[93] *Aux décorés de la Médaille de Sainte-Hélène. A propos de l'inauguration de la statue de Napoléon Ier à Rouen, le 15 août 1865.* Bib. Nat. YE-37738. 'Despite so much suffering/Despite so many setbacks/Laurels of our France/You will always be green!'

[94] An example: Report of Mayor of Behonne (Meuse), 17 August 1858. AD Meuse 73 M 6.

presence of the imperial veterans in the processions of the 15th of August was greeted with acclaim; and individuals, groups, and institutions all over France gave generously to help those Médaillés—a relatively small number—who were experiencing material hardship.

And what is more, the veterans seemed to appeal to all sections of society: young and old; rich and poor; bourgeois, worker, and peasant; agnostic and believer. We would particularly stress the appeal of the veterans in rural France, as highlighted by numerous administrative reports throughout the period. In 1869 the sub-prefect of Vitry-le-François (Marne) pointed out that the awards to the imperial veterans had given rise to sentiments of enthusiasm 'everywhere in our countryside'.[95] Long before the advent of the Third Republic and the alleged transformation of 'peasants into Frenchmen', the Second Empire had done much to transcend the popular antithesis between peasants and soldiers.

Through the active participation of the veterans in its ceremonies, we have also been offered promising glimpses of the complexity and richness of the festivities of the 15th of August. Away from Paris and other French cities and large towns, France's national festivity under the Second Empire appears in a fundamentally different light from the stereotypes later conveyed by the organizers of 'la fête républicaine'. These gatherings were joyful and festive, without any doubt, and attracted the participation of wide sections of local communities. But what also appears clearly is the catalytic effect of the imperial veterans, whose presence often engendered various forms of spontaneous social behaviour: acclamation of the procession, gestures of solidarity with the veterans against absent municipal councillors, and so forth. An equally forceful connection which emerges is the robust sense of civic pride which manifested itself during these festivities. The imperial veterans were incorporated into the public sphere of the commune, and their presence gave the official processions from the *mairie* a lustre which was carefully nurtured by local municipal officials. Contrary to the received wisdom about the 'religiosity' of the 15th of August, the veterans' presence thus demonstrated the existence of a powerful secular dimension to the festivities—a secularism which was explicitly brought into the open, and contested, in the clashes between the Médaillés—and municipal authorities more generally—and the Church authorities.

What, in fine, of the alleged 'militarism' of the 15th of August? The presence of the Médaillés at the festivities, and their repeated invocations of the memory of the great Bonaparte's romps across Europe might invite the rather simplistic conclusion that the veterans were mere instruments of French 'chauvinism', the lowest and most debased expression of French national sentiment in the nineteenth century.[96] But things were much more complex. We

---

[95] Report of the Sub-prefect of Vitry-le-François, 18 August 1869. AD Marne 30 M 31 (reports to the prefect 1869–1870).

[96] For a study of the resonance of this theme in French nineteenth-century writings, see Gérard de Puymège, *Chauvin, le soldat-laboureur: contribution à l'étude des nationalismes* (Paris, 1993).

have to be cautious in our conclusions about these Napoleonic manifestations of nationalism and patriotism because, although we know that the imperial veterans often spoke about 'some of their military feats',[97] as one report puts it, we have very few records of what they actually said. There is no doubt that the martial theme of Napoleonic domination and conquest was present and powerfully reverberated through the songs, poems, and dramas of the period. But it was most often celebrated alongside the civic and political aspects of the Bonapartist epic. Speaking at the ceremony at which the imperial veterans of Albi received their medals in 1858, the local Bonapartist deputy—a General and a Médaillé de Sainte-Hélène, as well as the mayor of Albi and President of the Conseil Général of the Tarn—spoke of 'the immortal glory of our great Emperor, who, *all at once*, was a man of genius, a warrior, a law-giver, and a profound political strategist'.[98]

It is even possible to argue that the militarist theme was overshadowed by two other motifs. The first was the age-old notion, shared by Bonapartists and Jacobin republicans, of 'France as the bearer of civilized values'—a progressive civilization which had disseminated the values of 1789 to Europe under the Revolution and Napoleon Bonaparte and was continuing to spread the message of Christianity to France's colonies. The second theme was peace. 'The Empire brings peace' was one of Louis Napoleon's slogans from the earliest days of the regime, and it assumed a strong place in the imagery and rhetoric of the festivities of the 15th of August. Even while they were listening to the imperial veterans recounting their past military exploits, local populations were enthusiastically chanting 'Long Live Peace!'.[99] This was not the smallest paradox of the festivities of the 15th of August, but it also demonstrated the continuing ideological vigour—and capacity of reinvention—of the Bonapartist tradition during the 1850s and 1860s. By drawing out and bringing together French populations around common civic and political themes, and redefining the essence of the Bonapartist epic, the festivities of the 15th of August in this respect also prepared the ground for the republican *fête du quatorze juillet*, that other 'invented tradition' which still today defines the mythology of the modern Republic.

---

[97] Report of Mayor of Tourtour, 18 August 1859. AD Var 6 M 18 (5).

[98] *Discours prononcé à la distribution de la Médaille de Sainte-Hélène aux anciens soldats de la République et de l'Empire de la commune d'Albi, le 24 janvier 1858, par M. le Général Baron Gorsse* (Albi, 1858), 4; emphasis added. Bib.Nat.LL24-4.

[99] Ibid.

4

The Prefect, Political Functionary of the Jacobin State: Permanences and Continuities (1870–1914)

JEAN-PIERRE MACHELON

AS one of the best-known historians of nineteenth century France, Vincent Wright could not have failed to be interested in the prefects. His doctoral thesis on the Basses-Pyrénées from 1848 to 1870 took him straight to the heart of a department of rural France at the time of the Second Republic and the Second Empire, where he was understandably fascinated by the contrast between the stability of the consular administrative institutions and the political and constitutional instability of the nineteenth century. Over a period of 30 years, starting in 1968, he wrote a number of important works on the prefectoral institution, which had long been taken for granted as being the backbone of territorial administration and the custodian of the Jacobin spirit. With Bernard Le Clère he wrote the definitive work on the prefects of the Second Empire.[1] He himself wrote a number of articles on the same period, in particular on 'Les préfets démissionnaires en decembre 1851' (1968), 'Le corps préfectoral et le *coup d'Etat* de décembre 1851' (1968), 'Les préfets d'Emile Ollivier' (1968), and 'Les préfets impériaux et le 4 septembre 1870' (1970). In addition, other very substantial contributions to the literature on the subject scrutinized in detail the prefectoral body during the tormented early days of the interregnum between the Second Empire and the Republic, a period about which little was known, as is the case with all transitional periods.[2] Vincent Wright's curiosity did not stop there. In addition to a methodological article on the historical sources relating to the prefectoral body, written in collaboration with Guy Thuillier,[3] our eminent historian wrote a number of articles clarifying the image the prefects had of themselves in the nineteenth century[4] or defining

---

[1] *Les préfets du Second Empire* (1973).
[2] 'Les préfets du gouvernement de la Défense nationale (6 September 1870–February 1871), (1975); 'Francs-maçons, Administration et République: les préfets du gouvernement de la Défense nationale. 1870–1871' (1987–88); 'Le système territorial en période de crise: le corps préfectoral républicain pendant la guerre de 1870–1871' (1998).
[3] 'Les sources de l'histoire du corps préfectoral 1800–1880' (1975).
[4] 'Comment les préfets se voyaient' (1978).

the place occupied by the institution at the time of the Third Republic and then under the Vichy regime.[5] The extraordinarily reserved behaviour of the prefects at the time of the Dreyfus affair gave rise to a particularly illuminating analysis of the way in which the prefectoral body evolved at the threshold of the twentieth century.[6]

In these few pages *in memoriam*, written with the sole ambition of providing a brief continuation of Vincent Wright's thought, I will examine the period from 1870 to 1914 in order to attempt to answer a simple question. How did the prefectoral institution, which was created by an authoritarian, centralized regime, adapt itself to the progress of political democracy? Under the Republic, changes were made to the organisation of the State. What effect, if any, did these changes have on the role of the prefects?

If one looks at the literature on the subject, the answer would seem to be fairly obvious. We are told that the sociology of the body, which from 1870 on was the most provincial and the least bourgeois of the great state bodies, was gradually modified and handed over to 'the new social stratum'.[7] The task and the behaviour of its members also changed. The prefects of Caillaux were prudent administrators who bore little resemblance to those of the heroic era of Gambetta 40 years earlier. The function of the prefects was transformed over a lengthy transition period that corresponded more or less to what is generally known as the Belle Epoque. According to Vincent Wright's analysis, in 1890 the 'Napoleonic model of an ordered, hierarchical, powerful body was replaced by that of the prudent, flexible, conservative, sceptical prefect, whose influence was based on observation of administrative and political constraints and not on official written texts ... We can talk in terms of a sort of Republican synthesis of a consular tradition, which was authoritarian and technico-administrative, and a parliamentarian, democratic tradition in which notables played a large part'.[8] There is, moreover, plenty of evidence to show that this process of evolution took place. 'The prefect no longer gives orders, he asks', wrote the experienced politician Gabriel Hanotaux in 1901.[9] Do we need to look any further? Did a genuine transformation really take place? It did, according to the prefect Bellion, keen to demonstrate the modernity of the body he belonged to, in a publication which attracted attention.[10] It was his view that between 1898 and 1914, as a result of the consolidation of the

[5] 'Les préfets de Vichy' (1992).
[6] 'La réserve du corps préfectoral' (1994). See also 'La carrière mouvementée du préfet Monteil : Préfet des Loges' (1973).
[7] J. Siwek-Pouydesseau, *Le corps préfectoral sous la Troisième et la Quatrième République* (Paris, 1969), 30.
[8] 'La réserve du corps préfectoral', 306.
[9] Gabriel Hanotaux, 'Impressions de la France: la province et Paris', *Revue des Deux Mondes* (1901), 5–29; reprinted in *L'énergie française* (Paris, 1902), 115–52, under the title 'La ville moyenne : Laon'. See G. Thuillier, 'Comment Gabriel Hanotaux voyait la préfecture de Laon en 1901', *La Revue Administrative*, 304 (July–August 1998), 482–88; and also C. Charle, *Les hauts fonctionnaires en France au XIXe siècle* (coll. 'Archives') (Paris, 1980), 85–6.
[10] R. Bellion, 'L'histoire intérieure de la France de 1898 à 1914 et les préfets de la République radicale', in 'Sept études pour servir à l'histoire du corps préfectoral (1800–1940)', *Administration* (special issue, n.d. (1983)), 196–8.

Republic, the political prefect was slowly but surely transformed into an administrative prefect, building a career within a body and representing the State in a sphere beyond the central power in place.

The prefect of the Belle Epoque was unquestionably no longer '*l'empereur au petit pied*'[11] of the beginning of the nineteenth century, and his career had become longer. Nevertheless, this all seems a little exaggerated and there is a danger of lapsing into anachronism. Let us say at the outset that the prefect of the Third Republic was always fundamentally a political functionary. To recall the distinction made by Carl Schmitt, which dates back to the 1920s, the task of the prefect, in 1914 as in 1870, came closer to being a form of mandate or delegation (*Stellvertretung*) relating to contingent interests, notably political interests, rather than a form of representation (*Repraesentation*) of an immutable, permanent State which he embodied locally, and in so doing transcended political contingencies.[12] In considering the evolution of the office of prefect, which was unquestionably becoming more professional, we must not lose sight of the essential (that is to say, the specifically political) continuity of the institution. Vincent Wright was quite rightly struck by this characteristic when he was investigating the image that the prefectoral body had of itself.[13]

If we examine the remit and the activity of the prefect, we are forced to acknowledge that, in spite of the republican legend, the degree of change that took place during the first part of the Third Republic was extremely limited. Not only did the prefect continue to be the representative of political authority, as under the Second Empire and earlier regimes, but he also continued to organize elections. It was his responsibility to keep the government informed and to see to the maintenance of order and public safety. He was in the front line in the event of any natural or accidental disaster. As in the past, he was expected to devote much of his time to the medical boards assessing fitness for military service, to the administration and supervision of the *departement*—all this, moreover, despite the fact that he considered himself to be the representative of his department in the state. The only novelty was an acknowledgement that the prefect had to endeavour to maintain a degree of neutrality in situations of social conflict.

On a day-to-day level, on the ground, the role of the prefect certainly does not appear to have been very different from what it was under the Second Empire. Criticized as it was (sometimes violently) particularly by radical republican factions,[14] the institution lived on. And, consistently close as it was to those governing the country, it remained Jacobin. This was in no way con-

---

[11] Literally, 'the small-footed emperor'.

[12] See O. Beaud, '"*Repraesentation*" et "*Stellvertretung*": sur une distinction de Carl Schmitt', *Droits*, 6 (1987), 11–20; S. Manson, 'De l'an VIII à l'an 2000: le préfet est-il encore un "fonctionnaire politique"?', *Revue du droit public et de la science politique* (2000–1), 201–19.

[13] 'Comment les préfets se voyaient', 145.

[14] Although doomed to failure, there were numerous proposals to abolish the prefects and the sub-prefects, particularly at the end of the century. See, for example, P. Guiral, 'Comment les Français voyaient leurs préfets' in *varii auctores, Les préfets en France (1800–1940)*, 162.

tradictory, for the Republic was far from being committed to decentralization. In this chapter, I shall stress the political aspect of the permanence of this institution and its major effects, looking successively at the body itself, the office of prefect, and his activities between 1871 and 1914.

The Prefectoral Corps

Like his predecessors, the prefect of the Third Republic did not enjoy any autonomy in relation to his political masters. He was necessarily in league with the government. Even if 'good elections' were no longer his sole concern, as had been the case in the time of Balzac and Stendhal, he was, in accordance with the tradition of the year VIII, the political functionary *par excellence*. There were but few changes, and no significant statutory changes at all, with regard to the preceding periods. The strictly relative professionalization of the prefectoral body continued to leave in place the customary relations of dependence of the representatives of the State on the governing powers.

In 1914, as had been the case in 1870, the prefect remained by statute at the mercy of the political powers and had no guarantee of tenure. There had been no change in this respect since the law of 28 Pluviôse of the year VIII (17 February 1800). As the person having sole charge of the administration, the prefect, according to consular and imperial reasoning, was the arm, the ears, and the eyes of central power. The government retained the greatest degree of latitude possible with regard to the nomination of prefects. Nominations were entirely discretionary and were made according to a system of recommendation and political patronage—from which vote-catching and even nepotism were clearly not excluded. Until 1928,[15] there was no legislation specifying the qualifications required to become a prefect, a sub-prefect, a general secretary of a prefecture, or a prefect's head clerk. There were no requirements in terms of either qualifications or seniority. All that was required was that the person should have reached majority (age 21). This is stated explicitly in the year-books of the end of the century:

No apprenticeship, no training, no competitive qualifying examination. Neither is any university education considered to be a requirement for entry into this career, since those who are admitted into this type of office must, above all else, possess certain qualities of mind and character which can neither be acquired through formal education nor attested by diplomas or examinations. Provided that these qualities of mind and character are present, there is nothing to prevent the functionary being an educated person, a good administrator, well-accustomed to the handling of public affairs, nor that he demonstrate in the accomplishment of his duties that good administration is one of the results of good political policy.[16]

---

[15] At this point, it was required that sub-prefects should have a university degree and three years' experience of working in a prefecture or administrative office. A little later, a decree of 31 July 1935 put in place a competitive qualifying examination for admission to the post of chef de cabinet to a prefect.

[16] Text cited by Siwek-Pouydesseau, *Le corps préfectoral*, 30.

This absence of prerequisites, whether in terms of qualifications or of education, for access to the position of prefect was unique in the higher echelons of the French administration. During the first part of the Third Republic, there was no comparable rank to which a person could expect to be appointed at the age of 40.[17] This no doubt added to the attraction of the position. There was, however, another side to the coin. There were no real guarantees of security attaching to the position. At best, pensions and non-activity payments were available according to certain conditions from the beginning of the Second Empire, as was a system of paid temporary leave of absence dating from legislation passed on 25 February 1901.[18] Before 1914, the promotion of prefects was not treated in the same way as that of members of a real body, these being governed by statute and organized according to an appropriate career structure. In the terms of the decree of 25 March 1852, prefectures were divided into three classes, to which was added an unclassed category consisting of the most important posts. Salaries varied according to this geographical hierarchy. This encouraged a certain degree of mobility on the part of the prefects, which prevented them from acquiring too much personal authority in a particular post and in so doing diminishing the role of central government and the political authorities. It was taken for granted that a prefect had no more right to a higher class of post than had a sub-prefect to become a prefect.[19] It was only at the very end of the period that a first step (and a very timid one at that) was taken in the direction of what would later become the prefectoral career structure. The decree of 19 October 1911 put in place a promotion scale for sub-prefects, general secretaries of prefectures, and second-class and third-class prefecture officials. But the discretionary power of the political authority remained entirely in place so far as the prefects themselves were concerned. They could be divested of their posts at any moment. Chosen as they were to be the executors of government policy within a department, they were regarded as being 'essentially responsible', in the famous expression of Chapsal,[20] and as a result could be relieved *ad nutum* of their functions.

---

[17] See Charle, *Les hauts fonctionnaires*, 105–6.

[18] The law stated, 'Prefects and sub-prefects may receive a salary during temporary leave of absence for a period not exceeding six years or half the period of their services rendered to the State; this payment shall not exceed 6,000 francs per annum nor half the average salary of the preceding year.'

[19] In 1870, the third class consisted of 43 departments, the second of 31, and the first of 14. Certain 'personal' classes existed in addition to these in order to allow the minister to grant certain prefects promotion in their posts. The division of prefectures into geographical classes was abolished by Clemenceau in favour of a system of personal classes (decree of 5 November 1907) and re-established by Caillaux on the grounds that this made it possible to avoid unjustified inequalities and run-overs in budget (decree of 19 October 1911). Subsequent measures abolished the unclassed category and modified the classification of the prefectures and sub-prefectures.

[20] Presenting the legislation of the 28 Pluviôse of the year VIII, Chapsal explained to the legislative body that 'the certainty of complete execution of the legislation and acts of the government . . . exists whenever the execution is placed in the hands of an essentially responsible man' (*Archives parlementaires*, second series (1800–1860)), I, 230.

The Diversity of Prefects

As well as having no autonomy in relation to central power, the prefectoral institution in the period concerned had no unity—which could only add to its docility. It consisted of extremely diverse personalities, whose appointment, which had little to do with the rituals of meritocracy or the conventions of local notables, always essentially depended upon political circumstances. The patronage of influential ministers or parliamentarians was standard practice and conformed to no pre-established system or rule. Moreover, bound up as political favour was with fluctuating networks of influence and difficult work on the terrain, which was appreciated or not according to political criteria, it often did not last long.

The most prominent prefects themselves showed all the signs of diversity, as can be seen very clearly from the *Dictionnaire biographique des préfets*.[21] One writer said rightly that 'the victorious Third Republic had no stereotypical prefects'.[22] The well-known figures came from every sort of background and constituted a portrait gallery of contrasting colours. The lawyer Louis Andrieux was a picturesque personality—and the natural father of the poet Aragon. He was a republican deputy and was State prosecutor in Lyon from 1870 to 1871. He owed his appointment to the position of prefect of police in 1879 to his friendship with Gambetta. He was subsequently ambassador to Spain while continuing to sit in parliament up to 1885 and from 1910 until 1924; at the age of 87, he defended a thesis entitling him to a doctorate of literature.[23] It was the protection of Jules Ferry and powerful support at the heart of the republican party (Jules Simon, Jean Casimir-Perier) that ensured the brothers Cambon entry into the higher echelons of the administration: without going through the stage of sub-prefect, Paul was appointed prefect of the Aube at the age of 29 (1872) and Jules prefect of Constantine at the age of 33 (1878). They may not have been geniuses in the academic sense, but they both lost no time in asserting themselves by means of their exceptional authority.[24] Eugène Poubelle, appointed to the prefecture of the Seine by Waldeck Rousseau in 1883 after having held several territorial posts from 1871on, was a professor of law. He ended his career as ambassador to the Holy See. 'Jews of State' such as Ernest Hendlé or Abraham Schrameck (the future minister of the interior of the Cartel des gauches) had yet another profile. Hendlé, after serving as private

---

[21] Ed. R. Bargeton (Paris, 1994).

[22] C.-L. Foulon, 'Les préfets de la république modérée (1877–1898)', in 'Sept études pour servir à l'histoire du corps préfectoral', *Administration*, 146.

[23] His *Souvenirs d'un préfet de police* (Paris, 1885) makes compelling reading.

[24] Jules Cambon, who in 1872 had failed the competitive qualifying examination for the Council of State, shared the opinion that prevailed in political circles at the beginning of the Third Republic on the mode of recruitment of high functionaries: 'Relying on examinations as the sole means of judging men is but a semblance of justice; outside pure knowledge, there is mastery of social relations, penetration of mind—in a word, intelligence, and that cannot be learned in any school'. *Le diplomate* (Paris, 1926), 63. On the exceptional careers of the Cambon brothers, see L. Villate, *La République des diplomates. Paul et Jules Cambon (1843–1935)* (Paris, 2002). See also, by the same author, 'Jules Cambon (1845–1935). An administrative career', DEA dissertation (Paris, 1990).

secretary to Jules Favre at the Ministry of Foreign Affairs (1870), was prefect of the Nord (1871), then of Loir-et-Cher (1873), a post from which he subsequently resigned in order to avoid serving the *Ordre moral*. He ended his career as prefect of the Seine-Inférieure from 1882 until his death in 1900. He remained the paragon of the republican prefect, a man of absolute integrity but nonetheless close to financial circles; a man of strong convictions, yet able if necessary to act as mediator between the Trappist monks, the Fathers of the Assumption, and the anticlerical republican leader Méline.[25] Quite different from these, but no less skilful, was Louis Lépine, the extremely media-conscious prefect of police during the Belle Epoque (1893–7 and 1899–1913), who thought nothing of taking personal command of the uniformed brigades of the municipal police, was not uninterested in 'plain clothes activities', and gave priority to improving the image of the police in the eyes of the Parisians.[26]

In any panorama illustrating the diversity of the profession, a place must be set aside for the sons of ministers—Martin-Feuillée and in particular Edgar Combes—as well as their brothers and nephews.[27] Justin de Selves, a 'classic prefect'[28] who was to become prefect of the Seine and Minister of the Interior and subsequently president of the Senate, was appointed prefect of Tarn-et-Garonne in 1880, at the age of 31, by his uncle Freycinet, at that time Prime Minister. The influence of eminent political leaders should be underlined: Léon Bourgeois (himself a former prefect) Waldeck-Rousseau, Sarrien, Leygues, and Constans, as well as Clemenceau, Briand, and Caillaux.[29] They sometimes counteracted one another. Certain heavyweight political personalities would, on taking up their positions, make haste to dismiss those prefects who had been favoured by their predecessors. Ministerial succession often introduced an even greater degree of variety into an already diverse group.

The fact that there was no such thing as a typical prefect should not lead us to conclude that the prefects did not have any common sociological characteristics. Some excellent studies have underlined a few dominant features that bring the prefectoral world even closer to the political world.[30] Amongst these was the geographic origin of the prefects, since they generally came from the

[25] Cf. P. Birnbaum, 'De génération en génération, une famille de Juifs d'Etat, les Hendlé', in P. Birnbaum (ed.), *Histoire politique des Juifs en France* (Paris, 1990); and *Les fous de la République. Histoire politique des Juifs d'Etat de Gambetta à Vichy* (coll. 'Points. Histoire') (Paris, 1994), 29–43, 231–6, and *passim*; C.-L. Foulon, 'Les préfets de la république modérée (1877–1898)', 145–6; Guiral, 'Comment les Français', 161.

[26] Cf. J.-M. Berlière, *Le préfet Lépine. Vers la naissance de la police moderne* (Paris, 1993); J. Porot, *Louis Lépine, préfet de police témoin de son temps (1846–1933)* (Paris, 1994); Foulon, 'Les préfets de la république modérée', 148; Bellion, 'L'histoire intérieure de la France', 200–2.

[27] Such as Thomson or Allain-Targé. See Pierre-Henry, *Histoire des préfets* (Paris, 1950), 225, 239.

[28] Foulon, 'Les préfets de la république modérée', 148. In addition, Bellion, 'L'histoire intérieure de la France', 202–4; Pierre-Henry, *Histoire des préfets*, 250–1.

[29] See C. Charle, *Les élites de la République (1880–1900)* (Paris, 1987), 206.

[30] Principally, Siwek-Pouydesseau, *Le corps préfectoral*, 21–35, and 'Sociologie du corps préfectoral', in *Les préfets en France (1800–1940)*, 168–72; Charle, *Les hauts fonctionnaires*, 103–7; *Les Elites de la République*, 204–10; 'Le recrutement des hauts fonctionnaires en 1901', *Annales E.S.C.* (March–April 1980), 380–405.

provinces and often from the south of France. In this they differed from the rest of high-level public service—in 1901, 8.7 per cent of prefects came from Paris and the surrounding suburbs, compared with 52.2 per cent of magistrates in the national audit office and 33.8 per cent of the members of the State Council; similarly, their social background was increasingly ordinary or, to a much lesser extent, *petit bourgeois*. Political clashes and upheavals had their impact on the social composition of certain groups and a certain number of analogies emerge between the prefects and the governing classes. The milieu was more or less the same: in 1901, 40 per cent of prefects were related, closely or distantly, to parliamentarians or local political figures; 27 prefects were themselves engaged in political activity. Other characteristics remained particular to the prefects, among them a complicated relationship with money caused partly by the drop in salaries (in 1810, a prefect in the highest class was paid 40,000 francs and in 1910 30,000 francs) partly by the uncertainty of finding employment afterwards—this being necessary on account of the brevity of the period of service: during the period under consideration, prefects were appointed at an average age of 41 and ended their term of service at the age of 51; and partly by increasing professionalization, which in practice was increasingly confined to the sub-prefects—91 per cent over the whole period. But, for all that, the prefects before 1914 did not constitute a body, even sociologically. They were in every respect too scattered to have any weight as a lobby. It is revealing that the Mutual Insurance and Assistance Association of the prefectoral administration, which was to broaden the scope of its activities to include institutional representation at ministerial and governmental level, was not founded until 14 December 1907.

The Prefect as Political Agent

Not only was the prefect, as an organ of the administration, dependent in the closest manner possible on his political masters, but his office was overtly considered to be political. Although often given a back seat, this aspect of the prefectoral institution was strongly underlined at the time by Hauriou and particularly by Jèze. In a note under the *Delpech* case, issued by the Council of State on 20 January 1911, the celebrated jurist had no hesitation about writing 'that the prefect in France is essentially an electoral agent for the government, that his future depends on how skilfully and successfully he is able to manipulate the electorate; and thus that, in order to be successful in his career, a prefect must be extremely flexible, have few scruples, and exercise a firm hand . . . in dealing with the government's adversaries'. He adds: 'The prefects of the Third Republic are the worthy successors of the First and Second

[31] G. Jèze, 'Du rôle des préfets en France', *Revue du droit public et de la science politique* (1911), 273. Note that G. Jèze, who considered the prefects to be 'the natural enemies of public liberty', cites at considerable length, in support of his opinion, Maurice Hauriou, who himself was in no way hostile to the prefectoral institution (277–9).

Empires. They continue that tradition.'[31] Nowadays such things are expressed rather less vehemently. Nonetheless, although far from engaging in polemic, some administrative historians stress the political role of the nineteenth century prefect, without making any exception for the first part of the Third Republic. Thus, Guy Thuillier and Jean Tulard assert that 'the job of a prefect . . . is essentially political, much more so than it is administrative, and [that] as political figures the prefect and the sub-prefect have to understand a great many things which are elusive, ephemeral, and imponderable'. They thus conclude that the history of the prefectoral body is 'first and foremost political history'.[32]

Official documents, particularly ministerial circulars, provide ample corroboration of this proposition. They are strikingly explicit, despite regular appeals for neutrality before every electoral consultation, from 1881 on.[33] With the advent of the 'Republic of republicans', the prefects were presented in high places as being political functionaries *par excellence*. In setting out their duties in a lengthy circular of 3 June 1879, the Minister of the Interior, Lepère, was not afraid to insist on this point, 'last but not least':

You must not forget, Monsieur le Préfet, that the essentially political nature of your office demands that you have a precise perception of the public conduct of the functionaries of every order that the government has placed in your department, and I reserve the right, as and when necessary, to communicate to my colleagues any observations I may wish to make on the information I see fit to require of you in this respect.[34]

When the regime had been fully established, the political nature of the office of prefect was in no way attenuated. If anything it was reinforced, as was the role of the prefect in his department. There was nothing fortuitous in this similitude. The importance of activity on the ground was regularly stressed, notably by Sarrien in 1888.[35] The prefect, charged with this responsibility for activity on the ground, saw his pre-eminence over the departmental functionaries sanctioned; it had not been particularly recognized earlier in the nineteenth century. Even at the time of Thiers and Mac Mahon, departmental councillors could communicate directly with heads of government departments without going through the prefect, whose position tended, in terms of protocol, to be under constant attack from the military authorities.[36] Things changed fairly quickly, even before the decree of 16 June 1907, 'concerning public ceremonies, precedence, civil and military honours' had put the pre-

---

[32] Guy Thuillier and Jean Tulard, 'Pour une histoire du corps préfectoral français', in *Les préfets en France (1800–1940)*, 174 and 175.

[33] In his circular to the prefects dated 31 July 1881, Constans, Minister of the Interior, went so far as to speak of 'absolute neutrality' and 'positively scrupulous distance'. *Bulletin officiel du ministère de l'intérieur (BMI)* (1881), 341–2.

[34] *BMI* (1879), 141.   [35] Circular of 15 February 1888, *BMI* (1888), 24.

[36] Cf. P. Aubert, 'Un siècle et demi d'histoire préfectorale', in 'Sept études pour servir à l'histoire du corps préfectoral (1800–1940)', 306.

[37] *BMI* (1907), 366. The report of the President of the Republic was entirely positive: 'One of the principal reforms is directed at the rank of prefect, who must take his place at the head of all the local

fects in the first rank.[37] At the same time, Clemenceau, who was greatly concerned about symbols, granted them the right to wear white feathers.[38] As early as 1886, Freycinet asked his ministers to issue a reminder that the prefect was, in his department, the direct representative of the State and that, this being the case, all functionaries must give him their loyal support. The Minister of Justice Demole wrote to the general prosecutors that 'the departmental prefects are, by the nature of their duties, the depositories of governmental thought',[39] while the Minister of Commerce and Industry, Eduard Lockroy, spoke of an 'active, deferential collaboration'.[40] The essential point had been made.

A variety of consequences ensued, beginning with a duty to ensure political surveillance. Even outside election periods, the prefects were frequently reminded of the need for vigilance. In this the republicans were doing nothing new. In 1874, on the subject of a projected visit to England for the 18th birthday of the Imperial Prince, son of Napoléon III, the prefects were invited to prevent any propaganda encouraging public participation from being displayed 'in public places' and to make sure that no functionary 'of any order or rank' joined the expedition.[41] Generally speaking, the prefect was required to pass on to the government all factual information, regardless of its importance, concerning political life and particularly to report on the state of affairs regarding the government in his department. This task, which the prefect was obliged to fulfil at the very least in his monthly reports, was insisted upon between 1889 and 1912, and was taken to extremes at the time of the Dreyfus affair and the 'defence of the Republic'. In the era of the Republic at war, the State was most concerned about the nationalists, the leagues, and their plots, real or imaginary. Equally, the prefect had to be consulted. In a circular issued on 11 January 1901, Waldeck-Rousseau gave this insistence on good administration a resolutely political twist: 'With a view to strengthening your authority and your political power of action, I have consistently expressed to my colleagues my desire that you should at all times be consulted where affairs likely to have certain political repercussions are concerned.'[42]

In parallel to this, the prefects were also entrusted with a mission to ensure the political management of their departments. This concerned first and foremost the public functionaries. Waldeck-Rousseau wrote in the most official manner possible: 'I ask you to take all necessary steps to ensure that all parties

authorities. This measure is justified first of all by the fact that the prefect is invested with a general mission and an extensive remit, thus setting him apart from and above the technical authorities, and making him the representative of all the ministers and heads of public departments. It is, moreover, justified in terms of the concern to ensure that the representative of the civil power should have preeminence over all the other authorities, a principle confirmed by Parliament every time it has been debated' (p. 370).

[38] Decree of 24 July 1907 concerning the formal dress of prefects, replacing the decrees of 1 March 1852 and 10 April 1873.
[39] Circular to the procureurs-généraux dated 31 January 1886, *BMI* (1886), 28.
[40] Circular of 30 January 1886, *BMI* (1886), 27.
[41] Circular issued by Broglie dated 19 February 1874, *BMI* (1874), 37.
[42] See particularly P. Sorlin, *Waldeck-Rousseau* (Paris, 1966), 415 ff.

concerned in the Administration are absolutely united so far as political management is concerned.'[43] This recommendation was of course directed primarily at their own duties, but not exclusively so.[44] From June 1902 on, Combes not only continued in the same direction as his predecessor but also consolidated his measures into a system. The duty of the prefect to carry out the 'political management' of the functionaries was more than ever a priority on the agenda. A celebrated circular of 20 June 1902 invited the 'representative(s) of central power and the delegate(s) of all the ministers' to 'exert active political control over all public services'; 'despite the fact that the heads of the various departments enjoy a certain amount of autonomy so far as the negotiation of administrative affairs is concerned and in this respect report to their hierarchical seniors, they should not forget that they are under a strict obligation to comply with your political management'.[45] How then could it be denied that the prefects, thus invested with a propagandist mission, were first and foremost in the service of the government?

Pushing the consequences of the politicization of public office to extremes, Emile Combes made loyalty to the Republic, as he understood it, the principal criterion for assessing the quality of the work of functionaries and the suitability of candidates for public office. This could lead prefects, charged as they were with the responsibility of keeping the government informed, to form judgements concerning the professional, and where necessary private, behaviour of government agents. They were, moreover, invited to 'reserve these favours which [it was in their power to dispense] solely for those amongst the administrative body who [had] proved unequivocally their loyalty to the Republican institutions'.[46] On two occasions, on 26 November 1902 and 18 November 1904, this government formula was officially reiterated and made known to the other ministers. 'The prefects are reminded that, as the delegates of central power, one of the essential duties attaching to their posts is to exercise, as their own responsibility, political control over all the public services and faithfully to keep the government informed so far as functionaries of every order and candidates for public office are concerned.'[47] Despite the reaction after Combes fell from power as a result of the *Fiches* scandal, the prefects were not discharged of all responsibility for political observation. A circular issued by the Minister for War, Messimy, on 31 January 1912, giving instructions as to the type of information they were expected to provide, specifically highlighted the need for intelligence on 'the political attitude of officers garrisoned in the department'.[48]

---

[43] Circular of 6 November 1900, included in Waldeck-Rousseau, *Politique française et étrangère* (Paris,1903), 76.

[44] For details of the attacks on the neutrality of the administration and the public services, see J.-P. Machelon, *La République contre les libertés ?* (Paris, 1976), 329–51.

[45] *L'Année Politique 1902* (Paris, 1903), 170.   [46] Ibid.

[47] Circular of 18 November 1904, *BMI* (1904), 445.

[48] See Bellion, 'L'histoire intérieure de la France', 195.

The Vicissitudes of Prefectoral Careers

So the prefect of the Third Republic was inevitably mixed up in political life and was thereby exposed to all its hazards. He thus acquired the 'adaptability' and the 'political flexibility' rightly stressed by Vincent Wright,[49] but he was forced to endure tremendous upheavals which were generally incompatible with any real career. Throughout the entire period, the administrative future of these political functionaries was extremely precarious. We must, however, make a distinction here between the period from 1870 to 1879 and that from 1879 to 1914.

Politics was preponderant in 1870–1. The memory of the Second Empire left little doubt about this; even less did the attitude of Gambetta's prefects, more than half of whom stood as candidates in the elections of 8 February 1871.[50] The movement of personnel that marked the beginning of the interregnum between the Empire and the Republic soon revealed the existence of a particularly close relationship between the prefects and the world of politics.[51] The prefects of la Défense nationale, who were appointed after 4 September, were a new type of man, two-thirds of them being either lawyers or teachers and all of them ardent republicans. Although, with the exception of four of them, they had practically no administrative experience, they were expected simultaneously to defend the territory, to ensure that the administration functioned properly, and to consolidate the new Republic. Their political and partisan role was no less important. The appointment of republican personnel within the department and the preparation for elections were obvious priorities. Many of these prefects subsequently played important political roles. Fifty-eight were parliamentarians, eight were ministers, two (Ferry and Freycinet) were prime ministers, and one of them (Sadi Carnot) even became President of the Republic. Only 27 of their number remained in the prefectoral administration after the elections of 18 February 1871.

In fact, immediately on coming to power, Thiers reshuffled the prefectoral body and had no hesitation in recalling to office several prefects of the Empire who had been relieved of their office by Gambetta. Between 23 February and 26 March 1871, he appointed 47 prefects. But his fall from power on 24 May 1873 and the election of Mac Mahon to the presidency of the Republic brought about a sudden change in political direction. The hour of the *Ordre*

---

[49] 'Comment les préfets se voyaient', 148.

[50] See Siwek-Pouydesseau, *Le corps préfectoral*, 73. Sixteen prefects and sub-prefects were elected. However, only eleven of these, who had resigned their office ten days before the vote, had their election confirmed. On the legal aspects of the problem, which were dealt with by the National Assembly amidst huge confusion, see J. Gouault, *Comment la France est devenue républicaine. Les élections générales et partielles à l'Assemblée nationale (1870–1875)*, (Paris, 1954), 46–50.

[51] See, as well as Vincent Wright's work, Pierre-Henry, *Histoire des préfets*, 213–18; Siwek-Pouydesseau, *Le corps préfectoral*, 77; C. Lobut, 'Le corps préfectoral entre le Second Empire et la République opportuniste (1870–1877)', in 'Sept études pour servir à l'histoire du corps préfectoral (1800–1940)', 119–37; P. Laharie, 'Le personnel de l'administration préfectorale : chiffres et graphiques. 1800–1914', *Histoire et archives*, 5 (1999), 53–101 *passim*.

moral had struck. Eleven prefects, including Calmont, prefect of the Seine, resigned. They were followed by 20 sub-prefects. Others were appointed to replace them and joined the new entrants to the prefectoral body, all of whom were resolutely conservative: this within the framework of a new prefectoral movement which, between May and September, affected almost two-thirds of posts. Sixteen prefects were relieved of office. Beulé, the Minister of the Interior, addressed the prefects in a highly political manner: 'Do not hesitate to speak out loud and clear to communicate your sympathies and our encouragements . . . Starting now, you must engage in constant communication with the people you administer . . . The clarity of your attitude will raise spirits, discourage anarchic tendencies, and ensure respect for the National Assembly and the law.'[52]

In 1877, the crisis of the Sixteenth of May caused the prefects to undergo another violent push to the right, the positively seismic scope of which caused everyone to forget the appointments in the other direction which had been made in the spring of 1876 in the wake of the republican electoral victory.[53] 'Changing the prefects has veritably become at once the general rule and the main form of amusement in the life of the nation', wrote *Le Constitutionnel*.[54] Scarcely had they been called to power by Mac Mahon than the Duc de Broglie and his Minister of the Interior, Fourtou, plunged, according to an expression of the time, into an 'administrative orgy'.[55] They got rid of the staff who had gradually been set in place by the conservative republicans in order to appoint functionaries who were 'strong men', either royalists or Bonapartists, but never republicans. The prefectoral body was naturally first in the line of fire. Right from the start, on 19 May, 62 prefects were replaced as a result of dismissal, granting of leave of absence, or resignation. The sub-prefects and general secretaries were not spared either, nor even were the prefecture staff. And the process was repeated several times. At the end of the day, it turned out that more than two-thirds of the functionaries of the prefectoral administration had been appointed by the *Ordre moral*, often after having served under the Second Empire. In the midst of the electoral confrontation that was raging at the time, the prefects could scarcely be unaware of their duty, which they were reminded of by the minister in extremely explicit terms in a lengthy circular published on 3 July. Given the 'great political interests' for which they had responsibility, it was incumbent upon them as a priority to 'enlighten public opinion', to 'protect it against the innumerable errors propagated by hostile parties', to 'unmask false devotion to the regime', and to 'unite all the conservatives' in support of the official candidates.[56]

[52] Circular of 23 September 1873, *BMI* , 478.
[53] This movement, which was directed by Dufaure and carried out after the general elections of 20 February 1876, in three waves on 21 March, 13 April, and 24 May, brought about a complete upheaval so far as appointments were concerned. However, only 13 prefects of the Moral Order left the body. Jules Simon carried out other, moderate changes on 6 January and 22 February 1877.
[54] Cited by Lobut, 'Le corps préfectoral', 135.
[55] M. Reclus, *Le Seize Mai* (Paris, 1931), 77, citing the expression used by John Lemoinne in the *Journal des Débats*.
[56] *Journal officiel* (1877), 5006 and 5007.

There is absolutely no doubt that the message was understood. According to Alexandre Pilenco, an attentive reader of parliamentary debates concerning the confirmation of the October 1877 elections, favours, gifts of money, railway lines, even garrisons 'hailed down', with the cooperation of the prefects, to promote the interests of the official government candidates.[57] By exerting pressure in various directions, the prefects applied themselves to obtaining the required number of withdrawals. The bargaining was sometimes difficult. For example, a lawyer from Agen demanded that he be appointed Councillor to the Court of Appeal of Alger.[58] The prefects themselves organized electoral tours in order to support the conservative candidates. They readily took the platform, even if this involved transforming extraordinary general sessions of local councils into electoral meetings.[59] A close watch was kept on licensed premises in order to track down anti-government propaganda. The administration frequently issued closure orders, which were promptly executed. It even happened, in the Haute-Loire for example, that licences permitting the opening of such premises, which had previously been issued by the departmental authorities, were declared null and void.[60] Needless to say, the posting and distribution of republican posters and, more generally, the circulation of republican newspapers came up against the greatest of difficulties. Peddlers' licences were frequently withdrawn.[61] Arbitrary intervention was given such a free rein that the prefect of Vaucluse was able to pride himself on having gained control of the *Journal du Midi* 'without paying a penny'. He did so by 'setting the prosecutor' on its manager and its editor, who, once they were locked up in prison, signed a complete capitulation.[62] At the same time the official press benefited from special conditions.

Despite all these efforts, the republicans won the elections of October 1877. The failure of the movement of the Sixteenth of May provoked a counter-purge within the prefectoral institution. On 19 December 1877, all the prefects but four, among them those of Alger and Oran, were replaced. On 26 December, it was the turn of the general secretaries, and on 30 December the sub-prefects. On 15 January 1878, almost all the prefecture staff were purged. One author, perfectly justifiably, said that 'no other year, not even 1815 or 1944 equalled 1877 for the rate, the number, and the scope of movement within the prefectoral body'.[63] The era of purges came to an end in 1879 with the advent of the 'Republic of republicans' following the resignation of Mac Mahon on 30 January. Two big episodes of change in May and December 1878 had brought the prefectoral body into line with the new political order. This personnel renewal had been facilitated by the relatively large number of resignations of prefects—26—and sub-prefects—65—following the convention observed at the time among the ruling classes.

[57] Alexandre Pilenco, *Les mœurs du suffrage universel en France (1848–1928)* (Paris, 1930), 96.
[58] Pilenco, *Les mœurs du suffrage universel*, 103–4.
[59] Pilenco, *Les mœurs du suffrage universel*, 113–16.
[60] Pilenco, *Les mœurs du suffrage universel*, 121–3.
[61] Pilenco, *Les mœurs du suffrage universel*, 135–9.
[62] Pilenco, *Les mœurs du suffrage universel*, 134.   [63] Pierre-Henry, *Histoire des préfets*, 219.

Although it did not result in such upheavals, in the form of either purges or counter-purges, the way in which political life evolved between 1879 and 1914 nonetheless continued to have repercussions on the appointment and career structure of the prefects. They were required to be entirely in agreement, sometimes in very precise terms, with the government.[64] Reflecting on the administrative upheavals of the end of the century, the non-conformist Henri Chardon said ironically: 'The principal task of the prefect is to represent one after another the different factions of the Republican Party as they come to power.'[65] The mission was sometimes impossible. On coming to power, Léon Bourgeois, radical Prime Minister and Minister of the Interior and furthermore a former prefect of police, dismissed 21 prefects and 68 sub-prefects. In a quite different spirit, Louis Barthou, moderate, his successor at the Ministry of the Interior in Méline's cabinet, did likewise a few months later, on 23 May 1896, not without being rebuked by Jaurès, who regretted the departure of the prefect of the Tarn.[66] Other changes followed shortly after. The waltz of the prefects continued after the move to the Left of 1898. Brisson, who installed himself in the Ministry of the Interior at the Place Beauvau just after the elections, on 28 June 1898, right in the middle of the Dreyfus affair, carried out two major prefectoral reshuffles. Over a third of departments changed prefect and ten 'Mélinistes', considered to be too moderate, left the body. Combes, in turn, on 9 September 1902 and 5 September 1904, decided on a number of changes of posting and dismissed eight prefects. Caillaux followed his example in October 1911.

These changes, which were obviously motivated by political considerations, were denounced as arbitrary. In particular, the steps taken by Brisson caused a great stir. One of his 'victims', Rozier-Joly, protested and addressed the minister in vehement terms: 'The truth of the matter, as can be seen quite clearly today, is that I carried out faultlessly the instructions I received and that the steps taken against me were clearly and exclusively of a political nature. According to what I was told at the Ministry—which, in its brutal simplicity, makes other argument superfluous—I was dismissed because "I was appointed by the others". It will be clear to everyone that such a crime calls for an exemplary punishment.'[67] Should people have been outraged? The measures criticized were part and parcel of what we may call, as does Siwek-Pouydesseau, the 'local politico-administrative system'.[68] By virtue of his role in electoral matters, the prefect maintained a close relationship with the deputies and the

---

[64] This point is stressed by Vincent Wright in particular, in his article on 'La réserve du corps préfectoral', 298–300.

[65] Henri Chardon, Le pouvoir administratif (Paris, 1911), 39. Chardon, who was very hostile towards the prefects, hastened to add that 'this mission, which was in itself singularly difficult, did not constitute representation of the Republic'.

[66] A long discussion ensued on 8 June 1896, in the Chamber of Deputies (Journal officiel. Débats parlementaires. Chambre des députés, 1886, 877–86).

[67] Cited by Siwek-Pouydesseau, Le corps préfectoral, 110.

[68] Siwek-Pouydesseau, Le corps préfectoral, 117. On the relations between prefects and members of parliament, see also P. Guiral and G. Thuillier, La vie quotidienne des députés en France de 1871 à 1914 (Paris, 1980), 207–14.

senators of his department. He was in a position to make various decisions in order to help them to become established in the department and to facilitate their political activity. In return, the parliamentarians were able to further the careers of the representatives of central government by making representations to the minister. Very widely and effectively practised as it was, despite the protests of Clemenceau,[69] this exchange of courtesies could nonetheless backfire. In the event of the balance of relations breaking down, there was every likelihood that the prefect would bear the brunt of the rancour of defeated, disappointed, or rejected parliamentarians.

The Beginnings of Professionalization

The political changes which took place in the last years of the nineteenth century had, moreover, given a greater degree of power to the deputy, a circumstance over which many prefects did not fail to take umbrage. Among them was the prefect Monteil, despite his unwavering political support for the radical Republic: 'Every time a prefect suits the local inhabitants, he is disliked by the deputies who, eighty times out of a hundred, will complain to the minister.'[70] The Palais-Bourbon, seat of the Chamber of Deputies, had become the primary political battleground, the locus of all ambition and all intrigue. It was the era of the 'contrôleur', beloved by Alain. The deputy had above all to make sure he defended 'the citizen against the powers'[71] and against all the Napoleonic Bastilles. How could the politicization of the prefectoral institution not have been sanctioned by parliament?

However, this politicization was incompatible neither with a certain degree of continuity nor with the beginning of a trend towards professionalization. Over the period we are concerned with, there were admittedly cases of extreme instability so far as terms of office were concerned—and not all of them corresponded to periods of crisis. In 1882, Floquet held the position of prefect of the Seine for barely ten months and Lépine was prefect of the Marne for only a few days—from 26 June to 11 July 1893. Nonetheless, there were a few examples of exceptional administrative longevity. Although far from equalling the record held by Bourgeois de Jessaint, who was prefect of the Marne from 12 March 1880 until 1 November 1938, Lefebvre de Grosriez held the prefecture of Savoie for 22 years until 1905, Estellé was prefect of the Dordogne for 20 years, and Hendlé stayed in Seine-Inférieure for 18 years (1882–1900). Eugène Poubelle was prefect of the Seine for 13 years (1883–96) and his successor, Justin de Selves, held the post for over 15 years. Although Lépine made only a

[69] In a famous letter dated 10 August 1907, Clemenceau, as Minister of the Interior, declared himself to be resolutely opposed to any intervention, however urgent, on the part of parliamentarians: 'If you know me, my dear deputy, you will know that I am unmoved by threats' (document reproduced by Siwek-Pouydesseau, *Le corps préfectoral*, 171).

[70] E. Monteil, *L'Administration de la République* (Paris, 1893), 67.

[71] The title of one of his most celebrated collection of 'propos' (Paris, 1926).

fleeting appearance in the prefecture of Versailles, he was prefect of police for
more than 18 years (July 1893–October 1897; June 1899–March 1913). In
total, 40 or so prefects held their positions for more than ten years. Over the
period from 1881 to 1914, the average tenure was two years and two months,
as against one year and four months for the period from 1800 to 1880.[72]

The professionalization of the prefectoral institution was a later phenomenon, the consequences of which began to become apparent at the end of the
nineteenth century before being further developed through the activity of the
Association de prévoyance et d'assistance. Contrary to 'prefectoral romanti-
cism', which glorified the political nature of the prefect's duties in order to
promote the prefect's liberty and responsibility, some people maintained that
the prefect was first and foremost an important civil servant whose duties were
to represent and serve the State as much as, if not more than, the interests of
the political powers. According to this view, the prefect was bound by bureaucratic rationality and administrative ethics and had the right to a proper career
within a proper body of civil servants.[73] In actual fact, from this time on, not
only were practically all the prefects appointed former sub-prefects, but career
movements increasingly rarely involved leaving the institution. Where this
did happen, due to at least a minimum of commitment to professional security, those dismissed from prefectoral positions generally obtained other posts
within the administration. From 1880 on, some positions as heads of the
Trésor Public, which were first-class sinecures at the time, were automatically
set aside for them and one in five prefects benefited from this between 1876
and 1918.[74] Other openings were found in central administrative bodies, hos-
pital establishments, and the revenue and tax offices and, for the prefects most
in favour, on the Council of State or at the national audit office. Some were
offered diplomatic or colonial posts.[75]

It should be stressed that there was no contradiction between the politicization of prefectoral duties and the professionalization of the body, between the
political vagaries resulting from governmental prerogatives and the preoccupations with career and security that were starting to appear. It was under
Emile Combes' government that the political demands made on the prefects
were at their most intense. However, it was also under Combes that the concern to find other posts for ousted prefects was most in evidence. At the political level, the prefect was dependent upon his function as the representative
of the government in a department. However, this did not alter the fact that
he could more or less count on continuing to occupy an honourable position
in the higher echelons of the administration. When considering this paradoxical reconciliation, the personal role played by Edgar Combes, the son of
the prime minister and himself a prefect and general secretary at the Ministry

[72] Laharie, 'Le personnel de l'administration préfectorale', 63.
[73] Siwek-Pouydesseau, *Le corps préfectoral*, 114–16.
[74] Cf. P.-F. Pinaud, *Les trésoriers payeurs généraux au XIXe siècle. Répertoire nominatif et territorial*
(Paris, 1983), *passim*.
[75] See Charle, *Les élites de la République*, 208–10.

of the Interior, is sometimes stressed.[76] He saw to it that the eight prefects who were dismissed in September 1904 were accorded honorary status and were actually appointed to other offices (Councillor of State, head of the *Trésor Public*, head of the Paris funding office, director of the body governing pawnshops and moneylenders . . .)

Foxes and Lions

On the ground, the steady politicization of the prefectures had various consequences and took diverse directions. The attitude of the prefects, which was sometimes dictated by circumstances, could vary from place to place and, moreover, some had neither the necessary skill nor style. To exaggerate slightly, and leaving aside the periods of crisis at the beginning of the period (1870–1, 1877), two different attitudes to the influence of political power can be discerned: that of the 'clever ones' and that of the 'combative ones'—in short, V. Pareto's 'foxes' and 'lions'.

Those in the first group, to which the 'great prefects' belonged, succeeded in harmoniously integrating politics into administration. Although they knew how to exert authority, they sought first and foremost to interpret the language of politics and to adapt the government's instructions to suit local conditions while avoiding falling into over-obedient inflexibility. In 1896, in *L'Orme du Mail (IX)*, Anatole France, thinking about the immutable Hendlé, depicted in archetypal—and critical—manner, in the person of Worms-Clavelin, the prudent, finely tactically skilled prefect who refused to serve simply as a communication channel for the Place Beauvau:

His administrative policies were based on the premise that ministers come and go. He took great care never to serve any Minister of the Interior with ardent zeal, refrained from pleasing any of them to excess, and avoided every opportunity to be seen to be over-successful in any undertaking. This attitude of moderation, maintained throughout one minister's term of office, ensured that that minister's successor would be sympathetic towards him, having been warned in advance in a manner sufficiently favourable to cause him to make do with a display of mediocre zeal, which in turn made him acceptable to a third parliament, and so on . . . Monsieur le préfet Worms-Clavelin did little administrating, communicated in the briefest of terms with the Place Beauvau, managed his offices carefully, and lasted and lasted.[77]

In some exceptional cases, 'skilful' prefects managed both to assert themselves and to stay in office without necessarily always being in sympathy with the government. Whereas Justin de Selves owed his immovability to the fact that he was related to Freycinet, Louis Lépine, on the other hand, asserted himself in the role of prefect of police and remained in office during the

---

[76] In particular by Bellion, 'L'histoire intérieure de la France', 162 ff. and 208.

[77] A. France, *Œuvres*, II, ed. La Pleiade (Paris, 1997), 782–3. It first appeared in *L'Echo de Paris* on 5 May 1896.

Combes period (despite disapproving of it) thanks to his popularity and, especially, to the balancing act he set up between central power and the municipal council of Paris, whose support he had succeeded in securing.[78]

At the opposite extreme was the group consisting of the 'combative' prefects, into whose number people moved through all sorts of transitions, some
of which were imperceptible. There were some notorious instances of militancy, such as that of Edgar Monteil, the *préfet des Loges* studied by Vincent
Wright. A former member of the Commune, fanatically anticlerical, and one
of the most prominent personalities of French Freemasonry, he established
files on the political adversaries of the government from his base in Limoges.
Other 'combative' prefects were more obscure and more discreet, but no less
active. Jèze was severely critical of the uses to which some of them put their
supervisory powers: 'They have no scruples about blocking *legal* decisions
taken by municipalities which are unsympathetic to the government in power
and they have no hesitation about letting through *illegal* decisions taken by
local administrations friendly to the government.'[79] Government litigation
provides innumerable illustrations of this somewhat polemical assertion in
politically sensitive areas, such as what might be termed 'everyday anticlericalism'. Fired by political passion, the prefects played their part in the
'tragedy—tempered by comedy' of French religious divisions'.[80]

In itself, the colourful record of court proceedings concerning bell-ringing,
which took shape at the beginning of the century subsequent to the legislation of 9 September 1905 concerning the separation of the Churches and the
State, is chock-full of cases of improper municipal rulings that were eventually
quashed by the Council of State, after having received—if this pun be
allowed—a ringing endorsement from the prefect. In a circular dated 21
January 1907, Briand asked the prefects to tread cautiously, 'the custom of
bell-ringing for religious ceremonies being the principle that is enshrined in
law, in order to ensure that the regulations governing bell-ringing do not lead
to the custom being halted or reduced in such a way as to impede the practice
of religion'. Nonetheless, there were clear cases of excessive zeal being detri-
mental to the freedom of religious practice. The prefect of the Var, for example, approved a municipal ruling which imposed strict limits on the number,
duration, and times of day of religious bell-ringing, at the same time giving the
municipal authorities unlimited powers to ring the bells, notably for civil
funerals.[81] The prefect of the Tarn, for his part, found no fault with a ruling
that ordered the church bells to be rung 'to signal mealtimes and the time to
go back again to work in the fields, when it was time to go to municipal council meetings, the opening and closing time of voting stations on election days,
to call children back into school, and to sound the death knell for members of
the community . . . '.[82]

---

[78] See Berlière, *Le préfet Lépine*, 94–100.   [79] *Revue du droit public*, 280.

[80] G. Le Bras, 'Le Conseil d'Etat régulateur de la vie paroissiale', *Etudes et documents* (du Conseil d'Etat) (1950), 64.

[81] Conseil d'Etat, 30 July 1909, Abbé Jourdan *et al. v.* the mayor of Besse (Var), *Recueil Lebon*, 781.

[82] Conseil d'Etat, 26 May 1911, Sieur Durand, curé of Parisot, *Recueil Lebon*, 620.

Generally speaking, the effects of the politicization of the role of the prefect on the French administration cannot be dissociated from the Jacobin spirit which prevailed at the time. The dependency of the prefect in relation to political power (that is to say, central power) could not but reinforce the centralization of the administration, which went hand in hand with the refusal of any 'political decentralization', a refusal which had been explicitly asserted in 1884, when the great municipal legislation of the Third Republic was passed.[83] The law of 5 April 1884 did not bring much in the way of innovation to the existing practices of centralization as it confined itself to replacing a very limited programme of centralization with a very moderate degree of decentralization. Municipal freedom of action continued to be closely monitored. No municipal ruling, however minor, could come into force without having been approved by 'the superior authority'. Procedures for the intervention of central government were set down with meticulous attention to detail, particularly where matters of budget and finance were concerned. Attached as they were to political centralization, which Tocqueville calls 'governmental', the republicans in office had been loath to learn any lessons from the existence of interests purely at the level of the *commune*; indeed, they did not even acknowledge these. The consolidation of the Republic had seemed to them to be incompatible with any recognition of genuine municipal power. The *communes* were supposed to confine themselves to purely administrative tasks. 'What we call administrative decentralization,' explained Antonin Dubost, formerly a prefect under Gambetta and future president of the Senate, speaking for the commission of the Chamber of Deputies, 'is nothing other than the ever-increasing extension of power to local authorities, without this ever going far enough to sever the ties of legislative subordination that link the *commune* to the State.'[84] Without going so far as to tip over into anarchy, declared the rapporteur de Marcère, 'municipal bodies cannot and must not be concerned with politics'.[85] In this spirit, the law '[forbade] all municipal councils to publish proclamations or statements, either to express political wishes or, apart from those cases provided for in law, to enter into communication with any other municipal council or councils' (Article 72, paragraph 1).

Politics was and had to remain the business of the State, its representatives, and its agents. Such then was the politics of the prefectoral body, which, in consequence, was expected to play an eminently centralizing role on the ground.

---

[83] See J.-P. Machelon, 'Pouvoir municipal et pouvoir central sous la IIIe République. Regard sur la loi du 5 avril 1884', in *L'administration territoriale de la France (1750–1940)*, 509–19; and, more generally on the subject of the uncertainties and limits of republican decentralization, 'La Troisième République (jusqu'à la Grande Guerre)', in L. Fougère, J.-P. Machelon, and F. Monnier (eds), *Les communes et le pouvoir. Histoire politique des communes françaises de 1789 à nos jours* (Paris, 2002), 351–441.
[84] 8 November 1883 (*Journal Officiel. Débats parlementaires. Chambre des députés, 1883*, 2261).
[85] 30 June 1883 (*Journal Officiel*, 1519).

Conclusion

In conclusion, I would suggest, in extending the scope of my remarks to include the whole of the higher echelons of the administration, that the proximity of prefects to political power reinforced the apparatus of the State itself and made it possible to make personnel changes according to no defined rules in cases of fluctuation or change in the elected rulers of the country. André Siegfried was fond of pointing out certain features that were common to the 'political leaders' and the 'top civil servants' under the Third Republic, particularly in its early stages. 'Their psychology of notables and their republican convictions', he wrote, 'went hand in hand with an unquestionable devotion to the State. This observation applies not only to great political leaders like Gambetta, Ferry, Waldeck-Rousseau, and Fallières, but also to top civil servants, residents, and governors and ambassadors, such as Cambon, Alapetite, and Hendlé, who were competent men but, at the same time, men of conviction who served the Republic with the same devotion as did its rank-and-file militants. This was a highly effective combination, in which competence was fired with passion, whilst, at the same time, government orthodoxy remained intact.'[86] Albeit expressed in laudatory mode, this remark goes directly to the heart of the matter and leaves no room for doubt that a regime that had inherited a great administrative tradition, but which was unsure about its legitimacy and its future and was constantly subject to revisionist assaults, was inexorably led to set in place a process of fusion between the militants and the 'men of skill', between State and government. The example of the prefects as political functionaries demonstrates the effectiveness of the system. It also affords us a glimpse of its limits.

[86] André Siegfried, *De la IIIe à la IVe République* (Paris, 1956), 26–7.

5

Fraternity, Solidarity, Sociability: The Grass Roots of the Grand Orient de France (1900–1926)

MAURICE LARKIN

> Lodges must never forget that our ideal is the pursuit of the moral perfection of humanity.
>
> Report of the Lodge, 'La Parfaite Unité' (Albi), 29 March 1922

FOR much of its existence, Fraternity was the neglected Third Person of the republican Trinity: it was the Jacobin equivalent of the Holy Spirit. Historians largely concentrated their attention on the creative and redemptive work of the other two persons of the trinity, Liberty and Equality, especially in those periods of social upheaval when Equality accused Liberty of ignoring its sufferings. Yet, like its divine counterpart, Fraternity inspired a steady if less spectacular devotion as the tangible expression of the bond between Liberty and Equality. During the nineteenth and twentieth centuries, however, nomenclature became increasingly a problem. Just as devout but status-starved women looked to Mariology and eventually to metaphors of 'the Motherhood of God' as antidotes to a male-dominated realm of concepts, so their secular counterparts claimed that 'Fraternity' would no longer do. 'Solidarity' slowly took its place; and then 'Sociability' made a belated entry in an untidy attempt to cover the issues that had somehow got lost in the change of names.

I have been privileged to read in typescript Vincent Wright's joint work with Sudhir Hazareesingh, *Francs-Maçons sous le Second Empire* (2001), one of the rare books to address these neglected matters. This chapter is a modest attempt to explore some of the issues that their book raises, but in the context of a later period. It is also an expression of gratitude to Vincent Wright for his help, advice, friendship, and unforgettable humour. As both perpetrator and victim of many practical jokes, he must surely have wondered whether it was sheer coincidence that decided the Grande Loge Mixte de France to set up its headquarters in the Rue des Ours a few doors from his Parisian *pied à terre*—a bold challenge to the strictly fraternal membership rules of the Grand Orient de France which he has analysed so well.

I should also like to take this opportunity to express my grateful thanks to M. Pierre Mollier, Mme Hélène Camou, M. André Combes, and their colleagues at the Library and Archives of the Grand Orient de France for their generous help and advice, and to the Faculty of Arts of the University of Edinburgh for kindly providing me with a research travel grant. I am greatly indebted to my wife Enid for her help with the archival research and subsequent statistical work.

Yet the flag of Fraternity still had its loyal upholders—and none more stalwart than the Grand Orient de France, the dominant branch of French Freemasonry. The close links between the Grand Orient and the Radical Party are well-known; and their roles in the campaign against Church influence in French education and politics have been extensively examined in a variety of publications. What is much less familiar is the role that the Grand Orient played in provincial life and in furthering the personal interests of its members. The first quarter of the twentieth century presents a coherent and rewarding period for enquiry in that it spans the years when the Grand Orient believed that its opportunities for influencing public life and society were at their most propitious. This was not consistently the case throughout the period. Both at the time and retrospectively, 1914–1924 appeared much less propitious than 1900–1914. But the coming to power of the Cartel des Gauches in 1924 struck optimists as offering the same sort of perspectives as the arrival in office of the governments of 'republican concentration' at the turn of the century, following fears of an anti-Republican *coup d'état* in 1899. But the inability of the Cartel to master the financial crisis of the mid-1920s and its failure to anticipate the unpopularity of its anticlerical proposals rapidly destroyed Masonic hopes of a return to the heady days of the pre-1914 period. Indeed, so great was the disappointment that the Grand Orient formally abandoned its traditional policy of openly backing parliamentary candidates who were sympathetic to its political aims; the 1924 election that had brought the ill-starred Cartel to office consequently became the last occasion on which politicians could look to public and formal Masonic endorsement. Thereafter the influence of the Grand Orient in electoral politics made itself felt through the industry of its members, acting in their own right as individuals but still campaigning under the guidance of the strategies and tactics that the lodges privately devised as appropriate to their localities.

The Legacy of the Past

For the Grand Orient, 'Fraternity' meant what it said. Female lodges had been grudgingly recognized by the Grand Orient in 1774 but their designation as 'loges d'adoption', with its oddly *orpheline* overtones, indicated the inferior role which women played in the Masonic scheme of things. Indeed, the expectation that they would dedicate themselves principally to charitable work put them on a level similar to that of nunneries within the Catholic Church, where the priesthood and senior ecclesiastical office were male monopolies; and the *loges d'adoption* largely sank from view during the Revolution. A minor strand of French Masonry, le Droit Humain, introduced mixed lodges into France in 1893; but the Grand Orient was extremely reluctant to follow suit. Proposals for admitting women to its all-male lodges were invariably rejected at its annual national gatherings. In 1907 the regional Congrès des Loges du Centre affirmed that 'women unknowingly possess in the depths of their being a grain of mysticism. Consequently, in our view, female postulants can-not be wholly free of religious ties'.[1] Significantly, support for the principle of mixed lodges was mainly confined to Paris and those areas where women were regarded as relatively emancipated from Church influence. Not that women were held irredeemably in low Masonic esteem. Suspicion centred on unre-generate womanhood, left to its own instincts before enlightened men and the forces of reason had redeemed it.

The Grand Orient's growing conflicts with the Catholic Church under the Third Republic sharpened these issues. Symptomatically the questionnaires that would-be members and their investigators had to answer before initiation was considered demanded explicit assurance on the attitude of their wives towards their husband's initiation; and investigators often added comments on the wife's moral probity if it fell short of what was expected of a Mason's soulmate. Indeed, a lodge report of 1922 claimed that failure to maintain a robust and wholesome wariness on wifely influence had led to a situation where 'timid and insufficiently sincere brothers dare not be Freemasons in their own homes, and insist that lodge invitations be sent to an alternative address lest Madame be upset!'[2]

Quite apart from matters of gender, 'fraternity' always meant much more to Masons than did its anodyne successors, 'solidarity' and 'sociability'. To out-siders, Masonic fraternity seemed to present something of a paradox. On the one hand, it appeared to believe in universal brotherhood, as a long-term pos-sibility if not necessarily in the realizable present. And yet it had many of the marks of a secret society, suspiciously vetting its members and distinctly reti-cent about what went on within its portals. Even in the late twentieth century a former Grand Master of the Grand Orient felt no embarrassment in publicly declaring that 'Masonry is elitist. We choose the best'.[3] Like so much else, this seeming paradox was partly a legacy of its eighteenth-century origins. A prod-uct of the Enlightenment, it was also part of the century's development of clubs and debating societies; and, like such clubs, its members were expected to be socially respectable, personally congenial, and intellectually capable of contributing to the discussions and life of the lodge. But Freemasonry went much further in its pursuit of Enlightened ideals. It sought to develop wisdom and equilibrium of life among its initiates in a much more vigorous way than the simple exchange of ideas that characterized a debating society. At the same time its members were expected to nurture close ties of mutual loyalty and friendship, and to come to each others' support in times of difficulty. These ideals continued to be reflected in the names of the Grand Orient's lodges in twentieth-century France: 'Aimable Sagesse' (Marseille), 'Auguste Amitié' (Condom), 'Rose du Parfait Silence' (Paris). Admittedly the title of the Nîmes

---

[1] Stephane Landemaine, 'Le Grand Orient de France dans l'Orne: la Fidélité, Orient d'Alençon (1899–1940)', Mémoire de maîtrise (Le Mans, 1996–7), 95–6.

[2] 'La Parfaite Amitié' (Albi), 29 March 1922. Archives du Grand Orient (Rue Cadet, Paris); hereafter AGO(RC) – 525.

[3] Jean-Robert Ragache, cited in Patrice Burnat and Christian de Villeneuve, Les francs-maçons des années Mitterrand (Paris, 1994), 262.

lodge, 'L'Echo du Grand Orient', might not suggest a strong propensity for bold initiatives. Like caviar, however, such finely honed qualities were not as yet for the general, even if the eventual perfectibility of mankind remained a distant hope in an unpredictable future. In the meantime Masonry saw its brotherhood as embracing not only enlightened minorities in other parts of the world but also the enlightened minorities of the past, to say nothing of the much larger numbers of the enlightened expected in centuries to come. But, like other strands of Enlightened thought, Masonry recognized that geographical and historical differences of space and time created diversity of perception and perspective among different societies, no matter how well-intentioned and well-educated. Masons should therefore be tolerant of differences of opinion and belief, recognizing them as chequered manifestations of the same ideals, until such time as the advance of knowledge and mutual understanding created a consensus on where perfectibility was to be found. Moreover, tolerance should extend to religious differences.

The ethos of eighteenth-century Masonry was predominantly deist—with notable national differences—and from its earliest days it laid emphasis on seeking the common denominators that underlay the great religions of the world, present and past. For all its faith in the prevailing force of reason, it recognized that religious instincts were a basic if not immutable part of human nature, with a potential force for creating solidarity. This recognition largely accounts for the enduring place of ritual and symbolism in Masonic activities, with their echoes of ancient religions that predated the religious divisions of the contemporary world. It ran parallel to Masonry's sentimental evocation of the medieval confraternities of itinerant stonemasons who travelled from country to country, contributing their skills to the great joint enterprises of architectural endeavour, the cathedrals and public buildings that symbolized the interaction of personal commitment and cooperative achievement. These confraternities were likewise seen as embodying the Masonic virtues of mutual help among brothers. Even in the twentieth century, the study reports prepared by Grand Orient members for lodge discussion were termed 'morceaux d'architecture'.

Although the Grand Orient famously dropped deistical references to the Grand Architect from its profession of beliefs in 1877, it continued to respect the principle that its members as individuals were free to profess whatever religion they wished, provided that the religion in question did not itself pose a threat to the principle of toleration. This was a key proviso which reflected the growing animosity between Masonry and the Catholic Church, with its assertive claims to being the One True Faith and its long history of enlisting the aid of governments to suppress its religious competitors. On 12 June 1910, the Conseil de l'Ordre of the Grand Orient issued a circular reminding lodges that, while in principle religion was a personal matter in which Masonry would not interfere, 'it is incompatible with the spirit of Masonry for a Mason to abdicate his personal responsibility and submit himself to the practice of a religion which teaches that outside it there is no salvation—a religion, moreover, which smothers reason and shackles science, a religion which claims to be ruler and mentor of mankind'.[4]

The old alliance of throne and altar was also a major factor encouraging the secrecy that characterized Masonry, especially in those countries where the Catholic Church was politically powerful and free from the tight restraint of an Enlightened monarch such as Joseph II of eighteenth-century Austria. Secrecy was also a consciously fostered ingredient in the emotional appeal of Masonic ritual and symbolism; but it principally sprang from the desire to protect its members from possible harassment at the hands of civil or religious authorities.

The aim of Masonry to make Enlightened principles a reality in the contemporary world also required that Masons should seek to acquire positions of influence in government service and elsewhere in society. Given the widespread suspicion of Masonry in conservative circles, this itself was a delicate and difficult matter, requiring discretion and secrecy in its negotiation. Even before the Grand Orient established a favour-seeking network under the Third Republic, the motives behind Masonic job-seeking were inevitably mixed: a genuine desire to change society for the better was often hard to disentangle from personal ambition and the basic human wish for secure employment. Similarly, the duty of Masons to help their brethren when the occasion arose became quickly enmeshed in this ambiguity. It was not easy to distinguish between affording sound men the opportunity to improve the world around them and simply giving friends a timely leg-up in the competition for jobs and promotion. These ambiguities became much more acute after the Dreyfus crisis of the 1890s.

An Unsavoury Image

Many political historians of the early twentieth century present a somewhat unedifying picture of the Grand Orient at national level. Its close association with the more punitive aspects of the anticlerical legislation of the Combes era gave its militancy an obsessively vindictive character in the eyes of many foreign observers—an impression which the strong phraseology of its political circulars seemed to confirm. Even in the 1920s, after the wartime Union Sacrée against a foreign enemy had helped to soften many of the political animosities of pre-war France, these circulars continued to speak the vituperative language of a past that many had hoped was mercifully dead. The terms 'réactionnaire et clérical' were still thrown around like custard pies at anyone or anything that seemed to be posing a minor difficulty for some local Masonic undertaking. Nor was it surprising that both friends and enemies of Masonry should attribute an excessive importance to its power and influence

[4] Yves Hivert-Messeca, 'La Franc-Maçonnerie en pays Niçois de la fin du XVIIIème siècle à la Seconde Guerre Mondiale'. Thèse de Doctorat du 3ème cycle, ii. (Nice: University of Nice, 1989), 313.

when over a third of the membership of the French houses of parliament were Masons of some sort in the opening decade of the century, as were at least a half the cabinet ministers. Moreover, the total membership of the Grand Orient grew by over a third in only five years: from 21,670 to 30,044 between 1903 and 1908, and its lodges within the Hexagon from 301 to 345.[5] In principle, the constitution of the Grand Orient prohibited lodges from establishing formal links with specific political parties; and between 1901 and 1907 its governing body, the Conseil de l'Ordre, repeatedly reminded lodges of this stipulation lest lodges became split over matters of political allegiance. Yet in practice about two-thirds of its lodges actively supported the Radical Party in 1905 and a third looked to the Socialists. This split in sympathies was not a major problem during the years of 'Republican concentration', when the two parties were in close alliance against the Church and right-wing subversion. But it threatened to create difficulties when the anticlerical programme was completed and social issues could no longer be left to simmer unattended on the back burner.

The inclination of many historians and contemporaries to exaggerate the political power of Masonry was encouraged by the fact that resolutions of the annual general assembly of the Grand Orient often featured in the following congress of the Radical Party, and in many major instances became a reality in the legislation and ordinances of predominantly Radical governments. Yet this did not necessarily make Masonry the inspiration and prime mover of these legislative changes, even if it significantly contributed to their initial momentum. Although many of the parliamentary and government figures who played a key role in the anticlerical programme were themselves Masons, it was rarely that Masonry had made them anticlericals in the first place, however much it may have strengthened their disposition to be such. Radicals, and then increasingly Socialists, became Masons primarily because the democratic and secular ideology of the Grand Orient corresponded to their existing beliefs; and they saw in Masonry a form of solidarity which gave protection and opportunities to men who shared these convictions. This was especially attractive at a time when French political parties had not yet developed an effective system of extra-parliamentary organization, least of all at regional level where Masonry was most effective. Masonic ritual and language were not taken with an oppressive seriousness by existing members, so interested outsiders were not significantly embarrassed or deterred from seeking initiation if it was otherwise to their advantage to do so. Indeed, many postulants found Masonic ritual a vaguely satisfying substitute for the more congenial aspects of the corporate religions that they had abandoned or had never had.

[5] André Combes, *Histoire de la Franc-Maçonnerie au XIXème siècle*, ii. (Monaco, 1999), 390–1. This book is the most recent source for general information of this kind. On Masonry under the Third Republic, including the inter-war years, Mildred Headings, *French Freemasonry under the Third Republic* (Baltimore, 1949) is still very useful. Pierre Chevallier's *Histoire de la Franc-Maçonnerie Française*, iii. (Paris, 1975) draws heavily upon Headings while adding rectifications of detail.

The annual assemblies of the Grand Orient saw a great deal of experimental kite-flying by ambitious young Radicals and also by their Socialist counterparts. While the 33 members of the Conseil de l'Ordre were predominantly Radical in their personal predilections, the study commissions that prepared the programme of debates on matters of current concern were increasingly dominated by men whose sympathies were Socialist, as was reflected in their choice of issues for discussion. But the Masonic assemblies were in the happy position of not being governed by political timetables, and were therefore able to give opinions on what was desirable as distinct from what was practically attainable. In a similar but more circumspect way, the rank and file of the Radical Party congresses were also safely distanced from the political high wire that the minister had to tread, and so were able to echo the bold proposals of the Grand Orient, even if their closer proximity to the realities of power generally made for greater caution in their formal resolutions compared with what emerged from Grand Orient assemblies. Boldness of utterance was no proof of where ideas originated; and whether these ideas became law or not depended on the men in government and on the members of parliament whose votes they needed. The voices and resolutions that came out of the Grand Orient assemblies and Radical Party congresses said little that they had not heard many times before—and which were often little more than echoes of what they themselves had urged in the distant days of their political youth. At the same time, when it came to the person-to-person diffusion of republican ideas at grass-roots level, it has often been argued, though it is incapable of proof, that the multitude of local shooting clubs were much more influential than the lodges in terms of breadth of contact. Nor should it be forgotten that the active membership of most Masons averaged only about five years and generally corresponded to periods when the member felt most in need of professional, political, or social advancement.

This raises the second aspect of pre-war Masonry that aroused sustained criticism among historians and contemporaries: its attempts to interfere in the recruitment and promotion of civil servants and army officers. This took the double form of seeking favours for fellow Masons on the one hand and sabotaging the career prospects of political enemies, especially strongly committed Catholics and individuals with right-wing sympathies, on the other. The military aspect of this reached its boiling point with the so-called Affaire des Fiches, which arose from the systematic attempt in the opening years of the twentieth century to block the promotion of committed Catholics in the commissioned ranks of the army on the grounds that they represented a potential threat to the security of the Republican regime. The War Ministry was secretly using the Masonic network of the Grand Orient to spy on officers and report on those who were assiduous churchgoers; and, when the system became publicly known in October 1904, the furore led indirectly to the resignation of the Combes government three months later. These attempts to 'declericalize' the army have been extensively examined; and, if the details of its parallel but more diffuse activities in civil service matters have been investigated far less closely, the fact of their existence was both known and deprecated by the bulk of commentators. However, their extent and the degree to which this may have changed after the First World War has not been systematically studied; and this chapter attempts among other things to take sample soundings of what *fraternité* meant when it came to favouring friends and tripping up enemies. As will be seen, the number of Masonic interventions was surprisingly high—averaging well over five a day during their peak during the opening years of the century—but the ascertainable success rate was remarkably low, well under one in ten producing the hoped-for result.

The general histories of these years that have tended to give the Grand Orient an unfavourable image pay insufficient attention to the other aspects of fraternity and sociability that the Grand Orient sought to embody, especially at local level. Its attempts to give meaning and balance to its members' lives, its fostering of serious debate on social and personal problems, and its charitable activities radiate much of the idealism that Masonry professed in the eighteenth century, and still professed even if its practice often seemed swamped by the need to defend the enlightened principles of the Republic against its political enemies.

Problems of Evidence

The relative neglect of these aspects reflects the current state of published research on Masonry under the Third Republic. In many ways the available literature is reminiscent of what was available 40 years ago on the Catholic Church during the same period, in that it is mainly concerned with the role of Masonry in national politics, with relatively little to say on its role in provincial life and in the personal development of its members. Even published regional studies tend to be concerned with the relations of the lodges with local politicians and with their influence on the implementation of national legislation in the area. The results of research on the non-political aspects of Masonry in this period are mainly found in Masonic in-house publications with limited circulation; and even the locally produced histories of individual lodges tend to be celebratory booklets, marking a centenary or similar chronological landmark. The most interesting work on lodges and Masonic sociability is to be found in unpublished *mémoires de maîtrise* and doctoral theses; but, as yet, little of this valuable work has found its way into print. Moreover, the constraints of completing dissertations on time has discouraged postgraduates from attempting bolder comparative projects, juxtaposing lodges from widely differing socio-economic contexts with contrasting political traditions.

This chapter tentatively suggests some patterns of change and continuity that such a broader study might produce. It is mainly based on the archival correspondence of eight provincial lodges, representing widely differing geographical and political circumstances. It does not pretend to analyse how these contrasting circumstances shaped the individual character of each of these lodges, which would be impossible in a single chapter of this kind. It attempts instead to see what general trends emerge from amalgamating evidence from a widely spaced if numerically sparse selection of provincial centres of Masonic activity. The following alphabetical list of the eight lodges indicates the departments in which they are situated, together with a measure of the strength and longevity of Radicalism in each of these departments at the beginning of the century, on an ascending scale of 0 to 8: Albi ('La Parfaite Amitié', Tarn, 1); Bayonne ('La Zélée', Basses Pyrénées, 1); Chartres ('Marceau', Eure-et-Loire, 3); Nîmes ('l'Echo du Grand Orient', Gard, 8); Périgueux ('Les Amis Persévérants', Dordogne, 1); Pons ('La Tolérance et l'Etoile de la Saintonge réunies', Charente Inférieure, 2); Rennes ('La Parfaite Union', Ile-et-Vilaine, 0); and Vitry le François ('Les Vertus Réunies', Marne, 7).[6]

The Pattern of Membership

To become members of the Grand Orient, applicants had to be at least 21 years of age;[7] of irreproachable reputation and morals; engaged in 'a free and honourable occupation'; educated to at least primary level 'so as to understand and appreciate Masonic truths'; and to have at least six months' residence within a 100-kilometre radius of the solicited lodge. Vetting of applicants was a serious business. Three independent unsigned reports were ordered from members of the lodge who either knew the man already or had discreet access to others who would give honest opinions of him. If he had recently come from elsewhere, inquiries would be made in his former locality. Each *enquêteur* was required to fill in a questionnaire concerning the applicant on the following topics: 'morality, reputation; character; qualities and deficiencies; relations; political opinions; education; social position, family position'. And the investigator was expected to conclude with his own preference for acceptance or 'adjournment'. These reports would then be considered by the Master Masons of the lodge and a vote taken. If it was negative, the candidate was entitled to make up to two further applications at yearly intervals; and until then the case was officially deemed to be 'adjourned' rather than rejected. But few postulants made subsequent applications to the same lodge; and if they applied to other lodges, these lodges would be informed by the Paris headquarters of the Grand Orient in the Rue Cadet whether these applications had already been turned down elsewhere. A further check on the quality of applications came in 1908 when the Grand Orient and its smaller counterpart, the Grande Loge de France, agreed that any applicant 'adjourned' by the one rite was ineligible for consideration by the other until a year had elapsed.

---

[6] The figures indicate the number of legislative elections between 1871 and 1898 in which the department elected at least one Radical deputy. The general observations on these lodges as a group are based on AGO(RC): 521–5 (Albi); 620–4 (Bayonne); 873–6 (Chartres); 1525–7 (Nîmes); 1611–15 (Périgueux); 1583 (Pons); 1662 (Rennes); 2048–9 (Vitry-le-François).

[7] Sons of active lodge members were eligible for consideration at an earlier age.

Being a Mason was not cheap. Before the First World War, the basic annual subscription in many lodges was as much as 30 francs, or about £50 today; and there were various one-off payments as members moved up the rungs of the Masonic ladder from Apprentice to *Compagnon* and then to Master, the interval between each grade usually lasting at least a year. Certain ill-paid occupations, such as the army and primary-school teaching, entitled members to reductions on some of these items. Even so, it was perhaps not surprising that the average age for initiations in most lodges was 31 or so in the 1900–14 period, and the average size of lodges was about 60 members. Given the entrance requirements, lodges were inevitably town rather than village institutions and were overwhelmingly middle-class, even if a sizeable proportion of members belonged to the lower fringes of the middle class.

The First World War, despite its attendant social changes, had a surprisingly modest impact on the occupational spectrum of Masonic membership.[8] According to the surviving lists of initiates for the sample group of eight lodges, civil servants accounted for about a fifth of the total: 21.9 per cent before 1914 and 19.4 per cent thereafter. Primary-school teachers, who were the next largest group, and increasingly attracted by Masonry, nevertheless fell slightly from 12.4 per cent to 10.9 per cent, perhaps as a result of heavy casualties during the war. Conversely, the numbers engaged in various kinds of commerce rose proportionally from 20 per cent to 23.8 per cent, probably as a result of the post-war decline in Masonic favour-seeking in the public sector, which left the private world of business contacts as the main area in which Masonic membership could bring material advantage.

The most dramatic change was in the proportion of career soldiers—down from 11.6 per cent to 5 per cent of initiations—reflecting not only the impact of war losses but also the virtual disappearance of the Masonic *piston* as an aid to military promotion. By the 1920s, few doubted the loyalty of the army to the regime, which removed any justification for the 'Republicanization' of the army pursued during the Combes years. Moreover, the experience of war had revealed the disastrous consequences of promoting officers on political rather than professional grounds. In the first four months of the war, Joffre had been obliged to transfer to less responsible posts 190 of the country's 425 senior officers. And of the 19 officers whose skills in 1914 earned them unusually rapid promotion, 14 had been victims of unfavourable Masonic *fiches* before the war—which suggests that their qualities had hitherto remained unrewarded.[9]

Artisans and other individuals engaged in manufacturing were up from 4.8 per cent to 10.4 per cent of *initiés*, a rise perhaps reflecting the gradual democratizing of Masonry, although the Masonic avoidance of the terms 'ouvrier' or 'manoeuvrier' makes it hard to distinguish workers from self-employed crafts-

---

[8] The following statistics are all based on information on initiates in the archival boxes listed in n. 6 above. They do not include members who were initiated before 1900, and these percentages do not therefore represent the overall social composition of these lodges. What they do indicate is the occupational spectrum from which Masons were drawn in the period under study, 1900–26.
[9] François Vindé, *L'Affaire des Fiches, 1900–1904: Chronique d'un scandale* (Paris, 1989), 187–8.

men. For what it is worth, the handful of worker members clearly identified in the Clermont Ferrand lodge in the pre-war decade were mainly skilled railwaymen and works foremen.[10] Many middle-class members felt that workers would be unlikely to contribute usefully to lodge discussion, but the size of the annual subscription was usually enough to keep them out. In the inter-war period, industrial workers in the Nice lodges accounted for only 1.9 per cent of the whole, and were mainly in printing, while of the 6.3 per cent who were artisans most were connected with the building trade.[11]

Given the predominantly town-centred nature of the Grand Orient, 'agricoles' were never likely to feature largely among the brotherhood; and yet, in the sample group of eight lodges, they rose from 3.6 per cent to a modest 4.5 per cent of *initiés*, despite heavy war losses, perhaps as a result of improving rural transport. Conversely, the less clearly specified 'propriétaires', which presumably included a number of landowners, fell from 4 per cent to 1.6 per cent.

Despite their restricted numbers in society as a whole, the liberal professions continued to hold a significant place in the Grand Orient. Marginally down from 8.7 per cent to 7.9 per cent of *initiés* in the sample group, they were initially headed by the medical profession—2.9 per cent to 2.7 per cent—and then by accountants—1.9 per cent to 2.9 per cent—with lawyers some way behind—1.4 per cent to 1.3 per cent. Magistrates' membership was viewed disapprovingly by the outside world, and their initiations were down from 1.6 per cent to 0.3 per cent, while secondary-school teachers rose from 2.6 per cent to 4 per cent. Surprisingly, journalists were very few—0.7 per cent, then 0.3 per cent—although in minor provincial towns it was often a part-time occupation combined with a small business that might pre-empt how the member was designated in lodge records. Given Masonry's concern for confidentiality, it might be expected that journalists would be regarded with some wariness, as were bar-owners and music-hall artistes, yet unlike their voluble counterparts they scarcely feature among 'adjourned' applicants.

Nor were the lodges the only source of fraternal support. Commercial travellers could look to the Union Maçonnique des Voyageurs et Placiers, while from 1907 the fast-expanding membership among railway employees had long-distance links in the Groupe Fraternel des Chemins de Fer. In their modest way, these leagues may possibly have helped to humanize the traditional war between the fare-dodging tactics of the *commis-voyageurs* and the carriage-hopping cunning of the *contrôleurs de billets*.

Those Found Wanting

The Dreyfus crisis of 1899, with its alarm call of 'la République en danger!', had spurred the Grand Orient into increasing its membership as part of a general

---

[10] Mathias Ganière, 'La Loge Maçonnique Les Enfants de Gergovie à l'Orient de Clermont-Ferrand (1876–1914)'. Mémoire de Maîtrise (Clermont II: Université Blaise Pascal, 1995), 206.
[11] Hivert-Messeca, 'La Franc-Maçonnerie en pays Niçois', ii., 448.

campaign of Republican defence against the alleged risks of clerico-military subversion. In 1906, for instance, only 8 per cent of the Grand Orient's total number of applicants were 'adjourned'; and the number of existing members expelled for absenteeism, non-payment of dues, or for other reasons was equal to only 18 per cent of accepted newcomers in the same year.[12] But, after the completion of the government's programme of anticlerical legislation, the task of increasing the numerical membership of the lodges no longer seemed quite so important now that the Republic was clearly out of danger. Moreover, the Radical presence in parliament was firmly buttressed by its success in the 1906 elections. From 1909 onwards the annual number of *initiés* dropped dramatically to a tenth of what it had been. This was the result of falling applications on the one hand but also of conscious retrenchment in recruiting on the other, with effects that lasted until after the war. With more emphasis on quality than quantity, the grounds for turning down applicants noticeably changed. Whereas many of the rejections in the earlier period were on political or semi-religious grounds—'opinions douteuses' or 'd'une famille très cléricale'—the later ones, especially in the 1920s, were mostly based on the intellectual or moral inadequacy of the applicant or occasionally the easy virtue or loquacity of their wives. The correspondence of the sample group of eight lodges indicates that during the high tide of government anticlericalism in 1902–6 the commonest stated reason for 'adjourning' applications was insufficient Republican commitment—23 per cent—closely followed by clerical connections of a personal, family, or associative sort—17 per cent; and the remaining 60 per cent of 'adjournments' were attributed to a wide assortment of reasons covering personality defects, moral deficiencies, inadequate education, and self-interested motives.[13] After the war, however, insufficient Republican commitment accounted for only 15 per cent of 'adjournments', while alleged clerical connections were down as low as 7 per cent, leaving personal deficiencies of one sort or another as the overwhelming basis for rejection. At the same time there was a significant fall in the number of applicants who were turned down because they looked to Masonry to further their careers—from a pre-war 8 per cent to a post-war 4 per cent. This in all probability reflected a fall in expectations of what Masonry could do in the immediate post-war climate, with the Bloc National in power and anticlericalism no longer the passepartout to government favour.

Lodges varied in the verbal subtlety of their verdicts. At its lowest level, Nîmes turned down a *propriétaire* in 1903 because he was a 'political chameleon, former pupil of the Jesuits, Jesuit himself',[14] while Albi refused an applicant in 1905 for being 'the son of a former *agent de police*; is said to be a *mouchard* himself'—indicating the ambivalent attitude that many Masons still had towards the police.[15] Other lodges preferred a vocabulary more in keeping

---

[12] Combes, *Histoire de la Franc-Maçonnerie*, ii., 392.
[13] These and the following percentages are all based on information on applicants in the archival boxes listed in the n. 6 above.
[14] 24 February 1903, AGO(RC), 1525.   [15] 28 November 1905, AGO(RC), 522.

with the high aspirations of Masonry. Thus Périgueux 'adjourned' an applicant in 1904 because he was not 'd'une délicatesse parfaite',[16] while Chartres
in 1921 felt unable to overlook the education 'très ordinaire' of a stained-glass
painter who 'merely repeats that "je n'aime pas les curés" and lacks properly
thought-out philosophical convictions'.[17]

There were three professions in particular that experienced periodic
difficulty in passing the portals of the eight sample lodges. Predictably
enough, these were commercial travellers, music-hall artistes, and bar-owners.
The postulants themselves and the lodges that considered their applications
generally preferred to bestow propriety on their occupations by describing
them as 'représentants de commerce', 'artistes lyriques', and 'limonadiers'.
Commercial travellers made up at least one in ten of the applicants whom the
eight lodges turned down. Their itinerant life-style did not augur well for regular attendance at lodge meetings, while reports on their morals tended to
confirm the assumptions of British seaside postcards; and, of those who were
accepted, a considerable proportion were later expelled for absenteeism and
non-payment of dues. Their loquacity was also a problem for a discreet if not
entirely secret society. Albi 'adjourned' one because he 'likes to hold forth in
bars, and does it with some success . . . but there is reason to fear that Masonic
society might suffer in consequence'.[18]

The term 'artiste lyrique' covered a broad spectrum of talents, ranging from
the rendition of popular items from the operatic repertoire to comic songs that
were often part of a comedy act. The peripatetic existence of such types told
against them, as did their propensity to frequent bars and speak their minds.
Indeed, they were unique in that the sum total of those turned away actually
outnumbered acceptances. In many respects the 'limonadier' was a static
counterpart to the itinerant 'artiste lyrique', both blossoming in human company and keeping late hours in similar establishments, albeit on opposite sides
of the counter. Since Masonic Apprentices were expected to keep silent during
their first year of lodge meetings, 'limonadiers' were widely recognized as a
potential problem since even those who managed to bottle up their reflections
during meetings might find it hard not to uncork them amid the bonhomie of
the bar afterwards, in full hearing of the *profanes*. The outcome was that
'limonadiers' accounted for over 10 per cent of the total of 'adjournments'
pronounced by the sample group of eight lodges.

The unashamed self-interest of some applicants and the sybaritic insouciance of others never ceased to amaze the guardians of Masonic membership.
In 1925 a business representative accompanied his application to join the
Chartres lodge with a request for a loan of 10,000 francs to ease his bank-
ruptcy.[19] But perhaps the most remarkable example of an applicant who
combined self-interest with an almost beguiling insouciance was the semi-
legendary garage proprietor of St Malo who in 1923 wished to be initiated into
the Rennes lodge, 'La Parfaite Union'; and nowhere was this perfect union

[16] 7 December 1904, AGO(RC), 1612.   [17] 5 April 1921, AGO(RC), 873.
[18] 8 May 1902, AGO(RC), 525.   [19] 3 May 1925, AGO(RC), 876.

better exemplified than in the brothers' unanimous dismissal of his application.[20] The first confidential report on his application described how he was
rarely to be found in his garage—which was three times mortgaged—and how
he 'divides his time between shooting, drinking and gambling. During the
winter he spends the greater part of his night in the bar with his mistress, who
is a prostitute and invites clients to gamble for high stakes.' The summer
nights were spent mainly in the St Malo casinos. For 15 years he had been
unashamedly living at the expense of a widow who provided him with meals
at her café but for which he steadfastly refused to pay, even after being beaten
up by outraged onlookers. At one point it looked as though he was about to
succeed in marrying the daughter of a Parisian industrialist, until her father
started to make inquiries in St Malo.

The report concluded: 'There is no ill-will about him; he is even anxious to
be obliging; but with him nothing is planned, he is incapable of a sane judgement or an elevated thought, he lives bestially, trapped in immorality, and
having only one object in life: gambling.' Another report began engagingly
enough: 'Allow me, I beg you, to present my modest offering of evidence on
the morality of the candidate.' Not only was he was renowned for his alcohol
consumption but 'some of his *parties de baccarat* have been quite sensational'.
Regularly arriving home drunk in the small hours of the morning, 'he often
likes to say that he knows the time perfectly when he arrives in a bar, but has
no idea at what hour he will leave it' Happening to encounter the writer of
the report in the doorway of a bar, the applicant cheerfully remarked, 'I expect
you know that I am about to become one of you lot', showing him a confidential Masonic letter concerning his application. Revealing nothing, the writer
asked why he wanted to become a Mason. 'A moment's pause, a smile, then
he replied, "oh well, it could be useful. There're chaps there who could help
me out!".' All this was assuming a sociability beyond the bounds of Masonic
precept, and the outcome of his application was ineluctable.

The Life of the Lodge

Initiation was but the beginning; becoming a *Compagnon*, then a Master—and
perhaps eventually a lodge officer—was the *gradus ad Parnassum*. In the sample
group of eight lodges, no 'artiste lyrique' appears to have made it beyond
Apprentice. Among the footloose fraternity, commercial travellers with their
more circumscribed circuits scored more highly despite a fair number of resignations and exclusions. At the same time their professional dedication to articulate
persuasiveness often gave them an advantage in lodge debates—as it did to other
manipulators of eloquence, the liberal professions and secondary-school teachers, all of whom achieved promotion more rapidly than other groups. Despite
their high rejection at initiation level, 'limonadiers' did better than 'artistes

---

[20] 7 May 1923, AGO(RC), 1665.

lyriques' when it came to promotion, doubtless due to their better opportunities for regular attendance and also perhaps their strong pecuniary interest in not offending brothers who were, or might be, among their steady customers.

Once one was accepted as a Mason, continued membership was contingent on observance of Masonic principles as well as on regular attendance and punctuality with payments. When in 1899 proposals were made at the general assembly of the Grand Orient to expel Masons who sent their children to Catholic private schools, the leadership circumvented this contentious issue by leaving the matter to individual lodges to deal with on an *ad hominem* basis. Many Masons were married to practising Catholics, and it was generally recognized that the threat of exclusion could create serious family tensions. Symptomatically, no one seriously proposed that a church wedding, baptism of children, or a religious funeral should be a matter for exclusion, since most Masons were married in church and had their children baptized to placate their wives. Lodges varied in what they did with the *ad hominem* flexibility that the Grand Orient had accorded them; but, apart from family rites of passage, a very serious view was taken of Masons or would-be Masons who went to Sunday Mass or took Communion at Easter.

The frequency of lodge meetings varied depending on the size of membership and the ease of access to books and to other sources of information. But once a fortnight was a widespread norm, even though the wealthier lodges with well-stocked libraries, like those of Nice, met once a week. Despite the penalties for poor attendance, the usual size of these weekly gatherings in Nice was only a quarter to a half of registered membership.[21] The written constitution of lodges usually stipulated complete attentiveness to the subject of discussion—no whispered conversations or slipping in and out of the debate—and no member was supposed to make more than three interventions in support of a particular argument.

The lodge correspondence for the pre-war years gives little indication of what individual lodges chose to discuss from the list of options that the general assembly of the Grand Orient prescribed for the coming year. Conversely, the post-war correspondence of the sample group of eight includes not only lists of subjects covered but also a number of reports that emerged from these debates. These reports—sometimes by men with little formal education beyond primary school—give a measure of the importance of Masonic study sessions to the inhabitants of small provincial towns, where the opportunities for informed discussion were relatively limited.

For the pre-war period, the lists of options proposed by the general assembly included a large number that were of specifically working-class concern. This reflected the strength of the Socialist presence in the preparatory commissions.[22] But the surviving evidence for what individual lodges chose to

---

[21] Hivert-Messeca, 'La Franc-Maçonnerie en pays Niçois', ii., 291–6.

[22] For an overall survey of the General Assemblies and the political context between 1900 and 1914, see Combes, *Histoire de la Franc-Maçonnerie*, ii., 287–396, and more particularly on the subjects chosen for study: 333–8, 344–9, 395–6.

discuss at their meetings indicates that there was much less interest in these issues in the small provincial towns than there was in Paris and in the various industrial belts. And, when these rural towns chose topics such as the reform of capitalism or the nationalization of parts of the economy, their conclusions tended to be negative.[23]

In 1908–9, a third of the Grand Orient's lodges opted to discuss syndicalism and the principle of the general strike; but only one in ten reported in favour of the general strike as an acceptable means of pressure.[24] The most popular topics with lodges were those affecting society as a whole, with no particular class interest at stake.[25] Thus in 1910 no fewer than 44 per cent of lodges opted to discuss the subject of illegitimate children, with all but 5 per cent of these favouring the identification of fathers. In the following year, over a third of lodges discussed whether serving soldiers should be given the vote after two years' service, with nearly two-thirds of these responding affirmatively; and in the same year nearly a third of lodges debated the problems of rural depopulation. Other general topics chosen by a sizeable number of lodges at this time (1909–11) were alcoholism (28 per cent), prostitution (20 per cent), the provision of apprenticeships (28 per cent), workers' pensions (21 per cent), and constitutional reform (15 per cent, with only a minority of these wanting significant change).

Socialist-inspired subjects like cooperatives and collectivism appeared on the general assembly's list year after year, but aroused little enthusiasm outside Socialist-dominated lodges. There was wider interest in the broad range of social issues such as public health, housing, industrial accidents, wages, profit-sharing, and working hours. Not surprisingly, the status of civil servants, administrative decentralization, and educational reform attracted the attention of the many lodges where these professions were strongly represented. But, given the government's vigorous campaign against Church influence in education and politics, anticlerical issues featured less often on the list of suggested topics than in the 1890s. Lodges concerned themselves instead with the post-clerical issue of reformulating moral principles on a non-religious basis, a popular topic that was on offer in successive pre-war years and typically came high on the winter programme of one of the Nice lodges in 1911–12. The Nice programme gives a fair idea of what interested a relatively prosperous lodge at this time: the defence of secular schooling; secular and scientific morality; the rural exodus; collectivism; the reform of criminal law; reforming the appointment of magistrates; workers' and peasants' pensions; alcoholism; the enfranchisement of serving soldiers; the exclusion of private-school pupils from military academies; the abolition of martial law in Algeria; reform of the *indigé-*

---

[23] For the sample group of eight, see sources listed in n. 6. By the 1920s some reports from these lodges were favouring the nationalization of the railways and the strengthening of workers' rights against employers.

[24] Combes, *Histoire de la Franc-Maçonnerie*, ii., 334 and 346.

[25] The following percentages are based on information in Combes, *Histoire de la Franc-Maçonnerie*, ii., 346–8.

nat in Algeria; Masonic symbolism; the creation of secular youth clubs; and the eligibility of women for Masonic membership.[26]

What is striking about the post-war subjects for discussion, as compared with the pre-war lists, is the growing importance of international issues. These had previously been relatively rare except in times of war or diplomatic tension, as in 1904–6 and 1911. The Second Moroccan crisis of 1911 found 20 per cent of lodges debating issues of pacifism, but with no clear current of opinion emerging.[27] Henceforward, international topics were a prominent feature, with reconciliation with Germany, the League of Nations, and the peaceful resolution of international differences high on the agenda. At the same time, the *détente* in Church-State relations that resulted from the war created unease in the Grand Orient and partially restored anticlerical topics to the list of options for lodge debate.[28] The Périgueux winter programme for 1927–8 did not belie the Lodge's title, 'Les Amis Persévérants': the relevance of Liberty, Equality, and Fraternity to the modern world; the nationalization of the service industries—which the speaker opposed; the rural exodus; modern youth, castigated as obsessed with sport and indifferent to social problems and things of the mind; and the revision of Masonic ritual.[29]

As in all organizations with high ideals, reality often fell far short of expectation. A member resigning from the Cognac lodge in July 1897 recalled that on joining the lodge he had looked forward 'with a naïve joy to mixing with men with cultivated minds, emancipated from the prejudices of the past'. And what did he find? 'Apathy and indifference, that is the ethos of the place . . . There is no attempt to get down to solid methodical work.'[30]

Charitable activity was a long-standing part of Masonic life; and it was usual for lodges to have a collecting box—usually called 'le Tronc de la Veuve' or 'des pauvres' or 'hospitalier'—into which members were expected to make regular payments. Priority was given to appeals made on behalf of fellow Masons in need and in support of the Masonic orphanage and other Masonic good causes. Given Masonry's traditional emphasis on brotherly concern, it was understandable that responding to these requests should account for the largest category of expenditure, especially since such appeals could not easily address themselves to non-Masonic donors, unlike other deserving causes. To take an example from an earlier decade, the Clermont Ferrand lodge had collected 1,737 francs in 1884, equivalent to just under £3,000 today. It distributed two-fifths of this during the current year: 21 per cent in food for the local poor, 7 per cent to various non-Masonic good causes, 10 per cent to the Masonic orphanage, and 35 per cent to appeals made by other lodges on behalf of needy members.[31] To ensure

[26] Hivert-Messeca, 'La Franc-Maçonnerie en pays Niçois', ii., 293.

[27] Combes, *Histoire de la Franc-Maçonnerie*, ii., 344.

[28] For the sample group of eight lodges, see the sources listed in n. 6. The 1920s also saw a growing interest in the widening of social access to State education.

[29] AGO(RC), 1615.

[30] Olivier Buherne, 'Etude d'une loge maçonnique charentaise: La Loge 'La Liberté' (Orient de Cognac), 1880–1928', Mémoire de maîtrise (Université de Bordeaux III, 1992–93), 43.

[31] Ganière, 'La Loge Maçonnique Les Enfants de Gergovie', 222.

an equitable distribution of these important funds, the general assembly of 1898 decided to channel aid to individual Masons through the Paris headquarters in the Rue Cadet rather than leaving lodges to deal with these issues between themselves. In the case of Nice during the early years of the twentieth century, lodge gifts to Masons in difficulty—'médailles'—were usually of the order of two or three francs, about £5 today; but, since such appeals were usually circulated to a large number of lodges, the cumulative sum that went to the recipient was often quite considerable.[32]

Nor was inter-fraternal help confined to financial aid. In 1929 two unmarried women, who were retired primary-school teachers 'in comfortable circumstances', informed the Chartres lodge that they wished to adopt 'a young orphan girl with the intention of raising her according to *principes laïques*'.[33] The request was eventually passed on by the Rue Cadet to the president of the Masonic orphanage, but the archives do not reveal what came of it.

Charity in a non-Masonic direction was given added stimulus in the late nineteenth century by the competition of Masonry's chief rival, the Catholic Church. Although the Church had been a leading dispenser of charity for nearly two millennia, Leo XIII's encyclical on social justice, *Rerum Novarum* (1891), had encouraged a significant increase in Catholic voluntary social work and donations to poor relief. Indeed, when it came to charity, the Church and the Grand Orient, albeit on the worst of terms, learned quite a lot from each other. Like a number of other lodges, Rennes set up a Comité de Dames patronesses des œuvres de bienfaisance maçonnique, consisting of Masons' wives, sisters, and daughters, who distributed food and fuel to the poor and mended old clothes for their use. Describing its activities in 1905, the head of the lodge—*le vénérable*—stressed the care it took not to offend the religious sentiments of its beneficiaries, particularly women in childbirth, who represented a major sector of its activities. He claimed that the committee was a necessary counterpart to the Catholic-dominated Société de bienfaisance de Rennes, which allegedly helped 'only those women recommended by the parish priest'. The *vénérable* remarked en passant that the lodge itself had just donated cutlery and crockery to the local municipal school canteen, together with an annual 60 francs, whereas 'the clerical municipality provides three to seven-year-old children with worn-out mess tins, and gives an annual subvention of only 50 francs'.[34] A member of the Cognac lodge alleged in 1899 that 'our enemies, the clericals' had not only set up a rival network of soup kitchens to compete with the lodge's own Fourneaux Economiques, but, somewhat implausibly, had paid agents to infiltrate the Masonic kitchen and sprinkle powdered glass in the food that it distributed.[35]

Generosity to non-Masonic causes was especially marked in Nice, perhaps on account of the town's relative prosperity, which assured fund-raising

[32] Hivert-Messeca, 'La Franc-Maçonnerie en pays Niçois', ii., 300–1.
[33] Vénérable to Rue Cadet, 27 October 1929. AGO(RC), 876.
[34] Undated report to Rue Cadet, AGO(RC), 1663.
[35] Buherne, 'Étude d'une loge maçonnique charentaise, 97–8.

events of a handsome response. In the pre-1914 decade, aid given to widows, the unemployed, and the victims of natural disasters, including some in distant countries, amounted to two or three times the amount given to Masonic causes.[36] During the Combes era, the two Grand Orient lodges of Nice were accustomed to have a joint meeting several times a year, which was always followed by a banquet to which members were encouraged to bring wives and friends. An after-dinner speaker would then address them on the aims and virtues of Masonry, or sometimes more pointedly on a topic such as 'the importance of municipal elections' as in May 1904. There would then follow a formal dance.[37] Conviviality also included 'fêtes de bienfaisance', fundraising occasions when the Nice lodges would arrange a public entertainment in the Grand Théâtre, from which the proceeds would be equally divided between the charity accounts of the two lodges and the municipal *bureau de bienfaisance*. In April 1900 such an evening raised 2,160 francs, the rough equivalent of £3,500 today.[38]

Le Piston

Material help to Masons in financial trouble was one thing; furthering the ambitions of those in the clear was another, and an aspect of Masonry that aroused apprehension and criticism outside the brotherhood. Research on this contentious issue is handicapped by the fact that many of the relevant documents at the Grand Orient's headquarters disappeared during the German occupation of 1940–4, notably the file copies of the headquarters' own letters to lodges and to other correspondents for the period after 1900.[39] The historian is consequently reliant on the incoming correspondence from lodges— and from the Grand Orient's political contacts—for evidence of Masonic influence in securing public employment and promotion. By its nature, this incoming material is boxed according to its provenance and date rather than its subject matter—which helps the chronological study of individual lodges but slows down the pursuit of particular themes, especially those involving a variety of lodges. Perhaps for this reason, existing postgraduate work on individual lodges has paid very little attention to the solicitation of favours, other than to make a few isolated comments on its much reduced incidence in the inter-war years.

The year 1900 was the last for which there survive file copies of the Grand Orient's correspondence with lodges and political contacts. In that year the quantity of requests for favours would appear to outnumber the notifications

---

[36] Hivert-Messeca, 'La Franc-Maçonnerie en pays Niçois', ii., 303.
[37] Hivert-Messeca, 'La Franc-Maçonnerie en pays Niçois', ii., 298–9.
[38] Hivert-Messeca, 'La Franc-Maçonnerie en pays Niçois', ii., 300.
[39] When the Germans were driven from France in 1944, they took much of this documentation with them, part of which was subsequently taken by the Russians from Germany to the Soviet Union. After lengthy negotiations with the Masonic authorities and the French government, the Russian government has now repatriated what survives of these archives to the Grand Orient.

of success by some 30 to one.[40] This should not be interpreted as implying a success rate of only one in 30. The coming to power of a ministry of 'Republican concentration' under Waldeck-Rousseau (June 1899—June 1902) had encouraged a substantial increase in requests for government favours in 1900 compared with earlier years;[41] and the modest harvest of successes reaped in 1900 would partially reflect the smaller number of requests processed in 1899, since appointments and promotions took time to come about. Similarly, the large number of requests received in 1900, averaging nearly five a day at their peak, could not necessarily expect an outcome, one way or another, before 1901 or later; and the Grand Orient has no records for these later years other than the incoming mail concerning individual lodges. Moreover, the number of government rejections, notified to the Grand Orient in 1900, was equivalent to only some 6 per cent of the requests received. Once again this partly reflected the fact that requests in 1900 were much more numerous than in previous years, when many of the rejected applications were initially submitted.[42] But it also corresponds to the unquestionable reality that the overwhelming majority of applicants were left in a limbo of uncertainty for considerable periods of time. In many cases this could last indefinitely, since an applicant with the necessary qualifications would not be straightforwardly rejected like an inadequate candidate but could remain on a waiting list for the rest of his career if subsequent applicants were better qualified or had more powerful backers.

While these various factors make it impossible to verify overall success and failure rates for Masonic favour-seeking, the initial impression suggests that the success rate was certainly lower than one in ten, and perhaps as little as one in 20. This impression is also reflected in the correspondence of the sample group of eight lodges, where the success rate seems to have been approximately one in twelve. On the other hand, David Parry's study of the Orléans lodge for the period 1890–1914 shows a considerably higher success rate of about one in eight.[43] This may well reflect the fact that the Orléans lodge was fortunate in having Fernand Rabier as its parliamentary Deputy (1889–1919), then Senator (1920–33), as well as Mayor (1912–14). Rabier was a leading member of the Grand Orient's Conseil de l'Ordre, renowned for his energy and lack of inhibi-

---

[40] Archives du Grand Orient (Bibliothèque Nationale)—hereafter AGO(BN)—FM¹ 523–41.

[41] AGO(BN): for 1898, FM¹ 496–508; for 1899, FM¹ 508–23. The growth of the Rue Cadet's correspondence is reflected in the number of bound volumes of file copies, which overlap December–January for each year: 1898, 13; 1899, 16; 1900, 19. In 1900, 7% of this correspondence concerned the solicitation of government favours. In earlier years the proportion appears to be substantially lower, but a precise overall count for the pre-1900 period was not attempted. For examples of pre-1900 correspondence, see Maurice Larkin, *Religion, Politics, and Preferment since 1890: La Belle Époque and its Legacy* (Cambridge, 1995), 119–27.

[42] It is possible that the eventual outcome of applications was not always reported to the Grand Orient's headquarters; and even when it was it may not necessarily have triggered an acknowledgement from the Grand Orient, with the result that the file copies would show nothing. But it is most unlikely that this possibility would account for more than a small part of this striking disparity between requests and results.

[43] David L. Parry, 'Friends in High Places: the Favours Sought by the Freemasons of Orléans, 1890-1914', *French History*, 12/2 (1998), 195–212.

tions about stretching to the utmost his political credit limit. He was especially motivated in pushing the cause of lodge favour-seekers since his reputation both as 'un bon maçon' and as a member of parliament who could produce the goods for his constituents was doubly at stake. In other respects the pattern of demand in the Orléans lodge was broadly similar to that in the sample group of eight, with applications peaking under the Combes ministry, notably in 1902–3. The post-war period shows scarcely any requests of this nature from the group of eight, thereby confirming occasional remarks contained in several postgraduate dissertations on reduced demand in other lodges.

The regional procedure was that a Mason wanting a public appointment or a promotion would in the first instance make a formal application to the relevant ministry, without mentioning his Masonic membership or the nature of his backing. He would then request the *vénérable* of his lodge to commend it to the Secretary-General of the Grand Orient in the Rue Cadet. The *vénérable* and his colleagues were expected to vet the request carefully before forwarding it; and the Secretary-General would not hesitate to admonish in forthright terms lodges that sent in unsuitable applications.[44]

During the 30 years from 1889 to 1919, the Secretary-General was Narcisse-Amédée Vadecard, a large and intimidating bearded figure. His role and personality were a Masonic counterpart to those of Charles Dumay, the massive Directeur-Général des Cultes, who vetted and dispensed ecclesiastical appointments with a similar ironic awareness of human limitations. Each had an encyclopedic knowledge of the field; and, if Dumay's inclinations of choice were always subject to the overriding whims of the ministers who came and went, at least he had the satisfaction of being a crucial part of a selection procedure that resulted in tangible appointments; whereas Vadecard was in the frustrating business of merely channelling other people's desires and fancies, in the full knowledge that the vast majority would come to nothing. He was a man who spoke his mind, especially if he felt that his interlocutor was putting self-interest before the interests of Masonry and Republican defence. At his funeral in 1923, his successor, apostrophizing Vadecard's departed spirit, described in metaphorical terms how such encounters could end for the imprudent or dishonest petitioner. 'At that point, head lowered, you would rush upon your interlocutor, be he powerful or humble, famous or obscure; you would seize him by the throat and you would not relax your grip until, overpowered and repentant, he admitted his faults and begged for pardon, not of you, but of the institution that he had dishonoured.' At the same time, the orator acknowledged that those who knew Vadecard well recognized that 'your rages were deliberate, your roughness was the transparent and imperfect mask which only half-concealed your unshakeable kindness'.[45] Those who knew him less well did not always have this inner reassurance.

---

[44] For examples and a description of the overall procedure, see Larkin, *Religion, Politics, and Preferment since 1890*, 120–5.

[45] Reported in 'Conseil du 5 Mars 1923', *Bulletin Officiel du Grand Orient de France* (Paris, 1923), 92–3.

With an inflow of requests, rising from two to five per day during the course of 1900, and probably much more by 1903, the Secretary-General was heavily reliant on the lodges' initial scrutiny; and the great majority of requests were fed into the system without further question. Such requests represented a mere 7 per cent of the Secretary-General's postbag, so keeping the incoming piles of paper on the move was inevitably a prime occupation. He would then decide which Masonic Deputy or Senator would be best placed to raise the case with the relevant ministry; and a standard letter would be sent setting out the nature of the request and usually concluding 'The office of the Conseil de l'Ordre would be grateful to you to be so kind as to attempt what is possible to obtain satisfaction for Brother . . .'. Only if there were particular circumstances or a very strong desire to press the case would the letter say more. Very often the chosen Deputy or Senator was one of the 33 members of the Conseil de l'Ordre. In some cases he might represent the locality of the supplicant; more often he was a member of a parliamentary committee that dealt with the concerns of the ministry in question, and was more likely to be heeded by those who made the appointments.[46]

At this stage, the request would find itself competing with all the other requests that members of parliament received from their constituents. The member would then have to decide where his own order of priorities lay. His own re-election might depend on the good will of some non-Masonic figure or interest group in his own constituency, whose protégés might therefore have a stronger claim on his support. This would determine whether his letter to the ministry was, at the lowest level, a mere printed pro forma, with filled-in blanks for the name and desired appointment, concluding 'Je porte un vif intérêt à Monsieur . . .'—but not *vif* enough for a handwritten request; or whether, at the top of the scale of insistence, the conclusion was 'J'exige satisfaction pour Monsieur . . . ', with the vaguely implied threat that an unfavourable outcome might possibly result in the Deputy withholding his vote in some crucial parliamentary division. Like the language of flowers, the format and wording of such a letter enabled the ministry to judge how seriously to take the request and respond accordingly. In most cases the reply would be just sufficient for the Deputy or Senator to be able to reassure the supplicant that he had tried hard on his behalf: it would regretfully state either that there was no suitable post available or that the field of applicants was particularly strong and the supplicant would be borne in mind for future vacancies.[47] The Rue Cadet itself shared to some degree in this complicity of reassurance. It needed to soothe lodges and their applicants, including those it scarcely knew. The archives contain various letters of complaint from disappointed candidates, alleging lack of effort on the Grand Orient's part: accu-

[46] Prominent among these Masonic parliamentary intermediaries were four Radical deputies: Jean Tavé—who handled a quarter of the requests from the sample group of eight lodges—Antonin Lafferre, Louis Massé, and Fernand Rabier. Tavé's success rate on behalf of the sample group was one in eight.

[47] On the overall question of how Deputies, Senators, and Ministers handled such cases, see Larkin, *Religion, Politics, and Preferment since 1890*, 85–7.

sations that irritated and sometimes upset Vadecard, who took his labours very seriously despite the vast quantity of demands that came his way.

The knowledge that members of parliament received calls for support from a wide range of powerful lobbies, many of whom they ignored at their peril, probably explains why Vadecard tended to rely on a surprisingly narrow group of tried-and-true Masonic stalwarts who could be relied on to put Masons high on their list of protégés.

The Pattern of Petitions

An examination of the occupations of petitioners in the sample group of eight lodges reveals that the army headed the list, with a third of the total.[48] In the first decade of the century, there were twelve requests for promotion or transfers and three appeals for other forms of help in military matters. There were also three demands from lodges for the removal or reprimand of belligerently anti-Masonic officers in local garrisons. Paradoxically, the scandal over the Affaire des Fiches in 1904 saw a rise rather than a fall in the number of military requests for Masonic help in securing advancement; it demonstrated to many officers of Republican sympathies just how useful the membership of a lodge could be, especially since the affair had not significantly diminished the number of Masons in government and positions of influence.

Unfortunately for the reputation of the Grand Orient, its one military success for the sample group of eight was also an occasion for deep embarrassment, underlying the risks of relying too simply on the assurances of lodge *vénérables* in the interests of keeping the sausage-machine turning. Lieutenant Lesne of the 49th infantry regiment, stationed in Bayonne, was a member of the local lodge, 'La Zélée'. Claiming to be a continual victim of ultra-Catholic superior officers on account of his Republican sympathies and non-attendance at Mass, he asked the lodge *vénérable* to initiate support for an exchange posting to an African regiment in Algeria. The *vénérable* accordingly wrote to the President of the Grand Orient, describing Lesne as 'un bon maçon, loyal soldat, et un bon républicain', whose behaviour in the lodge had revealed him as 'modeste, travailleur et assidu'. The Rue Cadet had transmitted the request to one of its leading agents in the War Ministry, Captain Mollin, and the transfer duly took place. Shortly afterwards, Lesne wrote to the *vénérable* of the Bayonne lodge asking for further support, this time for a transfer to *les affaires indigènes*, claiming that he was being even more badly treated than in his previous regiment, while the men under his command were 'crapules', totally without loyalty to their superior officers. At this point the *vénérable* might have been wise to be more cautious in renewing his support, especially as Lesne's letter was an extraordinary litany of vituperation against his various

---

[48] The following statistics for the group as a whole are based on letters contained in the archival sources listed in n. 6 above.

past commanders. However, the Masonic recommendation went through the
same channels as before, only to be met this time with a firm refusal from the
War Office, accompanied by a devastating list of Lieutenant Lesne's short-
comings. Not only was he 'peu zélé, indolent', but he had incurred a string of
punishments for various misdemeanours. Whereas his last letter to the
Bayonne *vénérable* had admitted to being punished for allowing his dog to
escape and join him on manoeuvres, it transpired that it was not just a four-
legged friend that had made an unwelcome appearance at a military event. He
was reported to have 'kept a mistress at the officers' dining table for several
days. Nightly uproar'—for which he had been sentenced to 15 days' *arrêt de
rigueur* in addition to shorter periods of incarceration for other offences,
including the infliction of unjust punishment on a subordinate, perhaps one
of the 'crapules' who offended his sense of honour.[49]

Among other petitioners from the sample group of eight, primary school
teachers came next in order of frequency, representing 17 per cent of the
total.[50] Thereafter there came various employees and would-be employees of
the Finance Ministry (14 per cent), Postes et Télégraphes (14 per cent) and
Assistance Publique (14 per cent), notably as *inspecteurs* and *dames visiteuses* in
the field of child care. Child care saw the largest proportion of rapid refusals,
partly because the previous experience of so many applicants was in other
forms of employment, and they seemed insufficiently equipped for the work.
Requests for other categories of public placement were fewer and more thinly
sprinkled over a variety of sectors.

Of the total of requests from the eight lodges for posts, promotion, or transfers to more congenial locales, only one in twelve met with unambiguous success, while one in three resulted in clear rejection. The outcome of the other
two-thirds has left no trace in the archives; in most cases, the supplicant, like
the historian, probably waited vainly for a decision that never came. The same
was true for the handful of Masonic recommendations for the Légion
d'Honneur and Palmes Académiques made in these years: all appear to have
remained in limbo.

Lodge worthies themselves were sometimes in need of fraternal help in high
places. The proprietor of the Hostellerie du Grand Saint Antoyne in Albi was a
prominent member of the local lodge and played a prominent part in initiating Masonic pressure on the War Office to remove from the locality three
officers who had implemented a regimental boycott of a local publisher with
strong Republican sympathies at the time of the Affaire des Fiches. One of the
officers had also harangued the NCOs of his company in unfraternal terms: 'I
know that there are Freemasons among the NCOs of this regiment. If there is
among you one of those creeping informers, and if what goes on in my com-

---

[49] See extensive correspondence, 12 April 1903–18 January 1904, AGO(RC) 621.
[50] This and the following figures are given in percentage terms to facilitate comparisons, but it
should be remembered that the actual numbers of applications from the eight lodges, as reflected in
what survives in the archives, are small: a total of 59, of which 37 specifically concern appointments
and promotions.

pany is reported elsewhere, I will personally teach him a lesson by booting him up the arse!' The War Minister, himself a Mason, simply replied to the President of the Grand Orient that the matter was not worth pursuing.

Having failed to put the regiment in its place, the lodge was acutely embarrassed when the hôtelier who had led the campaign was shortly afterwards faced with prosecution for travelling on an expired railway season ticket that belonged to someone else. The Prefect of the Tarn obligingly intervened to hold up judicial proceedings, while the lodge appealed to the Rue Cadet to make representations to the Prime Minister, Jean Sarrien, who currently held the Justice portfolio, and to Georges Clemenceau, Minister of the Interior and Sarrien's designated heir as prime minister. The lodge insisted that the hôtelier had reimbursed the PLM company for the cost of the fare, but 'because the company is riddled with reactionary agents' it was seeking to give the matter full publicity in the press 'which must be avoided at all costs'. It added: 'Our Brother, Adrien, Deputy of the Tarn, is leaving tonight for Paris to try to get the Minister of Public Works to intervene.' The archives do not reveal whether such energetic fraternal concern received its just reward.[51]

The counterpart to seeking favours from government was protecting and promoting the interest of Masons in the world of private business and family life. Much the greater part of this went on without involving the Rue Cadet, since job-seeking in the private sector mostly took place in the locality of the lodge where the petitioner lived; and Vadecard had no desire to exercise an overview of requests that did not affect the Grand Orient's relations with government. So the bulk of Masonic influence in the private sector left no trace in lodge correspondence with the Rue Cadet. Similarly, lodges would most often confer directly with each other in the case of members seeking situations in a specific locality. On the other hand, a petitioner wishing to investigate a much wider range of opportunities, without preconceptions as to where he wished to go, would frequently ask his lodge to seek the assistance or advice of the Rue Cadet. In 1898 the secretariat expressed its regret at not having the Masonic equivalent of a *Bottin par professions*, listing Masons by occupation as well as location;[52] but the fear that it could potentially offer a weapon to enemies always outweighed the convenience that it would have represented. When it came to matters of marriage, the Rue Cadet was always assiduous in initiating discreet inquiries into the financial and moral suitability of prospective sons-in-law when asked to do so by Masonic *pères de famille*.

The Affaire des Fiches undoubtedly engendered in the Grand Orient a certain wariness towards seeking favours in the public sector. Although there was a brief increase in military applications, requests for civil government favours started to fall rapidly after 1905. In the case of the eight sample lodges, the rate of requests in 1906–8 was only half of that in 1903–5, and a large proportion were military. After 1910, they virtually dried up.

---

[51] See extensive correspondence, 27 September 1905–15 October 1906, AGO(RC), 522; emphasis added.

[52] Bergère to Belisaire lodge, Algiers, 18 June 1898, AGO(BN), FM¹ 497.

This reflected not only the impact of the Affaire des Fiches but also a general feeling both inside and outside Masonry that the clerical and military menace to the Republic was under firm control. A large number of the religious orders had been evicted, a third of Catholic private schools had been closed, and the Church had been disestablished. Consequently the need to 'republicanize' the public services with Masons and other tried-and-true democrats was no longer such a plausible pretext for pushing the applications of ambitious Masons. Moreover, the gradual development of party organization in the early twentieth century slowly reduced the importance of Masonry in national politics, even if the lodges could still act as a very effective bond at local level between different parties that were currently pursuing goals that the Grand Orient favoured. Nevertheless, in March 1914 the Rue Cadet felt obliged to remind the Alençon lodge that 'lodges are not political committees'.[53] Vadecard himself, the one-time organizer of victories, eventually retired from his post in 1919. He claimed that both he and Captain Mollin at the War Office had been made the scapegoats of the Affaire des Fiches, not least by those who were equally responsible for what had happened.[54] He had received hate mail not only from Masonry's enemies but also from many Masons. A member of the Rennes lodge wrote, 'Well then, you should be pretty satisfied with the results of your *fiches*! Freemasonry compromised, perhaps ruined for ever'.[55] Denied the pension he requested on retirement, Vadecard wearily confided to a fellow Mason, 'so many of the other Masons have simply dropped me, like some nonentity they never even knew'.[56]

[53] 11 March 1914, cited in Landemaine, 'Le Grand Orient de France dans l'Orne', 141.
[54] Denis Lefebvre, *André Lebey, intellectuel et franc-maçon sous la Troisième République* (Paris, n.d.), 84–5.
[55] Albert Duvignand to Vadecart, 5 January 1905, AGO(RC) 1663.
[56] Lefebvre, *André Lebey*, 83 and 85.

6

Reform, Conservation, and Adaptation: Sciences-Po, from the Popular Front to the Liberation

PHILIP NORD

E MILE Boutmy founded the Ecole Libre des Sciences Politiques in 1872. France had just experienced a cataclysmic military defeat, and Boutmy blamed the nation's battlefield setbacks on failed political leadership. The Ecole libre, or Sciences Po as it came to be known,[1] was intended to make good that failing, to incubate a new generation of public servants who would over-see France's recovery to greatness.

Sciences Po from the outset enjoyed the patronage of the nation's liberal establishment. Hippolyte Taine delivered the school's inaugural public address, and Albert Sorel, of the Académie Française, organized the first lesson. At Boutmy's death in 1906, stewardship of Sciences Po passed to Anatole Leroy-Beaulieu, who was descended from a distinguished family with old ties to that stalwart of nineteenth-century French liberalism François Guizot.[2] Leroy-Beaulieu himself died in 1912 and was in turn succeeded by Eugène d'Eichthal, son of the Saint-Simonian Gustave d'Eichthal. The d'Eichthal family, Jewish by origin, had long since converted to Christianity. Eugène under-stood the school's mandate much as Boutmy himself had: the nurture of a governing class steeped in '*une culture libérale*', of an elite 'worthy of the name', as he phrased it in a commemorative essay which appeared in *La Revue des deux mondes* in 1927.[3]

Sciences Po's success at its self-appointed mission was nothing short of remarkable. In the inter-war years, the school, a private institution, charged annual fees in the range of 850–1,500 francs. The substantial costs of

---

[1] It appears that in the 1930s the school was known as *les Sciences Po* but that this usage dropped out of currency in subsequent years. On this point as on numerous others, many thanks to Claire Andrieu who was kind enough to read a draft version of the present chapter.

[2] Gérard Vincent, *Sciences Po, Histoire d'une réussite* (Paris, 1987), 53, 59–60.

[3] Fondation Nationale des Sciences Politiques, Archives d'histoire contemporaine, ELSP, 1 SP 14, *dossier 6, tiré à part*, d'Eichthal (December 1927), 13, 17. All archival references below are drawn from the ELSP series at the Archives d'histoire contemporaine.

enrolment restricted the student body to a well-to-do few, never more than
2,000–2,500 all told, recruited in the main from the Parisian upper-middle
classes. The school itself was located in a bourgeois neighbourhood, on the rue
Saint-Guillaume in the Seventh Arrondissement, which furnished it a sizeable
portion of its pupils.

Sciences Po awarded students a diploma after two years of general education. A significant minority continued their schooling, taking a third year of
more focused tuition aimed at preparing them to sit the admissions exams set
by each of the State's Grands Corps. In these tests, Sciences Po students swept
aside all competition. Between 1901 and 1935, the four major Grands Corps—
the Inspection des Finances, the Conseil d'Etat, the Cour des Comptes, and the
Corps Diplomatique—admitted a total of 740 new recruits. Of these, 685 or
92.5 per cent had studied at Sciences Po. To be sure, not all were Sciences Po
diploma-holders. A number had taken part in the school's third-year exam
preparation programme, but no more than that. The general point remains,
however: the ranks of *la haute fonction publique*, of France's senior civil service,
were dominated in the inter-war decades by men who had been trained at
Sciences Po.

Liberal, elitist, private, Parisian, bourgeois: is it any wonder that a school of
such description—a school, moreover, so implicated in the exercise of state
power—attracted the critical attentions of France's Left? In 1937, Jean Zay,
Minister of National Education in Léon Blum's first Popular Front government—a post he would occupy until 1939—formulated a bill which provided
for creation of a state-run Ecole d'Administration. Zay made no secret of the
fact that the new school was intended to supplant Sciences Po as the principal, even exclusive, training-ground of future *hauts fonctionnaires*. A version of
the Zay proposal made it through the Chamber of Deputies but was never
voted on by the Senate. At the Liberation in February 1945, Communist representative Georges Cogniot returned to the charge, proposing to the
Consultative Assembly that the State expropriate Sciences Po and turn its
assets over to a new public institution, the Left's much dreamed of Ecole
d'Administration. De Gaulle's provisional government stepped in at this junc-
ture with a scheme of its own: to wrap Sciences Po into the university system
and hence within the State's regulatory purview, yet to allow it to continue to
exist. The Gaullist scheme at the same time envisaged the creation of a gradu-
ate-level Ecole nationale d'administration (ENA), its student body selected by
exam from a range of undergraduate institutions, Sciences Po included; its
graduates with privileged access to the ranks of *la haute fonction publique*. This
was the arrangement in the end settled on.

Sciences Po found itself twice menaced by the Left and twice rescued. It is
right to tell the story of the school's survival as one of elite persistence.[4] The
creation of ENA was a major institutional innovation, but how much differ-

[4] This position is argued with cogency by Christophe Charle, 'Savoir durer: la nationalisation de
l'Ecole libre des sciences politiques, 1936/1945', *Actes de la Recherche en sciences sociales*, no. 86–87
(March 1991), 99–105.

ence did it make to the life of Sciences Po? The school changed its name from the Ecole libre des sciences politiques to the Institut d'études politiques (IEP). Yet it continued to recruit the bulk of its students from the well-heeled bourgeoisie of the Paris region. And it maintained, as ever, its grip on the formation of the nation's governing elite. Under the new post-war dispensation, the senior civil service was obliged to draft its members from the ranks of ENA graduates, and there were two routes into ENA: the first via an exam aimed at recent undergraduates, the second via an exam reserved for low-level civil servants who had accumulated a certain minimal work experience. Never more than a minority made it in by the latter path. The royal road to ENA was the undergraduate exam, and here IEP diploma-holders outperformed their competitors. Between 1952 and 1969, about half the students who took the exam, but more than three-quarters of those who passed it—77.5 per cent—were Sciences Po alumni.[5] It is still fair to ask, though, whether the IEP that took shape in the aftermath of the war was the same institution as the old Ecole libre. The answer to that question is 'no'. From the mid-1930s, the Sciences Po administration, led first by René Seydoux and then by his youngest brother Roger—there was a middle brother François—inaugurated a programme of reforms, in part generated from within, in part formulated in response to external pressures. The school on its own initiative sought closer ties to the University; it attempted to craft a more rigorous and up-to-date curriculum; and it modulated its long-standing commitment to the liberal pieties of laissez-faire and the night-watchman state.

This is not to say that the Ecole libre remade itself into a school for technocrats, but it did open itself to reforming currents. This conditioned how it responded to the Zay bill, to the war years, and to de Gaulle's ENA project. The Zay proposal did not die in the Senate, as often supposed. Indeed, it came close to realization, not in the form of a legislative enactment but as a 'convention' worked out between the Ecole libre, which had sought such negotiations, and the Ministry of Education. The war brought the discussions, then so near to successful conclusion, to a halt. During the war itself, school authorities first accommodated themselves to Vichy, making room on its teaching staff for a cohort of young experts, many with links to the Pétainist regime. In 1942–3, however, the Ecole redirected its allegiances from Vichy to the Resistance and, in particular, to the constitutional and technocratic reformers gathered in François de Menthon's Comité général d'études. At the time of the Liberation, then, the Ecole found itself in alignment with the technocratic current in the Gaullist camp. From such a vantage point, it was in a position to inflect the Gaullist project of state reform, adjusting to its own satisfaction Sciences Po's fit into the new structures of elite formation. The IEP that emerged from the process was still elitist in orientation, but it now had a patina of policy-making professionalism and scientific seriousness that assured it a secure future in the expert-guided France of the post-war era. From this angle,

---

[5] Jean-Luc Bodiguel, *Les Anciens Elèves de l'ENA* (Paris, 1978), 30.

Sciences Po's survival is not just a tale of a elite persistence but of elite self-transformation as well.

The 1930s: Culture and Tradition

There is no overstating how stuffy and conventional the Ecole libre became in the decades after the First World War. An aging d'Eichthal still presided over the school's fortunes. He was assisted by a Conseil d'administration populated by a dozen or so establishment types. Maréchal Lyautey joined the Conseil in 1928, died six years later, and was succeeded by Maréchal Pétain. Jules Cambon, a dean of France's ambassadorial corps and long-time board member, passed on in 1935. The marquis de Vogüé, president of the Suez Canal Company and of the Société des agriculteurs, was enlisted to replace him. Typical in many respects of the depression-era Science Po board member was Henri de Peyerimhoff: a Conseiller d'Etat, a respected business magnate who headed the Comité des houillères, and, in politics, a backer of the Fédération républicaine, mainstay of the 'classic Right'.[6]

In matters of economic doctrine, the school had a reputation as a 'bastion of liberal capitalism'.[7] The label was not undeserved. Sciences Po's professor of political economy, Clément Colson, was described by an unsympathetic former student as the 'Doctor Pangloss of economics' who radiated a laissez-faire optimism even in the midst of the Depression.[8] When Colson stepped down, his chair was taken over by a disciple, Jacques Rueff, an up-and-coming Inspecteur des Finances who was just as 'ferociously liberal' as his mentor.[9]

But the school's 'liberalism' consisted in more than laissez-faire partisanship. André Siegfried, far and away the Ecole libre's star teacher, is a case in point. Siegfried's course on economic geography was a staple of the Sciences Po curriculum, drawing more students than the school's lecture halls could accommodate, until a new building was constructed in the mid-1930s. What was it about Siegfried that appealed? As an intellect, he was a complicated figure. Siegfried was an acute observer, open to foreign cultures, who knew and wrote about the Anglo-American world with an unmatched familiarity. At the same time, he fretted about the new civilization rising across the Atlantic, the United States, whose mania for machines and production he found threatening to Europe's greatest achievement, the autonomous and critical-minded individual. Siegfried's reputation as a scholar rested on a massive study, the *Tableau politique de la France de l'Ouest* (1913), which pioneered the field of electoral geography. Through an analysis over time of voting behaviour and

    [6] 1 SP 30, dossier 4, Procès-verbal des séances du Conseil d'Administration (hereinafter Procès-verbal), 23 November 1934 and 21 November 1935; Vincent, *Sciences Po*, 192; Gérard Brun, *Technocrates et technocratie en France, 1918–1945* (Paris, 1985), 214.
    [7] Daniel Guérin, *Autobiographie de jeunesse* (Paris, 1972), 123.
    [8] Raymond Abellio, *Ma Dernière Mémoire*, ii. (Paris, 1975), 100. Colson taught at the Ecole des Ponts-et-Chaussées as well, which is where Abellio encountered him.
    [9] Claude Des Portes, *L'Atmosphère des Sciences Po* (Paris, 1935), 48.

its social determinants—property regime, pattern of settlement, and so forth—
the *Tableau* demonstrated the deep-rooted and enduring connections between
region and political opinion. But in later work Siegfried succumbed to the
temptation to present regions, and not just regions but entire peoples and civ-
ilizations, as bearers of a distinctive soul, fixed in character. Such a point of
view lent itself to reductionist, at times negative, stereotyping which targeted
Jews and non-whites. Such tensions were characteristic of a particular strain of
French liberalism, enlightened and critical-minded but anxious about the fate
of an old-world Europe beleaguered by American enterprise and peoples of
swarthy complexion.[10]

Siegfried's students may or may not have shared such ambivalences, but
they very much esteemed the man. He was remembered as '*un esprit latin*', an
elegant figure who lectured from notes, lorgnette in hand.[11] It was a manner
he wanted in some measure to pass on to his pupils. He explained to students
preparing Sciences Po's exam in economic geography what he wanted them to
learn: 'a general economic culture', how to situate that culture in the ensemble of knowledge, and how to express themselves in 'a civilized vocabulary'. 'It
is essential', he concluded, 'that such habits of mind become as though second nature'.[12]

In matters of *tenue*, however, Siegfried's students did not have that much to
learn. Uneven entrance requirements—not all entrants had earned their bac—
and hefty fees resulted in a student body that was select in background and
tastes. Sciences Po had an acknowledged snob appeal. It was a good place to
see and be seen, to share a cigarette with the right sort, and talk over the lat-
est issue of the *Nouvelle revue française*. The atmosphere was cliquish, social
relations patterned by pre-existing ties inherited from childhood days or the
collège privé. Provincials new to Paris had a hard time breaking in. Not least,
this was a well-dressed world. Chroniclers of the era argue about the students'
precise fashion preferences, but all insist that a certain formality, '*une parfaite
correction*', reigned, the young ladies decked out in hats—the school had begun
to admit women in 1919—the gentlemen in ties and suits of 'the most perfect
cut'.[13]

Students understood that a Sciences Po education was in part about style.
They valued the diploma as a 'brevet of culture'.[14] Graduates who sought entry
into the senior civil service took preparatory courses in their third year to gear
up for the Grands Corps exams. These courses, nicknamed *grandes écuries*, were
run by career functionaries on loan from their respective Corps. But the most

---

[10] André Siegfried, *Tableau politique de la France de l'Ouest* (Paris, 1913/1995); André Siegfried, *Les Etats-Unis d'aujourd'hui* (Paris, 1927); Pierre Birnbaum, *'La France aux Français,' Histoire des haines nationalistes* (Paris, 1993), Ch. 5.

[11] Des Portes, *L'Atmosphère*, 53–4; Vincent, *Sciences Po*, 358–9.

[12] 4 SI 2, dossier 3, 'Conférence de révision de géographie économique'.

[13] 1 SP 30, dossier 3, Procès-verbal, 27 February 1932; 1 SP 15, dossier 3, Présentation de l'Ecole des Sciences Politiques (1949), testimony of Jacques Belin, promotion 1923. See also Vincent, *Sciences Po*, 346, 349; Des Portes, *L'Atmosphère*, 74–80.

[14] Des Portes, *L'Atmosphère*, 78, 88.

intensive cramming was conducted in smaller, informal groups known as *petites écuries*. A 'little stable' consisted of a dozen or so self-selected students who met under the tutelage of a junior civil servant not many years past the exam himself. Here, aspiring bureaucrats learned the tricks of the ordeal that awaited them, 'the *spirit* and the *style* of the test' as one put it.[15]

The test itself was an intimidating affair. The Inspection des finances exam, for example, consisted of a written portion followed by an oral; the writtens were conducted in the dining hall of the Ministry of Finance itself; and, until 1937, the dress code obliged all aspirants to wear formal attire throughout. No wonder the inspectorate was renowned for its esprit de corps, its sense of itself as 'an academy, a tradition, a force'.[16] No wonder too that types who lacked the proper grooming had such difficulty gaining entry. Rueff was the sole Jew who belonged to the Corps, and his was altogether an exceptional case, related as he was by marriage to the Maréchal Pétain.[17]

The Beginnings of a Reform Agenda

The Ecole libre in the 1930s had begun to run down, mildewed in its leadership, lax in its standards, overcommitted to an outdated economic liberalism. As the decade wore on, however, the situation began to change, and the change started at the top. In 1929, the Conseil d'administration appointed René Seydoux to the post of secretary-general, elevating him in effect to d'Eichthal's second-in-command. D'Eichthal died in early 1936 and was replaced by a veteran civil servant, Paul Tirard, who shared authority with an altogether new body, the Comité de direction. Seydoux left the Ecole not long thereafter to take up a job with Schlumberger—he was the son-in-law of Maurice Schlumberger. René's youngest brother Roger became the school's secretary-general in November 1936. Tirard was a man old enough to contemplate retirement, but René and Roger Seydoux represented a generation just starting out, with promising careers ahead that would in fact play out well into the post-Second World War era.[18]

The new team began to plot out a reform agenda, however modest in scope at first. To accommodate an expanded student body, a new building was erected, equipped with a spacious entry hall and an amphitheatre, named after Boutmy, on the ground floor. The facility was completed in October 1934.

[15] Jacques Georges-Picot, *Souvenirs d'une longue carrière, de la rue de Rivoli à la Compagnie de Suez, 1920–1971* (Paris, 1993), 69–71; Des Portes, *L'Atmosphère*, 91.
[16] François Piétri as cited in André Ferrat, *La République à refaire*, 3rd edn (Paris, 1945), 143. See also Olivier Feiertag, 'Wilfrid Baumgartner, les finances de l'Etat et l'économie de la Nation, 1902–1978', doctoral thesis (Paris: Université de Paris X-Nanterre, 1996), i.: 44; François Bloch-Lainé, *Profession: fonctionnaire. Entretiens avec Françoise Carrière* (Paris, 1976), 43.
[17] François Bloch-Lainé and Claude Gruson, *Hauts-fonctionnaires sous l'Occupation* (Paris, 1996), 83–4.
[18] Vincent, *Sciences Po*, 96, 105; 1 SP 30, dossier 4, Procès-verbal, 6 March 1936 and 12 November 1936. The Seydoux brothers' father, Jacques, had been a career foreign officer and, in that capacity, had worked with Tirard, France's high commissioner in the Rhineland throughout the 1920s.

Additional funds were allocated in 1935 to fit out the basement as a *salle des sports*.[19] At the same time, the school moved to tighten its admissions requirements. The principal concern was how to handle applicants lacking the bac. It was decided that they be asked to sit a special entrance examination, and the elder Seydoux contemplated excluding non-bacs from the applicant pool altogether.[20]

The profile of the faculty began to change as well. Raoul Dautry, a polytechnicien and ex-government official who had managed the state railway service, was hired in 1937 to teach a course on public transport. That same year, the name of an up-and-coming scholar of foreign relations, Pierre Renouvin, appeared on the Sciences Po masthead for the first time. Elie Halévy, the school's much respected lecturer on the history of socialism, died in 1938. He was replaced by Maxime Leroy, who had as thorough an understanding of the French trade-union movement as any senior academic. There was movement in the junior ranks as well. In 1932, Sciences Po offered courses on public finance taught by Wilfrid Baumgartner and on private finance taught by Henry Davezac, both assistant professors. A third junior colleague, Auguste Detoeuf, headed a team-taught *conférence d'application* on problems of industrial and commercial organization. Three years later, Detoeuf had occasion to present a series of lectures at Sciences Po based on his unpublished book titled 'Death of Liberalism'.[21]

Three observations may be made apropos this roster of appointments. It is clear, first, that the school was determined to establish the bona fides of its academic credentials. Renouvin and Leroy were scholars of weight who went on to publish work still in use today. Second, the appointments indicate a willingness on the school's part to update its curriculum: to temper its traditional liberalism and take on the now-pressing problems of economic organization and management. In the process—and this is the third point—the school implicated itself in a wider movement of technocratic reflection. Davezac and Detoeuf, both major figures in the electrical industry, were two of the five founders of the *Nouveaux Cahiers*. The journal, which first appeared in 1937, was a gathering place for independent-minded businessmen and self-appointed experts willing to entertain non-traditional solutions to France's economic problems. Baumgartner was a regular member—along with his father-in-law Ernest Mercier—of the *Nouveaux Cahiers* luncheon club. In February 1939, the periodical sponsored a debate on 'The Reform of the State' which rehearsed the standard litany of technocratic complaint: France's executive was too weak and its parliamentary assemblies too strong. Davezac and

[19] 1 SP 30, dossier 4, Procès-verbal, 26 June 1935; 1 SP 15, dossier 3, clipping from *L'Illustration*, 19 January 1935.
[20] 1 SP 53, dossier 2, sdr f, 'Confidentiel no. 6, Observations faites depuis 7 ans, janvier 1936'. The dating and title of the document indicate that René Seydoux was the author. 1 SP 52bis, dossier 3, sdr a, clipping from *La Flèche*, 29 August 1936.
[21] 1 SP 30, dossier 4, Procès-verbal, 11 October 1937 and 24 June 1938; 1 SP 15, dossier 3, pamphlet, *Nos Grandes Ecoles* (1932), 114–16; François Perthuis, *Auguste Detoeuf (1883–1947), l'ingénieur de l'impossible paix* (Paris, 1990), 27.

Detoeuf took part, as did a young newcomer to the Sciences Po faculty, Jacques Chapsal.[22]

The Challenge of the Popular Front

Sciences Po in the 1930s had begun to take the first, hesitant steps to chart a new course. Such was the situation when the storm of the Popular Front hit. The school was at first put on the defensive but then gathered its forces, confounding its critics. Yet the matter did not end there. Zay's proposed civil-service act prompted the Ecole libre seriously to rethink its position vis-à-vis the State. The school extended an offer of collaboration to Zay. It conceded that elite education, for so long the near-exclusive prerogative of Sciences Po, might be managed in partnership, the State and the school working out a division of labour. Sciences Po pursued the path of collaboration down to the war's outbreak and beyond. Zay's tenure as minister of education opened with a threat. Sciences Po parried the stroke, turning a moment of danger into one of institutional opportunity.

A state-run school of public administration had functioned for a few brief months in 1848–9 under the auspices of the Second Republic.[23] In 1936, Blum's Minister of National Education Jean Zay set about reviving the project. On 1 August he drafted a general proposal, calling for creation of an Ecole d'Administration. Zay's *exposé des motifs* bristled with critical broadsides aimed at Sciences Po. Modern administration, the minister explained, required a technical expertise not taught at any existing educational institution. More serious still, he went on, the current, private system of civil service training was altogether unrepublican. It gave advantage to 'a narrow, privileged class whose interests might not coincide with those of the nation as a whole'.[24] Zay was more explicit on the point in his memoirs, accusing Sciences Po graduates of a lack of 'democratic zeal'.[25]

Zay established an inter-ministerial committee to work out the details of his proposal. The bill that resulted provided for a multi-layered training process. Students fresh out of the lycée would enter first a State-run Ecole d'administration. Ecole graduates were expected to work for a period of years in low-ranking civil service posts. They might then compete, alongside graduates from other state schools with similar work experience, for admission to a Centre des Hautes Etudes Administratives, also State-run. The top finishers at

---

[22] Jacques Barnaud, André Isambert, and Guillaume de Tarde round out the list of *Nouveaux Cahiers* founders. Perthuis, *Auguste Detoeuf*, 43; Brun, *Technocrates*, 45; Bernard Serampuy [François Goguel], 'La Réforme de l'Etat', *Nouveaux Cahiers*, 1 February 1939, 14–15.
[23] Vincent Wright, 'L'Ecole Nationale d'Administration de 1848–1849: un échec révélateur' (1976).
[24] Guy Thuillier, 'Les projets d'Ecole d'administration de 1936 à 1939', *La Revue Administrative*, 177 (1977), 240.
[25] Jean Zay, *Souvenirs et solitudes* (Paris, 1945), 315.

the Centre would be guaranteed positions in the senior civil service. They would not have to pass a qualifying exam to earn the honour.[26] There was no place in the scheme for a private institution like Sciences Po. Zay's inter-ministerial committee included a young Conseiller d'Etat, Michel Debré, not a half-dozen years out of Sciences Po himself. Debré was an ardent booster of a State-sponsored Ecole d'administration, but Zay's anti-Sciences Po bias exasperated him. The school had rendered signal services to the State, yet Zay and his associates seemed motivated by a reckless 'will to destruction'.[27] Debré's reading of the situation was not off the mark. The Zay bill was submitted to the Chamber of Deputies' Commission de l'Enseignement in February 1937, and Zay appeared before the body on the 24th to argue its merits. Gustave Doussain, the Commission's *rapporteur*, later recounted the tenor of the minister's remarks to Sciences Po officials. Zay, it seems, did not mince words, putting it to the commission that 'the Ecole des Sciences Politiques is called on to disappear'.[28]

Sciences Po was not idle in the face of such threats. It elaborated a two-pronged strategy. On the one hand, it set about armouring itself against Left criticism, doing what lay in its power to deflect or delay the Popular Front legislative assault. On the other hand, it attempted to short-circuit the parliamentary process altogether, approaching Zay directly in an effort to work out a negotiated settlement. Neither strategy met with much success at first.

There was a public relations dimension to Sciences Po's defensive tactics. In a show of social conscience, the school established the so-called Fonds Boutmy in May 1937, a scholarship fund earmarked for the support of a few score meritorious students.[29] Sciences Po also made overtures to the University in an effort to demonstrate its openness to public institutions. The Dean of the Paris Law Faculty Sébastien Charléty was invited to chair the Comité de perfectionnement, the school's curriculum committee. Charléty signed on in October, and he was a strategic choice on two counts. First, Sciences Po and the law faculty recruited from the same pool of students. The typical Sciences Po man, in fact, doubled as law student, taking courses at the law faculty in preparation for a *licence* even as he pursued a diploma at Sciences Po. Second, Charléty had useful connections outside the university world. France's newspaper of record, *Le Temps*, would prove itself a valued champion of Sciences Po's interests. Charléty joined the paper's administrative board in 1938, reinforcing the school's ties to the establishment press.[30]

[26] Thuillier, 'Projets d'Ecole d'administration', 242–3.

[27] Michel Debré, *Trois Républiques pour une France. Mémoires* (Paris, 1984), 366.

[28] 1 SP 52bis, dossier 2, sdr b, 'Visite de MM. Lebée et Roger Seydoux à M. Doussain, Député de L'Alliance Démocratique,' 4 March 1937.

[29] 1 SP 30, Procès-verbal, 5 May 1937. The first scholarships, it appears, were not awarded until 1938. See Marie-Christine Kessler, *La Politique de la haute fonction publique* (Paris, 1978), 25.

[30] Charle has apposite comments to make apropos the school's strategic turn in 1937. Charle, 'Savoir durer', 100. See also 1 SP 52bis, dossier 3, sdr b, newspaper clipping, 'L'Ecole d'administration,' *Le Temps*, 24 November 1937; and sdr c, newspaper clipping, 'M. Sébastien Charléty, employé intéressé de la féodalité de l'Argent', *La Lumière*, 20 May 1938.

The school spruced up its image, and it lobbied parliament hard. School authorities sought an interview with Doussain, who insisted that he had no intention of causing harm to Sciences Po. Indeed, Doussain went on, a solid minority in the Chamber, perhaps even a majority, felt much as he did, , and Zay had been made aware of the fact.[31] In November 1937, however, Doussain made no reference to any of these discussions when he reported on the bill in its first reading. The school's partisans did not abandon hope. Roger Seydoux composed a circular letter to sympathetic deputies, trying to line up support. A trio of loyalists were identified: Anatole de Monzie, Jean Mistler, and François Piétri, who exhorted Zay not to move ahead with undue speed. Additional backing came from the administrative departments of the Ministries of Finance and Foreign Affairs.[32] Such pressures resulted in a minor amendment to the Zay bill and slowed its parliamentary progress, but little more.

Sciences Po's efforts to strike up a dialogue with Zay were even less fruitful. Right from the outset, Sciences Po authorities gave thought to conciliatory strategies. A note, drafted in mid-August 1936, in all likelihood by Seydoux himself, contemplated conceding civil service exam preparation to the new Centre des Hautes Etudes. What Sciences Po wanted in return was an equal chance to compete against Zay's Ecole d'administration for access to the Centre. The note, in fact, sketched out a quid pro quo. Sciences Po would abandon its third, exam preparation year, provided the State reciprocated, recognizing the Sciences Po diploma as equivalent to a University degree and per mitting Sciences Po graduates to vie for admission to the projected Centre des Hautes Etudes.[33] For the moment, though, such thoughts were confined to internal memoranda.

Tirard mentioned none of this when he went to see Zay for a first time on 14 January 1937. The meeting was perfunctory and not at all encouraging. As the pressure on Sciences Po stepped up in subsequent months, the school administration steeled itself to offer a deal. On 15 November, just as the Doussain commission readied its final report, Tirard wrote to Zay proposing a 'solution de collaboration'. Ten days later, a delegation was dispatched, consisting of Tirard, Pétain, and Alexandre Celier, a senior figure in the banking world, to put the school's case to the minister. The meeting took place on 25 November.

Tirard underlined that Sciences Po was trying to mend its ways, to enable all worthy students to attend thanks to a generous scholarship programme. The school, he continued, had no objection to the proposed Centre des Hautes

[31] 1 SP 52bis, dossier 2, sdr b, letter from Seydoux to Hippolyte Ducos, Président, Commission de l'Enseignement, Chambre des Députés, 23 February 1937; and, in the same file, 'Visite de MM Lebée et Roger Seydoux à M. Doussain', 4 March 1937.
[32] 1 SP 52bis, dossier 2, sdr b, circular letter from Seydoux to various deputies, November 1937 and letter from François [Piétri] to Mon Cher Ami [Seydoux], 27 November 1937; dossier 1, sdr b, copy of letter from [René Seydoux] to Roger Seydoux, c/o Schlumberger, Houston, Texas, 16 December 1937.
[33] 1 SP 52, dossier 4, sdr a, typed note, 14 August 1936; see also 1 SP 53, dossier 2, sdr f, 'Note de Quatre Pages sur l'Ecole', 1 February 1937.

Etudes Administratives. All it asked was that Sciences Po students be afforded the same opportunity as graduates of State-run institutions to win admission to the Centre. Zay listened to Tirard's arguments and gave indications of flexibility. A few days later, he informed an unidentified member of parliament that he was willing to work with Tirard *et al.* And then contact was interrupted.[34]

So matters stood when the Zay bill came to a vote in January 1938. Sciences Po had presented the minister a choice: pursue the legislative path in the face of determined, although not insurmountable, opposition or come to the bargaining table and negotiate. For the moment, Zay stuck with the parliamentary option. The Chamber took up the Zay bill on 27 January. The debate was bruising for Sciences Po partisans. Communist and socialist deputies lambasted the school as anti-democratic, a tool of 'powerful interests', which bred in its students a 'caste mentality' and perpetuated 'the possessing classes' stranglehold on the administrative machine'. The system stood in urgent need of purification, and the Zay bill would cause the first, cleansing winds, a '*souffle républicain*' as Georges Cogniot put it, to blow.[35] The Popular Front majority in Parliament was still intact, and the Chamber ended up voting the bill by a lopsided margin, 422 to 137.

For the moment, Zay appeared in control. Yet in the year that followed he would perform an about-face, abandoning the legislative path in favour of Sciences Po's offer of collaboration. There were three factors which might account for the change of course. The obstacles the Zay bill encountered in the Chamber, even if minor, helped to soften the minister's stance. In March 1938, Zay was ready to engage in a third round of talks with Sciences Po officials. He had a 'cordial' meeting with Seydoux and Tirard on the 2nd. There was discussion of a signed 'convention' between the State and Sciences Po, and Zay invited Seydoux and Tirard to spell out what terms might be acceptable. A memorandum was forwarded to the minister on 21 March. The document invited the State to nominate representatives to the school's scholarship committee. In exchange, the State was summoned to fund 100 additional scholarships and to accept Sciences Po representation on the governing board of the new Centre des Hautes Etudes. In June, Zay met again with Seydoux and Tirard. He acknowledged receipt of the memorandum, signalled that the State wanted a say not just in scholarship selection but in staff appointments as well, and promised to formulate a counter-proposal. Months passed, however, and the promised document never materialized.[36]

All the while, the amended Zay bill ground forward on its parliamentary way. The sceptical reception it encountered in the Senate commission must

[34] 1 SP 52bis, dossier 1, sdr b, letter from Tirard to Zay, 15 November 1937; 'Memento', 25 November 1937; 1 SP 52, dossier 3, sdr a, typed note, 21 December 1937.

[35] 1 SP 53, dossier 1, *Journal officiel, Chambre des Députés*, séance du 27 janvier 1938, remarks by Cogniot and Pierre Vaillandet, 112–13, 115–16. The Left press was even more unrestrained in its attacks.

[36] 1 SP 30, Procès-verbal, 8 March 1938; 1 SP 52, dossier 4, sdr c, 'Réponse à M. Zay le 21 mars 1938', marked confidential; 1 SP 52bis, dossier 1, sdr c, 'Entretien', 8 June 1938.

have added to Zay's worries about the project's ultimate fate. Sciences Po officials appeared at least twice before the Senate's Commission de l'Enseignement, once on 16 February 1938 and again on 16 June. The school pressed two arguments to the body. Sciences Po was not hostile to reform: quite the contrary, borne out by its evident willingness to bargain with Zay. The school indeed made a point of sharing with the Senators the details of its dealings with the Ministry of Education. From Sciences Po's point of view, the outcome of the February meeting was heartening. 'There is no doubt as to the opposition of Senate moderates', summed up a school document. The June results were even better. Senators Pierre Jossot and Aimé Berthod, the president and *rapporteur* of the Commission, communicated to Tirard their shared preference for an 'agreement' and claimed that 'an important part of the Commission' was of the same view.[37] Just in case the Zay bill ever worked its way out of commission, Sciences Po officials busied themselves in late 1938, identifying and courting 'sympathizers' in the Senate at large.[38]

An impending Senate fight must have given Zay pause, even more so in the closing months of 1938 when the national political climate had taken such a decisive turn to the Right. In April, the Popular Front majority fell apart, giving way to a centrist coalition led by the Radical Edouard Daladier. The Munich crisis of September 1938 effected a sea change in national priorities. War preparedness, not social reform, now became the central business of government. The point was hammered home in November when Daladier, in the name of boosting defence production, gutted the 40-hour working week law, once the centrepiece of the Popular Front's reform agenda.

The new mood suited Sciences Po. In the face of Left critiques, it had always billed itself a national asset, 'part of the intellectual patrimony of France',[39] and now it had a chance to demonstrate just how serious its patriotic credentials were. Not long after Munich, school officials began discussing the creation of a chair in national defence. By January 1939, the chair had been scaled back to a course, but the project had lost none of its patriotic resonance, for the 'faculty member' placed in charge was none other than Philippe Pétain, the hero of Verdun. Pétain delivered the inaugural lecture on 3 February 1939 before an audience of 800.[40]

Looming opposition in the Senate and the rightward turn in the political climate persuaded Zay to explore the path of negotiation. In January 1939, he

---

[37] For the February meeting, see: 1 SP 52bis, dossier 2, sdr c, letter from Tirard, Romieu, and Siegfried to M. le Président (of the Senate Commission), 7 February 1938; 'L'Ecole d'Administration au Sénat', 17 February 1938. For the June meeting, see dossier 2, sdr c, 'Aide-mémoire pour la séance du 16 juin' and dossier 1, sdr c, letter from Tirard to Daniel Serruys, 29 October 1938.

[38] 1 SP 52bis, dossier 1, sdr c, letter from Maxime Leroy, November 1938; letter from François Goguel to Seydoux, 13 December 1938; dossier 2, sdr a, 'Sénateurs ayant été inscrits à l'Ecole'.

[39] 1 SP 52bis, dossier 1, sdr c, letter from Tirard to Serruys, 29 October 1938.

[40] Pétain's speech made clear that the course had a double purpose: to stiffen the nation's resolve in the face of foreign enemies and, on the home front, 'to block the advance of subversive doctrines and sowers of disorder'. 1 SP 62, dossier 1, 'Cours sur la Défense Nationale'. See also 1 SP 52bis, dossier 1, sdr c., letter from Tirard to Serruys, 29 October 1938; 1 SP 30, dossier 4, Procès-verbal, 23 January 1939.

invited Sciences Po representatives to attend talks. The Ecole's Conseil d'Administration considered how to respond. An accord, it was concluded, was well worth the effort, even at the cost of yielding a measure of school sovereignty. Creation of an Ecole d'Administration might even be conceded, but only on terms that respected Sciences Po's fundamental interests.[41]

In the event, the school got what it wanted. It helped no doubt that Sciences Po had important and well-placed friends. From February to July 1939, Seydoux and Tirard—on one occasion joined by Siegfried—entered into a series of conversations with Zay, Zay's chef de cabinet Marcel Abraham, and the Directeur de l'Enseignement Supérieur Théodore Rosset. The school got a welcome leg up from an outside source. At the very start of the talks, Debré weighed in, penning a note to Abraham—shared in confidence with Seydoux—which laid out the terms of a possible convention, in rough outline quite close to the terms that Sciences Po itself wanted. The school, moreover, was able to count on a phalanx of sympathetic and influential bystanders whom Seydoux took pains to keep abreast of the negotiations: Berthod, Jacques Bardoux, Senator from the Puy-de-Dome, and Emile Mireaux, editor of Le Temps. Its troops lined up and facing a now-weakened interlocutor, Sciences Po was in a position to bargain from strength.[42]

The deal worked out was all that Sciences Po could have hoped for. To be sure, the school gave ground on certain issues. From early on, it had been willing to allow the State a role in the selection of scholarship students. In an April 1939 communication to Zay, it went further, envisaging the creation of a new organ, a Commission des Etudes, slated to include three state representatives, of whom two would be from the University. The Commission would have the authority to review certain senior faculty appointments, which in turn would be vetted by the minister of education. Even in curricular matters, the school was prepared to show flexibility, however limited in scope, inviting the State to help establish exam juries for certain categories of students.[43]

On the major point, however, Sciences Po got its way. The Zay bill had imagined a two-storeyed structure of civil-service education: at the top a Centre des Hautes Etudes Administratives, at the bottom an Ecole d'Administration. At the outset, Sciences Po had hoped to insert itself on the ground floor as a rival to the Ecole d'administration. Over the course of the 1939 negotiations, however, it got a good deal more, shunting aside the Ecole d'administration altogether and substituting itself as the feeder institution for the new Centre.[44] Zay, it seems, would get his two-tiered system but now reconfigured: the Centre at the top and at the bottom a Sciences Po linked to the State but still independent.

[41] 1 SP 52bis, dossier 1, sdr c, letter from Zay to Tirard, 16 January 1939 and letter from Tirard to Zay, 23 January 1939; 1 SP 30, dossier 4, Procès-verbal, 23 January 1939.

[42] 1 SP 52bis, dossier 1, sdr c, letter from Debré to Seydoux, 13 February 1939; letters from Seydoux to Berthod and Mireaux, 7 February 1939; letter from Seydoux to Bardoux, 24 February 1939.

[43] 1 SP 52, dossier 4, sdr d, 'Exposé des discussions au Ministère de l'Education Nationale, 10 February 1939'; 1 SP 30, dossier 4, 'Projet de procès-verbal, 5 avril 1939'.

[44] 1 SP 52bis, dossier 1, sdr c, letter from Seydoux to Abraham, 5 August 1939.

The convention, however, was never signed, although for its part Sciences Po felt the deal had been all but struck.[45] This was, moreover, a deal the school did not want to slip away. Zay left office in September 1939 as war mobilization got under way to be replaced by Yvon Delbos. Tirard had a meeting with the new minister in December in the hope of keeping the convention talks alive but to no avail.[46]

Still, Sciences Po had come a long way. A private institution par excellence, it now had official ties to the university. And, in its dealings with Zay, the school had made manifest a willingness to accept yet closer ties to the State. Sciences Po's liberal anti-statism, in matters of both curriculum and institutional practice, was slowly becoming a thing of the past.

Vichy and the Occupation

The catastrophe of 1940 presented Sciences Po with a series of dilemmas: how to manage the Germans; how to deal with Vichy; how to regulate its internal affairs in a setting of war and occupation. In the first instance, Sciences Po made every effort to establish '*relations correctes*'.[47] In the second, a more intimate and symbiotic relationship developed, Vichy recruiting into its service a raft of Sciences Po faculty, Sciences Po in return inviting Vichy officials to teach and to speak. And in the third? Reforms of a professionalizing cast remained as before the war at the top of the school's agenda, although now pursued with a Pétainist inflection. In 1942–3, however, Sciences Po replotted its course, keeping its distance from Vichy. It swung into the Resistance, yet did so in a way that reinforced its increasingly technocratic orientation.

Sciences Po was closed down by the Germans on 26 July 1940. Seydoux telephoned and then met with Karl Epting of the German embassy to work out conditions for the school's reopening. Before the war, Epting had worked at the German Institute in Paris, and Seydoux and he had become acquainted at the time. Vichy authorities were also approached. A letter inviting Pétain's intercession was drafted although not sent. Sciences Po officials did meet with General de La Laurencie, Vichy's representative in the occupied zone, and with the new Minister of National Education Emile Mireaux, an old friend, to discover what they knew of German intentions toward the school.[48]

These communications made two points clear. The Occupation authorities were unhappy about the anti-German bias of elements of the school's curriculum. Nor did they care for certain—unidentified—instructors on its teaching staff. The school promised to be responsive on the first issue. It had on its

[45] School authorities, looking back from a post-war perspective, felt that an accord had been 'very close'. 1 SP 66, dossier 4, sdr a, 'Relations de l'Ecole et de l'Etat, février 1945.'
[46] 1 SP 30, dossier 4, Procès-verbal, 20 December 1939.
[47] 1 SP 30, dossier 4, Procès-verbal, 15 November 1940.
[48] 1 SP 66, dossier 1, 'Entretien téléphonique de M. Seydoux avec M. Epting', 29 August 1940; 'Note pour Monsieur le Maréchal Pétain', 23 August [1940], 'non-envoyée'; 1 SP 30, dossier 4, Procès-verbal, 15 November 1940.

own initiative dropped Pétain's course on national defence. Jacques Benoist-Méchin, a well-known Germanophile and right-winger, was asked to lecture on aspects of contemporary German history. It does not appear, however, that he ever actually took up the invitation. A course *was* offered, though, on 'German unity', taught by a less controversial figure, René Dupuis.[49]

On the question of personnel, the Sciences Po administration is supposed to have given assurances of its intention to discharge 'undesirable' faculty. Rueff, who was Jewish, did leave the school's service. The Gestapo made plain that it would not allow him to teach in Paris, obliging the veteran economist to quit the rue Saint-Guillaume. He headed south in search of a safe haven. Sciences Po's exact role in this parting of the ways, however, is not clear. Rueff's case apart, the school overall seems to have found ways to spare itself hard choices. Debré, of Jewish descent, was just the sort of colleague the Germans would have targeted. With André Ségalat, he ran an *écurie* under Sciences Po auspices to gear up candidates for the Conseil d'Etat exam. In 1940, however, the *écurie* was convened, not on school premises in Paris but at Clermont-Ferrand in the unoccupied zone, out of German reach. The school also opened a branch campus in Lyon. Chapsal—now Seydoux's secretary-general and right-hand man—Dautry, Davezac and Siegfried all relocated there in the early years of the Occupation. Baumgartner, who was reputed to be *persona non grata* with German authorities, divided his time between the capital, which was dangerous for him, and the safer terrain of the Lyon campus.[50]

To placate Occupation authorities, the school pledged itself to good behaviour, adjusting its curriculum and reshuffling its teaching staff. Such exertions proved sufficient, and Sciences Po was allowed to reopen in the late fall of 1940. Unlike the Germans, the Vichy regime was disposed in Sciences Po's favour, as well it might have been. Pétain still sat on the Conseil d'administration. Vichy's first two ministers of justice, Raphael Alibert and Joseph Barthélemy, were high-ranking Sciences Po faculty. Alibert had taught at the school in the 1930s. Barthélemy, when called to Vichy's service in 1941, was still an active member of the teaching staff and had to take leave of absence to assume his government duties. The school sent faculty to work at Vichy: Davezac and Detoeuf held down the two top posts on the Comité d'organization for the electrical industry.[51] And the school welcomed to its halls Vichy officials, both current and former, as speakers and colleagues. In January 1942, Jean Bichelonne, soon to be Minister of Industrial Production, delivered an address to the school on 'L'Etat actuel de l'organisation économique française'. Two months later, it was the turn of Jean Borotra, a senior official at the education ministry, who discoursed on the pedagogical virtues of sport.

---

[49] 1 SP 66, dossier 1, 'Visite à M. Mireaux, Ministre de l'Education Nationale', 4 September 1940; 1 SP 62, dossier 3, 'Bulletin 1940–41'.

[50] Philippe Burrin, *La France à l'heure allemande, 1940–1944* (Paris, 1995), 313; 1 SP 30, dossier 4, Procès-verbal, 15 November 1940; Feiertag, 'Wilfrid Baumgartner', i: 248; 1 SP 67, dossier 1, sdr a, 'Note sur la Proposition de Résolution no. 332'.

[51] 1 SP 62, dossier 3, 'Bulletin 1940-1941'; 1 SP 67, dossier 1, sdr a, 'Note sur la Proposition de Résolution no. 322'.

Then in July 1942, Sciences Po added a new member to its faculty, Jean-Jacques Chevallier, remembered today as Emmanuel Mounier's mentor at the Grenoble Faculty of Law and star speaker at the Vichy-sponsored Ecole des cadres at Uriage.[52]

Once the school's status vis-à-vis the Germans had been sorted out and Vichy's benevolent patronage assured, Sciences Po turned to its own affairs. Before 1940 was finished, the school had subjected its governing structures to an overhaul. Tirard was named president, in effect kicked upstairs to a more honorific post. The old Comité de direction was at the same time dismantled, leaving Seydoux alone in charge of the day-to-day running of the school.[53] The sitting Conseil d'administration also underwent a shake-up. A trio of long-standing members, among them Vogüé, were dropped. It was proposed to fill the seats made vacant with five replacements: Baumgartner; Georges Pichat, Vice-President of the Conseil d'Etat; Pierre-Eugène Fournier, President of the national railway company, the SNCF; Georges Ripert, Dean of the Paris Law School; and the Rector of the University of Paris, who attended a council meeting or two but then stopped coming. Baumgartner was deported by the Nazis in 1943. Three of the other new members, however, were destined to play important roles at Vichy: Fournier as director of the agency which oversaw the management of 'Aryanized' Jewish property in the southern zone, Pichat as President of the Secours National, and Ripert as Vichy Minister of Education. The purpose of such reshuffling was twofold: to clean out older, non-participating members and to substitute for them a more dynamic, less business-oriented team with ties to the university and state administration.[54]

Sciences Po, indeed, was keen to formalize its links to the Sorbonne. In the early months of 1941, a convention was concluded between representatives from the two institutions and ratified by ministerial decree in June. Under the terms of the agreement, the Dean of the Faculty of Law and the Dean of the Faculty of Letters were accorded ex-officio status on Sciences Po's governing board. The Rector of the university himself was not expected to serve, but the convention did confer on him authority to nominate delegates to Sciences Po organs dealing with curriculum oversight and examinations. The Sorbonne in return granted Sciences Po the right to affix the university's name to its diplomas.[55]

[52] 1 SP 62, dossier 3, 'Bulletin 1941-1942'; 1 SP 30, dossier 4, Procès-verbal, 17 July 1942. Borotra's brother had attended Sciences Po. Borotra himself was a graduate of the Ecole Polytechnique, and a star tennis player who helped bring several Davis Cup championships to France. As for Chevallier, he was an accomplished cyclist who discoursed to Uriage students on the virtues of 'a virile order' which placed a premium on physical courage and risk-taking.
[53] 1 SP 30, dossier 4, Procès-verbal, 26 December 1940. Seydoux's growing responsibilities were acknowledged in a series of title changes. He had been promoted to sous-directeur in 1938 and then in 1942 was made directeur, plain and simple. See 1 SP 30, dossier 4, Procès-verbal, 12 November 1942.
[54] 1 SP 66, dossier 1, 'Note sur la réorganisation de l'Ecole, sd [1940?]; dossier 4, Procès-verbal, 15 November and 26 December 1940.
[55] 1 SP 30, dossier 4, Procès-verbal, 17 July 1941; 1 SP 66, dossier 4, sdr a, 'Note sur les principales transformations apportées à l'Ecole des Sciences Politiques depuis 1940', November-December 1943; dossier 6, sdr b, 'Convention entre l'Université de Paris et l'Ecole Libre des Sciences Politiques,' nd.

Tougher standards had been an ongoing preoccupation ever since Seydoux joined the school administration in 1936. Two changes were effected in this domain during the Occupation years, both with Vichy overtones. No sooner had Sciences Po reopened in 1940 than the administration imposed a physical education requirement. The object? To boost student morale and habits of discipline. Borotra, who paid a visit to the school in March 1942, inspected the athletic programme and came away much impressed by what he had seen.[56] In 1941, a second new requirement was imposed. All incoming male students, with certain exceptions, were now expected to possess the bac. As for women applicants, bac-holders or not, they were obliged to take a special entrance exam, which proved no mere formality as more than half who sat it actually failed. The school did not want 'young ladies . . . who come here for reasons of snobbery'. The Vichy regime, moreover, had placed restrictions on female employment in the State administration. Sciences Po officials saw no point in training women for jobs that did not exist.[57]

Last of all, the school continued to rework its curriculum, the better to reflect what it understood to be present economic realities. A course titled 'Economie libérale et économie dirigée' was added to the school's curriculum in 1940, taught by a new professor recruited from the Faculty of Law, Gaëtan Pirou. Alfred Sauvy, France's premier economic statistician, joined the Sciences Po faculty the same year. Louis Chevalier came on board as a junior professor in 1941 and François Bloch-Lainé at the same rank in 1942—Bloch-Lainé had Jewish ancestry on his father's side but was raised a Catholic. The former would distinguish himself in later years as a crack demographer and historian, the latter as an architect of France's economic and financial reconstruction in the post-war era.[58]

Sciences Po had begun to temper its erstwhile economic liberalism in favour of more directive approaches, and in the process it drew closer to technocratic circles, both independent and Vichy-based. The defeat of 1940 had dispersed the *Nouveaux Cahiers* group. Several NC veterans, however—Detoeuf, Sauvy, and a young Raymond Barre—were determined to carry on their pre-war debates and soon reconvened as the Comité d'études pour la France. Seydoux prevailed on André Isambert, a *Nouveaux Cahiers* founder who had resettled in the south, to launch a Lyon-based think tank, the Comité d'études et d'informations, which included Siegfried among its number as well as Georges Villiers, mayor of Lyon and in the post-Liberation years president of Confédération générale du patronat français. In 1942, Bichelonne, now Minister of Industrial Production, charged a colleague with putting together an economic advisory board. The Conseil supérieur de l'Economie industrielle et commerciale, as it came to be known, was staffed by 'the elite of the *monde technicien*', including a trio of Sciences Po faculty: Davezac, Detoeuf, and

[56] 1 SP 30, dossier 4, Procès-verbal, 15 November 1940 and 10 March 1942; 1 SP 62, dossier 2, text of Borotra conference, 23 March 1942; dossier 3, 'Bulletin 1941–1942'.

[57] Vincent, *Sciences Po*, 313; 1 SP 30, dossier 4, Procès-verbal, 19 March and 4 November 1941.

[58] 1 SP 30, dossier 4, Procès-verbal, 15 November 1940, 4 November 1941, and 12 November 1942.

Pirou.[59] Wherever the nation's economic future was being planned, there Sciences Po faculty made their presence felt.

The Turn Towards the Resistance

But however close the ties between Sciences Po and Vichy, the connection did not prove unbreakable. Take the cases of Siegfried and Seydoux. Siegfried in the first years of the Occupation continued to print articles in the pro-Vichy *Le Temps*. Yet he was also known to dabble in activities of a more oppositional nature. Paul Bastid, a Radical deputy and no friend of Vichy, ran a discussion group which met in Lyon. The old republican Left set the tone, but Bastid's circle included a smattering of more centrist types, the Christian Democrat Champetier de Ribes, for example, and, from time to time, Siegfried himself. Siegfried was active as well in a second gathering, animated by Jean de Traz, which began as a discussion group but which by 1942 had begun to relay intelligence to the Free French in London.[60]

Seydoux's trajectory was similar. In the first years after the armistice, he appears to have kept up contact with Epting. But to Sciences Po undergraduates like Jean Lacouture, Seydoux made no secret of his dislike for Vichy. The Allied invasion of French North Africa in 1942 prompted the Germans to occupy the southern zone. Jean Chauvel, a senior official at the Ministry of Foreign Affairs, resigned his post, taking with him a number of young colleagues, including Seydoux's brother François. Chauvel intended to create a veritable shadow ministry that would chart out French foreign policy for a post-Vichy future. He approached Seydoux for assistance; Seydoux made Sciences Po premises available for planning meetings.[61]

The year 1942, and the German occupation of the southern zone in particular, appears to have been a turning point. Pétain's name still figured on the roster of Sciences Po's Conseil d'administration in July. By year's end, it had been dropped.[62] In 1943–4, the school's involvement in oppositional activity deepened. Barthélemy, having stepped down as Minister of Justice in the spring of 1943, sought to resume his teaching responsibilities at the rue Saint-Guillaume. The school refused to take him back. More consequential still were the school's efforts to preserve its students from the labour draft imposed by Vichy in February 1943. The Service du Travail Obligatoire conscripted military-age youth for labour service in Germany, and Sciences Po wanted no part of the operation, attempting to dissuade students from answering the call,

    [59] Brun, *Technocrates*, 56–7, 178.
    [60] Birnbaum, '*La France aux français*', 160; Diane de Bellescize, *Les Neuf Sages de la Résistance, Le Comité Général d'Etudes dans la clandestinité* (Paris, 1979), 33; Richard Kuisel, *Ernest Mercier, French Technocrat* (Berkeley and Los Angeles, 1967), 150.
    [61] Birnbaum, '*La France aux français*', 165–6; Jean Lacouture, 'La Mort de Roger Seydoux', *Le Monde*, 12 July 1985; Jean Chauvel, *Commentaire, de Vienne à Alger, 1938–1944*, i. (Paris, 1971), 302, 320–2). Many thanks to Patrick Weil for this reference.
    [62] 1 SP 30, dossier 4, Procès-verbal, 17 July 1942.

falsifying records, and providing cover to help out those who did not want to go. Such foot-dragging earned Seydoux a frigid interview with the Minister of National Education Abel Bonnard in May. Bonnard would not shake Seydoux's hand, treating him to a mixture of reproach and imprecation about Sciences Po's general political posture.[63]

Seydoux, however, was undeterred by Bonnard's threats. Over the course of 1943—the precise timing is uncertain—Seydoux struck up a collaboration with Philippe Viannay, a student turned journalist who managed a major resistance newspaper, *La Défense de la France*. Viannay furnished Sciences Po students and personnel with forged documents; Seydoux supplied Viannay information and contacts in the civil-service and business worlds.[64]

The Resistance in fact was coming to recognize in Seydoux a useful go-between in its dealings with France's administrative and economic elites. In October 1943, Admiral Gabriel Auphan, one-time Vichy Minister of the Navy, got in touch with Seydoux in the hope of cooking up a rapprochement with the Resistance. Seydoux hosted a pair of meetings between Auphan and Resistance representatives Michel Debré and Pierre-Henri Teitgen, but the negotiations came to nothing. Seydoux's interventions were more effective in the case of Jean Prouvost. The defeat of 1940 had found Prouvost, a textile magnate and press lord, in the post of Minister of Information, a position which he continued to occupy for a brief period under Vichy. He was publisher as well of a much-read newspaper, *Paris-Soir*, which did not cease publication until 1943, well after the German occupation of the southern zone. As the Liberation neared, Prouvost grew anxious about the ambiguities of his wartime record and approached Seydoux, who then called in Debré. Prouvost ended making a substantial cash contribution to the Resistance, getting in return a receipt which helped to bail him out at the Liberation.[65] The Seydoux-Debré connection was activated yet once more in the spring of 1944. Debré, now a senior Resistance official, was charged with putting in place the administrative apparatus of a post-Vichy France. Future prefects were designated, and Debré then met with them clandestinely in batches, region by region. The Gestapo almost broke up one such gathering, the delegates taking refuge on Seydoux's invitation in a room at Sciences Po.[66] It is not clear how much Vichy authorities knew of such goings-on, but they knew enough to conclude that Sciences Po harboured 'Gaullist and Anglo-Saxon sympathies' and that Seydoux himself was the man most to blame for this sorry state of affairs.[67]

[63] 1 SP 66, dossier 4, sdr a, 'Note sur l'attitude politique de l'Ecole depuis 1940'. The document, although not dated, was written after the Liberation. See also 1 SP 67, dossier 1, sdr a, 'Note sur la Proposition de Résolution no. 322' and 1 SP 66, dossier Affaire Bonnard, 'Entretien de M. Abel Bonnard et de M. Roger Seydoux', 18 May 1943.

[64] Philippe Viannay, *Du Bon Usage de la France, Résistance, journalisme, glénans* (Paris, 1988), 39, 85.

[65] The receipt worked its wonders at the Liberation, keeping the otherwise compromised Prouvost out of trouble. In 1949, he went on to found post-war France's most successful photo-journal *Paris-Match*.

[66] Lacouture, 'La Mort de Roger Seydoux'; Debré, *Trois Républiques*, 218–19; 221–3, 248–50.

[67] Thuillier, 'Projets d'Ecole d'administration', 252; 1 SP 66, dossier 4, sdr a, 'Note sur l'attitude politique de l'Ecole depuis 1940'.

The Resistance Embraced

The school had been Pétainist at the armistice; in 1942–3, it turned to the Resistance. In certain respects, though, Sciences Po's underlying loyalties remained unchanged throughout. Pétain was looked to as a figure of authority who in partnership with the competent elites might yet set the nation's house in order. The Maréchal, however, had not been up to the task. Nothing made that fact more patent than German occupation of the southern zone in 1942, crushing testimony to Pétain's inability to preserve even a semblance of national sovereignty. But might not de Gaulle succeed where Pétain had failed? Yes, a Gaullist triumph would bring parliamentary institutions back to France, but, it was to be hoped, a representative order now disciplined as it had not been in the chaotic 1930s: by the authority of a Gaullist executive, by the expertise of an administrative elite purified and hardened in the fires of the Resistance.

These were indeed the cherished themes of the Resistance currents with which Science Po aligned itself. Viannay's *Défense de la France* may be cited as an example. The first issue of the paper appeared in August 1941. It was anti-German but not anti-Vichy, persuaded that the Maréchal was engaged in a double game, preserving France's assets against the Occupier in preparation for a future call to arms. Viannay in the end gave up on Pétain but not until the spring of 1942; and even then he did not definitively opt for de Gaulle until the following year. The new Gaullist commitment, though, was sincere and deepened when a member of the General's own family, his niece Geneviève, joined the group in 1943.[68] The paper wanted a democratic future for France, but the democracy it dreamed of was 'authoritarian and progressive'. The nation stood in dire need of forceful executive action. What substitute indeed was there for the 'living' authority of the true leader who imposed himself by force of will? The Resistance had cast up such a leader, and it had cast up 'a new elite' as well, '*des hommes purs, des hommes efficaces*' who delighted in risk-taking and shunned the careful materialism of the petty-minded.[69]

Viannay's paper was among the most successful of the Resistance press, with a circulation in the hundreds of thousands. It was also one of the few to survive the Liberation in good health. In November 1944, the paper rechristened itself *France-Soir* and brought in new management. Aristide Blank, a 24-year-old fresh from Sciences Po, had worked alongside Viannay from early on. It was Blank who persuaded the veteran newspaper man Pierre Lazareff to join

[68] Claude Bellanger et al., *Histoire générale de la presse française*, iv. (Paris, 1975), 115; Henri Michel, *Les Courants de pensée de la Résistance* (Paris, 1962), 448; Viannay, *Du Bon Usage*, 50, 82.
[69] Robert Tennaille (Robert Salmon), 'Vers la Révolution', *Cahiers de Défense de la France*, March 1944, and Ph. Viannay, 'Le Combat pour une cité libre', *Cahiers de Défense de la France*, January 1944. Both articles are reproduced in Henri Michel and Boris Mirkine-Goutzévich, *Les Idées politiques et sociales de la Résistance* (Paris, 1954), 155–8, 209–11. See also *Défense de la France*, 20 May 1943, as cited in Brun, *Technocrates*, 246.

the staff. Lazareff had worked at Provoust's mass-circulation *Paris-Soir* in the 1930s and then spent the war years in the United States, familiarizing himself with 'American ways'. This was the experience he brought to bear as *France-Soir*'s new secretary general, and the paper went on to claim a place for itself as the best-selling evening daily of the post-war era.[70] In that capacity, it would have occasion to intervene on Sciences Po's behalf.

Viannay, however, was not Sciences Po's sole Resistance contact. The names of Paul Bastid, Michel Debré, and Pierre-Henri Teitgen have been cited. All three belonged to a Resistance organ, known first as the Comité des experts when it got started in July 1942 and then, from 1943, as the Comité général d'études (CGE). The Comité ultimately counted nine members in all: Jacques Charpentier, René Courtin, René Lacoste, Pierre Lefaucheux, François de Menthon, and Alexandre Parodi, in addition to the three already mentioned. Almost from the outset, the CGE enjoyed direct and regular contacts with London. There was every reason for de Gaulle's entourage to take a close interest in the Comité's work, for the CGE had assigned itself a most ambitious agenda: mapping out France's administrative and constitutional future for the post-war era.[71]

The CGE's privileged status, none too modest programme, and self-styled expertise earned it the suspicion of other Resistance groups. Pascal Copeau, a senior figure in the domestic Resistance, dubbed the CGE 'the synarchy of Catholic professionals', a dig at Menthon and Teitgen who were both Christian Democrats and professors of law.[72] Copeau was right enough about the professional profile of the CGE, which was composed almost in its entirety of jurists and civil servants. Lefaucheux, an engineer and future manager of the State-run Renault vehicle company, was the exception. But Copeau's characterization of the CGE's political orientation was less accurate. The Comité, to be sure, was not left-wing. No Communist belonged and just a single Socialist, Lacoste. But the CGE's two Christian Democrats were outnumbered by men, like Debré, of moderate if independent-minded republican background. The Comité was no Catholic conspiracy but, rather, a technocratic think tank, mainstream and reform-minded, which occupied itself devising programmes and policies to remake France's political institutions.[73]

Refaire la France was, indeed, the title of a slim volume Debré co-authored with fellow civil servant Emmanuel Monick during the war years. The text, written under the Occupation, appeared first in clandestine edition.[74] Its pages resonated with the themes which informed Debré's work for the CGE, which in fact patterned his entire political career. France's destiny was democratic,

[70] Viannay, *Du Bon Usage*, 183–4; Olivier Wieviorka, *Une Certaine Idée de la Résistance, Défense de la France 1940–1949* (Paris, 1995), 361–2.

[71] Bellescize, *Les Neuf Sages, passim*.

[72] Copeau might have been in a position to know. He was the son of a reborn Catholic, the great inter-war dramaturge Jacques Copeau. Cited in Bellescize, *Les Neuf Sages*, 258.

[73] Bellescize, *Les Neuf Sages*, 256, 258.

[74] It was published in regular edition in 1945, although even then the authors were listed as Jacquier-Bruère, the hyphenated code names of Debré and Monick.

the book made clear, but what France required above all was 'a virile and disciplined form of democracy'.[75] In all domains, private and public, new elites were called for, willing to think beyond individual interest, willing to cooperate. But in no domain was the need more pressing than that of public administration. *Refaire la France* urged creation of a State-run school of administration, and in this it is not hard to detect Debré's influence at work. The same may be said of the text's ringing endorsement of a strong executive. France craved a genuine '*Chef d'Etat*', a head of state who did not answer to representative bodies, who was, indeed, in a position to rein Parliament in with the threat of dissolution.[76] Debré used the expression 'republican monarch' to describe what he had in mind. The phrase first appeared in a CGE report, but a report he wrote with the text of *Refaire la France* lying at his elbow.[77]

At the Liberation

Sciences Po had little reason to fear the Liberation. To be sure, it might be held accountable for certain 'failings' in the early years of the Occupation, but it had in 1943 and 1944 more than made amends, compiling a modest but nonetheless solid record of Resistance. And what friends it had made in the Resistance: journalists and experts who were poised to occupy strategic positions of command in the post-war order. Such men had institutional renovation on their minds, but so too did Sciences Po authorities, and the two visions of reform were not incongruous. The disciplined democracy dreamed of by a Viannay or Debré left ample room for an elite institution like Sciences Po. And did Seydoux, so intent on reorganizing the school along professional, technical-minded lines, want anything different?[78] This compatibility of views assured that there would be a remaking of Sciences Po at the Liberation, but a remaking undertaken in accordance with, not against, the school's wishes. Such a happy prospect, however, almost came unstuck. Viannay's paper outsold its competitors; CGE veterans—Lacoste, Menthon, Parodi, Teitgen—graduated to ministerial ranks in de Gaulle's provisional government. But there was more to the post-war scene than *France-Soir* and the Gaullist executive. A Left, re-energized by its Resistance struggles, the Parti Communiste Français (PCF) in the lead, had its own plans for France's future. Had the PCF had its way, Sciences Po would have been abolished altogether.

There was then a confrontation at the Liberation between the reform-minded in France's establishment on the one hand and the Resistance Left on the other, the fate of Sciences Po hanging in the balance. In the event, the confrontation turned out one-sided. The Left was routed, and Sciences Po got a

[75] Jacquier-Bruère, *Refaire la France, l'effort d'une génération* (Paris, 1945), 111.
[76] Jacquier-Bruère, *Refaire la France*, 122.   [77] Debré, *Trois Républiques*, 213.
[78] Viannay, it should be added, was evolving away from a youthful conservatism toward the independent Left.

reform it could live with. The Liberation might be thought a time when a Left ascendant had the resources, both moral and political, to recast France's destiny. The fate of Sciences Po points to a different conclusion. Reform there was, but it was conservative reform, effected by deal-making not confrontation.

Already in the autumn of 1944, Sciences Po officials knew a fundamental change was in the offing. Interested parties in the provisional government and Conseil d'Etat had begun to explore schemes for creation of a State-run Ecole Nationale d'Administration. The gist of these discussions was communicated to Sciences Po administrators at a meeting in September.[79] Sciences Po readied itself to respond. Seydoux was absent at the time. He had enlisted in the Leclerc Division at the Liberation and so was away at the front for much of the fall. Chapsal, however, stepped into the breach, meeting with government officials, sending round to them all the documentation pertaining to the Seydoux-Zay negotiations of 1939.[80] More important still, the school remodelled its leadership team yet again. In the first week of January 1945, Tirard submitted his letter of resignation, pleading ill health. Siegfried was persuaded to step in as Sciences Po president. The old Conseil d'administration took the occasion to resign en masse. Siegfried then proceeded to appoint his own men to the board, a mix of old faces and new. Baumgartner, now back from deportation, was kept on, joined by newcomers like Georges Duhamel, secretary of the Académie française.[81] Gone were the discredited Pétainists Pichat and Ripert.

Duhamel was a kindred spirit to Siegfried in many ways. Duhamel's institution, the Académie française, was packed with Vichy sympathizers and would-be collaborationists, but he had manoeuvred with surprising success to preserve it from compromising actions. Siegfried might well have imagined that he had played a not dissimilar role at Sciences Po. The two men, moreover, were both exponents of a nineteenth-century liberalism that vaunted the rationality and refinements of Western civilization, but worried about twentieth-century threats to that achievement: fascism, communism, and American-style mass society.[82]

Without fanfare, Sciences Po had begun to clean house, burnishing its Resistance credentials and in the process casting itself a standard bearer of Western values. Indeed, the French delegation dispatched to San Francisco in

---

[79] 1 SP 66, dossier 7, sdr a, 'Entretien du 22 septembre 1944 avec MM Joxe, Hoffherr, Ségalat, Chatenet'.

[80] 1 SP 66, dossier 4, sdr c., letter to Louis Joxe, 24 November 1944. The author is not identified, but it was in all likelihood Chapsal; see also, 1 SP 67, dossier 1, sdr a, letter from Siegfried to Cogniot, 23 February 1945.

[81] 1 SP 31, dossier 1, Procès-verbal, 2 January and 6 February 1945, morning and afternoon sessions.

[82] On Duhamel at the Académie française, see Gisèle Sapiro, *La Guerre des écrivains, 1940–1953* (Paris, 1999), Ch. 4. Duhamel, like Siegfried, penned a critique of United States: *Scènes de la vie future* (Paris, 1930). As for Western civilization, Siegfried laid out his views on the matter in a series of lectures at the Collège de France in 1944, the first delivered in December. 4 SI 11, dossier 2, 'Cours sur *la Civilisation Occidentale, Collège de France*'. Siegfried engineered Duhamel's appointment to the Sciences Po board; Siegfried was in turn elected a member of the Académie française.

the spring of 1945 to attend the founding conference of the United Nations included the school's two most senior administrators, Seydoux and Siegfried. Hard decisions about Sciences Po's future loomed, but the school might well have felt it had prepared itself to meet them.

The Communist Challenge

The trouble was not long in coming. In late February 1945, Sciences Po's old nemesis, the Communist Georges Cogniot, submitted a resolution to the Provisional Consultative Assembly. The text ticked off the usual list of anti-Sciences Po accusations: the school catered to the few; its curriculum did not correspond to modern realities; it was a tool of 'the global trusts'. But a new and explosive charge had been added to the standard brief. Sciences Po, the resolution read, had 'supplied the commanding officers [cadres supérieurs] of treason and of collaboration with the enemy'. Under the circumstances, the people's representatives had a right to confiscate the school's assets and turn them over to a new institution that would be 'national and democratic'.[83] Cogniot's, moreover, was not a solitary voice. All proposals relating to civil-service reform had to be examined by the Provisional Assembly's Commission sur la Réforme de l'Etat, which counted among its membership Pierre Cot, a former Young Turk of the Radical Party and Léon Blum's Minister of Aviation. Cot, a man of decided leftist views, was known to have it in for Sciences Po. So too did Assembly member André Philip, a socialist with an unimpeachable Resistance record, who harboured a particular distrust of la haute fonction publique. He penned a preface, published in 1945, which in its animus against the civil-service regime en place echoed Cogniot's indictment almost charge for charge, and in the following year he floated a proposal—which came to nothing—to abolish the Inspectorate of Finances outright.[84] From a certain angle, it might well have appeared that the old Popular Front coalition, drawing fresh vitality from its Resistance exploits, was re-forming, this time to finish off the job begun in 1936: the demolition of Sciences Po.

Sciences Po, however, was not without allies. By its own count, eight of the 13 members of de Gaulle's provisional government were Sciences Po graduates.[85] The General himself was not about to allow the obstreperous Cogniot to steal a march on him in matters of State. De Gaulle wanted a government counter-stroke and turned to Michel Debré, who was brought on board in the first week in April. Debré, of course, had been thinking over just such a project for years, so it did not take him long to conduct the necessary negotiations and come up with a proposal. He sketched a two-tiered system, his own variation on Zay's old scheme. At the top, a State-run ENA would prime mature students

---

[83] 1 SP 67, dossier 1, sdr a, 'No. 322, Proposition de Résolution', 2, 4, 6, 11, 15.
[84] See Philip's preface to Ferrat's La République; Feiertag, 'Wilfrid Baumgartner', i.: 259.
[85] 1 SP 66, dossier 4, sdr a, 'Note sur l'attitude politique de l'Ecole depuis 1940', n.d. The document does not identify the eight ministers in question.

to sit a single Grands Corps exam; at the bottom, a small number of political science institutes—the most important situated in Paris—would offer a more general education but also prepare interested undergraduates for the ENA admissions test. Debré laid out what he had in mind to de Gaulle on 23 May 1945. The bill was fine-tuned by an inter-ministerial committee on 4 June and approved by the cabinet as a whole four days later. In the meantime, Debré had cabled San Francisco, alerting Siegfried and Seydoux to what was happening. The pair returned to France on 31 May.[86] It must have heartened them to learn that the minister in charge of presenting the Debré project to the Consultative Assembly was Jules Jeanneney. Jeanneney, a veteran of Third Republic Senate politics, was well-disposed to Sciences Po, all the more so as his son—and directeur de cabinet—Jean-Marcel was a loyal school alumnus.[87] The Debré ordinance, of course, had first to make its way through the Assembly's Commission sur la Réforme de l'Etat. This was Cot's bailiwick—he was in fact designated *rapporteur* for the Debré project—but not Cot's alone, for the president of the Commission was Siegfried's comrade-in-arms from war days in Lyon, Paul Bastid.

Sciences Po had numerous well-wishers in the Provisional Government. Its position in the Consultative Assembly was less assured but far from hopeless. In the spring of 1945, the most urgent tasking confronting Siegfried and Seydoux was conjuring Cogniot's threat of confiscation, and this they contrived to do, making the most of the connections and public relations resources available to them.

First, a 33-page in-house memorandum was drafted, enumerating and then refuting point by point Cogniot's various charges. The document went to particular pains to demonstrate that Sciences Po had undertaken to purge itself of all Vichy taint. To this end, it was pointed out, the school had of its own volition set up an internal Commission d'épuration, chaired by Siegfried himself, which had fired compromising faculty and administrators like Ripert.[88] Copies of the memorandum, with a covering letter by Siegfried, were circulated in mid-April to well over a hundred recipients, members of the Consultative Assembly in the main.[89]

---

[86] 1 SP 67, dossier 3, sdr a, 'Procédure et Marche du Projet, 7 juin 1945'. See also Debré, *Trois Républiques*, 346; 376; Kessler, *La Politique de la haute fonction publique*, 37. The sources disagree about the timing of these events. Kessler dates Debré's appointment to 28 April. Debré himself is less precise, invoking a mid-March date. According to Sciences Po documentation, the date was 5 April. Kessler and Sciences Po sources agree that the inter-ministerial committee convened 4 June, but Debré remembers it as 28 May. As for the general cabinet meeting, Kessler does not mention it. Debré says it took place on 6 June, but a Sciences Po document puts it on 8 June. I have followed the dating of the Sciences Po documentation.

[87] Jean-Marcel Jeanneney was also an old friend of Debré's. Debré, *Trois Républiques*, 86; Feiertag, 'Wilfrid Baumgartner', i: 146. There was some question that the younger Jeanneney might teach at Sciences Po in 1945–6, but he turned down the opportunity, explaining that he might be of more use to the school as his father's *directeur du cabinet*. 1 SP 67, dossier 2, sdr b, letter from Chapsal to Seydoux, 14 April 1945.

[88] 1 SP 67, dossier 1, sdr a, 'Note sur la Proposition de Résolution no. 322', 9, 12.

[89] 1 SP 67, dossier 1, sdr a, 'Envoi de la lettre Cogniot' and circular letter from Siegfried dated 16 April 1945. A second round of letters was sent out in mid-June. See. 1 SP 67, dossier 4.

Siegfried and Seydoux had recourse to the press as well. On 30 March, prior to departing for San Francisco, Siegfried delivered himself of a front-page interview to Viannay's *France-Soir*. Sciences Po, he explained at length, had not collaborated with the Vichy regime; on the contrary, it had worked in close liaison with Resistance networks like Viannay's own Défense de la France. Seydoux too talked to the newspapers, although the issue he addressed was not so much the school's war record as its alleged laissez-faire bias. In early June, just back from the United States, he spoke to *L'Université libre*. Yes, Seydoux conceded, free-market doctrine had in the past dominated the school's curriculum but no more, and he proceeded to tick off the names of various '*dirigistes*' on the faculty: 'Gaëtan Pirou, [Charles] Morazé, Davezac . . .'[90]

In the early weeks of June 1945, as the government readied Debré's ordinance for submission to the Provisional Assembly, Sciences Po concentrated its lobbying efforts more and more on the individual personalities best situated to shape the outcome of the debate. At a business-like meeting with Jeanneney senior on 11 June, Seydoux and Siegfried renewed Sciences Po's pledge to work with the State on civil-service reform. An appearance before the Commission sur la Réforme de l'Etat on 19 June was much less satisfactory. Cot in particular exhibited 'a pretty aggressive attitude', making plain his own preference for Sciences Po's outright 'expropriation'. The next day, Seydoux and Siegfried had an audience with General de Gaulle himself, with more reassuring results. The General dismissed Cot as prone to 'demagogic posturing'. The government, he explained, had not the least intention of doing in Sciences Po. On the contrary, the General concluded, 'the school should find its place in the new organization of things'.[91]

The Consultative Assembly took up the Debré proposal next day. Sciences Po came in for rough handling from a number of representatives, Cot and Philip foremost among them, who urged State seizure of the school's library and buildings. Similar demands were made in the press by *L'Humanité* and *Franc-Tireur*, a Resistance paper. Sciences Po's own assessment of the debate, however, was almost exultant in tone and for good reason. In the Assembly, Bastid and Viannay had both borne credible witness to the school's Resistance record. Seydoux and Siegfried had worked hard to shore up school flanks on just this point, and they had succeeded. The Assembly as a body, moreover, issued an endorsement of the Debré proposal, even if many representatives felt that it did not go far enough. As for the newspapers, few echoed Cot and Philip's confiscatory exhortations. *L'Aurore* and *Le Monde*, in fact, spoke up in defence of Sciences Po's interests. On the eve of the Assembly session, there had been predictions of Sciences Po's imminent demise, but in its aftermath

---

[90] 1 SP 67, dossier 1, sdr a, Siegfried interview to *France-Soir*, 30 March 1945; dossier 2, sdr a, undated typescript of Seydoux interview to *L'Université libre*.

[91] For these various meetings, see 1 SP 67, dossier 3, sdr c, 'Note pour l'audience du Général de Gaulle' and 'Note sur l'audience accordée par le Général de Gaulle à MM André Siegfried et Roger Seydoux, le 20 juin'.

school authorities congratulated themselves that the old 'cadaver' had life in it still.[92]

A Most Favourable Compromise

Sciences Po had warded off the Left attack. Debré's ordinance, not Cogniot's resolution, would determine the school's future. All depended now on how the ordinance was applied, and the Sciences Po leadership set to work devising an implementation scheme of its own. Discussion of the question, indeed, had got under way in early June, several weeks before the decisive Assembly debate. School officials conceived a two-part strategy. First, the old Sciences Po would dissolve itself, to be reborn as the Paris Institut d'études politiques. No doubt, the State would play a key role in administering the new IEP, but Sciences Po officials did not want the State to govern alone. What they had in mind, rather, was a condominium, the State working in collaboration with an altogether new body, a private Fondation of as yet unspecified composition and attributes. This was the second and in the event crucial plank of the Sciences Po plan.[93]

The State turned out to be a receptive and prompt interlocutor. Little wonder, as Debré remained in charge of the negotiations from the State's end. To Sciences Po administrators like Chapsal and Seydoux, he remained 'Michel', a devoted alumnus and negotiator of unalloyed 'good faith'.[94] All concerned, moreover, felt under time pressure. There was a new academic year to prepare for, and elections for a new Assembly—this one Constituent rather than Consultative—were scheduled in October, which might well complicate what was now a constructive political climate.[95] It did not take long for an agreement to be arrived at. The terms, indeed, had been settled before the autumn was out, and on all points the State proved accommodating to Sciences Po concerns.

Debré from the outset was attached to the idea of a Fondation, or Fondation nationale des sciences politiques (FNSP) as the institution came to be known.[96] There was much toing and froing about the composition of the FNSP board. The government at first insisted on a majority of state nominees but then hesitated. The matter was for the moment left half-resolved. The initial ordinance of 9 October envisaged a governing board composed of up to 30 members. Fifteen would be designated by the State. As many as 15 but no fewer than ten would be selected by the outgoing Sciences Po administration. Not left undecided, however, was the identity of the FNSP's first president. On

[92] See 1 SP 67, dossier 4, Journal officiel, Assemblée consultative, séance du jeudi, 21 Juin 1945, 1167, 1169–70, 1173–4, 1176–7; dossier 4, 'La Presse et l'Ecole libre des sciences politiques', 25 June 1945.

[93] 1 SP 67, dossier 3, sdr a, 'Note sur le Projet d'Ordonnance relative à l'éducation de certaines catégories de fonctionnaires', 6 June 1945.

[94] 1 SP 68, dossier 1, letter from Seydoux to Chapsal, 26 July 1945.

[95] 1 SP 68, dossier 2, letter from Seydoux to Debré, 7 September 1945.

[96] Debré, Trois Républiques, 374.

12 September, the State announced its intention to appoint André Siegfried to the post.[97]

Definition of the FNSP's actual mandate generated a fresh round of debate. On one point there was agreement: that the FNSP would take charge of managing the Sciences Po endowment, devoting a portion of the income to the advancement of political science—the publication of a review, of monographs, and so on—and the balance to the running of the IEP itself—the upkeep and expansion of its library facilities, and so on. But what role would the FNSP have in IEP governance?

The answer came in three parts. On 12 September, the State made public its selection for the new director of the IEP, Roger Seydoux. Seydoux was to be assisted by a Comité de perfectionnement. The Comité's composition in turn was fixed by a decree of 9 October, which provided for a board of 17 members: two ex officio—the president of the Centre national de recherche scientifique and the director of ENA—two selected by the State, seven by the University, and five by the FNSP itself, plus one IEP old boy. The remaining details of FNSP-IEP relations were settled by a convention of 27 October hammered out between Sciences Po and university representatives. The first article of the document spelled out in lapidary terms that the FNSP was responsible for the 'administrative and financial management' of the new IEP.[98] A final, albeit minor, piece of the puzzle was put in place at the beginning of November. Debré's major interest in the new architecture of civil-service education was the Ecole Nationale d'Administration. Sciences Po administrators had no role in the shaping of the institution, although, as it turned out, they would have a bit part in its actual functioning. Sciences Po and ENA representatives signed a convention on 2 November, naming the FNSP's president and senior administrator as ex-officio members of ENA's Conseil d'administration.[99]

The rough outlines of these various ordinances, decrees, and conventions were known as early as late July 1945, so that Sciences Po was ready then to try the package out on its backers. Diehards like Davezac were outraged at the concessions made to the State, but cooler heads like Monick and Peyerimhoff—the latter now retired from the school's Conseil d'administration but still an influential figure—were delighted, 'surprised that it was possible to obtain so much'.[100] The Sciences Po governing board approved the deal in early September; the Provisional Government followed suit a few days later; and then came the flood of ordinances and decrees.[101]

---

[97] For the various proposals re the FNSP's composition, see 1 SP 68, dossier 1, 'Projet de Statut (dernier état)', 30 July 1945; dossier 2, document dated 4 August 1945; and, last, the decree of October 9, 1 SP 69, dossier 3, *Journal officiel, Ordonnances et Décrets*, 10 octobre 1945, 6380–1. See also 1 SP 68, dossier 3, letter from René Capitant, Ministre de l'Education nationale, to M. le Président, 12 September 1945.

[98] 1 SP 68, dossier 3, letter from Capitant to M. le Président, 12 September 1945; 1 SP 69, dossier 3, *Journal officiel, Ordonnances et Décrets*, 10 octobre 1945, decree of 9 October, 6382–3; 1 SP 68, dossier 5, 'Convention', 27 October 1945.

[99] 1 SP 68, dossier 5, 'Convention', 2 November 1945.

[100] 1 SP 68, dossier 1, letter from Seydoux to Chapsal, 26 July 1945.

[101] 1 SP 30, dossier 4, Procès-verbal, 12 September 1945; Debré, *Trois Républiques*, 376.

How much, indeed, had Sciences Po been able to obtain: parity or near-parity on the FNSP board, a controlling hand in the IEP's finances, a say in its pedagogical affairs, and even a voice, however faint, in the governance of ENA. Not least, the State had named two Sciences Po old-timers, Siegfried and Seydoux, to pilot the new FNSP-IEP complex.

The tidings got even better as the new machinery cranked into motion. In the event, the actual size of the FNSP board was set at 27, conferring on State appointees a slim majority. But whom did the State designate as its representatives: the university professors Jules Basdevant and Jean-Jacques Chevallier, both one-time Sciences Po faculty; the Conseiller d'Etat André Ségalat, a Sciences Po alumnus who had directed a Sciences Po *écurie* at the beginning of the war. Add to this that the State's 15 nominees included the director of the IEP, at the time Seydoux, and it becomes clear that the new FNSP board remained very much in the hands, not of the State's agents, but of Sciences Po loyalists, however reform-minded they might have been.[102]

The State's dominion over the IEP was greater, although far from undiluted. All senior faculty appointments required the sanction of the Ministry of Education. The selection of the junior faculty, however, remained the exclusive prerogative of the Director, Seydoux, who was succeeded by Chapsal in 1947. A new system of State scholarships was expected to leaven the elitism of the Sciences Po student body. The grants, while more numerous and generous than the old Boutmy grants, did not suffice to support students lacking other resources. Sciences Po remained a fees-based institution, its finances administered by a quasi-private Fondation, its students recruited from the ranks of the well-to-do. As such, it constituted an anomaly within the State-run university system.[103]

Finally, there was the working out of Sciences Po's place in the new civil-service training hierarchy. It no longer fed its students straight into the Grands Corps, that distinction having passed to ENA. But Sciences Po did contrive to remake itself into ENA's principal feeder school. Its *écurie* system was adapted to ready students for the ENA admissions test. ENA itself followed suit, accreting 'stables' of its own which prepared candidates for the civil-service exam. Indeed, the two layers of *écuries* were often staffed by the same men, tightening the bonds between the two schools. There was even a physical dimension to the symbiosis between the IEP and ENA. The ENA set up its headquarters, provisional at first, on the rue des Saints-Pères. Debré expected the school to relocate to Versailles, but the move in the end never took place. The rue des Saints-Pères, as it turns out, was just one street over from the rue Saint-Guillaume. The Ecole nationale and Sciences Po backed onto each other.

---

[102] See Kessler, *La Politique de la haute fonction publique*, 46; and 1 SP 69, dossier 3, arrêté of 7 February 1946, *Journal officiel*, Lois et Décrets, 4–5 mars 1946, 187. There was, however, an injection of new blood. The State's contingent of appointees included four trade unionists, Léon Jouhaux among them, as well as prominent *universitaires*, like Lucien Febvre and Gabriel Le Bras, who had no Sciences Po connections.

[103] Vincent, *Sciences Po*, 115, 188; Kessler, *La Politique de la haute fonction publique*, 115–16.

Students graduating from one school to the next had but to cross a common courtyard.[104]

Conclusion: The Old School and the New

In certain respects, the new Sciences Po looked just like the old. As before, it remained a bastion of privilege, training the offspring of the well-to-do for posts in the senior civil service. Yet much had changed. The IEP was now in name and, to a degree, in fact a State institution. And the education it offered was much more professional in cast than in bygone years. To be sure, the school still cared about imparting a general, liberal culture to its students, but that liberalism was now more and more interventionist in bias. All first-year students were required to take an introductory lecture in political economy. Keynesianism, not laissez-faire orthodoxy, enjoyed pride of place here, at least as Jean Meynaud taught the course in the late 1940s.[105] A member of the class of '62 who went on to prepare the ENA entrance exam remembers the technocratic partiality of the instruction he received:

And so progressively, I came to embrace the values proposed to us . . . That is, that in our country there are problems, and to deal with them, there is a State. This State has a certain legitimacy, a technical capacity which is called upon to resolve these problems.[106]

The can-do *fonctionnaire* was not the sole model of professionalism the school held up to students. The IEP hired and promoted a cohort of academic social scientists who would leave an enduring imprint on their field. The names of Chapsal and Meynaud have been mentioned. Maurice Duverger joined the faculty after the war and Jean Touchard in the early 1950s. Such high-calibre personnel made Sciences Po the best place in post-war France for the systematic study of things political: parties, institutions, and, above all, elections. François Goguel, promoted to the rank of professor in 1948, carried forward Siegfried's pioneering explorations in electoral geography, elevating psephological analysis into a sub-discipline in its own right with the requisite maps, charts, and statistical tables to prove its scientific character. Even in the 'soft' discipline of social theory, Sciences Po made its mark. Young normaliens might tout Sartre, but Sciences Po had a master-thinker of its own, Raymond Aron, who was a fixture in the Sciences Po faculty for many years. Sartre cited Marx; Aron answered, invoking the classics of continental social thought: Durkheim, Weber, and, of course, Tocqueville.[107]

Sciences Po might well imagine itself the premier political science institution in France. It had the personnel to make the case; it had the institutional

---

[104] Debré, *Trois Républiques*, 377.   [105] Alain Besançon, *Une Génération* (Paris, 1987), 164.
[106] Vincent, *Sciences Po*, 379.
[107] On this point, see Pierre Bourdieu, *La Noblesse d'Etat, grandes écoles et esprit de corps* (Paris, 1989), 302–3.

connections as well. The first national political science organization, the Association française de science politique, was founded in 1949. Siegfried presided over the new organism, succeeded by Chevallier and Goguel; and the FNSP, more often than not, hosted its meetings. From 1951, the Association published the *Revue française de science politique*, for decades the sole specialist periodical of its kind. Here too the Sciences Po imprimatur was evident. School faculty edited the journal—Meynaud and Georges Lavau, for example; and over time, the publications of the FNSP's research laboratories came to dominate its pages.[108]

Not least, the ambience of the school had undergone a none-too-subtle transformation. Students remained conventional in dress, but gone was the buttoned-up formality of the 1930s, the bowler hats and the umbrellas. The fashion détente had its effect even on the faculty. Chapsal pedalled to work on a bicycle, clips around his ankles, exuding the rough-and-ready air of the boy scout.[109] That Sciences Po had become less snobbish did not mean, of course, that it was any less an establishment institution. Siegfried, after all, wrote a regular column for the principal conservative daily of the post-war era, *Le Figaro*; Aron became a member of the paper's board of directors. But the school's enduring establishment bias was now tempered by a more questing, even religious impulse. Jean-Jacques Chevallier rejoined the faculty after the war. 'Liberal, Christian-Democrat': that was how the future Russianist Alain Besançon, then a student, recalled the former law professor, concluding, 'such was the tone of the school'. The scout-like Chapsal, it was rumoured, was active in the affairs of his local parish church. Goguel's analyses of the first post-war elections appeared in Mounier's *Esprit*, a journal of independent Christian opinion. The Christian existentialism which *Esprit* dealt in may not have appealed to all Sciences Po undergraduates, but it did to at least one: Pierre Elliot Trudeau.[110]

Sciences Po did more than just survive the whirlwind of the Liberation. It beat back a Left offensive and then, working in close collaboration with a cadre of sympathetic State negotiators, it remade itself. Critics had inveighed against the school's general subservience to business interests, outmoded liberalism, and snobbish dilettantism. The school now changed its orientation, distancing itself from the private sector in favour of the university and State administration. The institution that resulted was a peculiar hybrid. In principle, Sciences Po had been absorbed into the State, but in practice it retained considerable autonomy. Along the way, the school sharpened its professional and technocratic profile. Aspirants to the nation's senior administrative ranks had, as in pre-war days, to pass through its classrooms, but a Sciences Po

[108] Pierre Favre, 'La science politique en France depuis 1945', *International Review of Political Science*, 2 (1981), 105–6.

[109] Or Uriage acolyte. See Besançon, *Une Génération*, 162; also Bloch-Lainé, *Profession: fonctionnaire*, 154.

[110] Besançon, *Une Génération*, 162, 165; Favre, 'La science politique en France depuis 1945', 98; Pierre Elliot Trudeau, *Memoirs* (Toronto, 1993), 40. Many thanks to Seth Armus for the Trudeau reference.

education was no longer what it once was. The school remained a training ground for the privileged few, but the elite it formed were to be the best and brightest, educated by political scientists and civil-service experts to wield the instruments of State. A general, liberal culture counted as always: a sense of the Western tradition and of France's special place in it. But there were new realities and values to contend with: efficiency, modernity, grandeur. Sciences Po never ceased to be a bastion of the 'classic Right'. In the 1930s, *Le Temps* had been its champion; now it looked to *Le Figaro* and *France-Soir*. Yet the post-war Sciences Po, mainstream as it was, proved itself hospitable to new currents: to Gaullism, of course, but also to Christian Democracy.

Emile Boutmy had committed himself to endowing France with a cohesive and high-minded civil-service elite and enjoyed remarkable success at the enterprise. The *hauts fonctionnaires* schooled at Boutmy's Sciences Po, however, were not always at home in the Republic they served. It is not necessary to rehearse here in detail the multiple defects they imputed to the old Republic, notably incompetence, petty-mindedness, and demagoguery. The disaffection ran so deep that few senior civil servants mourned the ignominious passing of the regime in 1940. Few too at first resisted the temptations of Vichy authoritarianism. Yet, for a saving remnant, the Occupation years had a sobering effect. Democracy was embraced as France's destiny. The problem was to create a new Republic armoured against the weaknesses of the old. Such an agenda took material form in the new scaffolding of elite education erected at the Liberation: the FNSP, IEP, ENA. The result was a new deal for *la haute fonction publique*: an expanded and more activist role in the management of national affairs. *La haute fonction publique* in return extended to democratic institutions an allegiance it had earlier withheld or extended but half-heartedly.

Sciences Po's remaking formed a piece of this historic compromise. The Left played a role in the process, but it was a walk-on part which consisted in the main of goading others to action. The principal architects of the transformation were, rather, the school's own administration, Roger Seydoux in the lead, seconded by civil servants like Michel Debré. Seydoux had from the outset wanted to professionalize Science Po: to raise academic standards for students, to recruit a faculty which understood the technocratic currents of the day, to draw the school within the university's orbit. The upheaval of the Liberation forced on Sciences Po a more intimate relationship with the State than it would otherwise have sought, but in practice the nationalization of the school turned out to be less a demotion than, in Debré's own words, a veritable 'consecration'. Little wonder, as so many of the parties to the deal, on the State's side as on the school's, were themselves distinguished Sciences Po alumni. This was a conservative reform, worked out among establishment insiders. And it was a reform freighted with consequence, which helped to stabilize democratic institutions even as it edged French democracy away from the Jacobin revolutionary republicanism that lay at its origins.

7

General de Gaulle and
the Restoration of the Republic

DOUGLAS JOHNSON

T HOSE historians for whom General de Gaulle has been the centre of their
preoccupations have concentrated their studies on certain periods of his
life. The creation of La France Libre in London and the broadcast of 18 June
1940; his entry into a Paris that had been liberated by the Resistance and by
General Leclerc's 2nd Armoured Division; his triumphal progress down the
Champs Elysées on 26 August 1944; the return to power in 1958 and the creation of the Fifth Republic; the ending of the war in Algeria; the influence of
de Gaulle in Europe and in the world. It is as if the historians of de Gaulle and
Gaullism have themselves become Gaullist.

The part played by de Gaulle in the Liberation of France has also been told
many times and it is seen as another Gaullist triumph. This is undoubtedly
true in so far as de Gaulle succeeded in overcoming certain considerable
difficulties. He had to face the hostility of the British and American leaders and
the danger of an Allied military government being installed in France; it was
widely believed that there was the possibility of a Communist revolution
which could well have led to civil war. But once de Gaulle had established
himself in France and had been accepted as the head of government this hostility declined, and at times disappeared.

Not everyone in the British government had been hostile to de Gaulle head-
ing the first provisional government that would be established in liberated
France. Anthony Eden saw this as natural and acceptable. In Washington,
Cordell Hull, who had had his moments of violent hostility to de Gaulle,
sought to find a solution, a practical means whereby the leader of La France
Combattante, as La France Libre had become, could play his role. But
Churchill spoke of 'de Gaulle and his gang' forcing themselves on France and
flying the Cross of Lorraine from every *mairie*. Roosevelt, who had no
confidence in the future of France, was the first to throw doubt on de Gaulle's
democratic principles and was particularly concerned by the suggestion, originally conveyed to him by General Giraud, that de Gaulle was attracted to the
Führer-Princip and would establish a dictatorship. The execution of the former

Vichy Minister, Pierre Pucheu, in Algiers was cited as a reason for this disquiet. 'It was not a crime to have supported Vichy', protested Churchill to the representative of the Conseil National in London, Pierre Viénot. This was in April 1944.[1]

Even after the Allied landings in Normandy on 6 June, Roosevelt and Churchill maintained their lack of confidence in de Gaulle—although Churchill sometimes hinted that he did not want to quarrel with Roosevelt and he did not consider de Gaulle important enough to justify such a quarrel. On 14 June, the day that de Gaulle went to France, Roosevelt prophesied to Stimson, his Secretary of State for War, that de Gaulle was going to collapse. After the Liberation of French territory other personalities would emerge and, compared with them, de Gaulle would become insignificant. 'I know these personalities', he concluded, doubtless relying on the anti-de Gaulle French who had formed a small colony in Washington.[2] Similarly Churchill, a week before the liberation of Paris, sent a personal minute to Eden saying that no decision should be taken about France

. . . till we can see more clearly what emerges from the smoke of battle. Should the great success of our operation secure the liberation of the west and south of France, including Paris, as could easily be the case, there will be a large area from which a real provisional government might be drawn, instead of being composed entirely of a French national committee whose interests in seizing the deeds of France is obvious . . . One does not know at all what may happen and it is as well to keep our hands free. I think a broader base should be established before we commit ourselves.[3]

It is difficult to see any coherent thought or signs of military intelligence in these opinions. They ignore the fact that de Gaulle had succeeded in imposing his authority in Algiers and had from 31 July 1943 acted as the undisputed President of the Comité Français de la Libération Nationale. This Committee, that met twice a week, worked seriously and effectively. It prepared for the Liberation of France and for the reform of the French state once independence had been restored. Above all, it prepared for the reassertion of French sovereignty and the conference that was held at Brazzaville from 30 January to 8 February 1944, which looked to the future of the French empire within a new French union. Many laws were passed, including the enfranchisement of women by a decree of 21 April 1944; an Assemblée Consultative, which met for the first time on 3 November 1943, was hailed by de Gaulle as being the start of the resurrection of French representative institutions. It was Algiers which organized the liberation of Corsica on 13 September 1943.

The successes of de Gaulle were not without certain disadvantages. Not everyone approved of his treatment of Generals Giraud and Georges, whom he dismissed from membership of the Comité. He would not have been able

---

[1] These discussions were seemingly endless. The examples given and very many others are to be seen in the Public Record Office, FO 371 41876; 41877; 41878.

[2] Roosevelt to Stimson, 14 June 1944. Quoted in Daniel Pierrejean, *L'Envers du jour J. 6 Juin 1944. Le guet-apens américain* (Paris, 1997), 151.

[3] Churchill to Eden, 18 August 1944. FO 371 41882.

to do this had it not been for the understanding and neutrality of Eisenhower.[4] There were those who wanted the Assemblée Consultative to have more powers. There were those who spoke of the ukases of a pro-Soviet general, and there were those who were alarmed at André Philip's celebration, in a BBC broadcast on 11 October 1943, of the Corsican insurrection as a prelude to the national insurrection of France.[5] But in April 1944 the Assemblée Consultative decreed that one year after the complete liberation of French territory a Constituent Assembly would be elected in France, the delay of a year being the estimated time it would take for prisoners of war to return home. The provisional government in Algiers was ready to become the government in France. On 2 June, as he was preparing to leave for London, de Gaulle announced that the Comité Français de Libération Nationale would henceforth be called the Gouvernement Provisoire de la République Française.

Restoring French Sovereignty

The story of de Gaulle's first visit to France since June 17 1940 has often been told. The visit that Churchill wanted to be strictly supervised and controlled, and that he had even considered cancelling as late as the evening of 13 June 1944, was a success for the General. In particular, when he and two companions were travelling from his landing place in Normandy, Courseulles, to Bayeux, they encountered two gendarmes cycling in the opposite direction. When de Gaulle stopped them they naturally saluted a general in uniform. But when he told them who he was they were galvanized, 'affolés', and at his request they turned about and headed towards Bayeux to announce his imminent arrival. This was unnecessary, since de Gaulle's representatives were already there, but de Gaulle drew his conclusions from their reaction. Turning to his companions, he said 'Messieurs la reconnaissance est faite'. By this he meant that the representatives of the law had recognized him as the head of the government.[6] A farmer, working on his land near to the Courseulles–Bayeux road, heard a rumour that General de Gaulle was there and he rushed to greet him. He was in his working clothes and by his own account he was filthy. De Gaulle reproved him for presenting himself in such a state to the head of the French government.[7]

---

[4] See the work of Mario Rossi, *Roosevelt and the French* (Westport, CT, 1994), referred to in Jean-Louis Crémieux-Brilhac, *La France Libre* (Paris, 1996), 567 and n. 3.

[5] On Corsica see Crémieux-Brilhac, *La France Libre*, 553–698, and 'Jeux et enjeux d'Alger', in Jean-Pierre Azéma and François Bédarida (eds), *La France des années noires*, ii.: *De l'Occupation à la Libération* (Paris, 1993), 179–218; Jean-Eric Callon, 'La libération de la Corse', in *Le Rétablissement de la Légalité Républicaine 1944* (Paris, 1996), 55–64; and Hervé Bastien, 'Les hommes d'Alger: quelle idée de la République', in *Le Rétablissement de la Légalité Républicaine 1944*, 87–100.

[6] Colonel Rémy gives this account in *Les Mains Jointes* (Paris, 1949), and it is quoted in René Hostache, 'Bayeux 14 Juin 1944: Etape décisive sur la voie d'Alger à Paris', in *Le Rétablissement de la Légalité Républicaine 1944*, 234–6.

[7] The farmer in question, who was later elected as Senator for the region, Senator André, told me this story in 1960.

In practice this meant that the Provisional Government was accepted. The *commissaire régional*, François Coulet, dismissed the sub-prefect who had been appointed by Vichy and succeeded in establishing himself as the civil author- ity with whom the military settled administrative matters. But it was only gradually that he succeeded in getting full agreement on the banning of the American-manufactured currency which the Allied armies had brought with them and which had been accepted by the French populations, 'avidly' according to the Americans. General de Gaulle had publicly denounced this currency as being incompatible with French sovereignty. Coulet therefore issued many instructions, banning its use and ordering French officials not to accept it in payment of taxes. But it was not until 18 August 1944 that there was an agreement between Coulet and the British officer, Lieutenant-Général Grasett.[8]

Not everyone agreed that the welcome to de Gaulle in Bayeux had been overwhelming and it was noted that calm rapidly returned to the town after the General had left.[9] The Resistance had not been particularly active in the area. The German occupying forces had behaved correctly and there were occasions when people accused the Americans of seizing farm stocks in a man- ner which was notably worse than anything that the Germans had done.

The French presence in the invasion of the south of France and the activi- ties of the Resistance greatly strengthened the Provisional Government and it was a very self confident de Gaulle who entered Paris on 25 August and was given details of the German surrender. He had planned what he would do. He went to the Ministry for War and entered the room he had used when he had been Under-Secretary of State for National Defence in the last legitimate gov- ernment of the Third Republic. He had left the room on 10 June 1940, but, as he said in a much-quoted passage in his *Mémoires*, nothing had changed. All was as he had left it. 'Nothing was missing, except the State. It was for me to re-place it.'[10]

By making this journey to the war ministry he had established a continuity between 1940 and 1944. There had simply been an illegitimate and false inter- ruption which did not mean that the Republic had ceased to exist. The Republic had existed in London and in Algiers, and he, de Gaulle, had been and was the head of the Republic. He summoned officials to discuss matters in his room in the war ministry. Afterwards as head of State he called at the Prefecture of Police, inspecting, as was normal, the forces of security. Only then did he proceed to the Resistance leaders waiting for him at the Hôtel de Ville, where he informed Georges Bidault, the President of the Conseil National de la Résistance, that there was no need to proclaim the Republic. On 26 August as head of State he displayed himself to the Parisians and to the rest

---

[8] François Coulet, *Vertu des temps difficiles* (Paris, 1967); Pierrejean, *L'envers du jour J. 6 Juin 1944*, 153–99.

[9] For different accounts of de Gaulle's reception see Hilary Footitt and John Simmonds, *France 1943–1945* (Leicester, 1988), 269–70, n. 45.

[10] Charles de Gaulle, *Mémoires* (Paris, 2000), 568.

of the world by leading a ceremonial march down the Champs Elysées, from the Tomb of the Unknown Soldier to Notre Dame. As the leading person in France he was followed by military commanders, his state officials and members of the Resistance.[11]

La France Libre, La France Combattante, Le Comité Français de Libération Nationale and the Gouvernement Provisoire de la République Française had all had the same aim of driving out the Germans and restoring French independence and sovereignty. It was for the restored State then to determine in what way France would be governed.

The committee in Algiers had made arrangements for the establishment of new authorities throughout France in preparation for the 6th of June. From March 1944 Alexandre Parodi was the representative of Algiers in France. On 31 July de Gaulle wrote to him:

> You are the representative of the Government. It is your orders that must prevail in the last resort . . . the nomination of new officials must not be determined by choosing them proportionally from different groups. Officials belong only to the State and serve the State only. The many groups and actions that come from our remarkable Resistance of the interior are the means whereby the nation struggles to save itself. The State is above all these groups and all these actions.[12]

The Formation of a New Government

On 12 September de Gaulle spoke to an audience of some 1,000 in the Palais de Chaillot. This came after the formation of a government that included the Third Republic's last President of the Senate, Jules Jeanneney, to whom de Gaulle wrote on 2 September expressing the hope that other Ministers of the Third Republic, Edouard Herriot, Léon Blum, and Jean Marin, would eventually join his government. It came too after the dissolution of the Resistance army, the Forces Françaises de l'Intérieur (FFI) and their transfer to the forces commanded by General Koenig, who had been appointed Military Governor of Paris. The role of the Conseil National de la Résistance was considered finished, and its members were to be transferred to the Assemblée Consultative that was moved from Algiers and its membership enlarged.

The audience at the Palais de Chaillot must therefore have been well aware of the direction that the government was taking. De Gaulle left them in little doubt. He spoke of the war that was not yet won and the liberation of French territory that was far from complete. He emphasized the need for France to regain its position in world affairs, which he called its 'rank', and the need to be able to maintain it. But when he looked at France he saw only confusion. And the answer to this was then for the State to be active and for the State to

---

[11] Serge Berstein, 'L'arrivée de de Gaulle à Paris', in *Le Rétablissement de la Légalité Républicaine 1944*, 357–71. In the discussion that followed during this colloque that was held at Caen, 6–8 October 1994, see the remarks of Monsignor Badée, 374.

[12] Charles de Gaulle, *Lettres, notes, et carnets Juin 1943–Mai 1945* (Paris, 1983), 275.

reject any other body intervening in matters of justice and administration. Referring to the FFI, he insisted that all the soldiers of France belonged to the French Army. The French Army, like the French State, was one and indivisible.[13]

De Gaulle himself sensed that his speech was not being well received. Claude Bouchinet-Sereulles, who had been his *chef de cabinet* in London and who had taken charge of affairs in Lyon, arriving there immediately after the arrest of Jean Moulin, did not hear the speech. But entering the Palais de Chaillot when the audience was beginning to leave he found his old Resistance companions deeply disturbed. Lucie Aubrac was in tears, others were angry. 'De Gaulle has betrayed the Resistance', said one. 'It is the spirit of the Resistance that they wish to kill', said another. Bouchinet-Serreulles understood that de Gaulle's priority was to restore the respect for the State and he attributed this to his realization that the French Communist Party (PCF) had made important gains in the machinery of the Resistance.[14]

Yet in many respects there was much that was successful from the government's viewpoint. De Gaulle toured the provinces and was welcomed by the populations, as he had hoped. The work of the administrative machinery established from Algiers to carry out the process of liberation was largely successful. Bouchinet-Serreulles was on his way back from Limoges and Toulouse when he arrived at the Palais de Chaillot and he was able to report later that the difficulties which had arisen between the Comités Départementaux de Libération and resistance forces had been resolved. 'Le bilan est très positif.'[15] Although much has been written about the excesses that took place in the punishment of collaborators, both real and alleged, in the country as a whole the authorities did not lose control. It can be argued that it was only in villages and small towns that personal jealousies and hostilities led to various types of violence.[16]

The experience of Liberation was varied. It has been estimated that the majority of French towns which were *chef-lieux* of their department or arrondissement did not experience any rising or insurrection against their enemy. Only five towns, including Paris, were liberated by their own fighters, using strikes or barricades. There were 28 towns where the inhabitants were largely spectators but where the resistance played an important role. Eighty-five per cent of towns saw the Germans withdraw without being driven out and without being attacked. This suggests there was no national insurrection.[17]

Nor was there any Communist plot to organize a revolution. The PCF was omnipresent in France. With some 60,000 members in the summer of 1944, it counted 528,700 by the end of 1944. Its propaganda, with L'Humanité selling

[13] De Gaulle's account of this speech is in *Mémoires*, 592–4.
[14] Claude Bouchinet-Serreulles, *Nous étions faits pour être libres. La Résistance avec de Gaulle et Jean Moulin* (Paris, 2000), 371–2.
[15] Bouchinet-Serreulles, *Nous étions faits pour être libres*, 370.
[16] For one example see the assessment made by a former résistant in Nantes, in Jean François Ercksen, *1944: L'Eté de la liberté* (Rennes, April 1994), 49.
[17] Philippe Buton, 'La France atomisée', in Azéma and Bédarida, *La France des années noires*, 403.

more copies than any newspaper, with its incessant claim that 75,000 Communists perished fighting in the Resistance, and the publicity given to national figures such as Joliot-Curie and Picasso joining the party, was effective. But it was not lasting and it was not followed by any action. It was left to certain dissidents in Seine-et-Marne to set up barricades in December, which led to many arrests.[18]

The government was able to pursue its reforms in the country's economic and social structure. The coalfields of the department of the Nord and Pas-de-Calais were nationalized on 14 December 1944; air transport was brought into the public sector, following the nationalization of the railways in 1937; other nationalizations occurred in sectors that were guilty of collaboration with the Germans, such as the Renault car works and the aviation motor constructors, Gnome and Rhône. Enterprise Councils were established on 22 February 1945 in businesses employing more than 100 workers, thus giving the representatives of the personnel certain powers of *co-gestion*. Most importantly, a system of social security was started by a series of decrees, beginning on 29 October 1945.

De Gaulle also succeeded in using a referendum—a method usually associated with Bonapartism—to decide whether the Assembly to be elected would be a constituent assembly with a lifetime of seven months only, but with the power to choose and to dismiss a prime minister. The result of the referendum was to approve de Gaulle's suggestions by considerable majorities, and the Assembly that was elected on 21 October 1945 was chosen, as de Gaulle had wished, by a system of proportional representation. On 13 November the new assembly, unanimously but for one abstention, chose de Gaulle as the President of the Provisional Government. De Gaulle was victorious. But nine weeks later he resigned and went into what has been called 'l'exil intérieur'. How can one explain this?

De Gaulle's Resignation

The details of de Gaulle's conflict with the Assembly suggest that he might have resigned after only four days as head of the Provisional Government. It was then that PCF leader Thorez requested that a member of the Communist Party, which was the largest party in the Assembly and had won some 26 per cent of the votes in the country, should have one of the three key ministries: the Interior, Defence, or Foreign Affairs. De Gaulle refused and Thorez claimed that this was an insult to the 75,000 Communists killed during the war—a figure that no one believed. On 16 November de Gaulle sent a letter to the President of the Assembly, placing his office as Head of the Provisional Government at the disposal of the Assembly. But although the rumours of his

---

[18] Philippe Buton, *Les lendemains qui déchantent. Le Parti Communiste Français à la Libération* (Paris, 1993); Philippe Buton, 'Le PCF à la fin de l'année 1944', in *Le Rétablissement de la Légalité Républicaine 1944*, 733–46; Philippe Buton and Jim Guillon, *Les pouvoirs en France à la Libération* (Paris, 1994).

resignation were widespread, and it was said that documents were being removed from his office, those who were close to him assured his allies that de Gaulle did not intend to resign.[19] In a broadcast on 17 November he explained why he could not give any of the three posts to the PCF, since the three were vital to the external relations of France, representing diplomacy, the army, and the police. The relations of the PCF with the Soviet regime were obviously a vital element in this explanation. De Gaulle concluded that he was ready to resign, 'without bitterness', but he would continue his work 'for the interests and the honour of France' if the Assembly confirmed him as the head of government.

Thus the problem was returned to the Assembly. In the light of publicity, would the Assembly accept de Gaulle's offer of resignation over a claim by the Communist Party to hold a particular office in the government? Could Thorez, who had been a deserter in 1939, prove stronger than de Gaulle? To make it all the more unlikely, a solution was found to the apparent unacceptability of Thorez's request. After 19 November, when the Assembly had confirmed de Gaulle as head of government, it was decided that part of the functions of Minister of War could be filled by a Minister for Armament and a Communist, Charles Tillon, was appointed to this post. Could this solution have been found before?

It could be that we are getting a glimpse of a Gaullist tactic that was to be used again, that of giving the impression of imminent resignation with the hope that this would cause alarm in the country. Certainly alarm was caused, as instanced by François Mauriac in *Le Figaro* claiming that if de Gaulle resigned France would become a battleground between the Soviets and the Anglo-Saxons. Thus de Gaulle was confirmed in his position and felt stronger. Since a solution had been found by the appointment of Tillon, he retained the support of the Communists which he needed in negotiations with the unions.

But the conflict continued. The Assembly adopted certain measures, the nationalizations and the creation of the Ecole Nationale d'Adminstration, but certain of its members criticized the budget. In particular certain Socialists demanded a 20 per cent reduction in the credits of the National Defence. Therefore de Gaulle, on 1 January 1946, put forward his idea of the constitution. He believed in a government that governed; he did not believe in an omnipotent Assembly which delegated a government to carry out its wishes. He gave a hint that he might retire, and in his *Mémoires* he states that on the evening of 1 January he made up his mind to do so.[20]

But this time there was a longer delay. Going to the south of France to attend his daughter's wedding, which took place on 3 January, he stayed there for some ten days. On his return he told various associates and ministers of his intention to resign, always swearing them to secrecy but invariably discussing the matter with them. According to Gaston Palewski and Georges Pompidou, it was on 16 January that his decision became irrevocable. On 20 January, con-

[19] Jacques Baumel, *De Gaulle, l'Exil Intérieur* (Paris, 2001), 68.   [20] *Mémoires*, 865.

vening a special meeting of his government, he rapidly told them of his resignation and immediately left the room. There is some doubt as to the precise
words used, but at the time particular attention was paid to the words used by
de Gaulle in the letter of resignation that he sent to Félix Gouin, the President
of the Assembly, in which he stated that everything in France and in external
affairs was going well. Malraux, a few days after 20 January, was to say that
what was worst was not the resignation but the regrettable 'tout va bien' in the
letter to Gouin. Particular attention has been given by historians to three
details.

The first is the preparation of a broadcast which the General intended to
give but which he cancelled, according to his *Mémoires*, because he thought
that his silence would 'weigh heavier' with the people. The second is his conversation with Francisque Gay, deputy Foreign Minister, on 18 January, when
he is reported as saying that before eight days after his resignation there would
be a delegation requesting him to return to power which he would then do on
his conditions. The third is the letter that General Billotte sent to Maurice
Schumann on 22 January in which he gave warning of the consequences
which would ensue if a government of Socialists and Communists came to
power: they would include civil war at home and the loss of the empire overseas. Billotte has claimed that this letter was intended to persuade the Social
Catholics to take part in the government. But the tone of the letter written by
the officer who was Deputy Chief of Staff and who had always been a loyal
Gaullist could well have incited certain deputies to raise the question of a possible request to de Gaulle that he should consider returning to power.[21]

One is tempted to see in these events an early version of what happened in
May 1968, when de Gaulle made his secret journey to Baden-Baden, giving rise
to the rumour that he was about to resign. His sudden return and a vigorous
broadcast made him politically stronger, the indispensable head of State at a
time of crisis. Was not the lengthy stay in the south of France and the prolonged discussions which followed a forerunner of this tactic?

But, as has been shown, public opinion was no longer as pro-Gaullist as it
had been.[22] There were many reasons for this, whether it was opposition to
what the Right called the 'Front Populaire numéro deux' or whether it was former members of the Resistance who had resented the General's demands for
exclusive control of the Resistance movement and his capacity for annoying
allies, especially the Americans.[23] But the greatest reason for his decline in
popularity must have been the overwhelming difficulties of life that persisted
throughout 1945. In almost every sphere of everyday life, 'la liberté retrouvée
n'est pas synonyme du bien-être tant espéré'.[24]

---

[21] These matters have been discussed by historians over many years. See Georgette Elgey, *La
République de Illusions* (Paris, 1965), 60–106; Jean Lacouture, *De Gaulle*, ii.: *Le Politique* (Paris, 1985),
225–49; Serge Berstein, *Histoire du Gaullisme* (Paris, 2001), 86–97.

[22] Jean Charlot, *Le Gaullisme d'opposition* (Paris, 1983), 43.

[23] Richard Vinen, 'The Parti Républicain de la Liberté and the Reconstruction of French
Conservatism 1944–1951', *French History*, 7 (1993), 201.

[24] Dominique Veillon, *Vivre et survivre en France 1939–1947* (Paris, 1995), 315.

The Weaknesses of de Gaulle

One is inclined to see in de Gaulle's failure three important weaknesses. The first came from the past. In 1943 he knew that he was in danger of losing his position as leader, with the Americans supporting a rival in North Africa. Therefore it was important for him to become the undisputed leader of the French internal Resistance. Hence the Conseil National de la Résistance was created by Jean Moulin, his representative. It consisted of different resistance networks, with representatives of the political parties that supported these movements. To the distress of some Resistance leaders, this meant the official return of the political parties. With the Liberation he found it natural that the parties would return. 'C'est dans la nature des choses', he told Baumel.[25] But just as the Conseil National de la Résistance was meant to ensure that he was the national leader, so the political parties were meant to accept him as a national leader. There were many details which were the natural preoccupation of deputies, the interests of their electors and regions, but they were not concerned with the essential business of the state. At the time of the Resistance this meant recovering the independence of France. After the war it meant a preoccupation with the international status of France and its continued independence, as well as producing a modern and socially well-organized nation. Thus the head of State and the National Assembly functioned together, and the head of State worked separately.

Together with the failure of de Gaulle to see that parliamentary democracy could mean more than playing a very secondary role to the head of the State, there was his whole conception of the State. The aim of de Gaulle was to drive out Vichy, not because he was ideologically opposed to Vichy but because Vichy had abandoned the French State through the armistice and collaboration. Once the French State had been restored, the Resistance had achieved its victory and should disappear. It was for the State to undertake its renovation. The contrary argument, held by politicians, was that the State was not an entity in itself; it was not an absolute reality. The State was what the social and political forces in the country made it.[26]

Third, there was de Gaulle's grand view of history and his contempt for those who did not share it. He complained of those who spent their time writing about their opposition to Maurras or Déat or to some other political enemy when they should have been writing about the reconstruction of the French Army, Leclerc's advance to Paris, the French troops in Strasbourg, and the maintenance of France in Indo-China.[27] As a man imbued with history he wanted to forget the quarrels of the past, the Dreyfus affair, Vichy, clericalism, colonialism. He wanted to concentrate on the great moments of French his-

---

[25] Baumel, *De Gaulle, l'exil intérieur*, 27.
[26] This argument was used to explain the failure of certain resistance organizations to survive the Liberation. See, for example, Henri Denis, *Le Comité Parisien de la Libération* (Paris, 1963).
[27] Claude Guy, *En écoutant de Gaulle* (Paris, 1996), 105.

tory as on 26 August 1944 when he strode down the Champs Elysées contemplating the Tuileries, la Concorde, le Louvre. After that it was difficult for him to adjust to the realities of politics in November and December 1945.[28]

[28] Odile Rudelle, 'Politique de la mémoire: politique de la postérité', *De Gaulle en son siècle*, i.: *Dans la mémoire des hommes et des peuples* (Paris, 1991), 149–63. Many criticisms of de Gaulle's thought are to be found in Nicolas Tenzer, *La face cachée du gaullisme* (Paris, 1998).

8

Emulation through Decoration: A Science of Government ?

OLIVIER IHL

IF we include the Croix de Guerre of the First and Second World Wars, the official number of French men and women who have been awarded decorations and are 'presumed alive' is estimated at over 2 million. How is this honours table made up? The Légion d'honneur has more than 200,000 honorands, the Compagnons de la Libération just under 1,000 members, including five towns and 18 regiments. There are over 560,000 holders of the *médaille militaire* and 130,000 of the Ordre du Mérite, to say nothing of the swelling battalions of the Mérite Agricole, the Croix de Guerre, or the Palmes académiques. Just one look at these figures is enough to confer upon these modest emblems the status of a systematic instrument of governance.

A Behaviour Police

Yet the deference accorded to such honours has been bitterly condemned over time, in a salvo of criticism for which Montesquieu vigorously opened the way. If you wish to form an opinion as to the nature of a government, he suggested to his readers, consider carefully how it rewards people. You will observe that, under a despotic regime, the moral value of the people is reduced to a material one: the prince 'can only offer money'. In a monarchy, on the other hand, honour encourages a cult of 'distinctions and preferences'. Dispensed by the sovereign, these can certainly lead to fortune, but that is not what they are essentially about. However, in a republic, distinctions of honour are purely symbolic. Awarded by the whole of society, they serve to sanction a virtue that is supposed to be sufficient unto itself. And the model for this? The use that ancient Rome made of rewards of honour, that is to say, simple wreaths of laurel or oak which were worn as a sign of civil or military distinction. However, even under these last two regimes the use of such an expedient is for Montesquieu a sign of decadence. It is so in a monarchy because the bait of material advantage ultimately perverts everything, including the sense of dignity, and it is so in a republic because the distinction of being a citizen should be virtue's sole reward[1]—which implies that in reality true nobility is that of the soul and can be inherited only though education.

During the French Revolution, Mirabeau came to much the same conclusion. In protest against the creation in the young American republic of the Cincinnatus Society, a new patrician body that was threatening to turn itself into a hereditary aristocracy, he wrote a virulent pamphlet. Anodyne, this badge of honour by means of which people sought recognition and distinction? Inoffensive, this medal in the form of an eagle borne on a blue ribbon and surmounted by an inscription alluding to the health of the republic? Quite the contrary. This was a frightening emblem, the weapon of an oligarchy aspiring to the privileges of nobility. Such, in his view, is the fatal power of 'opinion and petty human passions': 'the most frivolous symbols have played their part in tightening the chains that bind the people, have ennobled the powerful and, by enabling them to afford to be waited upon by the poor, have increased the servitude of the poor'. Is it not the case that to covet a reward is in some way to relinquish to others one's own means of defining oneself? And, for the sovereign, a means of gaining power over the course of a human life? After all, those people who have been decorated become exemplars only through the share of power that they receive: that is to say, through the visibility conferred upon them by the sign that they wear and, consequently, through the respect that results from this. Whilst the decoration provides visible proof of an action of sufficient grandeur as to be worthy of recompense, it is above all a manifestation of the power of the person awarding it. Its value is to be assessed in terms of a desire for power. This is why Mirabeau declares: 'The greatest of rewards lies in the esteem of one's fellow countrymen, for this is deserved and not exacted; the most glittering of decorations is a virtue which can be seen for itself, and the most noble of charters is that of a member of a collectivity which one has had the good fortune to enlighten though reason.'[2]

The warning did not fall upon deaf ears. For the French revolutionaries, there could be no worse manifestation of tyranny than the unbridled commerce in ribbons and distinctions. Not only did it stand in contradiction to the principle of equality but it had, moreover, lost its purpose with the demise of the nobility. The Constituent Assembly, convinced of just how noxious the custom was, abolished its essential mechanisms. This was the agenda of the celebrated session of 17 June 1790, which was devoted to 'signs denoting feudalism'. From monarchic protocol to titles of nobility and from orders of chivalry to diplomatic ceremonial, a whole gamut of distinctions was

---

[1] Montesquieu, *De l'Esprit des lois*, in *Oeuvres complètes*, ii., presented and annotated by Roger Caillois (Paris, 1951), 302. The same assertion is to be found in a number of other writings, including those of François de Neufchâteau, Charles Duclos, and Sébastien Mercier, as well as in *L'Essai sur le mérite et la vertu* published by Diderot in 1745.

[2] Comte de Mirabeau, *Opinion du comte de Mirabeau sur la noblesse ancienne et moderne. Considération sur l'ordre de Cincinnatus ou imitation d'un pamphlet anglo-américain* . . . , (Paris, 1815), 7 (1st edn 1784).

abolished in a matter of hours. It was said that all display of distinction had to be abolished, along with all extravagance of a sort likely to be reminiscent of a society founded upon the distribution of honours.[3] Proudhon was to take up the argument later: 'If citizens are equal before the ballot box and the law, there is no longer any reason for distinctions of nobility.'[4]

Yet the fact is that decoration has indubitably become the essential instrument for measuring merit. The France that was born out of the Revolution has instituted twelve times more honorary distinctions than her monarchical predecessor did in 500 years. Up to 1789, royalty had been 'satisfied' with four insignia, which, moreover, were rarely awarded: the crosses of Saint-Michel, Saint Esprit, and Saint-Louis, and the cross of military merit. In republican France just after the Second World War, there were over 60 official distinctions. Medals were doled out for an extraordinary variety of situations: to those who had reached the end of a professional career, to those who had performed an act of bravery or suffered an injury, and even to those who had achieved some prowess in sports or in the arts. In the form of stars, palm leaves, and medals, all these people were rewarded with visible emblems whose entire lustre was derived from the affirmation of a superiority sanctioned by convention. The Republic founded the cult of equality. But it did so only immediately to set about universalizing another principle, which deserves to be writ large across its monuments: emulation through decoration.

How are we to explain this paradox, that of a nation powerless to curtail a process which rocks the very principles of its citizenship? Rather than falling back on the perpetual *trahison des clercs* thesis or conjuring up the ghost of a Republic of dukes and dupes, as a certain type of historiography has applied itself to doing, I would like here to go down another route, which is that of the *majesty of the State*. It is impossible to discuss the seizure of power by the revolutionary bourgeoisie without confronting the problem of the conquest of the administrative apparatus—in the absence of which it could not have happened—of that 'bureaucracy' which, for Grimm, constituted 'the very spirit of French laws'.[5] Now, in order to move forward in this direction, it is important to look into political doctrines as well as to understand the strategic position they have occupied ever since the Middle Ages, which is that of a State deference which the democratic competition of interests and reputations had succeeded neither in replacing nor in discrediting.

[3] Article 1 of the decree of 19 June 1790 stipulates that: 'The right to hereditary nobility has been abolished forever; consequently, the titles of *prince, duc, comte, marquis, vicomte, baron, chevalier, messire, écuyer, noble*, and all other similar titles will neither be taken by nor accorded to anyone.'
[4] On the controversy sparked off by this 'democratization of honours', see William M. Reddy, *The Invisible Code. Honour and Sentiment in Postrevolutionary France, 1814–1848* (Berkeley, 1997), 6.
[5] Friedrich Melchior Grimm (baron de), *Correspondance*, iv. (1764), 11. Cited by Emile Littré in the entry 'Bureaucratie' of the *Dictionnaire de la langue française*, Supplement (Paris, 1878).

From Honour to Honours

In the Middle Ages, the orders of chivalry had a precise significance. Created by the nobles themselves, among them Boucicaut when he returned from his expedition against the Turks in 1400 and founded the order of the Dame blanche à l'écu vert,[6] they were based upon peer recognition. Above all, their purpose was to ensure that Christians were protected. Released from all dependence by the popes, as was the case for the orders of Saint-Sépulchre and Saint-Jean de Jérusalem, they admitted only the cream of the nobility. Indeed, their grand masters had no hesitation in considering themselves the equals of their sovereigns. Their members had taken vows of poverty and chastity, thus giving the nobility a reason to 'make a profession of honour' and enabling it to perpetuate its independence in the name of a model of excellence embodied by the gentleman warrior. For earlier European noble lineages, duty was—and this must be stressed—something which was bound up in divine will. Although its ultimate meaning was incomprehensible, it was, and continued to be, recognizable as a means of putting a state of grace to the test: this was the meaning of chivalrous 'prowess' or the 'sacrifice' on the part of the warrior. Sustained as it was by the fact of belonging to a group of noble lineage, this external conscience enjoined the knight to 'go out in quest of honour' or, at the very least, not to allow himself to be humiliated or demeaned—'the point of honour'.

Now this 'mark of consideration'—Lucien Febvre— this 'prejudice of person and condition'—Montesquieu—were gradually turned to their own advantage by the sovereigns of the first modern states in order to ensure the loyalty of the highest in their kingdoms. Louis XI was the first monarch to make use of the morality of feudal honour when in 1469 he created the order of Saint-Michel, thanks to which he was able to secure the deference of the high-ranking nobility. Henri II created the order of the Saint-Esprit, which transformed the knights into 'Knights of the Order of the King'. But it was, above all, Louis XIV who in 1692, with the order of Saint-Louis, turned this supreme and unconditional value into the mainspring of the monarchic administration.[7] The order, which was open to those commoners who had rendered outstanding service as officers and were practising Catholics, associated marks of honour with substantial incomes.[8] So what purpose did it serve? To turn the respect

[6] 'White lady with the green shield.'

[7] The edict which instituted this military order of which the King declared himself leader and sovereign grand master begins with the words: 'The officers leading our troops have distinguished themselves by so many outstanding acts of merit and courage in these victories and conquests with which it has pleased God to bless the justice of the causes in which we have borne arms, that ordinary rewards are inadequate to express our affection and the gratitude we feel for their services, and we felt ourselves to be under an obligation to seek out new means of recompensing their zeal and loyalty.' Cited in Abbé Bocquillon, *Discours sur l'institution de l'ordre militaire de Saint-Louis* (Paris, 1694), 6. For a general presentation of the cohorts and the functioning of the equestrian royal order, see Alexandre Mazas, *Histoire de l'ordre royal et militaire de Saint-Louis*, 3 vols. (Paris, 1860–1).

[8] The religious restriction disappeared, however, when Louis XV created the military order of merit for Protestant officers in 1759.

accorded to the pyramidal structure of lines of descent and military ranks to the service of the Crown. Let us not forget that, from the beginning of the seventeenth century, the monarch's jurists had been striving towards using the bond of deference as a means of maintaining social harmony:

> It is a necessary imperative that some command and others obey. Amongst those who command, there are several orders, ranks, and degrees and those who obey them are again separated into several orders and ranks. Thus, by means of these multiple divisions and subdivisions, a general order is created out of several orders, so that, in the end, through the power of order, a massive number becomes one.[9]

The range of ceremonial arrangements to which the Crown had recourse serves as an indication of the extent to which this segmentation was used as an instrument of State. The superiority of the rulers over the people was cause for celebration, as was that of the kingdom over its neighbours, of the great and the good over the common people, but over and above everything else the proclaimed superiority of a king, who was unique in his eminence. Sanctified as the purest form of majesty because the most absolute, royal power could claim to be omnipotent. It was thenceforth embodied in a figure who, in keeping with his unequalled rank, both dominated and gave ultimate distinction to the entire pyramid of men of distinction. In the words of the legal adviser, Guy Coquille: 'The royal majesty of the king is without equal.' To this principle of supremacy the theory of 'royal blood'—'the best, the most pious, the surest blood in the world', according to Jean de Rély—brought the guarantee of hereditary transmission.

In fact, in the same way as the Church, through the religious formalities of investiture, had imposed upon the vassals the obligation to defend it, the sovereign imposed through the oath of allegiance the obligation to protect the security of his crown. This shattered the traditional model of the *nobilitas*.[10] Stripped of its prerogatives and deprived of its legal and customary responsibilities, first in England and France then, after the First World War, in the rest of Europe, the nobility lost its role as the governing class and became no more than a dominant class, and then a mere citadel of influence. In France, the nobility, which had been abolished as a class in 1790, never reappeared. It is true that nobles were reinstated with the Restoration, and more titles were created with the July Monarchy as well as the two Bonapartist Empires; but, for all the regimes of the nineteenth century, nobility was no more than an honorary distinction attached to a name. Moreover, the member of the Legislative Corps who put forward the bill of May 1858 aimed at stopping the abuse and usurpation of titles affirmed this point from the assembly platform:

> We are unanimous in considering that today in France nobility cannot be anything other than an *honorary distinction*, devoid of any privilege and that it must no longer have associated with it any idea of difference of race or of caste. In order that there

---

[9] Charles Loyseau, *Cinq livres du droit des offices*, i. (Paris, 1613), 60.
[10] On the *nobilitas* that was born out of the heritage of antiquity, see Karl Ferdinand Werner, *Naissance de la noblesse. L'essor des élites politiques en Europe* (Paris, 1998).

should be no possible doubt about this, we have had the word *nobility* removed from the text of the bill and replaced it with *honorary distinction*, which is in our view the true definition.[11]

Thus, if it is the case that nowadays distinctions are founded upon a fiction of ennoblement, this has occurred through the force of history. Moreover, the way in which their status has evolved reflects this. Up to the seventeenth century, the title was only of minor importance—apart from that of *duc*, which was recognized and protected by law—as the only thing that counted was how far back in time the line went. Then, under the effect of the 'curialization' of social elites and the competition opened up by the affirmation of the bourgeoisie, those who were ennobled decked themselves out with grandiloquent titles. In this way the right to nobility was transformed into a right to titles which became the monopoly of the sovereigns. The movement gained momentum in the nineteenth century with the development of new forms of titled nobility and then the increase in the number of purely life honours, which were formally open to all. This was the era in which the meaning of distinctions, having broken away from the patriarchal logic of court society, became autonomous. Standardized, multiplied, and delegated, it was to serve to amalgamate within a new hierarchy the old nobility with the new, the aristocracy with the common people, the representatives of civil society with the officers of the armed forces. In truth, with the advent of monarchical power and the development of parliamentarianism, heroic grandeur was no longer deduced from a morality of self-sacrifice or heroic deeds, a morality by means of which the nobility had in former times been able to call upon public recognition or upon its own conscience. From this time on, it was founded upon signs of esteem delivered as a reward for virtues which had been certified by State administrations. The society of honour had just given way to the bureaucracy of honours.

A Deference of State

Let us not forget that in classical theory, majesty—*maiestas*—is that presence that gives shape and form to the superiority of a governing power.[12] Now, we have seen that, from the end of the sixteenth century, monarchic absolutism put this manner of dramatizing appearances at the service of the exclusive preeminence of the king, with the result that, in the writings of the jurists, sovereignty itself was declared as being the plenitude of a power unhampered by tutelage and without limit of time. Since it is not simply given over for temporary keeping, it can be exercised without exception over any person, as over any thing, coming within the jurisdiction of what was called, from the time of Henri III and particularly Louis XIII, 'the State'. All in all, what is to be seen

---

[11] Pierre de Sémainville, *Code de la noblesse française* (Paris, 1860), 734.
[12] Georges Dumézil, '*Maiestas* et *gravitas*', in *Idées romaines* (Paris, 1969), 125–52.

here is the ultimate degree of a principle of grandeur beyond which no one can climb, a 'height of power at which the State must stop and establish itself'.[13] Now, it was to this grandeur of State that the republic ended up by attaching its hierarchy of merit.

On the occasion of the session of the Conseil d'Etat of 14 floréal, year X, devoted to the adoption of the Legion of Honour, the first consul, the future Napoléon Bonaparte, made this overwhelming statement:

The revolution is behind us. We have destroyed everything; now we must recreate. There is a government and there are powers; but what is the rest of the nation? Grains of sand. We have in our midst people who were formerly privileged, who are organized by principle and interest and who know very well what they want. I can count our enemies. But we ourselves are scattered and without system, without any means of meeting or contact. As long as I am here, I will certainly answer for the Republic but we must look to the future. We must 'cast a few masses of granite upon the soil of France'; we must give the people a direction and we need instruments to do this.[14]

These instruments, Napoleon would find them in hierarchical signs and honorary rewards. Grades, ranks, costumes, and decorations: the external signs, both functional and secularized, by means of which the State would henceforth objectify merit. In fact, this technique was not new. It started in court society. There, every distinction provided an opportunity of obtaining power. Awarded by the king, a distinction had a prestige value which was both hierarchical and transmittable. This was a matter of more than respect, for it brought with it immunities, privileges, tax exemptions, positions, and lands. In the same way, at the basis of *étiquette* lay more than decorations. There were rules governing precedence, royal pensions, genealogical titles, gestures, and apparel of bodies and societies . . . in a word, all those things that, referred to in his writings as 'formalities', so obsessed the Duc de Saint Simon.[15] These were signs which, as acts of homage paid to lineage as much as to loyalty, had the effect of encouraging a commerce of favour, hanging as they did upon the arbitration of royal favour.[16] For the king finally managed to seize the power to confer nobility, either by the individual award of hereditary distinctions— the famous *lettres patentes*—or by collective ennoblement.

[13] Charles Loyseau, *Traité des seigneuries* (Paris, 1608), 60. For a general presentation of such a frame of research, see Olivier Ihl and Yves Deloye, 'Deux figures singulières de l'universel: la République et le sacré', in Marc Sadoun (ed.), *La démocratie en France*. i.: *Idéologies* (Paris, 2000), 138–246.
[14] Quoted in Charles R. E. de Saint Maurice, *Histoire de la Légion d'Honneur* (Paris, 1833), 30.
[15] The document recently discovered by Yves Coiraul in Saint Simon's personal papers, *Mémoire succint sur les formalités*, bears the signs of this. Written in August 1712, it was published in *Traités politiques et autres écrits* (Paris, 1996), 137–306.
[16] On the importance of ranks and distinctions in the seventeenth century, see Henri Brocher, *Le rang et l'étiquette sous l'Ancien Régime* (Paris, 1934); Norbert Elias, *La société de cour* (Paris, 1975) (1st edn 1939) and, more recently, Jacques Revel, 'La cour', in Pierre Nora (ed.), *Les lieux de mémoire*, (Paris, 1992), 129–93. And, for an understanding of the transformation of this curial etiquette into a state protocol in the nineteenth century, see Olivier Ihl, 'Les rangs du pouvoir. Régimes de préséances et bureaucratie d'Etat dans la France des XIXe et XXe siècles', in Yves Deloye, Claudine Haroche, and Olivier Ihl (eds), *Le protocole ou la mise en forme de l'ordre politique* (Paris, 1996), 233–63.

This was what happened in the sixteenth and seventeenth centuries in the case of the judicial magistrates, who were integrated into the *noblesse de robe*. In England, the creation of peerages had a similar effect. The same might be said of the distribution of the titles of baronet—invented by James I for tax purposes—knight, and esquire. These gave the right to the title 'sir' and allowed its beneficiaries to become part of the gentry and the public administration, a world that was coveted every bit as much as was that of the nobility.[17] In the Russia of former times, the *dvorianine* was the equivalent of this artificial nobility that was integrated into the royal administration. Those concerned were civil or military functionaries who had risen through one or more of the 14 echelons of the administrative hierarchy, or *tchine*. On becoming colonels or members of the Council of State they were awarded titles that were hereditary or at the very least for life. This led to conflict with the old hereditary nobility, which, by virtue of its antiquity as well as the purity of its bloodlines, was entitled to proclaim itself the only true Russian aristocracy. We have seen that, in court society, deference relied upon a system of prerogatives, organized though rivalries between the different ranks, rivalries that were fuelled and arbitrated by the royal administrations. This was the type of system that the 'science of government' of the Enlightenment was to rationalize by setting in place a 'democratic' exemplarity as the guarantee of a new regime that publicized merit.

The Science of Power of Count Gorani

In Paris in 1792, a work in two volumes with the title of *Recherches sur la science de gouvernement* was published.[18] The author, Giuseppe Gorani, was an Enlightenment 'adventurer', at once 'philosopher', courtier, and reformer. He was a transition figure between the worldly science of the eighteenth century and the academic science of the nineteenth.[19] Unlike such philosophers as

---

[17] Mervyn James, 'English Politics and the Concept of Honour 1485–1642', *Past and Present*, Supplement no. 3 (1978), esp. 22.

[18] This work was first published under the title, *Ricerche sulla scienza dei governa* by Heubach, Durand & Co. in Lausanne in 1790. However, substantial alterations were made for this French edition.

[19] Born in Milan in 1744 into an ancient and noble family, this *illuminista* is presented in the dictionaries of the Restoration as a man who 'sowed seeds of revolution and democracy in the Peninsula'. It is true that, as a member of the society *Il Caffe*, he played an important role in the spreading of 'philosophical ideas'. He was a friend of Beccaria, Verri, and Frisi and also, in France, of Voltaire and Holbach, and wrote several works including a *Traité du despotisme*, which moved Bailly to ask for French citizenship on his behalf in the National Assembly. As aide-de-camp to Mirabeau and the Girondins, his exploits caused him to be rejected by the Lombardy nobility. Banished and stripped of his possessions, he joined the service of the Comité de Salut Public and then, with the fall of Robespierre, withdrew to Geneva, where he died in 1811. The most comprehensive biography is still that of Marc Monnier, *Un aventurier italien au siècle des Lumières: le comte Joseph Gorani, d'après ses mémoires inédits* (Paris, 1884). On the context of these Italian figures of the Enlightenment, see Franco Venturi, *Settecento riformatore, V, L'Italia dei lumi (1764–1790), tomo 1, La rivoluzione de Corsica. Le grandi carestie deglianni sessanta. La Lombardia delle riforme* (Turin, 1987).

Montesquieu, Rousseau, or Dragonetti,[20] he made absolutely no attempt either to identify the most legitimate forms of government or to determine what proportion of liberty man might have received from nature. Casting aside these 'metaphysical speculations', he strove to establish a different order of discourse on the State, a rhetoric that owes much to the 'police science'—Polizeiwissensschaft—of the universities of the German-speaking countries and their teaching.[21] So what was his aim? To rebuild the grand edifice of social relations through a new code of public merit. His idea was to establish a 'treasury of honours and outward decorations in order to encourage emulation and in so doing reward services rendered to society'.[22] The degree of novelty in relation to the aristocratic orders of honour is undeniable and rests upon three points.

First, this 'currency of honour', entrusted as it would be to the public authority as the guarantor of its value, had to be the reward for 'a truth well known to the public',[23] a way of signalling that decoration no longer derived its capacity to distinguish its recipients from its rarity but rather from a state monopoly which sanctioned its legitimacy. Admittedly it would be the Prince who awarded these signs of greatness. But in so doing he would simply be following the wishes of the academies specializing in the adjudication of merits. The Prince would thus be obliged to reward only those people who were judged worthy of reward by 'senates' set up to judge the different types and degrees of virtue. From being a princely art favouring the ambitions of the court, the competition for honours would go through a metamorphosis: through being applied to a great number of people, it would become a matter of procedure, institution, verification, inquiry, classification: in short, a sort of bureaucratic instrumentation of distinction, which from then on would be awarded by a tribunal of opinion.

In the second place, the brilliance of these signs of eminence would be proportional to the degree of usefulness of the actions performed. Thus decoration would now be thought of as a means of recognizing 'fine deeds' as opposed to 'those distinctions and prerogatives that opinion attaches to birth'.[24] In other words, it could no longer be accorded to the grand figures of

[20] Giacinto Dragonetti, Traité des vertus et des peines (Paris, 1768), translated from Italian by J.C. Pingeron.

[21] Cameralism formed the basis of the political philosophy and the precepts regarding administration in a new form of power. Born out of the need felt by the absolutist princes to rationalize both their power and the techniques of training for public office, it managed to gain a hold over a large part of eighteenth-century and then nineteenth-century Europe. By absorbing certain concepts, but also certain claims, of the movement of the Enlightenment, it transformed itself into an instrument for the promotion of only such changes as increased the power of the great and the good and the aristocracy. The result of this was that its call for reform hampered the modernization of the State apparatus as much as it promoted it. On this movement, see Karl-Heinz Osterloh, Joseph von Sonnenfelds und die österreichische Reformbewegung im Zeitalter des aufgeklärten Absolutismus : Ein Studie zum Zusammenhang von Kameralenwissenschaft und Verwaltungspraxis (Lübeck, 1970); and Pierangelo Schiera, Il camerismo e l'assolutism tedesco: Dall'arte di governo alle scienze dello stato (Milan, 1968).

[22] Giuseppe Gorani, Recherches sur la science de gouvernement, trans. C. Guilloton de Beaulieu, i. (Paris, 1792), vii.

[23] Gorani, Recherches sur la science de gouvernement, 20.

[24] Gorani, Recherches sur la science de gouvernement, 21.

society, no matter who they were, simply on account of their birth. Finally, political interest demanded that the talents and virtues of the 'lower classes of society' be rewarded, both because these classes 'represented the greatest number of people' and because this would 'encourage improvements in agriculture and in the most useful crafts and trades'.[25] By means of sashes, medals, ribbons, and pins, the signs of exemplary activity, the ploughman's cottage or the craftsman's workshop, places that had until then been considered humble retreats, would be able to bathe in the 'light of doing good, of true politics, and of social interest'. This form of utilitarianism was founded upon political expediency. Gorani did not deny that some men might be quite happy simply to find within themselves the prizes for their good deeds, that they might be capable of doing good without making any claim for recognition. But he immediately added that such people 'are the exception to the rule and we have no need to concern ourselves with them . . . instead we must concentrate on the vast majority of people, who, when they render service to society, do so out of a desire to obtain proof of recognition, esteem, and consideration in the form of civil honours and distinctions and so to live on in the memory of posterity'. This disposition was very 'useful' to society, making it 'the duty and the wise economy of government to offer a permanent means of nurturing this ambition, a means which would enable it to reward services rendered, make the rewards proportional to the services and, through such examples of justice, provide those who need it with an example to be emulated'.[26]

It is quite clear that improving the lot of the 'most numerous and less fortunate classes' was not in this context dependent simply upon arrangements of political economy, whether that of the physiocrats defending the freedom of grain markets or, in the nineteenth century, that of Sismondi, Bastiat, or Dupont-White. It was born out of the action of the state upon society, notably by setting in place a new regime of publicity. For Gorani, publicity was not just a means of controlling the government, it was much more a means of giving the government control over each and every person,[27] for one thing because it made emulation and thus 'influence' possible.[28] In the chapter entitled 'Des ordres d'honneurs', Gorani insisted that: 'investitures must take place in public and must be carried out with solemn ceremony by the "senates of education"'. The names of the commanders and knights of the various orders had to be constantly on show in university lecture halls, council or academy

---

[25] Ibid.   [26] Gorani, *Recherches sur la science de gouvernement*, 272.

[27] This is confirmed in Parsonian sociology, particularly in William J. Goode, *The Celebration of Heroes: Prestige as a Social Control System* (Berkeley, 1978): the idea is that the process by means of which social honour is allocated is a major source of stability for political systems.

[28] The statesman and 'doctrinaire' historian, François Guizot, made this the linchpin of his theory of 'the government of minds': governing the administration requires 'direct and promptly effective action', while governing society, on the other hand, requires other means: 'When it comes to minds, it is above all through influence that the government must operate.' He further mentions, along with the fact of bringing the 'superior minds of the lettered and wise' round to 'living in a natural and habitual fashion with the state', a 'moral development of successive generations', once more in order to 'establish intimate bonds between these generations and the state'. *Mémoire pour servir à l'histoire de mon temps*, iii. (Paris, 1859), 17.

premises, printed in public papers and in the national almanacs.[29] How could there be any doubt about it? Politics was no longer the physical science whose features had been set out by Montesquieu and would later be amplified by Comte. Its realm was now the sphere of public opinion. Consequently, governing no longer consisted in subjugating bodies or souls but rather in regulating, ordering, and channelling obligations. This involved setting in place new instruments of action.

The concept of *exemplarity* was the lever for these new instruments. It was at the turn of the century that it came into French from English to denote 'the formative power of having a model to follow'. The logic was simple: if negative sanctions were used to penalize law breaking, then positive sanctions rewarded exemplary conformity.[30] Such positive sanctions would encourage mimetic behaviour, bring about emulation, in short, constitute a veritable workshop of virtue within which the sense of duty would be crafted. Now, it was this sense of duty alone which could reconcile glory with merit and morality in the political arena. For Gorani, the notion of politics was not based upon action or a type of relationship between subjects. It embraced the State in its entirety through the medium of regulation. The objective here was less to reflect on the legitimacy of power than to construct it. Hence the importance of these institutionalized signs of exemplarity. They served as the guarantee that all grandeur should be first and foremost a politically defined conformity. Having rid himself of the scruples of the philosophers and turned his back on the psychological categories of 'human nature', Gorani had no hesitation in making the desire for honours the mainspring of the democratization of virtue. Publicity was not only the remedy for reason of state and the stratagems of the secrecy of absolutism.[31] It was an instrument of public power: a 'science' intended for a State that was conceived as being a machine that should be set in motion in order to turn it into a 'government of Enlightenment'.[32]

---

[29] Gorani, *Recherches sur la science de gouvernement*, 278. Emulation is ensured by means of a hierarchy of distinctive signs and types of reward: 'This order of encouragement will consist of four classes, the first of 25 grand commanders who will each have a pension of one thousand livres and will be decorated with a gold medal of one inch and a half in diameter to be worn around the neck; they will have an embroidered gold star on the uniform. The second class will be made up of one hundred commanders who will have a pension of two thousand livres; they will also wear the medal around the neck but the star on their uniforms will be of only half the size. The knights of the second class, five hundred in number, will wear a medal similar to that of the first two classes, but in the buttonhole of the uniform, which will have no star; they will have a pension of three hundred livres. Finally, the one thousand knights of the fourth class will wear a medal one inch in diameter in their buttonholes and will have pension of only one hundred and fifty livres'. Ibid.

[30] Gorani is aware of this: 'Merited glory confers a great deal of authority on the person who obtains it, particularly within the class in which his merit places him, and it is this authority which causes people to desire glory so intensely, because it greatly enhances our moral existence and seems to multiply us in every situation where we produce some enjoyment'. *Recherches sur la science de gouvernement*, 273.

[31] As Keith M. Baker established in 'Politics and Public Opinion under the Old Regime: Some Reflections' in Jack R. Censer and Jeremy Popkin (eds), *Press and Politics in Pre-revolutionary France* (Berkeley, 1987), 204–46.

[32] In fact, an entire epoch endorsed the ambition of this 'science of government'. For Constantin-François Volney it constituted nothing more nor less than the health of the state. Its absence, on the

A Technology of Virtue

This scrupulous management of control and visibility also lies at the heart of the political philosophy of Jeremy Bentham. Of his numerous works, his *Théorie des récompenses* has received little attention.[33] It suggested, however, control procedures which were as important as those in the Panopticon, which became famous in the twentieth century through the writings of Michel Foucault. Here the mechanism was not one of rehabilitation or punishment but a 'cultivation of benevolence' which would be the product of emulation through decoration:

The Humane Society, established in England for the purpose of affording assistance to persons in danger of drowning, and providing the means of restoration in cases of suspended animation, distributes prizes to those who have saved any individual from death . . . An institution of a similar nature, for the reward of services rendered in cases of fire, shipwreck, and all other possible accidents would still further contribute to the culture of benevolence; and these noble actions, brought in the same manner under the eyes of the legislators, and inscribed in their journals, would acquire a publicity of much less importance to the honoured individuals than to society in general. Indeed, though the reward applies only to one particular action, the principal object designed is the cultivation of those dispositions which actions indicate: and this can only be accomplished by the publicity which is given to the example, and the public esteem and honour in which it is held . . .[34]

other hand, paved the way to decadence, as could be seen from 'the sovereigns of Egypt who, like these of Baghdad, failed to preserve the nation from a wretched destiny'. *Voyage en Syrie et en Egypte pendant les années 1783, 1784 et 1785* (Paris, 1787), 92. A view which is also expressed by the Abbé Raynal in his *Histoire philosophique et politique des établissements du commerce des Européens des deux Indes*, i. (The Hague, 1776), 26. Gabriel de Mably is even more critical and speaks of a golden age which 'began by being borne to perfection with the Rome of Romulus only to degenerate subsequently'; *Parallèle des Romains et des Français par rapport au gouvernement* (Paris, 1740), 238. This is also the path taken by Claude Adrien Helvetius, for whom 'whilst it is very dangerous to tamper too frequently with the machinery of government . . . there are times when the machine stops if one fails to renew its springs. The ignorant worker does not dare to perform this operation; and the machine self-destructs. This is not the case with the skilled worker. He knows how to maintain it by repairing it with a bold hand. But such wise boldness presupposes an in-depth study of the science of government; this is an exhausting branch of study, which one is capable of only in early youth and perhaps only in countries in which public esteem promises people considerable advantages', an 'education' which might 'in the great empires, cause talents and virtues to multiply *ad infinitum*'. *De l'esprit* (Paris, 1758), 643.

[33] This is all the more surprising because the work, which was written in 1775, was very successful in its time. First published in French by Etienne Dumont under the title *Théorie des peines et des récompenses* (London, 1811), it was republished in 1818 in Paris by Bossange et Masson and in 1825, again in Paris, by Bossange frères, before appearing again in vol. 2 of his *Oeuvres* published in Brussels (Société Belge de la Librairie) in 1840. An English version was published in 1811 by the *Edinburgh Review*. This was reprinted in 1825 in London by Richard Smith for J. & H. Hunt. Since the text had been substantially modified by Etienne Dumont, a Swiss jurist friend of Bentham's, whom he had entrusted with the translation, only to repudiate this interpreter as 'having understood not a word of my thought', it was the English manuscript that was used for this edition, the one which, under the title *The Rationale of Reward*, was published by his assistant and publisher, John Bowring, in *The Works of Jeremy Bentham*, ii. (London, 1838), 89–266.

[34] J. Bentham, *The Rationale for Reward*, in *The Works of Jeremy Bentham*, i. (London, 1838), Ch. 16.

Persuade everybody that their actions, be they good or bad, are watched over by the State: for Bentham, this was how to get positive actions performed, that is to say, by orienting and directing free behaviour. Defined as a 'means of remuneration', the policy of decoration was the antithesis of the modern idea of penalty: 'Every distinguished service might find a place in these annals; and the people, always prone to exaggerate the vigilance and the means of information possessed by their governors would soon be persuaded that a perpetual inspection was kept up, not merely with respect to their faults, but also to their meritorious actions.' Do we need to be reminded that Bentham's philosophy was, like Gorani's, inseparable from his political struggle?[35] Jostling as it did the positions of both the Tories and the Whigs, it had, as we know, a profound influence on English political life, particularly on the electoral reform of 1832, with the extension of voting rights, and in 1872, after his death, with the adoption of the secret ballot. Bentham, who was a 'democrat' through his attachment to the ideals of the Enlightenment, founded in 1824 with James Mill the *Westminster Review*, which was the spearhead for numerous constitutional and educational reform bills. His plans concerning teaching methods, and notably those promoted by Lancaster, demonstrated this: the 'science' of emulation is bound up closely with educational procedures. Speeches, structures of precedence, prize-giving ceremonies: these were all resources to be exploited in order to link honorific gratification with individual adherence to social norms.

In his *Déontologie ou Science de la morale*, Bentham explained the status of these 'means of remuneration', which required extremely careful attention on the part of the authorities: 'reputation, honour, fame, celebrity, glory, dignity' were merely 'fictitious entities'. But although they had in common with money or land the fact of being 'objects of possession', the difference was that going out in search of such goods, 'however substantial they may be, was not considered unseemly'.[36] Sanction thus had a double status in his system: in the judicial domain, it acted mainly through punishment, whilst in the administrative realm it operated through the channels of reward. And it is in this latter role that it 'it is applied to those virtues which are designated by the State as being worthy of being rewarded by it'.[37]

It is quite clear: for Gorani, as for Bentham, the art of government operated through the mysteries of a 'science of morality'. This art was founded on *technologies of exemplarity*: means of gratification—public office, promotion in society, indemnity, or decoration—which would quite simply be signs of validation that would make an example of types of behaviour which went

---

[35] Note that, like Gorani, Dumont was a secretary to Mirabeau, for whom he wrote a number of speeches. Similarly, although there is nothing to suggest that Gorani and Bentham knew each other, both were naturalized as French citizens by the same decree of 26 August 1792, along with Thomas Paine, George Washington, and Thadeus Kosciuszko. *Archives Parlementaires de 1797 à 1860*, 1ère série, 1787–1799, xlix. (Paris, 1879), 10.

[36] Jeremy Bentham, *Déontologie ou Science de la morale*, revised, published and collated by John Bowring, translated by Benjamin Laroche (Paris, 1834), 113. For the English version, refer to the edition prepared by Amnon Goldworth, *Deontology* (Oxford, 1983).

[37] Bentham, *Déontologie*, 125.

beyond mere legal obligations. Emulation through decoration was for them, and also for those who have followed in their footsteps, intimately linked to the hopes projected upon it;[38] and this still holds good even if not everyone is able to realise himself in this way, as can be seen from the redefinition of the systems of decoration in post-revolutionary Europe.

A Fiction of Ennoblement?

The 'democratic' operation of decoration comes down to two aspects which sum up its development over the last two centuries: the arbitrariness of the distribution of distinction is no longer a matter of the favour of a monarch, at one and the same time judge and part of the system, by whose hand the spectacle is initiated. It comes out of a whole machinery of administration, of forms to be filled in, letters of recommendation, reports of inquiries, consultations, and regulations, all of which contribute to a will for uniformity that causes the patriarchal aspect to recede from view. Moreover, as a means of reward, honorific gratification has been made accessible to every citizen and thus constitutes a pattern of gaps and differences, which has lost all consistency.

The creation of the Legion of Honour caused a confrontation which, more than any other, brought out the principal arguments provoked by the 'democratic' adaptation of the system of distinction. According to the partisans of the order, since it was intended to reward military and civil services, it did not create a new class of citizens. While respecting the equality of everyone, it merely established an 'honourable distinction between those who have served their country and those who have done nothing for it'.[39]

According to its detractors, however, the creation of the order was an affront to the very values of the Revolution because 'the proposed order leads to aristocracy. Crosses and ribbons are the rattles of monarchy . . . We no longer have classes, let us not move towards re-establishing them. In the Republic, magistratures and appointments must be the best rewards for services, talents, and virtues'.[40]

Another councillor of state, Thibaudeau, was equally hostile: 'This institution, which is considered to be a guarantee of the Revolution, seems to me to go against its aims and, as an intermediary body, to set out from a principle which cannot be applied to a representative government. I fear that the love of ribbons may do more to weaken the very sense of duty and honour than to

---

[38] Just one example: for Charles His, 'the government, made up as it is of men, can do nothing to prevent either the number or the diversity of human passions but it is possible to prepare the ground in which these passions may circulate without damaging society'. *Théorie du monde politique ou de la science du gouvernement considérée comme science exacte* (Paris, 1806), 209.

[39] Pierre-Louis Roederer, quoted in M. Saint-Maurice, *Histoire de la légion d'honneur* (Paris, 1833), 30.

[40] Théophile Bernier, quoted in Saint-Maurice, *Histoire de la légion d'honneur*, 35.

strengthen it and cause it to bear fruit.'[41] As we know, Bonaparte famously replied:

I challenge anyone to show me a republic, ancient or modern where there were no distinctions. So these are rattles, are they? Well, it is with rattles that men are led. Nations that are old and corrupt are not governed in the same way as were the virtuous peoples of antiquity. Interest is sacrificed to enjoyment and vanity. This is one of the secrets of the return to titles, crosses, and sashes. These are innocent trinkets likely to command the respect of the masses, whilst at the same time instilling self-respect.[42]

On the one hand, a denunciation of the oppressive power of decorations and, on the other, a search for new distinctions to stimulate ambitions: the terms of the controversy are clear. What was being invented here was a new concept of State dignity. Whilst admittedly the decoration had to individualize, it did so only in order to make comparison possible. It could no longer lead to a partitioning of social space, as was the case with monarchic deference. On the contrary, it had to eliminate all attachments to nobility, and remove those who placed inherited glory before acquired glory or the descendants of great men before the great men themselves. For Lucien Bonaparte, who put forward the bill to the Tribunat, this was the meaning of this 'currency of a quite different value from those that are in the public coffers. It is a currency whose title cannot be changed and whose appearance cannot become worn because it resides in honour. It is the only currency that can serve as the reward for deeds that are regarded as being superior to all forms of reward'.[43]

Such a position would have been unthinkable under the Revolution, and in particular under the Convention, which set out to proscribe the very principle of decoration.[44] It is worth stopping to consider this for a moment, as it is the point at which French State republicanism breaks with classical republicanism.

What the Conventionnels feared about the award of civil decorations was the idea of rewards which, worn as a clear and distinctive sign of superiority, would be at odds with that 'visible equality' (Michelet) which was inscribed upon the heart of republican citizenship. Evidence of this is to be found in the report demanded by the Legislative Assembly in its session of 15 December 1791 in the Committee of Public Instruction. Three commissioners were appointed: Vaublanc, Condorcet, and Jean de Bry. They drew up a bill which

---

[41] Saint-Maurice, *Histoire de la légion d'honneur*, 37.

[42] Saint-Maurice, *Histoire de la légion d'honneur*, 39.

[43] Saint-Maurice, *Histoire de la légion d'honneur*, 59. On the birth of this order of virtue, see Frédéric Caille's recent clarification, 'Une citoyenneté supérieure. L'improbable "fonction" des membres de la légion d'honneur dans la république', *Revue française de Science Politique*, 47/1 (1997), 70–88.

[44] This is shown by the decree which, in 1793, awarded an oak wreath and a copy of the Constitution to young prizewinners. On 4 August 1793, at the height of the Terror, the awarding of prizes for the general competition held between the Paris schools took place at a ceremony in the Salle des Jacobins. The orator, a certain Dufourny, explained the meaning of the prizes awarded: 'Children of equality, may your hearts not be fearful of your brows being encircled for a moment by these wreaths, for these shall not be the wreaths of pride nor yet those of tyranny: these are the wreaths of the emulation of the talents that have founded, illuminated, and defended republics.' Cited in Albert Duroy, *L'Instruction et la Révolution* (Paris, 1862), 64.

was adopted by the Committee and put to the Assembly on 28 January 1792. What were the broad outlines of this bill? The following sentence offers a summary: 'Since the Constitution is founded upon absolute equality, the rewards must be calculated in such a way as to do no harm to that equality'. It went on to suggest rewarding virtuous deeds rather than those who had carried them out, or else substituting truly political insignia for marks of wealth, as Rousseau had already recommended, drawing his inspiration from the model of republican Rome:[45] rewards would range from oak or laurel branches for the most brilliant deeds to gold medals and rings for those which were less remarkable.

It remains the case that, even in its 'republicanized' form, this projected national decoration was thrown out. On 20 April 1792, the deputy Treilh-Pardailhan tried again. He suggested an external sign of the simplest possible character—a civic wreath made of two laurel branches—but he was no more successful. There was then a new initiative: in the session of 9 August 1793, the Conventionnel Guillemardet suggested issuing a commemorative medal for the *fête de la Constitution*. But it was the deputy Delacroix who won the day by suggesting that such a medal should be considered to be 'a monument and that no one should be able to wear it'.[46] It was thus apparent that for the Convention there could be no exterior mark to single out heroism. No person should be able make of such an emblem a visible means of attesting superiority.

Here lies the very meaning of the rupture introduced by the Revolution with the order of merit of the *ancien régime*. In the public arena, exemplarity could not *oblige* for it was no longer a sign of *noblesse*. Generally speaking, nothing could stand in the way of the principle of equivalence, that of the *common measure* set in place by the civic order of the Republic. This approach would remain the bedrock of nineteenth-century radical republicanism. Thus, in 1850, the deputy Chapuys-Montlaville opened the entry '*décoration*' in the *Dictionnaire politique* with the following assertion: 'This is a means of government used by monarchies. Its origin is entirely feudal; it is the spent representation of feudalism; it is a mutilated form of chivalry, reduced to petty proportions.' He went on to call for another form of recognition:

So may he who desires to devote himself to the service of his country no longer hope for any ribbon, any cross of gold, any diamonds. May he rather put his trust in public recognition; his name will live on in the memories of men, through tradition and history; if he is met with ingratitude, he will always have the recompense of his own self-esteem, that internal satisfaction, the perfume of his own virtue, that will perish only with him.[47]

[45] In order to subject all the members of the Polish government to a 'gradual march', Rousseau suggested re-establishing the classes and insignia of the former equestrian orders. But rather than having recourse to 'ribbons and jewels', as under the monarchy, which had the appearance of feminine baubles, these insignia would take the form of plaques of different metals 'whose material value would be in inverse proportion to the grade of those who wore them'. *Considérations sur le gouvernement de Pologne* (Paris, 1990), 238.

[46] Saint-Maurice, *Histoire de la légion d'honneur*, 10.

[47] Benoist Chapuys-Montlaville, in *Dictionnaire Politique* (intro. by Garnier Pagès) (Paris, 1850), 308.

For the radical republicans and soon for the Socialists, the idea was clear: the Revolution brought with it equality in the eyes of the law but also the metric system, the Code civil, the reform of the calendar, and the nationalization of the language. It was essential to prevent this homogeneous political space from being ruined by the reintroduction of insignia and sashes which would have the effect of catalysing new forms of social fragmentation.

In the 'sister republic' of the United States, the debate was no less passionate. Should a system of civil rewards be set up? The question arose at the end of the War of Independence. Influenced by the writings of Guichardin on ancient Rome, John Adams was one of the most resolute supporters of decorations. In his view, titles were indispensable to a republic as they maintained the passion for rewards and consequently the passion for virtuous attitudes: 'Men aspire to acts of greatness when merit is dependent upon reward.'[48] This concept of emulation through honours played a central role in the revolutionary vision of the 'old Whigs'. If people of talent were encouraged to satisfy their need for decorations, it was because public performance was carried out for the benefit of the common good. In so doing, it worked towards forging a 'republican aristocracy', one in which distinctions would be dependent solely upon competence and not upon birth or money.[49]

But this position was contested. For Thomas Paine, the notion of decorations came straight out of the *ancien régime* and was just a form of mystification intended to keep the people in a state of ignorance and fear. Madison too thought that it was dangerous to ask the language of honours to command the respect of the people because, in a republic, 'passions must be controlled by reason alone'.[50] The House of Representatives put an end to the controversy. It decided that honours would be awarded only for acts of military bravery. Thus it was that in 1782 Washington created the Purple Heart Badge of Military Merit, a simple purple heart made of woollen cloth and silk to be worn on the left lapel of the tunic. On the other hand, in civilian life, the people preferred to applaud rich men rather than men of virtue. Or rather they would be persuaded to honour the latter whilst paying deference to the former. Tocqueville summed this up as follows: in such a commercial society, the point of honour is turned away from the values of the warrior and is instead focused upon the love of wealth. If honour is nothing other than that 'particular rule founded upon a particular state, with the aid of which a people or a class distributes blame and praise', what is surprising about this? In the absence of a tradition of nobility, and especially in the absence of any majesty

[48] John Adams, *A Defence of the Constitutions of Government of the United States of America*, in Charles Francis Henry Adams (ed.), *The Works of John Adams*, vi. (Boston, 1851), 105. The concept is developed even further in his *Discourses on Davila*; see *The Works of John Adams* vi., 243.

[49] John G. A. Pocock, *The Machiavellian Moment: Florentine Political Thought and the Atlantic Republican Tradition* (Princeton, 1975), 249.

[50] On this controversy between the advocates of classical republicanism and the partisans of liberal rationalism so far as honours are concerned, see John P. Diggins, *The Lost Soul of American Politics: Virtue, Self-Interest and Foundations of Liberalism* (New York, 1984).

of State, there was nothing to prevent 'commercial temerity' itself becoming a qualification for honour.[51]

The Republic of Honours

In France, old monarchic country by its history, the Republic was not free from the imperative of majesty. In order to colonize the nation's imagination, it exhorted honorific deference. And not just the deference brought about through decorations but also that attached to civil and military precedence, those marks of State which, just as much as public statues, the trotting out of hymns, or the names of streets, put in place an aura of sacredness, guaranteeing submission and loyalty. On this point, therefore, the Republic was more aristocratic than revolutionary.

Although this bureaucratization of the French Republic gave rise to substantial revisions and even deep rifts, the immediate result was to cause a profound split at the heart of the republican movement, particularly from the end of the nineteenth century. The firm reply to the opponents of decoration, whether they were Protestants, positivists, or socialists was:

Decorations are not, as has been said, an attack on the equality that must reign between men, nor are they simple trinkets of vanity; what must be seen in them is public recognition of services rendered and a powerful motivating force towards emulation and encouragement.[52]

And even when the profusion of honorary orders made them less enviable, when obtaining them turned out from time to time to be a matter of favours or courtesanry, there were no negative conclusions to be drawn from this so far as the institution itself was concerned. This is because, in the words of the publicist Henri Fouquier, 'whilst admitting that honorific distinctions do not create merit and that virtue in the broadest sense of the term has no need of them, they do encourage virtue and mark it out; and by the simple fact of doing so give it the value of an example, which is absolutely essential'.[53]

There is no denying it: the Republic most certainly defined a new form of honorific deference. It did not renounce decorations. Nor did it content itself with imitating the monarchic model by substituting new signs of merit for the old ones. What it in fact did was to coin a new usage of the sign of merit. Its first feature was that the business of state honours was no longer characterized by the hierarchy of hereditary conditions, much to the displeasure of the traditional elites, who had high hopes of using them as a means of defending themselves against 'the invasion of common men'. Instead, republican

---

[51] Alexis de Tocqueville, *De la démocratie en Amérique*, ii. (Paris, 1961), 318.
[52] Theodore Bachelet et Charles Dezobry, 'Décorations', in *Dictionnaire des lettres, des beaux-arts et des sciences morales et politiques* (Paris, 1879, 5th edn).
[53] Cited in Joseph Durieux, *Etude sur l'action disciplinaire de la Légion d'honneur* (Paris, 1900), 34.

decorations became non-hereditary.[54] The second feature was that honour was no longer at the service of the monarch but now operated in the name of a nation proclaimed as the sole proprietor of titles of dignity. This is why decorations were taken to maintain the sense of virtue, a sense that was judged to be all the more essential for having to counterbalance the invasive power of money. So what exactly did the award of a distinction represent? 'An act of sensible economy, a compensation for services rendered, and an invitation to render more. But it is a reward that does not call for more rewards: society and the citizen are even.'[55] This is tantamount to recognizing that, if the decoration makes a claim to being seen, its role is above all to see and allow oneself to be seen through it and to attract and retain the public attention which is directed upon it. So, by developing its own honours system, the Third Republic effectively appropriated this 'gaze'. In order to do this, it was only necessary to stop the awarding of titles of nobility or to decree that, so far as bureaucratic deference was concerned, honour conferred was not transferable and did not lead to any political entitlement. For Jules Simon, this was obvious: a distinction is merely a reward that honours and the honour awarded is a distinction that rewards: 'For public spirit to be formed and maintained, we need this great voice of the nation that accords praise and blame every day, that reminds us constantly of social principles, of common interests.'[56]

The reason the republic made this choice is no doubt that it had to face up to the majesty of State, and also because it had to confront the extravagant laws of a society of orders. So, far from abolishing them, it set out to redefine their content in order to appropriate for itself their power of subjection. An operation that was determined by its social context, which was that of a rapidly rising bourgeoisie, a bourgeoisie that was torn between the will to appropriate for itself the behaviour of the nobility, in the hope of acceding to it, and the affirmation of its own class values. There is an unambiguous sign of this in the fact that, unlike the Republic born in 1848, that of 1875 recognized titles of nobility as affixes to a name. It did not award such titles and only very exceptionally recognized the right to bear foreign titles. But it continued to confirm regular titles—and this is still the case today—by inscribing them in the registers of the Sceau de France. It even took over the arrangements set in place by the Second Empire to prevent titles being usurped and the falsifying of names in order to claim distinctions of honour.[57]

Generally speaking, the French Republic applied itself to fixing and protecting the bearing of distinctions. This was the aim of the decree of 10 March

---

[54] Gabriel Tiersonnier, *Le nombre et le mérite. Lois constitutionnelles basées sur le mérite* (Paris, 1901), 5.

[55] Anon. (signed M. P.), *Des décorations dans une démocratie* (Angoulême, 1908), 4.

[56] Jules Simon, cited in the article 'Publicité' in Maurice Block (ed.), *Dictionnaire général de la politique* (Paris, 1863).

[57] This protection, which had been abolished by the July Monarchy, was re-established in May 1858. It was intended to guarantee the purity of titles of nobility but also to combat the fraudulent use of 'airs of nobility' such as that of adding a particle to the patronymic. On the reactions provoked by this initiative, see de Sémainville, *Code de la noblesse française*, 740.

1891 which laid down the etiquette for wearing these State honours: the Legion of Honour took precedence over the Military Medal, commemorative medals, university decorations, the Agricultural Order of Merit, and the Medal of Honour; foreign decorations were relegated to the bottom of the list and, significantly, were to be worn to the left of national orders. So far as the legal protection accorded to these tributes of honour was concerned, there can be no doubt: the prison sentences and fines set out in article 259 of the code pénal were every bit as severe as those put in place in its own code by the Italian monarchy in 1889. In both cases, the aim was to guarantee that State honours be accorded the deference that was their due. Everything thus points to the conclusion that, whatever the type of government, the capacity to award an honour had become a princely right. 'There is no honour but in the State and the State alone can dispense it', as Emile Worms revealingly put it.[58] From then on, those external demonstrations by means of which eminence achieved recognition would be in the control of the State. Now, by claiming this prerogative, the European bureaucracies took over the monopoly of *signs of validation* of merit. Consequently, they were able to transform certain modes of behaviour—what one might call *poses of grandeur*—into recognized and coveted forms of worth. All in all, they had succeeded in setting down the rules governing the forms taken by social esteem and in using these all at once as a tool for regulating ambitions, as a bonus to encourage loyalty, and as a means of making certain modes of conduct serve as examples to others.

The Bureaucratization of Honours

Since the nineteenth century, bureaucracy in Europe has taken on the guise of a workshop in which innumerable forms of honorific gratification have been crafted. Not only are there rules of precedence, military parades, escorts, and other codes of salute, funeral honours, or official customs, there are also decorations of every sort: marks of consideration awarded to certain bodies and certain people on account of their role or their worth.

In France a plethora of distinctions has been added to the Legion of Honour: the award known as the Rescue Medal (1820), the Cross of the July Combatants (1830), the Military Medal (1852), the medals of Sainte-Hélène (1857) and of the Mutual Aid Societies (1858), the China Medal (1861), the Post and Telegraph Medal (1882), the Forestry Officials' Medal (1883), the Tonkin Medal (1885), the Labour Medal (1886), the Madagascar Medal (1896), the Prison Administration Medal (1896), the Indirect Taxes Medal (1897), the Public Works Medal (1898), the Colonial Prisons Medal (1898), the International Exhibition Workers' Medal (1899), and the Firemen's Medal (1900). In Imperial Germany too, the bureaucracy set out to create new

---

[58] Emile Worms, *Les attentats à l'honneur : diffamation, injures, outrages, adultère, duel, lois sur la presse, etc.* (Paris, 1890), 23.

honours. So it was that the Royal Prussian Cross of Merit was introduced in October 1910. It was widely awarded and was intended not as 'a guaranteed honour for specific ranks, but as a visible demonstration of the monarch's favour, based on personal judgement of individual services'. Added to this were the Cross of Female Merit in 1906 and the Mark of Honour in 1911, and above all, the title *Rat*. This was extended to a number of activities including business, law, medicine, secondary school teaching, finance, and agriculture and gave its holders the right to be addressed as *Excellenz*. This explains its considerable success throughout the country.[59]

In the Italy of the *Risorgimento*, the notables of the economy and the liberal professions rushed to lay their hands on the titles of the traditional nobility and in so doing reinforced its social and cultural hegemony. But the bureaucracy knew precisely how to fuel this passion by creating new cohorts of distinctions, which this time were not hereditary. If we leave aside commemorative and military medals, four of these decorations played a key role. They were the Medal for Civil Valour (*medaglia al valor civile*), created by Victor Emmanuel in 1851, which rewarded acts of altruism and civic responsibility at first with gold insignia, then silver, and eventually bronze, in the face of the flood of people who rushed to claim them. Next came the Medal of Devotion to Public Health (*benemerenza alla salute publica*), created in 1854 by the King of Sardinia and reorganized by Victor Emmanuel II in 1867 in order to reward acts of courage in times of epidemic. This was followed by the Medal for Devotion to Public Instruction (*peri benemeriti dell'istruzione pubblica*), created in 1904 for 'people who have singled themselves out by their contribution to making the advantages of primary instruction and the education of children more widely available'. Finally came the Star of Labour Merit (*stella al merito del lavoro*), which was put in place by Victor Emmanuel III in 1923 to reward blue-collar workers in the industrial, agricultural, or business sectors who had displayed exemplary conduct.[60] In England, it was left to a subtle variation in the use of the adjective to distinguish between degrees of honour. These ran from the 'most distinguished', through 'the most noble order', the 'most exalted', the 'most honourable', to the 'most illustrious'.[61]

It would be mistaken to see this inflation of honours as being nothing more than a survival from the past, the imprint of a nobility which, having disappeared as an order, continued to impose its customs on the rest of society: in short, the result of a fascination on the part of bourgeois Europe for the aristocratic lifestyle.[62] This explanation does not go far enough. Admittedly, the

[59] Karin Kaudelka-Hanisch, 'The Titled Businessman : Prussian Commercial Councillors in the Rhineland and Westphalia during the Nineteenth Century', in David Blackbourn and Richard J. Evans (eds), *The German Bourgeoisie* (London and New York, 1991), 87–114.

[60] On these new 'honorific nobilisations', see Gian Carlo Jocteau, *Nobili e nobilità nell'Italia Unita* (Rome, 1997), 24–86.

[61] On the transformative processes of aristocratic honour in England, see Abraham D. Kriegel, 'Liberty and Whiggery in Early Nineteenth-Century England', *Journal of Modern History*, 52 (1980), esp. 266–78.

[62] This of course is Arno Mayer's thesis in *La persistence de l'Ancien Régime. L'Europe de 1848 à la Grande Guerre*, trans. J. Mandelbaum (Paris, 1983).

new titles could be seen, as was the case with the superior grades of the orders of Saint Anne and Saint Stanislas in Russia, to constitute the antechamber to true ennoblement. But, more often than not, these decorations were purely personal and were thus only honorary *titles*. Since behind them lay no territorial fiefdoms, their function was to reward the services of agents or professions over which the bureaucracy wished to gain control. This was the case in Germany with purely honorary titles of first or second class, such as *Kommerzienrat*, *Justizrat*, *Baurat*, *Medizinalrat*, or *Regierungsrat*. Just as significantly, in France, after the creation of the Legion of Honour, the conseil du Sceau had to establish a distinction in order to protect the ancient noble title of knight (*chevalier*): 'The appellation *chevalier de la Légion d'honneur* . . . must always be placed after the name rather than before it, given that it is in no way a title but merely a qualification.'[63] This did not prevent the noble title from suffering from the competition with the bureaucratic distinction—to such an extent that around the 1830s it dropped out of use except amongst older generations.[64]

Even if the inflation of honours and decorations in the nineteenth century was a means of reaffirming the pre-eminence of the old ruling class and of keeping control over the fortunes of the 'new men', it nonetheless had another mainspring, as can be seen even from the changes that took place in government practices. Let us not forget: everywhere on the European continent, new administrative tasks made it necessary to set up permanent offices and organizations and to define areas of jurisdiction and procedures. The administration of the State was transformed into the hands of the new elites: it moved from a prebendary-patrimonial logic to one of bureaucratic rationality. This reorganization of departments, which continued at an intense pace right through the century, brought with it an explosion in the number of public employees. The new status conferred upon employees and clerks, who had previously been paid as their superiors saw fit but were now placed under the control of assemblies, also offered new opportunities. Now under State control, the management of administrative personnel prepared the way for the advent of the modern figure of the civil servant. With this, functions that had up to then been the monopoly of ecclesiastical and municipal administrations were taken over, from the civil registry to the education of the people and aid for the poor.

This is also the context in which the bureaucracy generalized the use of honorific means of gratification. It was a question of ensuring systematic mastery of the conduct of civil servants. Professional qualifications alone were no guarantee that the means of administration would be rationalized. Something else was required: purely honorary rewards that would make it possible to forge the alliance between the princes and the bourgeoisie against the privileges of the high nobility. The German example is an eloquent one. Unlike what

---

[63] This session of 19 April is discussed by Jean Tulard, *Napoléon et la noblesse d'Empire* (Paris, 1979), 156.

[64] David Higgs, *Nobles, titres, aristocrates en France après la Révolution, 1800–1870* (Paris, 1990), 63.

happened in France, unification did not lead to a national system of honours. Quite the contrary. It encouraged a proliferation of titles of distinction and of ennoblement in the 25 states that made up the Empire, with the exception of the city states of the Hanseatic League such as Hamburg, Bremen, and Lübeck.[65] These means of gratification thus served to 'feudalize' the German bourgeoisie, and in particular the middle classes, who renounced all autonomy and rushed to get their hands on those aristocratic orders that were most highly prized, such as the Red Eagle, the Black Eagle, and the Cross of the Knight of the House of Hohenzollern. The result was that, in this 'Prussianized' society, the ethical models and the codes of behaviour of the military nobility became generalized.[66]

But there were higher stakes than this behind these means of gratification. They were intended to reconstitute a type of autocratic authority *at the very heart* of the imperial bureaucracy. This can be seen from the way in which the system of decorations was set in motion in concrete terms by the machinery of State. Although Wilhelm II was presented as being a 'fountain of honours'— his reign coincided with an expansion of the practices of ennoblement[67]—the independence that the State had managed to grasp for itself was very real. This stood out very clearly on the occasion of the centenary of the University of Berlin in 1910. The Emperor protested about the composition of the list of honorands, which contained more government 'officials' than university figures, but the bureaucracy haughtily ignored his injunction. And it went still further: it continued to make use of each and every occasion to reward those from its own ranks. For was it not the bureaucracy that actually handled the management of honorary titles? It was indeed the case that requests were addressed to the General Orders Commission, a body which had no power of decision but which, nonetheless, handled the material procedures: the updating of registers, the awarding of medals, the organization of annual celebrations. It was the Prussian cabinet (*Geheiles Zivilkabinett*) which was the principal arena of discussion and decision. It appointed the special commissions that examined the merits of civil servants. Their number had undergone an explosion between 1882 and 1907, rising from 251,000 to 945,000, that is to say, from 3 per cent to 5.2 per cent of the active population. The honours that were introduced during this period thus had two objectives: to respond to a growing demand for distinctive signs of merit and to develop a new system of bureaucratic control.

There is no getting round it: the bureaucratization of honours is essential to any modern definition of merit. The respect for State action does not spring

[65] For a presentation of the way that the awarding of decorations was orchestrated by the Prussians in imperial Germany, see Alastair Thomson, 'Honours Uneven: Decorations, the State and Bourgeois Society in Imperial Germany', *Past and Present*, 4 (1994), 171–204

[66] This thesis is argued by Norbert Elias, *The Germans: Power Struggles and the Development of Habitus in the Nineteenth and Twentieth Centuries* (London, 1996).

[67] To take just one example, the Black Eagle, which was the highest order in Prussia, became 'a very common animal'. Originally limited to 30 members, it rose above this threshold in 1890 and practically doubled its numbers in 1912.

from a purely formal belief in the regularity of its rulings or directives. Like the old *noblesse de robe*, the functionaries operated on the basis of an ideal that was at once heroic and utilitarian. In so doing, their propensity for docility was increased by their attachment to the prerogatives of honour. This encouraged a sense of duty that was increasingly perceived as being a vocation. One might speak in terms of a form of hierocracy or even of 'slavery without a master'. On might also, more cautiously, suggest that, contrary to the prophecies of Max Weber, the rationalization of the forms of government did not exclude from modern bureaucracy 'love, hate, and all purely affective personal elements'[68] likely to prevent objectivity from holding complete sway, that objectivity of which the State had been proclaiming itself the guarantor since the nineteenth century.

Since the prescriptions of honour have dwindled considerably since society ceased to be divided into different castes[69] and also since the bureaucracy has been generously awarding its own insignia of virtue, the forms according to which heroes have been created have undergone profound modifications. At the same time as they became public property servicing a network of clients, a means of distinction, and social mimesis, the orders of merit made it possible in the Europe of bourgeois democracies to invent a bureaucratic form of deference which concentrated all the justifications of this new form of authority: from the assertion of the superiority of individual virtue over inherited glory to the exaltation of altruism, the criticism of the venality of noble orders, and devotion to 'the public domain', here taken to include public service as well as public opinion.

But behind these changes, real as they were, was a structural continuity. Behind the references to democracy lay, above all, State action. Throughout the century, one principle was never questioned: the monopoly that had been attributed to central authority in the creation of signs denoting greatness. In France, on 10 July 1816, just after the Restoration, Louis XVIII defined the scope of this phenomenon. He signed an *ordonnance* according to which acts of public homage were to be included in the category of princely powers:

The right to award signs of recompense is an inherent right of the crown. In a monarchy, all favours must emanate from the sovereign; and the appreciation of services rendered to the state and the distribution of awards to those whom we regard as being worthy of such is our prerogative and ours alone . . . From now on, no act of homage and no reward can be voted for, offered, or awarded as a sign of public recognition by municipal councillors, national guards, or any other civil or military body without prior authorization.[70]

---

[68] Max Weber, *Wirtschaft und Gesellschaft*, ii. (Cologne-Berlin, 1964), 718.

[69] Tocqueville noted: 'it was dissimilarities and inequalities that created the honours system'. It can only dwindle when these are removed and disappear with them. *De la démocratie en Amérique*, 333.

[70] Ordonnance No. 198, in *Bulletin des lois du Royaume de France, (1816)* (Paris, 1817), 4. On the science of government that inspired this monopolization of the signs of public recognition, see Olivier Ihl, *La fête républicaine* (Paris, 1996), 62.

Léon Morgand, who was chief of staff at the Ministry of the Interior, provided the following reminder of the state of affairs at the beginning of the Third Republic: 'The right to award tokens of public recognition is an essential attribute of the state. No person can substitute himself for the state nor speak in the name of the state.'[71] Same situation in Italy, where in 1889 the House of Savoy set up the register of the *Consulta Araldica de Regno* (Office for the Titles of the Kingdom) in order to channel and control the norms of use applying to titles. In Imperial Germany, the Almanac of German Orders (*Deutscher-Ordenliste*) provided the means of keeping scrupulously up to date the list of more than a 100,000 names that made up this hierarchy of orders. The great and the good of the kingdom had gilded copies whilst other, more modestly produced versions were available in all the administrative centres of Prussia and the Reich.

Setting itself up as the producer of sociability, the State apparatus in a number of European countries took control of the dissemination of signs denoting homage. It was as if the *persona ficta* of the republic, kingdom, or empire was but a screen behind which another project was being carried out, that of a bureaucratic structure subordinating the new elites of commoners by developing a deference that was modelled on the *mores* of the former court nobility. This is why the existence of honorary distinctions cannot be explained simply in terms of the function they served, which was that of making certain moral and civic qualities visible. To leave it at that would be to reduce the decoration to a mere sign and consequently to forget its specifically administrative dimension. There is no way of avoiding the fact that the value conferred upon these marks of glory is first and foremost that of the political mechanisms that promote its recognition. Although democratic distinction confers *gravitas* upon an exemplary figure, this figure exists only through his encounter with the bureaucracy. It is the State that, since the end of the orders of chivalry and nobility, has dispensed and protected honorary rewards, insignia that it endows with what the inventor of semiotics Charles S. Peirce called a 'representative quality',[72] insignia in which, since that time, it has concentrated its power in order to establish itself in grandeur and dazzle the eyes of all.

---

[71] Léon Morgand, *Des hommages publics décernés par les corps administratifs ou autres* (Paris, 1884), 4.

[72] C. S. Peirce, *Ecrits sur le signe*, trans. G. Deledalle (Paris, 1978), 178.

9

The Republic and its Territory: The Persistence and the Adaptation of Founding Myths

YVES MÉNY

IN his classic *The Government and Politics of France* (1989), writing in almost Tocquevillian style, Vincent Wright presented young students from the English-speaking world with the specific features and intricacies of 'Provincial Pressures in a Jacobin State'. In this fine and balanced analysis Wright, as was his habit, took pleasure in emphasizing the paradoxes and contradictions of French political practice. The theory and practice of French territorial organization was presented successively from the contrasting viewpoints of the Jacobins on the one hand and the provincials hostile to the capital on the other. These two opposing, antagonistic, sometimes caricatured visions enabled Wright to reveal to his readers the excesses of the positions held by the protagonists. It also allowed him to sketch with impressionist brushstrokes a portrait of a France that was, and indeed remains, more complex than it seems: neither completely centralized, as the *Ancien Régime* monarchs and their Jacobin successors wished, nor totally enslaved as the aristocrats subjected to royal power and the court complained—as did, after the Revolution, all those frightened by the power and the blood-letting in the capital.

'Traditionally', wrote Wright, 'the capital was depicted as the malevolent centre of Revolution which, in 1789, 1814–15, 1830, 1848 and 1871 disturbed the contented and peace-loving provincials.' On the contrary, the Jacobins saw the capital 'as an island of culture, a city of enlightenment, a torchbearer of the progress assailed by oafish—and reactionary—rural clods, the ignorant troops of the church and the château. Like the monarchs of the *Ancien Régime* they imposed centralization as their means of strengthening the regime against internal opponents, but also against external enemies.'[1]

It is clear that Wright was following in Tocqueville's footsteps, highlighting the continuity of underlying State structures despite successive upheavals and revolutionary shocks. As recently stressed by the Italian scholar Stefano

---

[1] *The Government and Politics of France*, 255.

Mannoni in a brilliant study on the history of administrative centralization in France,[2] Tocqueville's contribution to the question is so fundamental that it bears down like a lead weight on thinking in this area. The thesis of the continuity of *Ancien Régime* centralization through the Revolution and the regimes that succeeded it has become so influential and decisive as by now to seem undisputed and unchallengeable. In Mannoni's words: 'The "Tocqueville paradigm" has exercised, and continues to exercise, an undisputed hegemony of which lawyers and historians are not always aware'.[3] But Wright departed from Tocqueville in seeing not only permanence and stability over and above the superficial agitation. He instead stressed throughout his chapter in *The Government and Politics of France*, and throughout his scholarly work, how the complexity of things ran counter to simplistic discourses and mystifying rhetoric. In particular he highlighted the collision of Jacobin and republican aspirations with local resistances, a state of affairs which led to compromises and nuanced solutions rather than to categorical outcomes. The process was never linear but full of contradictions that run against received ideas and common opinions.

Events in the summer of 2000 brought a remake of this comedy, sometimes tragic but most often magniloquent or simply ridiculous, of what Théodore Zeldin called the French passions.[4] Minister of the Interior Jean-Pierre Chevènement's resignation following disagreements with Socialist Prime Minister Lionel Jospin on the handling of the Corsica issue was a good illustration of the twofold tension Wright identified: defending the Republic against its internal adversaries—the Corsicans and other centrifugal forces—but also outside ones, forces hostile to the nation, such as an integrated Europe, American imperialism, and other forms of globalization. If continuity is to be found, it is perhaps more in perceptions, representations, myths, and rhetoric than in the increasingly complex realities themselves, which do not always show through in official discourse. To be sure, observers of French political and administrative reality tend less than in the past to take as gospel truth the antagonistic discourses structured around the two poles of Jacobinism and Girondinism: Jacobins the triumphant upholders of national unity and State centralization, Girondins the eternally defeated promoters of provincial unity.

But this more realistic and nuanced perception, now largely accepted, should not cause us to forget our debt to such pioneering spirits as Wright, who have enabled the French to 'revisit' their own history and the vision handed down to them by politicians and the dominant historiography: a vision crystallized in the conformist categories of legal discourse or ideologies comfortably resting upon certainties that are as untouchable as they are reassuring. Nonetheless, these legal and political stereotypes do present advantages for analysis. They constitute obligatory reference points around which

---

[2] Stefano Mannoni, *Une et Indivisible. Storia dell' accentramento amministrativo in Francia* (Milan, 1994), vi–vii.

[3] Mannoni, *Une et Indivisible*, vi.   [4] Theodore Zeldin, *France 1848–1945* (Oxford, 1977).

political thinking, action, and struggle can take shape. They scarcely provide information on the actuality of the organization of the territory, but condition and determine it as ideological and legal 'fixed points'. The problem becomes not so much transcending or erasing them—sacrilegious hypotheses—as accommodating them or surreptitiously deviating from them: practice triumphs over discourse, reality over myth, the unspoken over what is proclaimed.[5]

It is in relation to these so-called immovable boundaries that movement can be measured. At the dawn of the twenty-first century, France is changing but does not know it, or does not want to know it, or denies it like Molière's *Tartuffe*: 'Hide that breast, I cannot see it.' Vincent Wright, who knew better than anyone the vices and virtues of France and the French, had no equal in making them swallow a few home truths by using his favoured techniques of paradox or confrontation between thesis and antithesis. Having brought out everything the French were accustomed—and eager—to hear, he delighted in taking the question up again from a quite different angle, stressing all the aspects or facets of the problem that the national blinkers no longer allowed to come into view.

Political Unity and Administrative Uniformity

That the principle of unity is one of the pillars of the French nation and one of the values constantly affirmed by the Republic is hardly surprising given the way the nation State and the monarchy were created from the early Middle Ages though to the nineteenth century. Starting from the central core of the *Ile de France*, the monarchical State never ceased seeking to expand until it reached its alleged 'natural frontiers', in order where appropriate to extend the principle beyond those physical limits and claim new territory.

Until the mid-twentieth century the policy begun ten centuries earlier continued in similar terms. On the eve of the Second World War, for instance, de Gaulle could still seek to assert French claims over the Saar or the Val d'Aosta using arguments that had first been deployed by the monarchy and then the Revolution. Likewise, the principle of unity has been extended, though with more difficulties, to territorial configurations beyond the metropolitan continent: to the overseas departments, particularly Algeria, albeit in this case at the cost of a bloody and eventually unsuccessful war. And to Corsica, where nationalist claims are presently creating conditions for a new collective psychodrama around that indefinable yet emotion-laden, passion-charged concept, the Republic. By absorbing areas and populations with distinct traditions, local languages, and cultures, the State has from the outset opted for integration, absorption, unification, seeking to eliminate anything that might appear as centrifugal forces: most notably religious or social pluralism, and cultural or linguistic diversity.

[5] Yves Mény, *Centralisation et décentralisation dans le débat politique français* (Paris, 1974).

Unity has since the outset been understood as uniformity, but it was the Revolution and then the Empire and the ensuing regimes that gave full meaning to this original choice. Under the monarchy, the principle of unity meant unchallenged affirmation of the monarch to the detriment of feudal structures. The institution of the Court by Louis XIV and the domestication of the provincial aristocrats is an illustration of this monarchical conception of centralization. The elimination of Protestantism, not the Prince's religion, constituted another.[6] But the monarchy was never capable of bringing to full realization this principle of political unity conceived as administrative uniformity. There still survived institutions, rules, and traditions associated with localities and particularisms. The obsession with rational uniformity brought by the Revolution is where the strategic interests of the State and the intellectual heritage of Enlightenment philosophy came together. Rationality was imposed everywhere—to Burke's great regret—in the boundaries of administrative units, in the development of the revolutionary calendar, and in the creation of new weights and measures. Coupled with equality, this unitary principle was intended—and expected—to produce uniformity: what might be termed 'unity-as-uniformity'.

More than two centuries later this principle is still almost as vigorous. Yet, as Wright stressed, given the State's inability to constrain reality and shape it in its image, adjustments and exceptions have proved necessary. These derogations have indeed been frequent as long as lip service has been paid to the sacrosanct principle of unity-as-uniformity. The most glaring manifestation of this obsessive pattern can be found in the establishment and development of local institutions. From the outset one thing was understood: the new administrative structures would be founded on the same principles, provided with the same powers, and equipped with the same institutional features. In the case of departments—which some zealots would have liked to draw with the geometrical regularity of a chessboard—the rule was applied to its full extent: the new institutions were similar in size and identical in their powers. The determined will of the revolutionaries to get rid of the provinces of the *Ancien Régime* was to prove very effective.[7]

By contrast, despite several efforts it was much harder to eliminate the parishes in a rural world where they still possessed a powerful sociological presence. The salami tactics applied to the departments were to prove impossible, but the principle of unity-as-uniformity was to be reflected in the absolute egalitarianism of institutions and powers, despite historical, sociological, and especially demographic differences that set the sparsely populated communities against the towns.[8] Needless to say, the conception of the 'commune' defined as a sort of 'enlarged family' is scarcely compatible with the cre-

    [6] On this theme see the works of Emmanuel Leroy-Ladurie, notably *L'Etat Royal* (Paris, 1987) and *L'Ancien Régime* (Paris, 1991).
    [7] See Roger Dupuy (ed.), *Pouvoir local et Révolution* (Rennes, 1995).
    [8] Vivien A. Schmidt, *Democratizing France. The Political and Administrative History of Decentralization* (Cambridge, 1990).

ation of genuine urban government. It was to take a century and a half, and the economic, industrial, and urban transformation of France, for the specific features of towns and conurbations finally to start being taken account of.[9] But even in 1982–3 the projects to differentiate powers in accordance with the size of municipalities brought a circling of the wagons and a return to ideological orthodoxy under pressure from the Senate, the guardian of conservative vested interests in the republican order. It was once again asserted that no hierarchy could exist among territorial collectivities—for instance, between the departments and the municipalities—and that no 'discrimination' could be practised according to, for instance, the size of municipalities. As in Alice in Wonderland, 'all must have prizes'.

Obviously, once the inflamed proclamations of the politicians had subsided and the laws had been entered in the *Journal Officiel*, the reality principle came back with a vengeance to haunt the memories of local and central actors. The exceptions originate first from insurmountable political circumstances. Thus, from the Revolution to the present, Paris has constituted the main derogation from the principle of unity-as-uniformity. The capital was too specific—a demographic dinosaur in the predominantly rural world of the *hexagone*—too socially different, too politically turbulent, to take the risk of giving Paris the same powers as other French municipalities. We had to wait until 1975 for President Valéry Giscard d'Estaing finally to give the capital its necessary autonomy. But it is noteworthy that the democratization and modernization of Paris's territorial regime were carried out, not in the name of the special needs of a city at the centre of one of Europe's main conurbations, but, perversely, by invoking the sacrosanct principle of unity-as-uniformity. This did not prevent the distinction from being consolidated in the same move, since uniquely in this case the city of Paris at the same time handles the functions elsewhere devolved to departments.

The same compromise with the reality principle could be found in Alsace-Lorraine. After the province's re-integration into the Republic in 1918 it was to prove impossible to eliminate some of the reforms introduced by Bismarck or to go back on the Concordat with the Vatican, denounced by the Republic but still in force in Strasbourg. Local law thus continued to apply in these eastern departments because the wounds in the relationship between France and Germany were still too raw to allow the rigid application of the principle of unity-as-uniformity. French Jacobinism showed remarkable capacities of flexibility and adaptation in this case—not for the first time, nor indeed for the last.

Another illustration came in 1945 when the elites in the older colonies forcibly demanded departmentalization of the overseas territories, the only measure that would in their eyes enable them to be aligned with the situation in the metropolis. Equality was again to be secured through recourse to uniformity—of status, of rules, of institutions. But in the rush—and in order to

---

[9] François Ascher, *La République contre la ville* (La Tour d'Aigues, 1998).

take account of local specificities—it had to be accepted that the legislator could depart from certain provisions of the law in order to adjust them to very contrasting economic and sociological realities. More recently, the French Constitutional Council cancelled the provisions regarding overseas regionalization to take account of the fact that by contrast with the mother country some of these territories—Guadeloupe, Martinique, Guyane, Réunion—contained only one department. Nothing happened: the Constitutional Council rejected this scandalous 'discrimination' and compelled the government and the National Assembly to have recourse to a solution that was both costly and absurd, namely, the creation of single-department regions: a single territory, but with two assemblies, two budgets, two sets of powers and of taxes, two distinct types of majority because of different electoral systems, and so forth.

At municipal level the absurdity is even greater, since France is still divided into over 36,000 theoretically autonomous communes, each with a municipality responsible among other things for pursuing economic development in full freedom or devising its land-use plan. No one can be surprised at the contradictions of this sort of system and the results of such political and bureaucratic anarchy: had all the optimistic forecasts of these municipalities been realized, France would have long exceeded a hundred million inhabitants. Had there not been a number of features which have re-balanced the system, the competition would have proved costly and perverse in fiscal, urban, and environmental terms. One can, moreover, see some of these effects on the periphery of the big cities, where territorial competition does have real meaning.

In order to tackle these problems, palliatives have had to be dreamed up. The first of these, provided for by the constitution of the Fourth Republic, consisted in breaking the uniformity taboo by devising a special status for cities. It is significant, however, that this Article in the Constitution was to remain a dead letter. The Fifth Republic revisited the issue, but avoiding anything that might look like an attack on the unity-as-uniformity principle; solutions were thus offered in order to enable the municipalities to strengthen their horizontal cooperation. Forty years later, despite the official Jacobin vocabulary which describes it, the French territorial panorama resembles the disordered and confused landscape presented by Tocqueville in his picture of France on the eve of the Revolution: a jungle of institutions, tax systems, rules, and rights.

At the institutional level the complexity arises from the 20,000 or so more or less sophisticated cooperation bodies that have become stratified since the 1960s. Some are special-purpose bodies while others are huge conglomerate agencies running big budgets; some structures are highly regulated and entitled to levy taxes whereas others are demonstrations of mayors' powers and act almost invisibly through commercial or social-type structures, which often have recourse to the 1901 law for associations operating for non-profit purposes. In short, even the best specialists get lost in this labyrinth, where the confusion has ultimately one basic reason for existence: to solve questions of social complexity while claiming to retain without concessions the famous

Republican principles. An American political scientist who had undertaken to compare the British and French local systems without any particular *parti pris* had to confess his surprise and perplexity, reflected in his book's title: *British Dogmatism and French Pragmatism.*[10]

If truth be told, the paradox goes still further: so-called French pragmatism is the necessary outcome of dogmatic rhetoric. While it is not possible to change either the dogma—since that is too painful—or the reality—since it resists the dogma—the only solution remaining is to adapt State practice and behaviour, but on condition of not admitting it or even denying that the sacrosanct principles are being breached. It is this pious Noah's cloak that deceives many of the French and not a few foreign observers. From a distance, one indeed sees the French-style formal garden that the 'tourist guides' announce. A closer look, however, reveals that the landscape looks more like a British 'mixed border', except that the mixture and confusion of species and colours is less an artistic effect than the outcome of muddling through.

The same hypocrisy or, if we wish to be a bit more neutral, the same tensions between rhetoric and practice can be seen over and above the institutions in the *policies* pursued by the territorial authorities or imposed by the republican State. The claim to unity-as-uniformity resulting from the fundamental principle of equality comes up against an obstacle of size, the extreme fragmentation of the national territory into tiny units. Some of their powers are identical, but there are immense disparities in their resources, their constraints, and their ideological and political preferences. This differentiation has been taken in manifold directions that cannot be analysed in detail, though a few manifestations can be highlighted: what, for instance, could be more important or more symbolic than the proclamation of free, compulsory secondary education, conceived of as the instrument of republican unification, at the dawn of the Third Republic? Yet a fifth of the children are still taught privately, and this percentage goes up to almost 50 per cent in certain departments in the west. Likewise, the education system has had to do violence to itself to accept that the social segregation in the suburbs, the rise of illiteracy, and the educational catastrophe in certain establishments called for ad hoc measures, most notably the creation of priority education zones in the suburbs. The very idea of differentiation was seen in some circles, in particular by teachers, as tantamount to segregation, whereas for others it was the de facto segregation that necessitated diversified treatment. In the opposite direction, however much the education system may call itself national, this does not prevent parents from knowing the 'good' secondary schools and pursuing location strategies in order to be able to enter their children there.

The same phenomenon has appeared in the area of social policies, especially up to the Second World War. A major part of assistance to the poor, in the nascent welfare state, was handed over to the local authorities, forcing some of them to shoulder intolerable burdens because of the characteristics of their

---

[10] Douglas Ashford, *British Dogmatism and French Pragmatism* (London, 1982).

populations—workers, immigrants. The creation of social security and its nationalization in the aftermath of the war in part responded, yet still very unequally, to the concern to make social protection fairer. This did not prevent on-the-ground social policies, particularly assistance to the underprivileged, from diverging greatly according to perceived local needs and available resources. It was, and still is, better to be poor in Paris—a rich city—or in Corsica or an overseas department such as Réunion island—wallowing in State aid—than in the working-class suburbs of Paris, Lille, or Lyon. Other social policies, for instance, the distribution of services or the construction of public infrastructures, are highly disrespectful of the principle of unity-as-uniformity, offering the whole range allowed by the combination of fragmentation and political competition. The amount of local services on offer has long been a function of two parameters: local wealth and ideology. Where the local authority is on the Left, public services have often been multiplied for populations whose incomes did not allow them access to certain private or collective goods: municipal shops, hygiene or sanitary services, crèches for children, and public housing. It was even possible to speak of 'municipal socialism' in the 1930s, until the Conseil d'Etat came along to set limits to this endless expansion of local interventionism. In parallel, thanks to the *'cumul des mandats'*—multiple office-holding—clientelism in favour of municipalities run by national politicians was going ahead full steam. Under the cover of republican egalitarianism and economic and administrative rationality, some elected representatives, as in the United States, did not stint in order to 'bring home the bacon'. Paradoxically, never has the Jacobin national, unitary, and rationalizing discourse been so well accommodated to the clientelist facilitations brought by economic growth than under the Fifth Republic. On the one hand was the rhetoric of *'aménagement du territoire'*—a concept untranslatable into almost any other language because there is no functional equivalent—and on the other practices worthy of the Third Republic and its notables: the revenue school at Clermont-Ferrand—Finance Minister Giscard d'Estaing's fief—the police school at Vannes—the mayor of which was Minister of the Interior. The list of such 'rational choices' in the Republic of *égalité* is endless.

The Republic and its Democracy

The conditions of monarchical collapse and the radicalization of the process of establishing the Republic have never allowed genuine political liberalism to become rooted in French political culture. Even economic liberalism became established under special conditions. 'Laissez-faire, laissez-passer' as an objective and as a slogan was applied first and foremost to the social obstacles that nascent liberalism might encounter, starting with the guilds.[11] But it never

---

[11] François Burdeau, *Liberté, libertés locales chéries. L'idée de décentralisation administrative, des jacobins au Maréchal Pétain* (Paris, 1983).

prevented or hindered State intervention in producing rules, taxes, or even goods. Liberalism applied to the State was then limited to non-intervention in the social sphere.

The Republic was thus born in specific conditions. It was first and foremost egalitarian and individualist in its principles. Thus, it meant universal suffrage and abolition of all organizations that might act as a screen between the individual and the State. Of course the gap between proclamations and the realization of political ideas was sometimes a chasm: the universal suffrage proclaimed in 1793 did not become a reality until 1848 for men, and 1945 for women, who were suspected of lukewarm republicanism; slavery lasted until the Second Republic in the colonies, and its official suppression did not prevent similar forms of exploitation; the 'social question' began to be tackled only after the 1848 Revolution—and even then Gambetta later denied its existence; the programme aimed at finally letting citizens enjoy concrete civil and political freedoms began to come in only in the early Third Republic, between 1880 and 1900. The realization of republican principles was thus particularly slow and long. But the key feature lies in the original matrix. This mould was all the more crucial because its chaotic and uncertain implementation strengthened and mythologized the founding principles. Two centuries after the French Revolution, the key word, the political and ideological panacea, remains the Republic. Where in other countries social and political figures would use the word 'democracy', the French prefer to use a term sufficiently imprecise in its meaning to give rise to plural or even divergent interpretations, but sufficiently precise in historical practice and memory immediately to arouse coherent images, values, traditions, and rules associated with it.

Basically, what characterizes this French-style republicanism is on the one hand the concentration of sovereignty at the centre, in the hands of the people's representatives—like the Republic, sovereignty is one and indivisible—and on the other hand the assertion that the citizen is the bearer of rights and duties, the holder of a portion of sovereignty, which, however, he cannot exercise in practice except in a merger with his fellow citizens on the occasion of elections. Everything that might act as a barrier to this direct link, this 'dialogue' between the sovereign and the atoms that make it up, is banished: only the family, as a sociological reality hard to overcome, survives; but let us recall that only the men voted, and that heads of families, especially after the First Empire, remained household despots.

The Revolution and its Jacobinism completed what the monarchy had been unable to accomplish, namely, the destruction of social structures capable of opposing the central power. At the same time, it delegitimized the social and political pluralism guilty of fragmenting or endangering the principle of sovereignty. Without being aware of it, the Republic combined and took over two heritages it condemned: those of the monarchy and the Roman Church. The monarch had his subjects, the pastor his flock, and the Republic its citizens. This conception of power has profound implications for the organization of the territory. Local communities no longer have rights by themselves linked to, say, their history, their linguistic, cultural, or demographic peculiarities, or quite simply their existence as a social group. They are no more legitimate in spatial terms than are parties or professional or trade-union organizations in functional terms—all being suspected of divisiveness or 'factionalism'.

However, the reality principle tempers the radical visions and anthropo-morphic interpretations of a Republic that, like the human body, lived only from the impulses coming from its head. Not everything could be run from Paris. It was therefore necessary to accept territorial divisions, though only as the remote expression of the power of central command. That meant strict equality, absence of autonomy, and subordination in implementing the orders of the sovereign power. There resulted the creation of the depart-ments—with their neutral geographical nomenclature—and the hostility to provincial particularism; the unavoidable tolerance of the communes as con-stituting a sort of 'enlarged family', but initially with powers delegated by the State to the mayor as an agent of the central power who chose and appointed him; and the creation of executive prefects of departments and wardens of communes. On this radical republican view, the territory exists only as a space to be administered, not as a human and social collectivity. Let us repeat: terri-torial pluralism has no more place here than social pluralism. Political plural-ism is expressed only through radical, simplistic cleavages—revolutionaries against moderates, monarchists against republicans, Catholics against the lay—while the notion of party was just as suspect in the Republic as it had been in a different context under the monarchy. At no time were territorial authorities perceived as the legitimate basis for, or the natural components of, a democratic system. Those who defended the communes or the ancient provinces were liberals—though with moderate democratic beliefs—or monar-chists—whose primary concern was to rebuild the past.

The emergence of the local units as a focus for democracy and expression of a specific social link was therefore to be very slow. In successive stages, the election of town councils went from a property suffrage to universal manhood suffrage, then women were added; mayors, first appointed, were progressively chosen by the town council. The rule was first adopted in 1848 for mayors of municipalities with over 6,000 inhabitants, then extended to the rest of France, except Paris, in 1884. But the process was much slower for the depart-ments. Despite an attempt after the Second World War—the constitution of the Fourth Republic provided for the prefect to be discarded in favour of the chairman of the General Council in departments—it was only with the Defferre law of 1982 that the executive of a department came to be elected by its assembly. The minimalist process of 'democratization' was completed, although still arousing numerous reservations and fears as to the risks the Republic might incur because of such a reform. Throughout the past two cen-turies the political elites in power have mistrusted the application of universal suffrage. Until the Fifth Republic, the fear of division, of federalism, haunted the political class. The arguments heard in, say, the 1848 'Departmental and Communal Administration Committee' were to be repeated almost word for word in the constituent debates in 1945–6. In 1848 a member of the Favart Committee fully expressed the dominant viewpoint:

What makes France's strength is centralization and the unity of power. Forming department administrations made up of members appointed by election clearly means weakening central authority, replacing a unitary republic by a federative republic.[12]

The debate continues in contemporary France, even if the forms are a bit different: one of the reasons behind Chevènement's resignation from the Jospin government had to do with the reforms contemplated for the new Corsican region at the discussions in Matignon in spring 2000. The project was to eliminate the two departments and create a single territorial entity in the island, with a council elected by proportional representation. Both aspects ran smack up against the Jacobin republican tradition, since they sought to make an administrative entity coincide with a territory coherent in spatial, cultural, and linguistic terms—whereas the whole aim of the departments had been none other than to break this coherence. Moreover, the project risks, through the ballot box, clearly identifying and giving voice to the important nationalist minority. In addition, the granting, albeit more symbolic than substantive, of legislative power to the Corsican region makes a mockery, in the Jacobins' eyes, of the indivisible nature of the State embodied in French public law.

But the reticence regarding universal suffrage does not stop here, and perpetuates the great gap between rhetoric and reality that marked the practice of the revolutionaries—who except in 1793 were content with property suffrage—and the Third Republicans—who resisted extension of the suffrage to women. Thus, the 20,000 or so supra-communal cooperation bodies that often hold the bulk of power of taxation and decisions on investment are run by boards and executives generally unknown to citizens because their members are appointed by local municipal councils. Elected by indirect suffrage they are both invisible and unaccountable to the electorate. Still worse is the position of senators, whose democratic legitimacy is scarcely greater than that of the British Lords. Elected for nine years and invariably re-elected, they very well fit the definition of American Supreme Court judges, 'who never resign, and rarely die'. Their so-called democratic legitimacy is a sham. Their electorate is reduced to a few thousand people in each department and includes on the one hand the elected representatives in that district—regional and departmental councillors, mayors, town councillors of the biggest municipalities, according to population—and on the other hand the 'grands électeurs' of the cities, selected at the discretion of the municipal council from among sympathizers of the governing party or coalition.

Paradoxically, these reservations towards basic democratic rules have helped to turn the French second chamber, the Senate, into a quasi-federal assembly and a powerful, influential, and determined mouthpiece for territorial interests. No territorial reform is possible in France under the Fifth Republic

---

[12] Cited by Mannoni, *Une et Indivisible*, 235–6.

'without the advice and consent of the Senate'. Without being aware of it the Republic, whose democratization is incomplete, has in part become a prisoner of its own local authorities. The periphery controls the centre thanks to the veto power granted to the Senate or conquered by it.[13] This revenge of the territories has been still further accentuated by an old phenomenon, born with the Third Republic, that has considerably grown and become systematic under the Fifth Republic, namely, the *'cumul des mandats'*. This effective, functional way of linking centre and periphery has in fact spread widely because of the weakness of French political parties—local roots guarantee re-election better than party membership—and the decline of Parliament—with its boringness compensated by local administrative activism.

The low democratic content of the local system does not only have to do with inadequacies in the application of universal suffrage. It results also from many other factors, with legal ones supporting sociological ones and vice versa. The quasi-monarchical nature of the local executives is a product of a convergence of various features: the concentration of power in the hands of the executive, especially the mayor; the lack of separation of powers—the executive also chairs the assembly; the political subordination of the municipal council, the majority of which is carefully selected by the leader; the length of terms of office—six years for municipality and department, five years for the regions; the absence of equivalence, except at municipality level, between the electoral apportionment and the political and administrative territory. For instance, councillors of departments are elected in phantom electoral districts or wards, whereas regional councillors are elected from departmental lists, to prevent the emergence of regional representation. Only at the municipal level is there a proper alignment between the electoral and the political administrative territory. But this apparent harmony is increasingly fictitious because of the multiplication of supra-communal bodies and of de-alignment between urbanized territory and electoral district. Today's paradox is that a rural commune of 50 people continues to survive and defend its 'autonomy' while having the greatest difficulty in finding enough councillors to elect, whereas vast neighbourhoods of 20,000 or 30,000 people in France's suburbs have no specific representation to defend their interests or represent their problems. The territory of France at present takes the form of a jungle of institutions, structures, and rules that favour neither democracy, nor transparency, nor efficiency, nor responsibility. But reform is almost impossible because of the combination of the conservatism and corporatism of the notables and the permanence of abstract republican principles. However much they may be leaking on all sides, their symbolic value and their veto capacity remain as potent as ever.

---

[13] Yves Mény, 'Central control and local resistance', in V. Wright (ed.), *Continuity and Change in France* (1984).

Conclusion

For how long will the monarchical and Jacobin heritage continue to resist the pressures from the rank and file—local demands—and from the top—Europeanization, or globalization? The tensions are increasingly strong between the institutions and the ideological structures that perpetuate the old patterns and the development of a society seduced by pluralism, particularly in cultural respects, dominated by the market, and aspiring to internationalization. For the moment the apparent, surface changes are minor since the taboos to be broken are still too strong. It is therefore only in a sideways, unspoken, complex way that incremental transformations come, changes by addition and superimposition more than in any rational, pondered, or planned way. The debate on these questions is striking for its repetitiveness and its weary arguments. Yet the gap is widening between public opinion and the views of the political elites on this point, as on many others.[14]

Reform is thus possible, but it would still take a political shock to shake up received wisdoms and vested interests. The territorial order of the Republic is dysfunctional and schizophrenic: it no longer corresponds either to its own organizational schema or to rules of economic efficiency, and even less to the needs of democracy. Without any doubt the necessary preconditions for change—the 'objective conditions', as the Marxists used to say—are present. However, they are not pressing enough to overcome the multiple veto points that guarantee the permanence of the old structures. Once again we see proof of De Gaulle's aphorism that 'France can pursue reform only through the process of revolution'.

---

[14] P. Bréchon, A. Laurent, and P. Perrineau, *Les cultures politiques des Français* (Paris, 2000).

10

Making Citizens in an Increasingly Complex Society: Jacobinism Revisited

DOMINIQUE SCHNAPPER

VINCENT Wright was one of the few foreigners to express some sympathy for Jacobinism. For did he not say, with a humour that he would have forgiven me for describing as British, 'the nation state, with all its problems, remains, for most citizens, the principal repository of legitimate authority. In arguing this case, I am aware that I lay myself open to the not entirely unjustifiable accusation of being an old-fashioned Jacobin, perverted by a nostalgia for the 1950s and 1960s, by a penchant for limited social democratic distributionalism, and by an admiration for the French prefectoral administration'.[1] It seems to me that any lover of France should share this sympathy— even if it can only be critical—in so far as it was this very Jacobinism which built the nation.

It is, however, important to understand this Jacobinism for what it is, and not to take at face value the descriptions and the justifications which its own theorists provided. In this homage to Vincent, I would like to offer a few thoughts on what it was and on the problems encountered today by the heritage of Jacobinism, a legacy that is nowadays criticized in two respects. On the one hand, it is said to be alien to the great liberal tradition of the British, further developed by the United States and the democracies of northern Europe; and, on the other hand, it is viewed as inappropriate to the style of modern civilization, which is founded upon individual initiative. The rigidity of Jacobinism, like that of the traditional nation state, is believed to meet neither the conditions governing the functioning of modern democracy nor the demands of a liberal and internationalized economy.

An Ancient Political Project

According to the celebrated formulation of Bernard Guenée, in France the State preceded and created the nation. It is impossible to understand the role

[1] Vincent Wright, 'The Path to Hesitant Comparison' (1997), 174.

of the State if we forget how the French nation was constituted. This latter is the fruit of a political will put into action by the central State, successively monarchic and republican, which strove to constitute around itself, inscribed upon the national soil, a nation culturally and politically unified by its action across time. Jacobinism does not date from the Revolution. It is to be seen, as Tocqueville established, as part of a wider tradition dating from earlier times. The political, administrative, and educational institutions which were put in place by the Revolutionaries at the end of the eighteenth century and the republicans at the end of the nineteenth were descended, despite the rupture of political legitimacy, from institutions which in some cases had existed for centuries. The first elements of the State were created by Philip the Fair. Over the centuries, the king's civil servants, jurists, and military men gradually built up the State in close symbiosis with the nation. The monarchy was so bound up with the nation that, as Renan observed, when France transformed herself into a republic the nation remained: 'This great French royalty had been so thoroughly national that, on the morrow of its fall from power, the nation was able to carry on without it.'[2] In French history, the birth of the idea of nationhood ran parallel to the setting up of political and State structures, which, within relatively stable frontiers, embodied and symbolized the unity of the nation.

By affirming the legitimacy of citizenship beyond dynastic and religious allegiances and independently of the historical bond which, over the centuries, had united the nation, the monarchy, and the Roman Catholic Church, the Revolutionaries of 1789 suddenly created a new principle of legitimacy. The principle of citizenship succeeded that of dynasty and religion, which had held together the society of the *Ancien Régime*. The secular Republic was built up in opposition to and on the model of the Church: it had its ceremonies, its altars, its saints and martyrs, its missionaries, and its priests—the schoolteachers in particular and, in a more general sense, the intellectuals. The sacredness of the Catholic monarchy and of monarchic religion was transferred to the Republic and to the Nation and its primary instrument, secular education. Schoolteachers were given responsibility for training the citizen and celebrating the great national commemorative occasions, which were a sort of secular form of the Catholic mass. The prefects were entrusted with the organization of politics and administration. But the republicans continued the political project of the monarchy, whose aim it was to merge cultural and political unity; they developed the Jacobin institutions through which this project took form and meaning.

These institutions were also reinforced by the demands for social integration in a country where immigration was high. From the end of the Napoleonic wars and up to the Second World War, France was unique in Europe in 'importing' people while most other European countries during the same period were 'exporting'[3] them. From the Restoration on, English and German

[2] Ernest Renan, *Qu'est-ce qu'une nation?* (1885) (Paris, 1992), 44.
[3] Gérard Noiriel, *Le creuset français* (Paris, 1998).

engineers, Belgian workers, and Swiss soldiers entered the country and settled there. With the growth of industry in the second half of the nineteenth century, these were succeeded by numerous waves of Italians and Poles, then by Jewish refugees fleeing persecution at the hands of the Tsarist empire, Russians after the 1917 revolution, Ukrainians, and, from the start of the twentieth century, peoples such as North Africans and Senegalese, coming from the colonial empire. The low birth rate from the beginning of the nineteenth century, national ambition in an era of triumphant nationalism, and the traditional fusion of political and cultural unity explain the policy followed in relation to immigrants, which was to transform them, or at any rate their children, into French citizens.

The integration of the immigrants, like that of the whole of the population, was realized around the political project born of the values embodied by the Revolution, around the idea of individual citizenship, and in opposition to any acknowledgement of particular communities.[4] This policy, referred to until the 1970s as a policy of 'assimilation' and now called a policy of 'integration'—the change in terminology reflects a change in the *Zeitgeist* but not in the content of the policy—does not imply, contrary to what was voiced in no uncertain terms by those who sought to condemn the Jacobinism of the nation state in the 1970s, that all the distinguishing features of those population groups being gradually integrated into the French nation should be eliminated. This is, moreover, neither possible nor desirable. Democracy is founded on the distinction between the private, which is the domain of individual liberty, and the public, which is a place of unity between all citizens; on the Hegelian distinction between the distinguishing features of the private individual and the universalism of the citizen. In private life, all individuals can use their own language, remain faithful to a particular culture, or practise their religion as they wish, so long as these practices do not pose a threat to the public domain. But this policy implied that all distinguishing features be kept within the private domain and that individuals complied with 'French' reasoning within the public domain. There was no room for public recognition of particular 'communities' formed through immigration. The so-called 'assimilation policy' never forbade multiculturalism in the conduct of personal and social life, but it did forbid its manifestation in public life. It is as if political society had been influenced by Rousseau's idea of the General Will, which is premised upon an inveterate hostility to all intermediate bodies.

The logic behind this policy was to grant nationality and thus citizenship widely, if not to immigrants themselves, at least to their children. It was both for reasons of national ideology—accessibility of citizenship within a political nation—and in order to meet demographic and military needs that French nationality law was, until the 1980s, the most 'open' in Europe.[5] Only those of the United States and Argentina, which were both founded on immigration,

---

[4] Dominique Schnapper, *La France de l'intégration. Sociologie de la nation en 1990* (Paris, 1991).
[5] In the course of the 1980s, the other European countries, which had in their turn become countries with high immigration, modified their nationality rights in the same direction.

were more liberal, in that they granted the right to citizenship by simple virtue of birth on national soil. Since the law of 1889, legislation has accorded considerable space to the right to citizenship by virtue of birth on national soil, in particular through articles 44 and 23 of the nationality code, which have become symbols of the 'accessibility' of French nationality to the children of immigrants.[6]

This policy of integration was effective, even if it was sometimes brutal and accompanied by violent outbreaks of xenophobia. In Aiguemortes in 1893, the population committed a veritable massacre of Italians.[7] At that time, hostility and prejudice against Italians were as violent as they were uniformly widespread. But the effectiveness of the policy was tragically demonstrated by the experience of the 1914–18 war, in the course of which immigrants and their children fought like everyone else. After the war, military medals and photographs of sons who had become French and had lost their lives in the trenches of the First World War were to be seen pinned up on the walls in the homes of Lorraine steelworkers, immigrants of Italian or of Spanish origin, as in those of the Polish miners of the Nord. It was in the name of individual citizenship that the population of foreign origin formed the French population. today the number of French people having at least one grandparent born outside France is estimated to be over 18 million.

Integrative Institutions: School and Army

I shall discuss briefly the role of the Republican school system and Army as they were created by the Third Republic, expressly in order to build the modern nation and to 'republicanize' France at the end of the nineteenth century, but we should not forget that these institutions are the continuation of a very ancient history and that other institutions had also worked in their own way towards the process of national integration. The revolutionaries of 1789 had replaced the terms, formerly in use, of *maître d'école*, *régent*, and *recteur* with that of *instituteur* because, from that moment on, the task of the latter was to 'institute' the nation. From then on, the school became the school of the citizen. The 'republican school' was the prime instrument of the 'republican model', that is to say, the model of national integration.

In establishing the foundations of State schooling, the republicans of 1880 saw themselves as the sons of the Revolution and the inheritors of the

---

[6] Precisely because of the symbolic value of article 44, its terms of application have been modified regularly. The reform of 1993, known as the Méhaignerie law, laid down that persons born in France to foreign parents and who had been resident in France for the five years preceding their majority must demonstrate their desire to claim their right to acquire French citizenship. The Socialist government made this acquisition automatic once more in 1998. But whatever modifications are made to how article 44 is applied, its result since 1889 has been to grant French nationality to all children born and educated in France when they reach majority. Of the 30,000 or so children born in France to foreign parents, fewer than 2,000 on average do not become French when they reach majority, and this because they refuse to do so.

[7] Noiriel, *Le creuset français*, 57.

philosophy of the eighteenth century.[8] In accordance with this philosophy, it was important to tear the individual away from his or her distinctive features; education and secularism were liberating forces, instruments of freedom and reason, of the autonomy of judgement against the tyranny of traditions and distinctiveness, against religious fanaticism and extremism. Only through the State school could people be educated to be free and thus to become citizens.

From the starting point of this purely philosophical concept, the State school had the responsibility of spreading a political culture whose secularity was essential to it, even if, as Péguy has already observed, republican morality, inspired by the teachings of the Church, was essentially a Christian morality without God. The exclusive learning of the common language became an instrument for the emancipation of mankind, while the role of the teaching of history was to arouse feelings of historical community and constituted an important means of disseminating a truly national education amongst all citizens-to-be. The narrative of past events, scientifically established, would make it possible to assert a sense of collective identity and to encourage contemporary society, the designated inheritors of this glorious history, to extend the inheritance of the past and continue to engage in common action. We know that, in all countries, nations have to some extent been invented by historians. 'Republican' historians such as Ernest Lavisse were no exception to the rule.

Beyond the actual content of the teaching, the school, for the republicans, constituted a fictional space which mirrored political society and within which the pupils, like citizens, could be treated as equals, regardless of their family or social characteristics. It was a space, in both the physical and the abstract senses of the term, which was constructed to stand against the real inequalities of social life and to resist the movements of civil society. The order of the school, like that of citizenship, was impersonal and formal. The abstract nature of school society was to train the child to understand and master the abstract nature of political society. The Jacobinism of the primary school, that is to say, the imposition of the same teaching programme for every school—the same content, the same methods, the same timetables, the recruitment of teachers by national competitive examinations, right down to the most remote of the France's 36,000 *communes*—was a direct consequence of this education towards citizenship. What is today referred to as 'multiculturalism', that is to say, the recognition, in one way or another, of differences in background, was inconceivable within the school system of the Republic. It would have called into question the social functions, the moral and political justifications, and the values and ambitions of an education system which saw itself first and foremost as the school of the citizen.

The Republic also set out to emancipate the people and ensure the promotion of the best. To give education to all was to offer the citizens of tomorrow equal chances of promotion and, by getting rid of ignorance, to eliminate the

    [8] Serge Berstein, 'La culture républicaine dans la première moitié du XXème siècle', in Serge Berstein et Odile Rudelle (eds), *Le modèle républicain* (Paris, 1992), 165.

fundamental causes of poverty, injustice, and the class struggle. It was the responsibility of the school to ensure the promotion of the most deserving of the sons of the people or, in modern terminology, to combat inequality, to enable social mobility, and to favour equality of opportunity. Hence the role, essential in real terms and perhaps even more so symbolically, of the scholarships which would make it possible for the most gifted children, whatever their social or national background, to obtain the education and life chances to which their gifts entitled them.

The effort of the school system was continued by the Army, where it was often the case that the *instituteurs* would carry on the schooling of recruits and the diffusion of patriotism. The myth of the armed nation and the citizen-soldier, as well as the civil role conferred upon the army, belong within the national tradition. Once the principle of military service for all young men, which became necessary because of rivalry between the countries of Europe, had been established in 1873—although it did not in fact become universal until 1905—it thereby offered a means of generalizing instruction. Military instruction was inseparable from the mission to educate and train the citizen.

The Army contributed to the nationalizing and modernizing of its recruits. In mixing together sons of immigrants from every background and young people from every region of France and every social class, the army offered them, according to their circumstances, what might have been their first opportunity to travel outside their own region, their first encounter with a certain level of material comfort, and contact with other French people from different backgrounds and regions. The *instituteurs*, now non-commissioned officers, were to continue with their dual mission: to teach the recruits to read and write but also to make patriots of them. Instruction in civic responsibility and patriotism was an integral part of military training. At the end of their military service, young recruits were to feel that they were the inheritors of the armed *grande nation*, which was an integral part of the revolutionary and patriotic mythology. The enthusiastic departure of young Frenchmen for the war in 1914, when of course nobody knew what that war was going to be like, came as a 'divine surprise' to the government. This collective spirit showed that the Army had been an effective vehicle of civic sentiment. This explains why the decision to end conscription was not taken until 1996, long after this had happened in Britain and the United States. And even then the French population was continuing to accept it, perhaps without enthusiasm, but also without revolt—even in 1968—and was not clamouring for it to be abolished.

The Limits

As Vincent Wright aptly said, 'The centralised state is far from perfect, but centralisation . . . is much more flexible than we generally tend to think . . .'.[9]

---

[9] Vincent Wright, 'Questions d'un jacobin anglais aux régionalistes français' (1981), 119.

French Jacobinism was a principle of action and a policy, a regulating principle of political life. It was never a description of social reality. The national is always based upon the local. The Jacobinism of the administrative organization and the education system has never excluded negotiation with local bodies, nor has it excluded local adaptations of national regulations and informal recognition of the distinctive features of pupils or constituents, be they national, regional, religious, or social. We must not confuse a regulating principle with social practice.

To return to the school system—the primary instrument and means of expression of Jacobinism—it was not just a space in which regional cultures were broken down by fanatical Jacobins: indeed, quite the contrary. It 'cultivated the sense of belonging to a local community as an indispensable preliminary to that of belonging to the national community'.[10] In the name of the national ideology of 'unity in diversity', 'local communities' were systematically celebrated in the teaching of history, geography, and French. Local knowledge was given pride of place, national textbooks had departmental editions, networks were set up to bring together the *instituteurs* of each department around projects to increase local patriotism, which was presented as the precondition for national patriotism. It was envisaged that the child's sense of belonging would pass through successive concentric circles, starting with the family and moving out through the school, the region, and finally into the nation. According to the mythology of this civic patriotism, 'the great voice of France . . . is made up of individual voices singing in unison'.[11]

Beneath the apparent administrative centralization of the national education system lay the de facto pluralism of secondary education and the great independence of the teaching profession and of university teachers. The secular State has always negotiated with religious authorities, taking into account local circumstances, the dates of holidays, and the closing of schools on Thursdays to enable children to attend catechism classes. As noted in Chapter 9, it maintained the Concordat and the obligations attached to it when Alsace became French again after 1918. In reality, as recent historical research has shown,[12] the principle of secularism, which was central to the ideology of the Jacobins, never excluded local arrangements and adaptations to allow for particular cases. Local schools in districts of Paris with high Jewish populations took account of the Sabbath and Jewish festivals. Some closed on Saturdays and stayed open on Thursdays. Jewish children everywhere stayed away from school on Yom Kippur with the tacit agreement of all concerned. This was not a right laid down in law, nor was it even demanded. It was an agreed practice which, moreover, did nothing to hamper the assertion of and obedience to the Jacobinism of the education system. Nor did it hamper the sometimes brutal insistence on all children learning French, regardless of their origins. Even if it

[10] Anne-Marie Thiesse, *Ils apprenaient la France. L'exaltation des régions dans le discours patriotique* (Paris, 1997), 1.
[11] Thiesse, *Ils apprenaient la France*, 18.
[12] Jean François Chanet, *L'école républicaine et les petites patries* (Paris, 1996).

was the responsibility of the school to form the citizen, how could it not have adapted to take into account local circumstances? Institutions do not deal with 'the citizen' as an abstraction but with concrete individuals. Universal principles are inevitably modified and adapted to cater for particular cases.

The school system is not the only example of the capacity of Jacobinism to adapt to circumstances. In a study carried out in the 1960s, which has become a classic of its kind, Pierre Grémion showed that the role of the prefects could not be seen to be simply the mechanical application of instructions issued by central power.[13] The prefects, who were the agents par excellence of the Republican State, negotiated incessantly with local institutions and notables in order to establish their power in collaboration with these bodies. The concept of the State as neutral and universal, analysed in ideal-typical terms,[14] has always been a regulating idea and a principle for action, not a description of the day-to-day functioning of the State. If a study of the same type as Pierre Grémion's had been carried out at the end of the nineteenth century, it would have revealed the same flexible adaptation to the realities of the 'locality' on the part of the Jacobin system.

The prefect was never simply the representative of central government with responsibility for applying its directives; he was also himself a notable, inserted into the local community. His technical or legal capacities went hand in hand with his participation in local society. The relationships formed between the civil servant, the elected representatives, and the local notables made it possible to adapt the apparent rigour of the centralized system and very often to turn the situation to the advantage of that system. 'Administrative centralization does not eliminate all power at a local level. It generates specific forms of such power, no doubt vaguely defined and often running parallel to state power, but sufficiently established to counterbalance the power at the top.'[15]

There are many examples of the notable-civil servant alliance succeeding in blocking changes to the system decided at the top. The administration at local level has often 'swallowed up' reforms that the political powers wished to introduce. Pierre Grémion has studied the failure of the administrative reform of the 1960s, which became bogged down in the wake of these 'mechanisms of institutionalized inter-control between bureaucrats and notables in the local politico-administrative system'.[16] It could be said that the decentralization of 1982 to a certain extent came up against the same problems. This explains why France, which in 1789 wanted to rationalize the administration on the model of a vertical structure of State-department-canton-commune, is now going through a process of reorganization which is multiplying the number of administrative divisions and territorial levels to the point of absurdity. On to the Jacobin State-department-canton-commune structure, which was

---

[13] Pierre Grémion, Le pouvoir périphérique. Bureaucrates et notables dans le système politique français (Paris, 1976).

[14] Bertrand Badie et Pierre Birnbaum, Sociologie de l'Etat (Paris, 1989).

[15] Grémion, Le pouvoir périphérique, 12.   [16] Grémion, Le pouvoir périphérique, 364.

the inheritance of the 1789 Revolution, is now being superimposed the type of organization which came out of the 1982 decentralization legislation, a decentralization founded upon the hierarchy State-Regions-*Communautés urbaines*,[17] not forgetting the legislation, known as 'PLM', which governs the administration of Paris, Lyon, and Marseille.[18] The proposals of the Mauroy Commission on Local Administration (2000), according to which certain of these divisions which had become unnecessary would be abolished, caused a public outcry. In this particular case, local interests are obviously overriding the general interest represented by the Jacobin State. The more apparently rigid the system is, the more parallel circuits gain in importance. On the ground, Jacobinism is held in check by this peripheral politico-administrative system which balances and compensates for centralization. The interplay of forces on the periphery retains its autonomy and its effectiveness in blocking the 'rational' reforms proposed by the State.

What can be seen is that the Jacobin State has always been bound up with 'the extraordinary vitality of the rural communes, even the smallest of these'.[19] Out of the 36,565 communes in France—a figure far higher than in any other European country—34,000 are rural and a strong tradition of direct democracy at village level still lives on today. This is borne out by the turn-outs for municipal elections—which, along with those for presidential elections, are the highest in the country—not forgetting the maintaining of the Senate, the 'grand council of the small communes of France' and the national expression of this local democracy, which has continued to exist despite every effort that has been made to 'modernize' public life from General de Gaulle to Lionel Jospin. Every politician at the national level is also the mayor of a commune. No politician with ambitions at the national level can afford to neglect his or her roots in a local community, which are supposed to provide a close link with the '*peuple*' or '*la France profonde*'.

The limits of the effectiveness of the Jacobin State are also perceptible so far as the cultural homogenization of the population is concerned. Every nation is a blend of different populations and France is no exception to the rule. Long before the mass migrations of the end of the nineteenth century, monarchs were increasing the diversity of the population by assimilating neighbouring provinces into the kingdom of France. The political drive to homogenize the subjects of the King goes back a long way. French was imposed by the monarchy as the official language of the kingdom in 1539 in the celebrated Villers-Cotterêts decree. The *Académie Française* was declared guardian of the language in the seventeenth century. But there were always limits to this effort towards linguistic and cultural homogenization, for it is an endless process which has never excluded the possibility of maintaining all sorts of specific features.

---

[17] Literally, 'urban areas'.
[18] Pierre Grémion, 'Région ou département: les raisons d'un non-choix', *Intervention*, 3 (March–April 1983), 18–25.
[19] Henri Mendras, *La seconde révolution française 1965–1984* (Paris, 1988), 234.

When the education system of the Republic was organized by Jules Ferry, French was a foreign language for half the pupils. In 1914, even before Alsace was returned to France, several regional languages were spoken—German, Alsatian, Breton, Basque, Occitan, Catalan, and Corsican—not counting, obviously, the languages spoken by immigrants in the privacy of their own homes.[20] Breton soldiers died in the trenches because they failed to understand the orders given in French by their officers. Village priests were preaching in Breton in the countryside of Finistère and the Côtes-du-Nord into the 1960s. Languages related to Occitan were still spoken by the oldest people in the villages of Provence and Languedoc up to the same date. We should rather be surprised that, after the efforts of so many centuries to homogenize the population, 'regional diversity gave way only very recently' and that regional diversity and political centralization can sit alongside policies of cultural unification at such a profound level.[21]

What assessment can we make today of what may be called 'historical' Jacobinism? The idea and the ideal of the universal republican principle applied by the institutions of Jacobinism had three major effects. They legitimized the opening up of the right to nationality by freely granting French nationality to the children of immigrants born and educated in France, thus promoting social integration in a country with a high level of immigration.[22] They justified the organization of the republican school system on a universal basis by deliberately setting aside the historical and religious origins of the pupils. The school system of Jules Ferry effectively acculturated the children of peasants by teaching them French and arithmetic and by forbidding them to speak patois. It had the same effect and the same degree of effectiveness on the sons and daughters of immigrants: by treating them in the same way as everyone else, regardless of their origins, it turned them into citizens who shared the same language and the same historical and cultural points of reference. Finally, the republicans put in place political practices according to which the deputies did not represent one particular group but rather the whole of the political body of the nation and disregarded the idea that 'communities' or particular 'ethnic groups' could be recognized *as such* within the public domain. Particular historical or religious features, while being neither denied nor proscribed, were left to individual choice within the private sphere and were not to be recognized as such in public life. These three institutions—the right to nationality, the republican school system, and political legitimacy founded upon the concept of individual and universal citizenship—were the primary instruments of a mode of civic integration which can be called integration *à la française*.

---

[20] Eugen Weber, *Peasants into Frenchmen: The Modernization of Rural France 1870–1914* (Stanford, 1976).

[21] Mendras, *La seconde révolution française*, 215.

[22] On the nuances and criticisms which should be brought to bear on what the French sometimes complacently refer to as the 'liberalism' and the 'accessibility' of the right to nationality, too big a topic to be pursued here, I take the liberty of referring the reader to my book *La France de l'intégration*, esp. Ch.1.

To repeat, Jacobinism has never been a simple description of reality but rather a *principle* of integration and a political ideal directly linked to French national mythology. It asserted that every person, regardless of origin or beliefs, could be integrated into political society as a citizen, provided they received a *national* education by means of which diverse individuals, who de facto remained linked to 'small communities' each one different from the next, also became French citizens. It was the advocates of the *Ancien Régime* and the anti-republicans who for decades invoked local or historical identities and the authenticity of cultural 'roots', claiming that these were in contradiction with national citizenship, and asserted that the son of an immigrant or a Jewish child would always be incapable, whatever their education, of understanding Racine.

The Test of Modernity

Today, we readily make the comparison between a France of the past, seen to have been united by the institutions of Jacobinism, and a new society viewed as multicultural, multi-ethnic, and multi-faith. We have seen the extent to which the idea of the effectiveness of Jacobinism must be qualified. This is equally true with respect to the contemporary notion of 'multiculturalism'. Not only is the present population no more diverse in its origins than it was in the past, but it has also probably never been as homogeneous as it now is.[23] But the national institutions and the project of the Jacobin State, which strove to increase the homogeneity of populations in the name of a particular concept of the nation, legitimized by universal philosophical concepts and the value attributed to the unity and homogeneity of the population, are now increasingly contested.

Three factors appear to be central to this. The Jacobin State, both political and military, was founded upon the idea and the value of individual citizenship, the classic representative political institutions, and the great national institutions—the school and the Army. It thus becomes essentially a welfare state. The political State, which claims sovereignty, sees its power and liberty of action de facto increasingly limited by the construction of Europe and by the claims of the regions. State intervention in economic life, through its great technical and administrative bodies and through the network of relationships which had been created between the politico-administrative elite and those involved in the economy, finally becomes less and less justified and effective in a climate where a growing share of economic life is dependent upon transnational or 'global' markets.

---

[23] Schnapper, *La France de l'intégration*, Chs 3–5.

The Welfare State and Republican Jacobinism

Let us return to the example of the school system. Universal principles are still asserted but, given the overall expansion of education, how could it have been possible to avoid adapting it to suit particular populations, as had always been done? Contrary to what was the case in Germany, for example, the possibility of providing a special education system for foreign children was not opened up to debate. Classes to bring children who have arrived in France at an age where they are already socialized in another language up to the required standard are purely transitional: the aim is to get these children into the general education system as rapidly as possible.

Policies of increased financial aid to schools situated in the *zones d'éducation prioritaires* (ZEP) are not aimed at children from particular ethnic, national, or religious backgrounds. Rather, they are directed at a whole district deemed to be educationally underprivileged, regardless of the origin of the children, and this despite the fact that the number of foreign pupils is one of the criteria taken into account when a school in a ZEP is being classified. Any consideration of particular national, ethnic, or religious features is still perceived and experienced as a form of stigmatization. This can be seen, for example, in the reactions to the application of the European directive on the teaching of Langues et Cultures d'Origine (ELCO) since 1975. Teachers from the country of origin, that is to say, the country of origin of the parents, provide a particular form of teaching for particular pupils within the normal school syllabus, within the school itself, and during normal school hours. This is an exception to the general principles of the unity and universality of the education system and has been found largely unacceptable by all concerned—pupils, parents, and teachers—precisely because it goes against the logic of national and educational policy. It remains the case today, as perfectly captured in the quip made by Cavanna, the son of an Italian immigrant, that 'a person's native language . . . is the language of his or her school'.

The affair of the 'Islamic headscarf', which sparked off a grand ideological debate on the model, *mutatis mutandis*, of the Dreyfus affair, revealed the degree of resistance on the part of teachers to accepting the manifestation of religious beliefs in the public domain.[24] In order to understand what was at stake, we must remember that the logic of national integration requires French people of the Muslim tradition to reinterpret two aspects of that tradition.

---

[24] The affair started in September 1989, when the principal of a middle school in a Paris suburb, who was of West Indian origin, excluded from the school three young Muslim students who refused to remove their headscarves during classes. The decision sparked off an impassioned debate on liberalism and secularity. An *avis* from the Conseil d'Etat ruled largely in favour of religious freedom, providing that the means of showing religious affiliation were in no way 'ostentatious'. First Lionel Jospin and then François Bayrou, successive education ministers, strove to resolve the conflicts by inviting school heads to negotiate with pupils and families, but both reaffirmed the need to avoid any form of proselytism and any wearing of ostentatious signs as well as the need to make attendance in classes of all subjects compulsory for all pupils. Almost all of the conflicts were resolved through negotiation at local level. Nonetheless, 200 young Muslims stopped attending school.

They are expected to renounce those aspects of personal law which are founded upon inequality of status between men and women and to accept the rules which ensure the separation of the political from the religious, that is to say, in French political parlance, 'secularism'. The Islamic headscarf affair was directly linked to these two requirements. Despite the fact that every survey so far undertaken indicates that the Muslim population is moving in this direction both in so far as the status of women is concerned and in the acceptance of the necessity to separate the political from the religious, and despite the fact that the Islamic headscarf is sometimes for young Muslim women a means of obtaining a certain degree of independence by ostensibly honouring tradition,[25] the majority of teachers felt that the values of 'the Republic' were being challenged. What is interpreted by our friends abroad as flagrant proof of French non-liberalism was perceived by teachers as the logical expression of the concept of the school of the citizen, within which no religious or cultural affiliation may be expressed.

The effectiveness of the education system has been maintained up to the present day so far as the acculturation of foreign children is concerned. Every survey has shown that foreign children, when they are educated in France starting from primary school, have the same tastes, the same body of knowledge, and display the same behaviour as French children of the same social class. If one takes into account the social class they belong to, their school results are even slightly better than those of French children from the same social class.[26] But at the same time, in an indirect and little recognized manner, the school system guides its pupils in different directions, according to their abilities as these are perceived by the teachers. Moreover, in many respects, it has adapted to particular demands since, for instance, more than 300,000 children now study regional languages within the public system, and the huge range of foreign languages which can be presented for the *baccalauréat* accords symbolic value to the variety of national origins.

The school system is a particularly significant case of a more general process of evolution which has taken place in Western democratic societies. Republican Jacobinism has adapted to the needs of a differentiated society and the State has become first and foremost a welfare state. Its political drive as a whole can be interpreted as being a vast mechanism of social transfers aimed at correcting the shortcomings of universal policies. Today's Jacobins have taken on board the criticisms levelled at republican universalism, according to which there is a constant risk of it serving to legitimize inequality. They have rallied to the idea that, in the name of national solidarity, those individuals who are most marginalized have a right to receive more than others. The reasoning behind public intervention is less and less that of the Republican State, seen in ideal terms as the rational, neutral referee whose claim is to be univer-

[25] Françoise Gaspard and Fahrad Kosrokhavar, *Le foulard et la République* (Paris, 1997).
[26] See the work of Serge Boulet and Danièle Fradet, particularly *Les immigrés et l'Ecole, Une course d'obstacles* (Paris, 1988). The statistics produced regularly by the Ministry of Education since the publication of their book have confirmed their conclusions.

sal. If the managing of the nation by the State has always taken account of specific situations and circumstances, this has become increasingly the case as the State intervenes more and more in the economic and social domain, which is the domain par excellence of the individual.

The Jacobin State has thus moved away from its universalist logic towards diverse and increasingly finely tuned forms of categorization. This is particularly to be seen in the multiplicity of categories addressed by social policies. Given the purpose of its interventions, State action takes increasing account of the diversity of individual cases and of what may be called the 'ethnic' dimension of social situations. Recent urban policies—*'politique de la ville'*—for instance, grant financial aid to associations of an 'ethnic' nature, which are deemed to encourage the integration of children of immigrants. As a result of the measures taken by Socialist Minister Martine Aubry concerning the creation of jobs for young people, many State-subsidized vacancies are filled by social workers, who have come to be known as *grands frères* and whose responsibility it is to supervise or control young people of the same origin as themselves in the suburbs of big cities.

Such measures are breaking with 'republican' tradition, according to which origin was not taken into account when recruiting people. The police are also aiming in large suburban areas to recruit police officers of the same 'ethnic' origin as the young people whose behaviour they will be monitoring. It is felt that they will have a greater understanding of particular situations as well as more authority. They will act as models that their *'jeunes frères'* may be likely to follow. In a more general context, social workers, whose numbers are constantly increasing, are taking more and more account of the 'cultural' traditions of the communities in which they work. 'Multicultural' awareness is considered to be of paramount importance. Albeit covertly, since it is against the law, those people responsible for the running of social housing take account of national origin and distribute populations accordingly in order to avoid the creation of ghettos.

The 'ethnicization' of social policy is growing apace. France refuses in principle to pursue the multicultural route taken by Canada and Australia, for instance, invoking in a sometimes incantational manner 'the republican model'; but there nonetheless exist forms of the welfare state which may be called 'ethnic' in American terms. A share of public funding is given to particular groups to enable them to keep up their own particular culture. Libraries, cultural associations, and Jewish and Armenian schools, for example, are subsidized through public funding, even if this is officially justified in universalist terms. There are Jewish and *'beur'*—the name given to themselves by young French people of North African origin—radio stations. In the name of social solidarity and the policy of integration, associations set up by French people of North African origin are given financial aid. References to an 'imaginary Jew' or an 'imaginary *oummah*', that is to say, the expression of ambiguous and contradictory identities, no longer arouse suspicion in the way that they did in the era of the triumphant nation State. In fact they are now seen as a source of prestige. The formal judicial recognition by the *Assemblée Nationale* in May 1998 of the Armenian genocide is part and parcel of the increasing ethnicization of political life. Equally, the prime minister delivers an address every year to the 'Jewish Community', assembled by the *Conseil Représentatif des Institutions Juives de France* (CRIF), despite the fact that the very idea of a 'Jewish community' is in flagrant contradiction with the traditional model of national integration. The vast and varied activity of the Ministry of Culture has led to the development of increasingly 'ethnic' forms of culture. Caught up in its own dynamic, the tendency of the Jacobin welfare state, whether through social, cultural, or ethnic intervention, is towards a movement from the collective to the individual, from the universal to the singular.

Europe and the Regions

Jacobinism is also being challenged by the development of transnational phenomena. While the philosophy of Jacobinism was founded upon the point of convergence of political organization, economic practice, and national identity, these are becoming increasingly dissociated in the modern world.[27] We are experiencing the emergence of a transnational society whose expansion can be measured by looking, for example, at the number and scope of activities of non-governmental organizations (NGOs), actions undertaken by international associations such as Amnesty International or Greenpeace, membership figures of supranational organizations, the number of different populations with whom these are directly concerned, and so on. Through its media campaigns, Greenpeace has been more effective than national States in forcing multinational companies to modify their behaviour and policies. It is suggested in some quarters that CNN has a more powerful effect on the development of people's minds than does the national or State education system of individual countries. An increasing number of problems cannot be dealt with in an exclusively national manner: the environment, transport systems, demography, population migrations, economic development, to cite but a few. Throughout the world the sovereignty of national states is weakening, as is their ability to act alone.[28]

The construction of Europe has also played a part in limiting the power of the national State and in eroding political and identity-based investment towards the nation. The powers that be in the European institutions are objective allies of the regional governments which equally desire to assert themselves against the nation-state. Direct relationships between the new institutions of the European Union and the regions are growing in number in France, as they are in all the member countries. Regardless of national bound-

---

[27] This theme is developed in Dominique Schnapper, 'From the Nation-State to the Transnational World: On the Meaning and Usefulness of Diaspora as a Concept', *Diaspora*, 8/4 (1999), 225–54.
[28] Bertrand Badie, *Un monde sans souveraineté. Les Etats entre ruse et responsabilité* (Paris, 1998).

aries, the regions are establishing new links with neighbouring provinces, which are closer to them than the capital of their own nation-state, or with its distant cities.[29] The city of Marseilles and the Provence-Côte-d'Azur region, for example, are developing a policy of direct exchanges with the Mediterranean countries without going through the ministries in Paris. The 'natural economic territories' identified by such economic exchanges will now play a greater role than those areas defined by the central political institutions of the State. The monitoring of the flow of immigrants is now carried out within the Schengen area rather than at national frontiers, as was previously the case.

By increasing economic integration, the construction of the European Union has also played a part in restricting the autonomy of national policies. When the Socialist government introduced radical changes in French economic policy in 1981, European economic pressures forced it to make another radical change in the opposite direction in 1983. It is common knowledge that increased economic interdependence is putting limits on the sovereignty of the national state so far as economic—and thus social—policy is concerned. Equally, from a judicial point of view, national sovereignty has been eroded. The European Court receives complaints from individuals against their own states. In a number of cases, it has upheld the complaint of the citizen and found the French State guilty of 'torture' under European human rights legislation.

It is, moreover, true that the policy of 'assimilation' pursued by the Jacobin State in order to integrate populations now seems less and less compatible with values of individual authenticity and freedom. The French are asking themselves questions about the sense and value of their traditional policy which consisted in transforming the children of immigrants into French citizens without leaving any space for their distinctive features in the public domain. But it is also true that the level of debate between the 'integrationists' and the partisans of multiculturalism has not gone very far. No one has thought of challenging the instruments of law which allow the children of migrants to become French citizens, that is, the nationality law and the process of socialization through the school system and the language of the nation. The project to make Corsican virtually obligatory within normal school hours in State primary schools scandalized the majority of French people, who remain attached to the 'language of the Republic', in this respect supporting former Minister of the Interior Jean-Pierre Chevènement, without necessarily endorsing his nationalistic sentiments.

There is increasing criticism of the difficulty the Jacobin State is experiencing in sorting out the problems of the distinctive features of communities, given that these are now recognized as legitimate. Yet the Jacobin State is often more open and more flexible than is civil society. The population has put up more resistance than has the State to the recognition of certain distinctive features of social groups. Successive Ministers of the Interior, Pierre Joxe (Parti

---

[29] Badie, *Un monde sans souveraineté*, 168.

Socialiste), Charles Pasqua (Rassemblement Pour la République), and Jean-Pierre Chevènement (Mouvement des citoyens), who also have responsibility for legislation governing religious worship, strove to bring forward a representative Muslim body in order to regularize religious worship and respond to particular demands such as availability of *hallal* meat, recognition of public holidays, provision for the training of French imams, and so on. Although nobody publicly questions the right of Muslims to their own places of worship nor for their religion to recognized as one of the religions of the country—which involves allowing Muslims to benefit from legislation on secularity—the social inscription of Islam upon the French landscape continues, more often than not, to bring local populations up in arms. And yet Muslim authorities regularly affirm their allegiance to secularism and to the Republic. In the context of the great Middle East crises, and again after the events of 11 September 2001, they have always striven, on behalf of the Jewish and Arab communities in France, to ensure that external conflicts are not imported into the public domain in France. It is probably less Islam itself than memories of colonization and the Algerian war which lie behind the reservations and the passions which come out every time a new mosque is planned and every time there is a decision to give Muslims their own area within a municipal cemetery. In the same way, in the Islamic headscarf affair, the government and the Conseil d'Etat reacted in a more 'liberal' manner than did the teachers, who were imbued with the spirit of an uncompromising 'secularism'.

Finally, it is worth noting that the difficulties encountered in the integration of populations of foreign origin seem to be linked more to social problems associated with the economic crisis and problems of social disintegration in the suburbs of big cities. Of course, there is no guarantee that specifically 'ethnic' problems will not arise in the future, possibly linked to manifestations of transnational Islamism. But, on the whole, Jacobinism has remained as effective a means of integrating new immigrants as it was in the past.

Globalization

'Colbertism', that is to say, the dynamic role played by the State in economic development, is a French invention. The programmes of French industrialization put in place by General de Gaulle and his Prime Minister, Georges Pompidou, in the course of the 1970s and then the Socialist government's nationalization programme in 1982 were probably the final manifestations of this historic policy. President Mitterrand still presented the nationalization programme to the nation in these terms: 'We have made a choice on the basis of effectiveness in improving our economy.' Although a country which is the fifth exporting power in the world is now being affected by globalization, there remain today three specific traits which are the inheritance of Colbertism: the share of the public sector within the national economy; the transfer of the political and administrative elite into the governance of big companies through the intermediary of the large administrative and technical bodies; and the high number of people working in the public service, which employs 25 per cent of the active population and almost 30 per cent of the working population. This sector includes national and local public services and companies having 'special' status, such as the Régie Autonome des Transports Parisiens (RATP), the Société Nationale des Chemins de Fer Français (SNCF), Electricité and Gaz De France (EDF-GDF), and Air France.

The process which has taken place over the last 20 years has had various effects on these three dimensions of 'modern Colbertism'. In 1982, Socialist Prime Minister Pierre Mauroy nationalized five industrial groups, Péchiney (PUK), Saint-Gobain, the Compagnie Générale des Eaux (CGE), Thomson Brandt, and Rhône-Poulenc. The State also became the majority shareholder of Dassault, Matra, Honeywell-Bull. The nationalized companies constituted a third of France's industrial production. The State also acquired a predominant position in basic industry and an important place in the advanced technology industries. The big banks which were still in the private sector were also nationalized.[30] As we know, this massive programme of nationalization at the beginning of François Mitterrand's first term was followed by an equally massive programme of privatization, adopted by the *cohabitation* government between 1986 and 1988 and continued by the subsequent Socialist governments.[31] The 1986 programme reversed not only the nationalizations of 1981 but also part of de Gaulle's nationalization programme of 1945. A total of 65 State-controlled companies were privatized, including major industrial companies, the most important banks and insurance companies, and the television station TF1. These represented a third of market capitalization at the time.[32] To a certain extent, this policy was a point of no return. The age of nationalization seems to have come to a definitive close, despite the fact that the managers of EDF, Air France, and France Télécom continue to have reservations about the process of liberalization which has been imposed by the European authorities.

As far as the recruitment of the economic elite is concerned, the opening up of the economy to globalization and the liberal policy of the European authorities are beginning to have their effects. It is true that company directors, like high-placed civil servants and politicians, continue to come from a tiny number of educational institutes: Hautes Etudes Commerciales (HEC), Polytechnique, and the Ecole Nationale d'Administration (ENA). These people, who are recruited very young through competitive entrance examinations, have then to get through the various stages of this veritable *cursus honororum*. The elite thus consists of a restricted number of people recruited from a narrow sector

---

[30] For more details, see for example, Bele Balassa, 'Une année de politique économique socialiste', *Commentaire*, 19 (1982), 415–28.

[31] On the reasons behind this policy, which was in line with a movement which affected all the countries of Europe, it is instructive to read Vincent Wright's remarkable introduction to the book he edited, *Les privatisations en Europe. Programmes et problèmes* (1993), esp. 42.

[32] For an analysis of this policy, see the article on France by Hervé Dumez and Alain Jeunemaitre, in Wright, *Les privatisations en Europe*, 105–32.

of society, and is very homogeneous.[33] In general, it welcomes neither new talent nor original personalities. The success of people who have made their way up through companies is little valued. The original diploma delivered by these *Ecoles de l'Etat* continues to play a decisive role in career structure, much more so than is the case in other European countries.[34] The chief executive of Renault, Louis Schweitzer, an alumnus of ENA and a member of Laurent Fabius's cabinet when the latter was prime minister, is still today an ideal-typical example of this career *à la française*. This traditional model is the inheritance of State action over the centuries: the first prestigious training centres in engineering were created by the State in the eighteenth century in order to train the engineers it needed. It was reinforced by the creation of ENA, the increase in State intervention in economic and social life that has taken place since the Second World War, and by the waves of nationalization of big companies in 1945 and 1981.

But this model is crumbling under the effect of the globalization of the economy. The opening up of big business capital means that, on the model of economic liberalism that the French refer to as 'Anglo-Saxon', it is the shareholders who hold the essential power. Foreign shareholders on the boards of French companies know nothing about the positions of the State and the imperatives of a career directed by service to the State. Moreover, the Crédit Lyonnais scandal revealed in brutal fashion the extent to which 'capitalism *à la française*' was dysfunctional in that too few people, all alumni of the prestigious state institutes, working through an excessively restricted network of relationships and in an environment of interlinked participation in capitalization, had no real control over the decisions taken in companies. The link between state and business had resulted in political will and group solidarity taking pride of place over economic logic. The scandal played a part in accelerating a process of evolution imposed by the globalization of the economy. It is no longer the case that the leaders of industry necessarily come from the prestigious State institutes, as can be seen from the examples of Bernard Arnault and François Pinaut. Capitalist logic is now gradually imposing itself at the expense of Jacobin state control.

On the other hand, to the extent that they constitute a sector which is protected by the State and which is unaffected by globalization, the 'special regimes' that deal with the status and the careers of a quarter of the active population—employed by organizations which have, in many cases, become purely commercial companies—are successfully resisting any realignment of their status, however partial, on the private sector. A growing percentage of the active population is made up of civil servants and people who, by right or de facto, fall into this category. Local administration employees—whose numbers were increased by the decentralization legislation of 1982—and the employees of the SNCF, Air France, the big nationalized companies, and 'pro-

[33] Pierre Bourdieu, *La noblesse d'Etat. Grandes écoles et esprit de corps* (Paris, 1989).
[34] See the various publications of Michel Bauer and Bénédicte Bertin-Mourot, particularly *L'accès au sommet des grandes entreprises françaises 1985–1994* (Paris, 1995).

tected employment markets' fall into a category of administrative regulations based on those applying to public servants, which offers them guaranteed career and salary structures. The 'public service salary scale', invented in 1946 by a Communist minister, which governs the careers of public servants according to a single model from beginning to end, remains the model which applies to all those whose careers and salaries are governed by 'special regimes'. The number of these has been increasing steadily in both absolute and relative terms, moving from less than 20 per cent of the active population, excluding unemployed people, in 1968 to almost 30 per cent from the end of the 1980s.[35] It is particularly difficult for Socialist governments to reverse this process, given that the parties of the Left draw their voters and their party activists from these 'public sector people', to borrow the expression used by François De Singly and Claude Thélot who demonstrated systematically 'the great divide', in social and political terms, separating those who belong to the exposed world of the private sector and those who enjoy the relative advantages of the protected world.[36]

These relative advantages compared with the private sector in terms of career security, working hours, pension rights, benefits in kind—the rich works council of EDF, which is granted 1 per cent of the company's turnover, is the most spectacular example of these—and even salary levels are rendered all the more difficult to challenge by the fact that the unions also draw the vast majority of their members from this protected sector. It was by conceiving the project to bring the pensions of those people benefiting from 'special regimes' gradually into line with those of the private sector that Alain Juppé sparked off the massive strikes of December 1995, which paralysed the country for more than a month. Between 1997 and 2002 the Socialist government of Lionel Jospin, having learned a lesson from that episode, did not venture to bring up the matter for further discussion.

Conclusion

The erosion of Jacobinism is unevenly spread. Those sectors of the economy which are exposed to the global market are gradually losing their specificity and are falling into line with capitalist logic, albeit reluctantly and with something of a lag. On the other hand, the political and social weight of a protected sector which is the inheritance of Jacobinism, reinforced by the politics of social democracy, will doubtless resist any plans for reform for some time to come.

It is particularly at the political level that there are questions to be asked. Is Jacobinism as hostile as its detractors suggest to the recognition of the cultural

---

[35] Dominique Schnapper, 'Rapport à l'emploi, protection sociale et statuts sociaux', *Revue française de sociologie* (1989), 3–29.

[36] François de Singly et Claude Thélot, *Gens du public, gens du privé. La grande différence* (Paris, 1988).

diversity to which the citizen of the modern democracy aspires? I am tempted to think that by laying down the principle that, beyond the normal and desirable diversity of modern societies, it is important also to maintain a common culture which enables people to 'make society', Jacobinism, which has nowadays become more flexible, may be less outmoded than the theorists of postmodernism think. There remains, however, a fundamental question to which I have no answer. The state and the national institutions have been weakened by the globalization of the economy and the building of a Europe in which the economic and social dimension is predominant. They have also been weakened by the effects of democratic individualism and claims made for the recognition of distinctive features. How can a political nation which is organized by State institutions of ancient origin adapt and reinterpret the Jacobinism which has constituted it over the centuries without challenging the national bond, that is to say, the social fabric? To what extent can local democracy and particular identities, which have always existed alongside Jacobinism—more so than recognized by republican ideology—be accepted in the public domain without challenging everything that has constituted the history of this particular society?

The problems posed for all the nations concerned by the construction of Europe are accentuated in the case of France, which is more political, more State-controlled, and more centralized than most of its partners, even if, paradoxically, it was the French who were the originators of the modern European project. Even though we continue analytically to hold up a more liberal 'British' model of citizenship against a more republican, more State-controlled 'French' version, I have no doubt that the Europe that is being built will be closer to the model that has come out of British history. This model, which integrates economic and political liberalism with a great respect for the law, is more in line with current social and political trends than the model of complete citizenship which has been that of the French Republic. I suspect that Vincent Wright shared this analysis. Susceptible though he was to the charm of 'the French exception', he must also have recognized that it was not destined to last for ever.

APPENDIX

The Works of Vincent Wright

Ph.D. thesis

'The Basses-Pyrénées from 1848 to 1870. A Study in Departmental Politics' (London University, 1965).

Books

Le Conseil d'Ftat sous le Second Empire (Paris: Armand Colin, 1972).

With Bernard Le Clère, *Les Préfets du Second Empire*. Cahiers de La Fondation Nationale des Sciences Politiques, 187 (Paris: Armand Colin, 1973).

With Frédéric Marx, *Les Universités Britanniques* (Paris: Presses Universitaires de France, 1973).

The Government and Politics of France (London: Hutchinson Press, 1978; American edition 1980; 2nd revised and updated version 1982; 3rd revision 1983; 3rd edition 1989, 4th edition, with Andrew Knapp, Routledge, 2001).

With Jacques Lagroye (eds), *Local Government in Britain and France: Problems and Prospects* (London: Allen and Unwin, 1979; French edition 1982).

Editor and contributor, *Continuity and Consensus in France* (London: Frank Cass, 1979).

Editor and contributor, *Continuity and Change in France* (London: George Allen and Unwin, 1984).

With Yves Mény, *La Crise de la sidérurgie européenne 1974–1984* (Paris: Presses Universitaires de France, 1985).

With Howard Machin (eds), *Economic Policy and Policy Making under the Mitterrand Presidency* (London: Frances Pinter & Co., 1985).

With Yves Mény (eds), *The Political Management of Industrial Crisis: The Case of Steel 1974–1984* (Berlin: de Gruyter, 1986).

With Rod Rhodes (eds), *Tensions in the Territorial Politics of Western Europe* (London: Frank Cass, 1987).

With John Vickers (eds), *The Politics of Privatization in Western Europe* (London: Frank Cass, 1989).

Editor and contributor, *The Representativity of Public Administration* (IISA: Brussels, 1991).

Editor, *Les privatisations en Europe: programmes et problèmes* (Paris: Actes-Sud, 1993).

Editor, *Privatization in Western Europe* (London: Pinter Publications, 1994; revised and updated edition of above).

With Yves Mény (eds), *La Riforma Amministrativa in Europa* (Bologna: Il Mulino, 1994).

With Wolfgang Müller (eds), *The State in Western Europe: Retreat or Redefinition?* (London: Frank Cass, 1994).

With Sabino Cassese (eds) *La recomposition de l'Etat en Europe* (Paris: La Découverte, 1996).

With Paul Heywood and Martin Rhodes (eds), *Developments in West European Politics* (London: Macmillan, 1997).

With Luisa Perrotti (eds), *Privatization*, 2 vols. (Aldershot: Edward Elgar, 1999).

With E. Page (eds), *Bureaucratic Elites in West European States: A Comparative Analysis of Top Officials* (Oxford: Oxford University Press, 1999).

With B. G. Peters and R. A. W. Rhodes (eds), *Administering the Summit: Administration of the Core Executive in Developed Countries* (Basingstoke: Macmillan, 2000).

With Hussein Kassim and B. Guy Peters (eds), *The National Co-ordination of EU Policy: The Domestic Level* (Oxford: Oxford University Press, 2000).

With Anand Menon (eds), *From the Nation State to Europe? Essays in Honour of Jack Hayward* (Oxford: Oxford University Press, 2001).

With Jack Hayward, *Governing from the Centre: Policy Coordination in France* (Basingstoke: Palgrave, 2001).

With Hussein Kassim and B. Guy Peters (eds), *The National Co-ordination of EU Policy: The European Level* (Oxford: Oxford University Press, 2001).

With Sudhir Hazareesingh, *Francs-Maçons sous le Second Empire* (Rennes: Presses Universitaires de Rennes, 2001).

Articles

'Les préfets démissionnaires en décembre 1851', *Revue Administrative*, 121 (January–February 1968).

'Le corps préfectoral et le *coup d'Etat* de décembre 1851', *Revue Administrative*, 122 (March–April 1968).

'Les préfets d'Emile Ollivier', *Revue Historique*, 260 (July–September 1968).

'Le Conseil d'Etat et l'affaire de la confiscation des biens d'Orléans', *Etudes et Documents du Conseil d'Etat*, 1968.

'La Loi de Sûreté Généralé de 1858', *Revue d'Histoire Moderne et Contemporaine*, 16 (July 1969).

'The Reorganisation of the Conseil d'Etat in 1852: The Study of a French Elite', *International Review of Social History*, 14 (1969).

'Religion et politique dans les Basses-Pyrénées pendant la IIeme République et le IIeme Empire', *Annales du Midi*, 81 (October 1969).

'La presse dans le département des Basses-Pyrénées de 1848 à 1870', *Bulletin de la Société des Sciences, Lettres et Arts de Pau*, 4e série (4) (1969).

'L'enseignement primaire, les instituteurs et la politique dans les Basses-Pyrénées de 1848 à 1870', *Bulletin de la Société des Sciences, Lettres et Arts de Pau*, 4e série (4) (1969).

'Les préfets impériaux et le 4 septembre 1870', *Revue Administrative*, 123 (January–February 1970).

'La structure du pouvoir local dans les Basses-Pyrénées de 1848 à 1870', *Bulletin de la Société des Sciences, Lettres et Arts de Pau*, 4e série (5) (1970).

'La vie politique dans les Basses-Pyrénées: de la proclamation de la République à l'élection présidentielle, février à décembre 1848', *Bulletin de la Société des Sciences, Lettres et Arts de Pau*, 4e série (5) (1970), Nouvelle série, no. 122.

'La vie politique dans les Basses-Pyrénées: des élections législatives de 1849 au coup d'état', *Bulletin de la Société des Sciences, Lettres et Arts de Bayonne* (1970), Nouvelle série no. 123.

With Jack Hayward, 'The 37,708 Microcosms of an Indivisible Republic: The French Local Elections of March 1971', *Parliamentary Affairs*, 14/4 (1971).

'L'épuration du Conseil d'Etat en juillet 1879', *Revue d'Histoire Moderne et Contemporaine*, 19 (October–December 1972).

'Enseignements tirés de recherches sur l'Administration française au XIXe siècle', *Histoire de l'administration*, Cahier de l'Institut Français des Sciences Administratives (Paris, 1972).

'L'archevêque d'Aix devant le Conseil d'Etat', *Revue d'Histoire de l'Eglise de France*, January 1973.

'La carrière mouvementée du préfet Monteil: Préfet des loges', *Revue Administrative*, 153 (May–June 1973).

With Jack Hayward, 'Presidential Supremacy and the French General Elections of March 1973'; Part 1, *Parliamentary Affairs* (July 1973), Part II, *Parliamentary Affairs* (September 1973).

'Administration et politique sous le Second Empire', *Procès-Verbaux de l'Académie des sciences morales et politiques, Institut de France* (May 1973).

'La réorganisation du Conseil d'Etat en 1872', *Etudes et Documents du Conseil d'Etat 1972* (Paris: Conseil d'Etat, 1973).

With Howard Machin, 'The French Socialist Party in 1973: Performance and Prospects', *Government and Opposition*, 9/2 (1974),

'Politics and Administration under the French Fifth Republic', *Political Studies*, 22/1 (1974).

With Jack Hayward, '"Les deux France" and the Presidential Elections of May 1974', *Parliamentary Affairs*, Summer 1974.

'Presidentialism and the Parties under the French Fifth Republic', *Government and Opposition*, 10/1 (1974).

With Howard Machin, 'The French Socialists: Success and the Problems of Success', *Political Quarterly*, 64/l (1975).

With Howard Machin, 'The French Regional Reforms of July 1972: A Case of Disguised Centralisation?', *Politics and Policy*, 2/3 (1975).

'Les préfets du gouvernement de la Défense nationale (6 Septembre 1870–Février 1871)', *Bulletin de la Société d'Histoire Moderne et Contemporaine* (1975).

'L'élection de Jean-Jacques Weiss au Conseil d'Etat', *Revue Administrative* (March–April 1975).

With Guy Thuillier, 'Les sources de l'histoire du corps préfectoral 1800–1880', *Revue Historique*, 253 (January–March 1975).

Chapters VII (Second Republic), VIII (Second Empire), and IX (early Third Republic), of *Le Conseil d'Etat, son histoire à travers les documents d'époque* (Paris: Editions du Centre National de la Recherche Scientifique, 1974).

'Politique et administration en temps de guerre', *Bulletin de la Société d'Histoire Moderne et Contemporaine* (1975), Quinzième Série, No. 11–12, 74e année.

'The Coup d'Etat of December 1851: Repression and the Limits to Repression', in Roger Price (ed.), *Revolution and Reaction: 1848 and the Second French Republic* (London: Croom Helm, 1975).

'Souvenirs d'un ancien élève de l'Ecole d'Administration de 1848–1849', *Revue Administrative*, 168 (November–December 1975).

'L'Ecole d'Administration de 1848: Un échec révélateur', *Revue Historique*, 255 (January–March 1976), 21–42.

With Guy Thuillier, 'Pour l'histoire du coup d'état de décembre 1851: une source à exploiter', *Mouvement Social*, 94 (January–March 1976).

'L'administration du Ministère de l'Intérieur en temps de crise: le cabinet de Gambetta à Tours en 1870', *Administration* (Autumn 1976).

'Les secrétaires généraux et les directeurs des administrations centrales: pou voirs et pouvoir', in *Les Directeurs de Ministère en France*, Cahier de l'Institut Français des Sciences Administratives (Geneva: Droz, 1976).

With Howard Machin, 'The French Left under the Fifth Republic: The Search for Identity in Unity', *Comparative Politics*, 10 (1977).

With Jack Hayward, 'Governing from the Centre: The National Significance of the 1977 French Local Elections', *Government and Opposition*, 12 (1977).

'Les épurations administratives pendant la deuxième moitié du XIXème siècle', in *Les Epurations Administratives*, Cahier de l'Institut Français des Sciences Administratives (Geneva: Droz, 1977).

'La vision interne du corps préfectoral', in *Les Préfets en France (1800–1940)*, Cahier de l'Institut Français des Sciences Administratives (Geneva: Droz, 1978).

'Comment les préfets se voyaient', in *varii auctores*, *Les préfets en France (1800–1940)* (Geneva: Droz, 1978).

'The Referendums of the French Fifth Republic', in David Butler and Austin Ranney (eds), *Referendums: A Comparative Study of Practice and Theory* (Washington: AEI, 1978).

'"La divine surprise": The French Elections of March 1978', *West European Politics*, 3/1 (1979).

'Les préfets de police 1851–1880: problèmes et personnalités', in *L'Etat et sa police en France 1789–1914*, Cahier de l'Institut Français des Sciences Administratives (Geneva: Droz, 1979).

'Parlementarismes britanniques et français', in F. Bédarida, F. Crouzet, and D. Johnson (eds), *De Guillaume le Conquérant au Marché Commun: Dix siècles d'histoire franco-britannique* (Paris: Albin Michel, 1979).

'La Préfecture de police au XIXe Siècle', in *L'Administration de Paris*, Cahier de l'Institut Français des Sciences Administratives (Geneva: Droz, 1979).

Preface to Guy Thuillier, *Regards sur la haute administration de la France* (Paris: Economica, 1979).

'Les protestants dans la haute administration 1870–1885' and 'Allocation de clôture', in A. Encrevé and M. Richard (eds), *Les Protestants dans les débuts de la IIIe République* (Paris: Société de l'histoire du protestantisme français, 1980).

'Regionalisation under the French Fifth Republic: The Triumph of the Functional Approach', in Jim Sharpe (ed.), *Decentralist Trends in Western Democracies* (London: Sage, 1980).

With Howard Machin, 'Centre-Periphery Relations in France', in George Jones (ed.), *New Approaches to the Study of Central–Local Government Relations* (London: SSRC, 1980).

'The Change in France', *Government and Opposition* (Autumn 1981).

'Questions d'un Jacobin anglais aux régionalistes français', *Pouvoirs*, 19 (1981).

With Howard Machin, 'Why Mitterrand Won: The French Presidential Elections of April–May 1981', *West European Politics* (Autumn 1981).

'Parlement et administration aux débuts de la Troisième République: la crise', in Charles Debbasch (ed.), *Parlement et Administration en Europe*, Cahier de l'Institut Français des Sciences Administratives (Paris: Editions du CNRS, 1982).

'Prise de décision et processus de réforme en France', *Administration 1982* (Paris: Institut International d'Administration Publique, 1982).

'La Presidencia Mitterrand: el primer ano del experimentao socialista en Francia', *Revista de Occidente*, October 1982.

'The French Communist Party During the Fifth Republic: The Troubled Path', in Howard Machin (ed.), *National Communism in Western Europe: A Third Way for Socialism* (London: Methuen, 1983).

'Socialism and the Interdependent Economy: Industrial Policy Making under the Mitterrand Presidency', *Government and Opposition*, 19/3 (1984).

'Regions and Regionalisation in France, Italy and Spain—Some Concluding Remarks', in M. Hebbert and H. Machin (eds), *Regionalisation in France, Italy and Spain* (London: ICERD, 1984).

'Regione e Regionalizzazione in Francia, Italia e Spagna', *Le Regioni*, 12 (November–December 1984).

'Francia', in *L'Amministrazione Nella Storia Moderna*, ISAP-Archivio-Nuova series e, ii. (Rome, 1985).

With Yvonne Fortin, 'Chronique de l'administration à l'étranger: Grande-Bretagne 1984–85', *Administration 85* (Paris: Institut International d'Administration Publique, 1986).

'L'administration locale sous le gouvernement Thatcher—problèmes et paradoxes', *Revue Française d'Administration Publique*, 38 (April–June 1986).

Contributions on 'Declaration of the Rights of Man', 'Tutelage', 'Bonapartism', and 'Anti-clericalism', in Vernon Bogdanor (ed.), *The Blackwell Encyclopaedia of Political Institutions* (Oxford: Basil Blackwell, 1987).

'Débat: la politicisation du Conseil d'Etat: mythe ou réalité', *Pouvoirs*, 40 (1987).

'Francs-maçons, Administration et République: les préfets du gouvernement de la Défense nationale, 1870–1871', *La Revue Administrative*, 240 (November–December 1987), 517–26, and 241 (January–February 1988).

With Martin Rhodes, 'The European Steel Unions and the Steel Crisis, 1974–84: A Study in the Demise of Traditional Unionism', *British Journal of Political Science*, 18 (1988).

'Le privatizzazione in Gran Bretagna', *Rivista Trimestrale di Dirritto Pubblico* (January 1988).

'Oeffentlicher und privater sektor in Grossbritannien–die Privatisierungs-politik der Thatcher-Regierung', in *Verwaltungswissenchaftliche Inform-ationen*, 16/3–4 (1988).

'La restructuration des rapports des relations pouvoir central-pouvoirs locaux en Europe', in *Forces et faiblesses des collectivités locales européennes avant 1993* (Paris: Fondation pour la gestion des villes, 1989).

With H. Machin, 'Les élèves de l'Ecole d'Administration de 1848–1849', *Revue d'Histoire Moderne et Contemporaine*, 36 (October–December 1989).

'The Administration of British Universities: The Managerial Impact Of Recent Developments', *Rivista Trimestrale di Diritto Pubblico*, 3 (1989).

'The French Administration: Old Dilemmas and New Problems', in Peter Hall, Jack Hayward, and Howard Machin (eds), *Developments in French Politics* (London: Macmillan, 1989).

'Las privatizaciones en Gran Bretaña', *Documentacion Administrativa*, 218–219 (April–September 1989).

'Convergence and Diversity in Western Europe: The British Case' in Henri Mendras and Dominique Schnapper (eds), *Six Manières d'Etre Européen* (Paris: Gallimard, 1990).

'The Nationalisation and Privatization of French Public Enterprises 1981–1988: Radical Ambitions, Diluted Programmes and Limited Impact', *Staatswissenschaften und Staatspraxis*, 2 (1990).

'The History of French Mayors: Lessons and Problems', in *Yearbook of European Administrative History*, ii. (Baden-Baden: Nomos, 1990).

'Evolutions et perspectives: un regard britannique sur la politique française', *Autrement*, 122 (1991).

With Hussein Kassim, 'The Role of National Administrations in the European Community Decision-Making Process', *Rivista Trimestrale di Diritto Pubblico* (Spring 1991).

'"Les Frères en lutte"? Provincial Freemasonry on the Eve of the Third Republic', *French Politics and Society*, 9 (Winter 1991).

With Sonia Mazey, 'Les préfets de Vichy', in Jean-Pierre Azéma and François Bédarida (eds), *Le régime de Vichy et les Français* (Paris: Fayard, 1992).

'Explaining *Relance*: European Integration as Model, Myth and Instrument', in A. Clesse and R. Vernon (eds), *The European Community after 1992: A New Role in World Politics* (Baden-Baden: Nomos, 1991).

'Representative Bureaucracy: Summary Report', *Cahier d'Histoire de l'Administration*, 3 (1992).

'Les leçons des privatisations britanniques ou les dilemmes de l'Etat libéral', *Revue Française d'Administration Publique*, 61 (May 1992). Reprinted in *Problèmes Economiques* (Paris: La Documentation Française, No. 2362, February 1994).

'Redrawing the Public–Private Boundary: Privatization in the United Kingdom 1979–1991', in Karl Rohe *et al.* (eds.), *Deutschland-Grossbritannien-Europa*, Bochum 1992.

'La relación Estado-Mercado en Europa', *Boletin Informativo* (Madrid: Fundacion Juan March, August–September 1992), 222.

With Roger Morgan, 'Introduction to "The Origins of the European Community Administration", *Yearbook of European Administrative History*, 4 (Baden-Baden: Nomos, 1992).

'The Administrative System and Market Regulation in Western Europe: Continuities, Exceptionalism and Convergence', *Rivista Trimestrale di Diritto Pubblico*, 4 (1992).

'La machine administrative: vieux problèmes, nouveaux dilemmes', in Peter Hall *et al.* (eds), *L'évolution de la vie politique française* (Paris: PUF, 1992).

'Décentralisation et société française (deuxième table ronde)', in Guy Gilbert and Alain Delcamp (eds), *La décentralisation dix ans après* (Paris: LGDJ, 1993).

'Public Administration in the Nineties: Trends and Innovations', in International Institute of Administrative Sciences, *Public Administration in the Nineties* (Brussels: IIAS, 1993).

'The President and Prime Minister: Subordination, Conflict, Symbiosis or Reciprocal Parasitism?', in Jack Hayward (ed.), *De Gaulle to Mitterrand: Presidential Power in France* (London: Hurst, 1993).

'State Withdrawal and Market Regulation: Situating the Greek Case', in Loukas Tsoukalis (ed.), *Greece in the European Community* (Athens, 1993).

'Les bureaux du ministère de la guerre', *Revue Historique des Armées*, 3 (1993).

'Public Administration, Regulation, Deregulation and Reregulation', in K. A. Eliassen and J. Koolman (eds), *Managing Public Organisations: Lessons from Contemporary European Experience* (London: Thousand Oaks; New Delhi: Sage, 1993).

'Whitehall et le local governement à l'épreuve du thatchérisme', *L'Administration territoriale en Europe* (Paris: La Documentation Française, Dossiers et Débats, 1993).

'Reforming the Machinery of State in Western Europe: Convergent Pressures, Developing Responses, Divergent Outcomes', in Karin Pinter (ed.), *Eine neue Rolle für den Staat?*, 3 (Vienna: Bundesministerium für Finanzen, Schriftenreihe, 1993).

'Le corps préfectoral et le Conseil d'Etat dans l'histoire des institutions françaises', *L'Etat de Droit au Quotidien* (Paris, 1993).

'La réserve du corps préfectoral', in P. Birnbaum (ed.), *La France de l'Affaire Dreyfus* (Paris: Gallimard, 1994).

'Collectivités locales et sécurité: les ambiguités du système français', *Cahiers de la Securité Intérieure*, 16 (Paris: La Documentation Française, June 1994).

'El Estado y las grandes empresas', *Boletin Informativo* (Madrid: Fundacion Juan March, August–September 1994), 242.

'Reshaping the State: The Implications for Public Administration', *West European Politics*, 17/3 (1994).

'Introduction', *The Napoleonic Administrative Model in Europe* (Brussels: IIAS, 1994).

'The State and Major Enterprises in Western Europe: Enduring Complexities', in J. Hayward (ed.), *Industrial Enterprise and European Integration* (Oxford: Oxford University Press, 1995).

'Leadership local et leadership du local en Europe occidentale: la contradiction croissante', in Claude Sorbets (ed.), *L'Intérêt Territorial* (Paris: Pedone, 1995).

'Le Conseil d'Etat', in Jean Tulard (ed.), *Dictionnaire du Second Empire* (Paris: Fayard, 1995).

'Conseil d'Etat e Consiglio di Stato: le radici storiche della loro diversità', in Yves Mény (ed.), *Il Consiglio di Stato in Francia e in Italia* (Bologna: Il Mulino, 1995).

'Il gruppo di lavoro sulla "storia dell'amminstrazione" dell'IISA', *Storia Amminstrazione Costituzione*, Annale ISAP, 3 (1995).

'The Local Management of a Financial Crisis in France', *Yearbook of European Administrative History*, 7 (Baden-Baden: Nomos, 1995).

'The Industrial Privatisation Programmes of Britain and France: The Impact of Political and Institutional Factors', in Peter Jones (ed.), *Party, Parliament and Personality* (London: Routledge, 1995).

'El Neoliberalismo en Europa Occidental: un balance', *Boletin Informativo* (Madrid: Fundacion Juan March, August–September 1995).

'Aspetti comparativi', in *Rappresentanti dello Stato Sul Territorio e Autonomie Locali* (Rome: Ministero dell'Interno, 1996).

'Quelques commentaires sur l'ENA', *Revue Administrative*, 49, special issue (1996).

'Privatizzanione industriale e bancaria in Europa occidentale: alcuni para-dossi', *Stato e Mercato*, 47/2 (1996).

'The Administrative Coordination of European Affairs: Negotiating the Quagmire', in J. J. Richardson, (ed.), *European Union: Power and Policy-Making* (London: Routledge, 1996).

'La réforme administative en Grande-Bretagne: le démantèlement du système traditionnel', *Revue Française d'Administration Publique* (1996).

'Redefiniendo el Estado: las implicaciones para la Administracion Publica', *Gestión y Análisis de Politicas Públicas*, 7–8 (September 1996).

With B. Guy Peters, 'Public Policy and Administration: Old and New', in Robert E. Goodin and Hans-Dieter Klingemann (eds), *A New Handbook of Political Science* (Oxford: Oxford University Press, 1996).

With Paul Heywood, 'Executive Power in Western Europe: Increasing Strength in a Weakening Policy Environment', in Martin Rhodes, Paul Heywood, and Vincent Wright (eds), *Developments in West European Politics* (London: Macmillan, 1996).

With Robert Elgie, 'The French Presidency: The Changing Public Policy Environment', in Robert Elgie (ed.), *Electing the French President: The 1996 Presidential Election* (London: Macmillan, 1996).

'The Development of Public Administration in Britain and France: Fundamental Similarities Masking Basic Differences', *Yearbook of European Administrative History*, 8 (Baden-Baden: Nomos, 1996).

'Die Demontage der traditionellen Verwaltung in Grossbritannien', *Verwaltungswissenschaftliche Informationen*, 24 Jahrgang, Heft 3-4 (1996).

'Privatization Programmes in Western Europe: Managing Contradictions', *Epicentre* (September 1996).

'Démocratiser l'élite administative française: regard d'un Britannique', *Pouvoirs*, 80 (1997).

'The Path to Hesitant Comparison', in Hans Daalder (ed.), *The Intellectual Autobiography of Comparative European Politics* (London: Cassell, 1997).

'Relations intergouvernementales et gouvernement régional en Europe: réflexions d'un sceptique', in Patrick Le Galès and Christian Lequesne, *Les Paradoxes des Régions en Europe* (Paris: CERI, 1997).

'Intergovernmental Relations and Regional Government in Europe: A Sceptical View', in Patrick Le Galès and Christian Lequesne (eds.), *Regions in Europe* (London: Routledge, 1997).

'France: la fin du dirigisme?', *Modern and Contemporary France*, 5/2 (1997).

'The Paradoxes of Administrative Reform', in Walter J. M. Kickert (ed.), *Public Management and Administrative Reform in Western Europe* (Cheltenham: Edward Elgar, 1997).

With Guy Peters and Rod Rhodes, 'Introduction: Tendances convergentes et spécificités nationales', *Revue Française d'Administration Publique*, 83 (July–September 1997).

'Amministrazione e costituzione: la lettura francese', *Storia, Amministrazione Costituzione: Annale dell' Istituto per la Scienza dell' Amministrazione Pubblica*, 5 (1997).

'Redefiniendo el Estado: las implicaciones para la Administración Pública', *Gestión y Análisis de Políticas Públicas*, 7–8 (1997).

'Le système territorial en période de crise: 1870–1871' and 'Rapport de synthèse', in Michel Pertué (ed.), *L'administration territoriale de la France, (1750–1940)* (Paris: Presses Universitaires d'Orléans, 1998).

'Le Conseil d'Etat et changements de régime: le cas du Second Empire', *Revue Administrative* 51; Special issue on Le Conseil d'Etat et les Crises, (October 1998).

'The French Administration: Letter to an American Colleague', in Françoise Gallouédec-Genuys (ed.), *The French Administrative System* (Paris: IFSA, Documentation Francaise, 1998; in English and French).

'L'Etat n'est pas mort', in Dominique Jacques-Jouvenot (ed.), *L'oeil du Sociologue* (Besançon: Presses du Centre Unesco, 1998).

With Christopher Clifford, 'La politisation de l'administration britannique: ambitions, limites et problèmes conceptuels', *Revue Française d'Administration Publique*, 86 (April–June 1998).

'Paradojas de la reforma administrativa en Europa Occidental', *Foro Internacional*, 38 (April–September 1998).

'La fine del dirigisme? La francha negli anni novanta', *Stato e Mercato*, 54 (1998).

'Reshaping the State: The Implications for Public Administration', in C. Amirante and A. Cattanio (eds), *Efficienza, Trasparenza e Modernizzazione della pubblica amministratione in Europa* (Rome: Univerista di Roma la Sapienza, 1998).

'From the *droit de l'Etat* towards the *Etat de Droit*', *Rivista Trimestrale di Dirritto Pubblico*, 1 (1999).

'Dirigisme: Myth and Reality', in E. Bort and R. Keat (eds), *The Boundaries of Understanding* (Edinburgh: Social Sciences Institute, University of Edinburgh, 1999).

With G. Pagoulatos, 'The Politics of Industrial Privatization: Spain, Portugal and Greece in a European Perspective', *Rivista trimestrale di diritto pubblico*, 3 (1999).

'The Fifth Republic: From the *Droit de l'Etat* to the *Etat de Droit*?', *West European Politics*, 4 (1999).

'Blurring the Public–Private Divide', in B. Guy Peters and Donald J. Savoie (eds), *Governance in the Twenty-first Century: Revitalizing the Public Service* (McGill-Montreal: Queen's University Press, 2000).

'L'effacement de la ligne de demarcation entre public et privé', in B. Guy Peters and Donald J. Savoie (eds.), *La gouvernance au XXIe siècle: revitaliser la fonction publique* (Quebec: Les Presses de l'Université Laval, 2001).

'From the *Droit de l'Etat* towards the *Etat de Droit*', in Peter Hall, Jack Hayward, and Howard Machin (eds), *Developments in French Politics*, ii. (London: Macmillan, 2001).

With Sudhir Hazareesingh, 'Le Second Empire', in L. Fougère, J.-P. Machelon, and F. Monnier (eds), *Le communes et le pouvoir: Histoire politique des communes françaises de 1789 à nos jours* (Paris: Presses Universitaires de France, 2002).

INDEX

Pons 97
Popes 60, 161
Popular Front 17, 116, 122–8, 155
populist tradition 8–9
Post and Telegraph Medal 177
Poubelle, Eugène 73, 83
Poupon, André 51, 52
poverty 41, 46, 47, 83, 201
power 5, 94, 164, 191, 206
  absolute, royal 162
  attitudes to the influence of 85
  bureaucratic 17
  central 9, 70, 71, 73, 78, 86, 87
  concentration in hands of executive
    194
  confiscation by sectional groups 10
  desire for 159
  juridical 5
  legitimacy of 168
  local 203
  manifestation of 159
  means of gaining 159
  monarchical 163
  municipal 87
  opportunity of obtaining 164
  prefects 203
  seizure of 160
  share of 159
  territorial 2, 12
  unhampered by tutelage 163
  unity of 193
  veto 194
Precurseur (republican paper) 36
prefects 4, 12, 69–88, 113, 133
  executive, creation of 192
  Gambetta's 21, 38, 39, 69, 73, 79, 87
  organization of politics and adminis-
    tration 197
  role of 203
  war veterans and 50, 52, 58, 60, 63
  see also Bellion; Bourgeois; Calmont;
    Cambon; Combes; Dubost; Estellé;
    Floquet; Jessaint; Lefebvre du
    Grosriez; Lépine; Martin-Feuillée;
    Monteil; Poubelle; Rigault; Rozier-
    Joly; Selves
press 32, 134 see also newspapers
Prison Administration Medal 177
private sector 214, 215
privatization 213
privileged class 122, 146, 159, 164, 179
processions 63, 65, 66
  civic 56–8, 61, 62
  municipal 60

religious 62
  torchlight 64
promotion 93, 102, 107, 109, 112
  equal chances of 200
  unusually rapid 98
propaganda 28, 77, 81, 152–3
proportional representation 153
prostitution 104
Protestantism 5, 161 n., 186
Proudhon, Pierre-Joseph 9, 160
Prouvost, Jean 133
Provence 205, 211
Provisional Consultative Assembly 138,
  139, 140
Provisional Government 142, 150, 153
Prussia 26, 180, 182 see also Franco-
  Prussian war
public opinion 80, 168, 181
public sector 18, 98, 153, 212–13
Public Works Medal 177
Pucheu, Pierre 148
Purple Heart Badge of Military Merit
  174
Pyrenees 34

Quinet, Edgar 12

Rabier, Fernand 108–9
Racine, Jean 206
Radical Party, radicalism 8, 13, 40, 90,
  94, 95, 97 100, 138
radio stations 209
Ragghianti, Renzo 7
Rat (title) 178
rationalism/rationality 12, 190
  administrative 190
  bureaucratic 84, 179
  imposed everywhere 186
  liberal 174 n.
RATP (Régie Autonome des Transports
  Parisiens) 213
reality 185, 187, 189, 192, 206
  economic and sociological 188
  political and administrative 184
  rhetoric and 193
  State's inability to constrain 186
reason 24, 159, 198
  instruments of 200
  passions must be controlled by 174
referendums 153
reform 120–2, 126, 192
  administrative 203
  capitalism 104
  conservative 137, 146

Lightning Source UK Ltd.
Milton Keynes UK
UKHW010907100223
416739UK00004B/646

9 780199 256464